Stanley Porter is Professor of Theology in the Department of Theology and Religious Studies at Roehampton Institute London.

Dennis Stamps is Director of the West Midlands Ministerial Training Course, Queen's College, Birmingham.

JOURNAL FOR THE STUDY OF THE NEW TESTAMENT
SUPPLEMENT SERIES
180

Executive Editor
Stanley E. Porter

.

Sheffield Academic Press

The Rhetorical Interpretation of Scripture

Essays from the 1996 Malibu Conference

edited by
Stanley E. Porter
and Dennis L. Stamps

Journal for the Study of the New Testament
Supplement Series 180

Copyright © 1999 Sheffield Academic Press

Published by Sheffield Academic Press Ltd
Mansion House
19 Kingfield Road
Sheffield S11 9AS
England

Typeset by Sheffield Academic Press
and
Printed on acid-free paper in Great Britain
by Biddles Ltd
Guildford, Surrey

British Library Cataloguing in Publication Data

A catalogue record for this book is available
from the British Library

ISBN 1-85075-959-6

CONTENTS

Contents

Part IV
RHETORICAL INTERPRETATION OF HEBREWS AND IGNATIUS

EDITORS' PREFACE

This volume contains the edited proceedings of the fourth international conference on rhetorical criticism organized by Thomas Olbricht with Stanley Porter, and sponsored by Pepperdine University, Malibu, California. During 9–12 July 1996, a group of approximately 30 participants from around the globe gathered at the scenic Pepperdine University campus. Surrounded by views of the Pacific ocean and supported by some of the finest educational facilities in the United States, the conference explored once again the ongoing developments and debates in the rhetorical criticism of Scripture. This was the smallest of the conferences so far, marked by the absence of the usual contingency from South Africa and by the absence of a number from the European countries. Yet, seven different countries were represented: the United States, Canada, Great Britain, Sweden, Finland, Spain and Japan. As can be seen in this collection of essays, the breadth of interests and issues that are encompassed by this group remains widespread. This conference was marked by the fact that a sizable number of individuals in the group has regularly attended previous conferences. This growing familiarity enabled the discussion of the papers to proceed quickly to the heart of issues with a frankness and candor (yet in a congenial manner) not seen before. Though the group shares a common interest in exploring the importance of rhetorical criticism for biblical studies, there is no common perspective as to the nature, method and significance of this discipline. But the important and rewarding aspect to these ongoing conferences is the fruitful exchange of ideas and even our disagreements. Some of this exchange is recorded in the papers of this volume.

If readers of this volume wish to follow up previous conferences, the papers are published by Sheffield Academic Press. The proceedings of the first conference have been published as *Rhetoric and the New Testament: Essays from the 1992 Heidelberg Conference* (ed. S.E. Porter and T.H. Olbricht; JSNTSup, 90; Sheffield: JSOT Press, 1993);

the second as *Rhetoric, Scripture and Theology: Essays from the 1994 Pretoria Conference* (ed. S.E. Porter and T.H. Olbricht; JSNTSup, 131; Sheffield: Sheffield Academic Press, 1996); and the third as *The Rhetorical Analysis of Scripture: Essays from the 1995 London Conference* (ed. S.E. Porter and T.H. Olbricht; JSNTSup, 146; Sheffield: Sheffield Academic Press, 1997). The proceedings from the fifth conference held in July 1999 at the Pepperdine University Facility in Florence, Italy will be published in 2000.

This volume is significant in that it is dedicated to Professor Thomas H. Olbricht. The participants from the four conferences on rhetorical criticism wish to honor Tom. It was through his impetus that these international forums came to exist. It was through his diligence that funding and support for these exchanges came through Pepperdine University. Tom also has been the key organizer of the conferences and has been the co-editor of the previous three collections of essays. On a wider scale, Tom has been an important contributor to the academic community in many areas, particularly rhetoric. Richard T. Hughes, a close colleague of Tom, offers a more personal summary of his personal and academic career in the dedication; also included is a selected CV and bibliography of his writings. An up-close and personal insight into Tom's perspective on rhetoric and the interpretation of Scripture is offered in the interview with Tom by his daughter, Erika Mae. We offer this volume to Tom as he retires in appreciation for his past (and anticipated ongoing) contribution to these conferences and to the scholarly study of rhetoric, and for his kind and gentle friendship.

Finally, it is important that we say thank you for the ongoing financial and material support of Pepperdine University for these gatherings. We remain very grateful to Sheffield Academic Press for their willingness to publish the proceedings of these conferences. We also thank the individual academic and other institutions who provide support and resources in order that work and research can continue through these conferences and through the writing and discussion of the individuals who attend these conferences.

ABBREVIATIONS

AB	Anchor Bible
AnBib	Analecta biblica
ANRW	Hildegard Temporini and Wolfgang Haase (eds.), *Aufstieg und Niedergang der römischen Welt: Geschichte und Kultur Roms im Spiegel der neueren Forschung* (Berlin: W. de Gruyter, 1972–)
ARW	*Archiv für Religionswissenschaft*
ASNU	Acta seminarii neotestamentici upsaliensis
BAGD	Walter Bauer, William F. Arndt, F. William Gingrich and Frederick W. Danker, *A Greek–English Lexicon of the New Testament and Other Early Christian Literature* (Chicago: University of Chicago Press, 2nd edn, 1958)
BBR	*Bulletin for Biblical Research*
BDF	Frederich Blass, A. Debrunner and Robert W. Funk, *A Greek Grammar of the New Testament and Other Early Christian Literature* (Chicago: University of Chicago Press, 1961)
BETL	Bibliotheca ephemeridum theologicarum lovaniensium
BFCT	Beiträge zur Förderung christlicher Theologie
BHT	Beiträge zur historischen Theologie
Bib	*Biblica*
BibRes	*Biblical Research*
BJS	Brown Judaic Studies
BSO(A)S	*Bulletin of the School of Oriental (and African) Studies*
BU	Biblische Untersuchungen
BZ	*Biblische Zeitschrift*
CBQ	*Catholic Biblical Quarterly*
ClQ	*Classical Quarterly*
ConBNT	Coniectanea biblica, New Testament
CRINT	Compendia rerum iudaicarum ad Novum Testamentum
EBib	Etudes bibliques
EKKNT	Evangelisch-Katholischer Kommentar zum Neuen Testament
ExpTim	*Expository Times*
FFNT	Foundations and Facets: New Testament
FRLANT	Forschungen zur Religion und Literatur des Alten und Neuen Testaments
GTJ	*Grace Theological Journal*

HbAltW	Handbuch der Altertumswissenschaft
HNT	Handbuch zum Neuen Testament
HTKNT	Herders theologischer Kommentar zum Neuen Testament
HUCA	*Hebrew Union College Annual*
HUT	Hermeneutische Untersuchungen zur Theologie
ICC	International Critical Commentary
IDB	George Arthur Buttrick (ed.), *The Interpreter's Dictionary of the Bible* (4 vols.; Nashville: Abingdon Press, 1962)
Int	*Interpretation*
JAAR	*Journal of the American Academy of Religion*
JBL	*Journal of Biblical Literature*
JBLMS	Journal of Biblical Literature Monograph Series
JQR	*Jewish Quarterly Review*
JSNT	*Journal for the Study of the New Testament*
JSNTSup	*Journal for the Study of the New Testament*, Supplement Series
JSOTSup	*Journal for the Study of the Old Testament*, Supplement Series
JSS	*Journal of Semitic Studies*
LB	*Linguistica biblica*
LCL	Loeb Classical Library
LEC	Library of Early Christianity
LSJ	H.G. Liddell, Robert Scott and H. Stuart Jones, *Greek–English Lexicon* (Oxford: Clarendon Press, 9th edn, 1968)
MeyerK	H.A.W. Meyer (ed.), Kritisch-exegetischer Kommentar über das Neue Testament
MGWJ	*Monatsschrift für Geschichte und Wissenschaft des Judentums*
Neot	*Neotestamentica*
NICNT	New International Commentary on the New Testament
NIGTC	The New International Greek Testament Commentary
NovT	*Novum Testamentum*
NovTSup	*Novum Testamentum*, Supplements
NTD	Das Neue Testament Deutsch
NTS	*New Testament Studies*
NTTS	New Testament Tools and Studies
OTP	James Charlesworth (ed.), *Old Testament Pseudepigrapha*
RB	*Revue biblique*
RelS	*Religious Studies*
SBG	Studies in Biblical Greek
SBLDS	SBL Dissertation Series
SBLSBS	SBL Sources for Biblical Study
SBLSP	SBL Seminar Papers
SCHNT	Studia ad Corpus Hellenisticum Novi Testamenti
SEÅ	*Svensk exegetisk årsbok*
SJT	*Scottish Journal of Theology*

SNT	Studien zum Neuen Testament
SNTSMS	Society for New Testament Studies Monograph Series
Str–B	[Hermann L. Strack and] Paul Billerbeck, *Kommentar zum Neuen Testament aus Talmud und Midrasch* (7 vols.; Munich: Beck, 1922–61)
SVF	*Stoicorum Veterum Fragmenta*
TDNT	Gerhard Kittel and Gerhard Friedrich (eds.), *Theological Dictionary of the New Testament* (trans. Geoffrey W. Bromiley; 10 vols.; Grand Rapids: Eerdmans, 1964–)
THKNT	Theologischer Handkommentar zum Neuen Testament
TU	Texte und Untersuchungen
TynBul	*Tyndale Bulletin*
TZ	*Theologische Zeitschrift*
VF	*Verkündigung und Forschung*
WUNT	Wissenschaftliche Untersuchungen zum Neuen Testament
ZAW	*Zeitschrift für die alttestamentliche Wissenschaft*
ZNW	*Zeitschrift für die neutestamentliche Wissenschaft*
ZTK	*Zeitschrift für Theologie und Kirche*
ZWT	*Zeitschrift für wissenschaftliche Theologie*

LIST OF CONTRIBUTORS

J.D.H. Amador
Santa Rosa Community College, Santa Rosa, California

L. Gregory Bloomquist
Saint Paul University, Ottawa, Ontario, Canada

Anders Eriksson
University of Lund, Sweden

Glenn S. Holland
Allegheny College, Meadville, Pennsylvania

Richard T. Hughes
Pepperdine University, Malibu, California

Ira J. Jolivet, Jr
Pepperdine University, Malibu, California

Gustavo Martín-Asensio
Roehampton Institute London, England

Erika M. Olbricht
Pepperdine University, Malibu, California

Thomas H. Olbricht
Pepperdine University, Malibu, California

Dale Patrick
Drake University, Des Moines, Iowa

Mary W. Patrick
Drake University, Des Moines, Iowa

Stanley E. Porter
Roehampton Institute London, England

Allen Scult
Drake University, Des Moines, Iowa

Timothy W. Seid
Smith Neck Friends Meeting House, South Dartmouth, Massachusetts

Dennis L. Stamps
Queen's College, Birmingham, England

Lauri Thurén
Åbo Academy, Åbo, Finland

Duane F. Watson
Malone College, Canton, Ohio

Kota Yamada
Keiwa College, Tokyo, Japan

Introduction: The Malibu Conference and the Ongoing Debate

Stanley E. Porter and Dennis L. Stamps

In 1992 when the first international conference on rhetorical criticism was held in Heidelberg, Germany, the methodology and practice of rhetorical criticism was still emerging, especially in New Testament studies. Today, rhetorical criticism seems firmly entrenched as a specialized field of biblical interpretation. As has been evident from the beginning, rhetorical criticism is not a univocal perspective or practice; one should really speak of rhetorical criticisms. Equally, there remain important hermeneutical issues to ask and explore before the practice of rhetorical criticism can have greater influence in the historical and theological interpretation of Scripture: there is still a great deal of scepticism among traditional biblical scholars as to the value and significance of rhetorical criticism. But this collection of essays demonstrates that the discipline has moved to a level of sophisticated engagement and analysis which requires some reckoning by the established practice of biblical studies.

In what follows, an introduction to the essays is given which is far from comprehensive, but hopefully one which highlights some of the significant content and debate which characterized this particular conference. Instead of following the order in which the essays appear in the volume, the essays are commented upon according to some of the issues which emerged from the conference. Also, the introductory comments are meant to place the essays against the backdrop of the larger debate within rhetorical criticism itself and biblical studies in general.

First, what is the general aim or purpose of rhetorical criticism? Dale Patrick with Allen Scult suggest that rhetorical criticism as an analysis of persuasion offers a more balanced approach to assessing the ideological nature of biblical texts than certain modern practices of ideological and political criticism, as seen, for example, in the work of

Robert and Mary Coote, *Power, Politics and the Making of the Bible.*[1]
A different approach is suggested by Erika Mae Olbricht in her interview with her father, Thomas Olbricht. In this wide-ranging interview
on Olbricht's theory and practice of biblical interpretation as a
rhetorician and as a leading academic in theological education for the
Church of Christ, Olbricht suggests that rhetorical criticism and a God-
centred hermeneutics offer ways for finding what a text meant when it
was written and what a text means in the belief and practice of the
Church today. Gustavo Martín-Asensio recognizes the multi-dimen-
sional interpretative goals rhetorical critics are attempting to combine
in their analysis, but suggests that these complex goals are perhaps best
accomplished through the analysis of texts according to Hallidayan
functional grammar. As is evident from these essays, the interpretative
goal of rhetorical criticism is not a singularly stated and agreed
assumption.

One aspect of rhetorical criticism is that of assessing the nature and
strategies of argumentation. J.D.H. Amador, in dialogue with previous
papers from the conferences, raises the important question as to the role
of the author in a rhetorical-critical interpretation: is it the desire to
have an author in control and as an able practitioner of rhetoric which
gives our interpretation as rhetorical critics its interpretative unicity?
Using a more eclectic understanding of rhetoric, he shows in his
analysis of 1 Corinthians 11 that Pauline rhetoric or argumentation is
not as coherent and polished rhetorically as is often suggested. However, Anders Eriksson, in his rhetorical interpretation of 1 Corinthians
8–10, seeks to show how well Pauline argumentation follows a rhetorical plan which is consistent in terms of logos, ethos and pathos. The
larger question of Pauline argumentation is explored by Dennis L.
Stamps as he seeks to find what distinguishes Pauline theological
rhetoric from traditional forms of argumentation.

Another issue which rhetorical critics continue to explore is how
rhetorical criticism contributes to historical reconstruction and theological analysis. Both Thomas H. Olbricht and Duane F. Watson discuss
the way classical Greco-Roman rhetorical theory aids in the historical
reconstruction of the situation to which a text is addressed. Olbricht
offers a sharp critique of the way biblical scholars have used classical
rhetorical criticism to reconstruct the situation behind a text, and

1.   R. Coote and M. Coote, *Power, Politics and the Making of the Bible: An
Introduction* (Minneapolis: Fortress Press, 1990).

instead offers an expansion of his proposal for 'church rhetoric' to help define the situation and purpose of biblical texts in their original situation. Watson, however, in a comprehensive essay on methodology, gives a point-by-point prescription for the way classical rhetorical theory can illumine the original rhetorical and historical situation of New Testament texts. Lauri Thurén goes further in his 'derhetorizing of Galatians'. He suggests that a careful analysis of the rhetorical devices used by Paul in his letter to the Galatians suggests that the typical historical and psychological reconstruction of an angry Paul behind the letter needs re-evaluation. If the rhetorical devices in Galatians actually reveal a careful and calculating orator at work, then the theology of Paul as worked out in Galatians also needs re-evaluation. Rhetorical critics have claimed that rhetorical criticism offers new and valuable insights into the history and theology of biblical texts; these essays attempt to substantiate this claim.

In the end, rhetorical criticism is a method for interpreting the text. As in the earlier collections of essays from the previous conferences, a good number of essays offer rhetorical-critical readings of New Testament texts. In this collection, there has been particular focus on the Lukan writings. Kota Yamada offers a re-examination of how the preface to Luke's Gospel functions in comparison with the theory and practice of history-writing in the Greco-Roman period. L. Gregory Bloomquist offers a multi-textured reading of Luke 21 from the perspective of socio-rhetorical analysis in order to discern the particular nature of apocalyptic argumentation. His focus specifically examines the use of enthymemes in this text. Ira J. Jolivet, Jr, suggests that the discrepancies between the accounts of Paul's conversion in Acts 9, 22 and 26, particularly between Acts 9 and 26, can be addressed by using Hermagorean stasis theory instead of Aristotelian stasis theory. In so doing, the different literary functions of the two accounts are assessed and the defense strategy of Paul before Agrippa is revealed. Though thinking primarily of Paul, Stanley E. Porter also looks at the rhetoric of the Pauline speeches in Acts. His concern is to discern the persona of Paul as a rhetorician. Porter suggests that the two main bodies of potential evidence for Paul the rhetor are his letters and the speeches in Acts. He argues (as he has previously) that letter-writing bears little or no resemblance to the practice of rhetoric in the Greco-Roman period. However, in the speeches of Paul recorded in Acts, recognizing the influence of Lukan historiography, we have possible summary accounts of actual speeches of Paul which do have traces of Greco-Roman rhetorical practice. As one can observe, though these essays employ rhetorical criticism, each of them employs a different rhetorical theory and strategy exposing the diversity of rhetorical criticisms.

Three other essays offer rhetorical-critical readings of texts. Glenn S. Holland tackles the interpretative conundrum of the use of 'I' in Rom. 7.7-25. By examining the rhetoric of the use of 'I', Holland shows how this fits with the larger rhetorical strategy and intentions of the letter and how Paul deliberately employs the *topos* of self-example from the Hellenistic moral philosophers. Timothy W. Seid uses the Hellenistic rhetorical category of synkrisis (comparison) to address and solve the exegetical problems confronting the exegete when reading Hebrews 7. For Seid, synkrisis combined with the tactic of exhortation not only suggests a way to organize Hebrews 7 structurally, but also is a means to determine the function of the text. In a wide-ranging and comprehensive rhetorical reading of Ignatius of Antioch's *Philadelphians*, Mary W. Patrick examines the rhetoric of the text as a means for filtering the rhetorical self-presentation of Ignatius so that the critic can arrive at a more balanced assessment of his pastoral strategies and of his historical representation of his opponents. In each of these three essays, a rhetorical interpretation of the texts suggests that certain interpretative problems which have remained unsolved or unsatisfactorily solved can be resolved through rhetorical criticism. One of the goals of rhetorical criticism is to cast new light on old problems.

What is the essence of rhetorical criticism? How does rhetorical criticism conceive and analyze modes of argumentation? Can rhetorical criticism provide new and improved insights into the historical and theological questions of biblical interpretation? How does one's theory of rhetoric shape the way one interprets the rhetoric of biblical texts? Does applied rhetorical criticism offer better solutions to exegetical problems of biblical texts? The panoply of essays offered in this volume attempts to address these interpretative questions. They do not agree in the answers they suggest, either in method or in practice. It is equally important to recognize that these questions remain at the heart of the internal debate among rhetorical critics themselves. Though rhetorical critics debate among themselves, they seek to offer through their discipline new insights into the wider, ongoing debate of the interpretation of Scripture. These essays are meant as a contribution to the ongoing debate.

DEDICATION: A TRIBUTE TO THOMAS H. OLBRICHT

Richard T. Hughes

In 1985, the Religion Division at Pepperdine University launched a search for a new chairperson. This position would be difficult to fill since the division housed Old Testament scholars, New Testament scholars, specialists in theology and ethics, church historians, a scholar who taught in the field of world religions, and others who taught homiletics and practical ministry. Everyone hoped that the incoming chairperson would be at home with all these specialties, though no one seriously expected that the division would find someone with this kind of breadth. Then someone suggested that the division take a look at Thomas H. Olbricht.

It is rare to find a scholar of genuine breadth in this age of narrow specialization, but Olbricht fits that description about as well as anyone I have known. In fact, Olbricht is in many ways a Renaissance man. Broadly trained in biblical, theological and historical studies, Olbricht also earned a doctorate in speech and nurtured throughout his career a lively interest in the history of rhetoric. He has authored first-class academic treatises in all these fields, and has held leadership positions for over 30 years in professional organizations dedicated to the study of both religion and communication.

Partly because of his extraordinary breadth, Olbricht proved to be far more than a chairperson. He emerged instead as a genuine academic leader, a man who regularly engaged every person in the division in serious, scholarly conversation about his or her discipline. Olbricht provided academic leadership not only by words but also by deeds. Although he devoted much of his career to administrative tasks—he served once as a dean and on three different occasions as a departmental chairperson—he never allowed those tasks to undermine his work as a serious scholar. During his years at Pepperdine, he regularly rose at 4 a.m. in order to spend several hours at home on a scholarly article, a chapter in a book or a paper he was preparing for an academic meeting, before going to his office at Pepperdine. For this reason, he was—and continues to be—one of the most productive scholars I have known.

One cannot understand Olbricht, however, by simply gauging the breadth, depth and profundity of his scholarship. Olbricht was and is a man driven by his allegiance to the Christian faith and by his membership in the American-born Churches of Christ that descend from the Stone–Campbell movement of the early nineteenth century. Many years ago, Olbricht determined that he wanted to make a difference in the quality of preaching in this tradition, and that commitment drove him to combine an expertise in biblical and theological studies with an expertise in speech, communication and rhetorical studies.

Olbricht's commitment in this regard has borne abundant fruit. First, it is safe to say that he likely would not have blessed those of us in the academic community with the kind of high-level scholarship he has generated over the years had it not been for that commitment, made many years ago. Secondly, Olbricht's commitment has, indeed, made an enormous difference in both the quality of preaching and the quality of theological thinking that today characterize the pulpit of the Churches of Christ. In truth, it is difficult to think of anyone whose influence has been more pronounced in this regard. Scores of first-rate pulpiteers who studied at Abilene Christian University from 1967 to 1986, or at Pepperdine University from 1986 to 1996, readily acknowledge their debt to this man.

One example will suffice. Some years ago, the pulpit minister at the University Church of Christ in Abilene, Texas, preached a particularly fine sermon, informed throughout by the best insights of biblical theology. At the sermon's conclusion, I paid the preacher the highest compliment I knew how to give. 'Sir', I said, 'that was a marvellous sermon and you are an extraordinary theologian'.

'I am a student of Tom Olbricht', he quickly replied.

Finally, this sketch would not be complete unless we took note of Olbricht's commitment to generate serious conversation among scholars with common concerns. I have seen this happen any number of times over the years. Three examples will illustrate the point. First, in 1981, Olbricht founded the Christian Scholars' Conference, a meeting that evolved into the only annual conference that regularly brings together scholars who represent a variety of disciplines but who all happen to belong to the Churches of Christ. Secondly, while at Pepperdine, Olbricht organized a monthly discussion group that involved scholars from several disciplines who shared a common interest in the history of the Stone–Campbell movement in the United States. Thirdly, Olbricht provided the leadership that created the series of conferences on 'Rhetorical Criticism of Biblical Documents'. Without his leadership, this current volume would never have come to fruition. It is altogether appropriate, therefore, that here in this book we pay tribute to Tom for the quality of his scholarship and for giving so much to so many of us who work in the several fields of religious studies, rhetoric and communication.

CURRICULUM VITAE

Thomas H. Olbricht

Thomas H. Olbricht received his BS degree from Northern Illinois University in 1951, his MA from the University of Iowa in 1953, his PhD from the University of Iowa in 1959, and his STB from Harvard Divinity School in 1962.

Olbricht was Assistant Professor of Speech and Director of Forensics at Harding University from 1954 to 1955, and then Assistant Professor and Chair of the Speech Department at the University of Dubuque from 1955 to 1959. From 1962 to 1967, he went from Instructor to Associate Professor of Speech and Humanities at the Pennsylvania State University, and then from 1967 to 1986 at Abilene Christian University, he was Professor of Biblical Theology, as well as Dean of the College of Liberal and Fine Arts (1981–85) and Chair of Graduate Studies in Religion (1985–86). From 1986 to 1996, Olbricht was at Pepperdine University, where he was Chair and Professor in the Religion Division, and Distinguished Professor of Religion from 1994 to 1996. He is now Distinguished Professor of Religion Emeritus (1997–).

Besides serving as minister in various Churches of Christ in Illinois, Iowa, Massachusetts, Pennsylvania, Texas and California, Olbricht has held a number of positions in various service clubs and professional organizations. He has also been active as editor for several major journals. He was associate editor of *Speech Monographs* (1964–67), the *Quarterly Journal of Speech* (1968–71), the *Southern Journal of Speech Communication* (1974–77), and *Philosophy and Rhetoric* (1968–69). He also was associate editor and then editor of *Restoration Quarterly* (1963–87). He has served on the editorial boards of *Philosophy and Rhetoric* (1968–97) and of *Restoration Quarterly* (1987–). He was President of *The Second Century Journal, Inc.* (1981–96), as well as Director of Abilene Christian University Press (1985–86).

Olbricht has been honored as a Danforth Foundation Associate (1955–59) and Senior Associate (1959–80), and has won awards for his writing from *Restoration Quarterly* (1961) and *Twentieth Century Christian* (1987). He was also honored with a special issue of *Restoration Quarterly* on his sixty-fifth birthday (36.4 [1994]).

The prolific writing that Olbricht has done includes numerous books, chapters and articles. Among these, his most significant books include: *Informative Speaking* (Glen Ellyn, IL: Scott–Foresman, 1968); *The Message of Ephesians and Colossians* (Abilene, TX: Abilene Christian University Press, 1983); *Hearing God's Voice: My Life with Scripture in the Churches of Christ* (Abilene, TX: Abilene Christian University Press, 1996). With Stanley E. Porter, he has co-edited *Rhetoric and the New Testament: Essays from the 1992 Heidelberg Conference* (JSNTSup, 90; Sheffield: JSOT Press, 1993); *Rhetoric, Scripture and Theology: Essays from the 1994 Pretoria Conference* (JSNTSup, 131; Sheffield: Sheffield Academic Press, 1996); and *The Rhetorical Analysis of Scripture: Essays from the 1995 London Conference* (JSNTSup, 146; Sheffield: Sheffield Academic Press, 1997).

Chapters in books include significant entries on preaching, the early church, and various biblical topics. Several worthy of specific mention include: 'An Aristotelian Rhetorical Analysis of 1 Thessalonians', in D.L. Balch, E. Ferguson and W.A. Meeks (eds.), *Greeks, Romans, and Christians: Essays in Honor of Abraham J. Malherbe* (Philadelphia: Fortress Press, 1990), pp. 216-36; 'Amplification in Hebrews', in Porter and Olbricht (eds.), *Rhetoric and the New Testament*, pp. 375-87; 'The Rhetoric of Colossians', in Porter and Olbricht (eds.), *Rhetoric, Scripture and Theology*, pp. 308-28; 'The Flowering of Rhetoric in America', in Porter and Olbricht (eds.), *The Rhetorical Analysis of Scripture*, pp. 79-102; 'Delivery and Memory', in S.E. Porter (ed.), *Handbook of Classical Rhetoric in the Hellenistic Period 330 B.C.–A.D. 400* (Leiden: E.J. Brill, 1997), pp. 159-67; 'Exegesis in the Second Century', in S.E. Porter (ed.), *Handbook to Exegesis of the New Testament* (NTTS, 25; Leiden: E.J. Brill, 1997), pp. 407-23. Tom has also contributed numerous dictionary entries for such publications as the *Dictionary of Christian Ethics* (ed. C.F.H. Henry; Grand Rapids: Baker Book House, 1973); *Dictionary of Christianity in America* (ed. D.C. Reid, R.D. Linder, B.L. Shelley and H.S. Stout; Downers Grove, IL: InterVarsity Press, 1990); *The Blackwell Dictionary of Evangelical Biography: 1730–1860* (ed. D.M. Lewis; Oxford: Basil Blackwell,

1995); *Historical Handbook of Major Biblical Interpreters* (ed. D.K. McKim; Downers Grove, IL: InterVarsity Press, 1998); and the *Dictionary of Biblical Intepretation* (ed. J.H. Hayes; Nashville: Abingdon Press, 1999), with forthcoming entries in the *Dictionary of New Testament Background* (ed. C.A. Evans and S.E. Porter; Downers Grove, IL: InterVarsity Press). Olbricht also published extensively in the *Restoration Quarterly*, with articles appearing in 1961, 1962, 1963, 1965, 1966, 1968, 1972, 1979, 1980, 1982, 1988, 1991 and 1995, as well as in other journals and more popular level publications.

Part I

THE THEORY OF RHETORIC AND BIBLICAL INTERPRETATION

ACTING ON THE CENTER: AN INTERVIEW ON RHETORIC
AND HERMENEUTICS WITH THOMAS H. OLBRICHT IN THE WAKE
OF *HEARING GOD'S VOICE*

Erika Mae Olbricht

1. *Introduction*

For the 1996 Malibu conference, I had decided to write a paper on the
rhetoric of autobiography. I knew that Thomas H. Olbricht was writing
a new book that would be an autobiographical reflection on hermeneutics and Scripture, a format that interested me greatly. I thought that
it would give me the perfect opportunity to continue with some of the
ideas I posed in my paper from the 1995 conference in London on the
author-function, by asserting that the act of writing the self is an
(unsuccessful) attempt to override interpretive instability.[1]

But something did not sit right with me about this approach. While I
still hold those theoretical principles and find them rich and necessary
for understanding the status of texts and our own disciplinary use of
texts in a postmodern context, I thought it would be strange to discuss
Olbricht as an author-function, knowing that he would be present at the
conference. After a bit of hedging around a couple of other topics, I
finally decided that I would conduct an interview with him that would
address issues connecting this conference series with his new book,
*Hearing God's Voice: My Life with Scripture in the Churches of
Christ*.[2] However, I do not want to pretend that interviews are exempt
from any interpretive instability, nor do I want to claim that they are
outside of critical scrutiny—they themselves proliferate the author-
function, they do not suspend it.

---

1. E.M. Olbricht, 'Constructing the Dead Author: Postmodernism's Rhetoric
of Death', in S.E. Porter and T.H. Olbricht (eds.), *The Rhetorical Analysis of
Scripture: Essays from the 1995 London Conference* (JSNTSup, 146; Sheffield:
Sheffield Academic Press, 1997), pp. 66-78.
2. Abilene, TX: Abilene Christian University Press, 1996.

Hearing God's Voice, as I have just pointed out, establishes an autobiographical context for Olbricht's works and beliefs. It begins with his earliest childhood memories and the family members and friends that people them. Drawing on what he learned from their example, especially that of his mother, father and grandfather, he sets the stage for discussing the choices that he has made in terms of life commitments, scholarly pursuits and choices of career. At the center is a concern for the Scriptures and how they are interpreted and organized, both in church communities and in academic circles. *Hearing God's Voice* was written for a non-academic audience. Therefore, one of the primary goals that I have tried to accomplish in the questions I ask is to make connections to specific classes that he has taught, and to other of his scholarly interests.

2. *Interview*

In the introduction to Hearing God's Voice, *you state a couple of reservations about writing an autobiography. Reflect a bit on the process of writing a book like this. Did you have a model for it? Does its form place the book in a tradition with something like Augustine's* Confessions?[3]

For some years, students had asked that I write a book on hermeneutics. I had reflected a lot on hermeneutics, had taught it as part of various classes, and did give serious thought to writing such a book. My only problem, though, with writing it was that the book my students had in mind would be something of a cookbook—that is, some kind of a quick set of rules for settling hermeneutic matters. I decided that a book of that sort would be misleading and I didn't have much interest in writing it. In the midst of hearing about autobiographical theology, it dawned on me that here was a manner of pointing out my perspectives on hermeneutics without simply laying out a schematic 'how to' manual. I can't say that I had specifically thought a lot about autobiographical theology or even how to do it, though I had always been interested in autobiographical statements by theologians and had read several such items, including Augustine's *Confessions*. For that reason, I am sure

3.   This interview was conducted via email and in person between 28 June and 8 July 1996. Final revisions were made in July 1997.

that I had accumulated considerable acquaintance with autobiographical discourse, but I didn't really set out to write this book with any specific theory of autobiography in mind. Having read autobiographies that involved name-dropping and efforts to enhance self-importance, I set out to avoid these ends as much as possible. I could have told the story in a different manner through incorporating a different set of details. I do think the autobiographical aspects of this work are different in that I did not attempt to include every aspect of my upbringing and career, but only those dimensions having to do with the church and the interpretation of the Scriptures in it.

What, then, does autobiographical writing accomplish for you? Is (auto)biography a means of getting at the 'meant' rather than the 'means' (Krister Stendhal's distinction)?[4]

I do not have, I think, a foundational philosophy of autobiography. Philosophy itself, so I think, has no universal ontology from which to lift itself up. I therefore commence with the commitment that God is the point of departure. God is, above all, personal. He defines, in word and work, personhood. Since personhood is fundamental, any account of persons entails the totality of what they do or say, along with their reasons.

As I have argued in two journal articles,[5] reasons detached from persons are impersonal and therefore disingenuous. The effort to inform or persuade a person without being up-front in respect to reasons is manipulation. Therefore communication occurs fullest and best through autobiography, since the personhood of the author/speaker is thereby disclosed. The best way to try to help people think through 'what it means' is to try to follow in the footsteps of an author as he or she explains how they arrived at the point where they find themselves.

4.   The distinction is between what the biblical text meant in its original setting, and what it means now. The hermeneutical task is to construct a bridge between the 'meant' and the 'means'. K. Stendhal, 'Biblical Theology', in *IDB*, I, pp. 418-32.

5.   See 'The Self as a Ground of Persuasion', *The Pennsylvania Speech Annual* 21 (1964), pp. 28-36; and 'Speech and Commitment', *Today's Speech* 12 (1964), pp. 7-8.

I know that your interest in biography and autobiography carries over into the classes you teach. In particular, you have taught a first-year seminar at Pepperdine entitled 'Biographies in Christianity and Human Rights'. Will you comment on the class, and on the importance of accounts of lives of people for understanding something like human rights, or Christianity? There seems to be a connection between the importance of biography in your teaching and Hearing God's Voice. *Was your thinking about autobiography shaped and influenced by the course or vice versa?*

When I first designed this seminar I did it biographically for the reasons stated above. But I did not have students read biographies. They complained, and with justification, that the readings didn't match what went on in class. I explained that I wished the readings were better adapted to the course, but I couldn't find readings of that sort. Then it occurred to me that I should cut down on the topics and read, with the students, biographies of selected persons. In this manner not only are human rights on the table, but also the reasons why specific persons acted, wrote and spoke as they did in regard to human rights. We read biographies of Martin Luther King, Jr, Cesar Chavez, Elizabeth Cady Stanton and Jane Addams—four who at least commenced their life-long commitment to human rights from Christian motivations. So even though we covered fewer topics, the ones we took up were more vivid and related to persons. And, after all, that matched my vision, because ideas don't float in the universe. They are always attached to persons who hold them. Students surface as persons through that apprenticeship in which they struggle with the reasons advanced by persons, as well as with conclusions.

At several points in Hearing God's Voice, *you talk about the difference between rationality and storytelling—one tending toward the analytical and logical, and the other tending toward the emotive. Hauerwas and Burrell use Augustine's* Confessions *as a centerpiece of their article on narrative as the alternative to rationality.[6] Quickly, their central thesis is that moral codes are determined from and redisseminated within narrative (or more specifically, story). In the light of narrative theology*

---

6. S. Hauerwas and D. Burrell, 'From System to Story: An Alternative Pattern for Rationality in Ethics', in S. Hauerwas and L. Gregory Jones (eds.), *Why Narrative? Readings in Narrative Theology* (Grand Rapids: Eerdmans, 1989), pp. 157-90.

and the ways that you have discussed your upbringing, is there a way to dovetail theories of rational logic and emotive storytelling? Better yet, do you find the answers that the Hauerwas school gives to the question satisfying?

This is a good question which I did not undertake to address in *Hearing God's Voice*. I employed narrative in my book because of the conviction that good hermeneutical insights must always be incarnated, since it is in this manner that the interpretation of the past, so as to create a present, always occurs in 'real' life. I think the Hauerwas school is correct that models for life and the codes contained therein are most fully passed generationally through narratives. I am reluctant, however, to pinpoint the difference in the emotive over and against the logical. Narratives may be essentially logical as is the case with two novels of Umberto Eco: *The Name of the Rose* and *The Island of the Day Before*. As novels they are imaginistic (that is, these novels include philosophical or scientific reasoning, yet they aren't written like philosophies), but they are written from the perspective of logical coherence. The novels of Charles Dickens, in contrast, are fictional and center on the subjectivity of the characters. These subjectivities are not just emotion or feeling, but existential concerns embracing both reasoning and feeling. Anthony Trollope, in contrast, presents the noetic and emotional side of his characters, but has some difficulty integrating the two. For me a holistic approach to narrative is represented in the historical writings of Daniel Boornstin, for example, his book *The Creators*, and that of Samuel Eliot Morison, *The Great Explorers*. It is difficult to characterize their approach as either emotional or logical, but rather as a constant combination of both. In any case, their works are highly imaginistic. Many of the biblical narratives possess these same characteristics, for example, the succession narrative of the Deuteronomistic historian and the Gospel of Luke. I have tried to present a coherent view of interpreting Scripture in an imaginistic manner, which contains the discrete and the emotional, but without either upstaging the other. Since this is a characteristic of much biblical material, a helpful hermeneutic must, therefore, somehow incorporate these and whatever other features the Scriptures exhibit.

Is autobiography, then, an 'alternative' to rationality without also losing its 'logicalness'?

Yes, and with my commitments it is more responsible since it is a means of apprenticeship into personhood. I argued this point in a book on informative speaking.[7] My epistemological commitment favors a strong preference for coherence. And with my prior commitments, logicalness is the 'inner logic' of a person, the prime example being the logicalness of God, who is, above all, a person. So rationality is not to be discovered in the universe as such, but in the coherence of the person—that is, God, or those made in his image. The universe is not without coherence, but its coherence is because of who God the creator is as a person.

In keeping with your autobiographical methodology in Hearing God's Voice, *I'd like you to 'tell the story' of the international Rhetoric and Scripture conferences.*

There is some description of the beginnings of the international rhetorical conferences in the introduction of the Heidelberg volume.[8] In 1990 considerable interest in the rhetorical criticism of the Scriptures was in evidence among persons at the meetings of the Western region of the Society of Biblical Literature, including Wilhelm Wuellner, Burton Mack, James Hester, Stanley Porter, Jeffrey Reed, Ronald Hock, James M. Robinson and myself. It was obvious, too—especially to Wilhelm Wuellner—that several scholars in other countries had developed an interest in rhetoric.

In 1989 it came to my attention that the Borchard Foundation in Los Angeles owned a chateau in France which they encouraged groups to use for scholarly activities. So in consultation with James Hester and Wilhelm Wuellner I made a proposal to the Foundation, which, however, was not approved. But we had through this effort discovered that several persons, especially in Europe and South Africa, were interested in such a conference. So in 1992, I made arrangements with Dr William B. Phillips, Dean of International Programs at Pepperdine, to use the facilities of Pepperdine's Heidelberg Program, the Moore

7. T.H. Olbricht, *Informative Speaking* (Glen Ellyn, IL: Scott–Foresman, 1968).

8. S.E. Porter and T.H. Olbricht (eds.), *Rhetoric and the New Testament: Essays from the 1992 Heidelberg Conference* (JSNTSup, 90; Sheffield: JSOT Press, 1993), pp. 9-10.

Haus. Since then we have had conferences in Pretoria (1994) and London (1995), and now this one in Malibu (1996).

How would you have fitted the story of the conferences and your involvement in them in Hearing God's Voice *topically, and what would you have to say about hermeneutics vis-à-vis the idea of the conference series?*

I think hermeneutics and rhetoric in the history of the interpretation of the Scriptures, especially the New Testament, are obviously connected as is shown through the works of biblical commentators from the fourth century through medieval times, and especially in continental renaissance and eighteenth-century biblical scholars. But the question is how, with my concerns, did I connect the two? One might say it was more accidental than intentional. My scholarly interests in the 1960s and 1970s revolved about rhetoric as a means of understanding discourse. In the 1960s, when I took up biblical studies at Harvard, I did not direct much attention to rhetorical analysis of the Scriptures. What work in rhetoric I did do was more directed toward the history of preaching and various other genres of discourse. My love, as it turned out, was biblical theology, especially inspired by G. Ernest Wright, but also Amos Wilder, Krister Stendahl and Abraham J. Malherbe. I became interested in biblical theology not as an arcane discipline, but as a special foundation for the theology proclaimed in the Church. I perceived biblical theology as the lens through which the theology of the Scriptures was to be mediated to the Church. It was for this reason that I got involved in controversies concerning hermeneutics. I never chose the role of an expert on hermeneutics, but I was drawn into it because of these interests. It became my conviction that it was imperative for the Church to develop a sense of biblical theology if it were to focus on the centers of the faith rather than the peripheries. Therefore, I concluded that biblical theology was a necessary *prolegomenon* for proper appropriation of the Scriptures, that is, hermeneutics.

When biblical scholars became newly interested in rhetoric in the late 1970s I became interested because of my past training and teaching. But what I saw was the embracing of many of the same freeze-frame perspectives which persons in speech rhetoric had managed to overthrow. I therefore tried to suggest new trajectories, but by then I had so many others matters to address that I had little time to turn out scholarly articles on rhetorical criticism.

I do think that one manner of interpreting the Scriptures is rhetorically, that is, through rhetorical analysis. I think it proper for rhetorical interpretation to take its place among other forms of criticism. Hermeneutics, as I understand it, has to do with the larger philosophical commitments and insights from which discourses are analyzed. Since rhetorical analysis is one valid aspect of this enterprise, then anyone interested in how Scripture is incorporated into the life of the church, that is, hermeneutics, and who has training in rhetoric, must, of course, relate the two. It is therefore not accidental that I relate my rhetorical backgrounds to hermeneutics in *Hearing God's Voice*.

For other scholars, in the meantime, philosophical and theological hermeneutics—especially in France and Germany in the twentieth century—have created new perspectives on discourse and those who originate it. These recently minted hermeneutics, in turn, have generated new rhetorics, which have been applied to literature and speech forms and likewise employed in the rhetorical analysis of the Scriptures. As yet, however, much rhetorical analysis of Scripture has drawn upon that classical rhetoric which is contemporary with the New Testament period.

Since hermeneutics and rhetoric are intricately related, as you've just pointed out, I would also like to ask about the Pepperdine graduate course in hermeneutics you have taught with Ron Highfield (Professor of Theology). What is the organization and focus of the class? What things have come together to make this class feasible and useful in an academic setting?

Actually the course Ron Highfield and I just completed was not focused, as such, on hermeneutics. We did teach such a course four years ago. But rather than resurrecting the hermeneutics course, I wish to talk about the course I'm presently teaching with him, since, though it did not occur to me as we put the course together, I did draw heavily upon my backgrounds in rhetoric, hermeneutics and biblical theology. We titled the course, 'Scripture, Theology and the Sermon'. For its purpose, we set forth:

> A study of the manner in which memorable sermons exhibit theological acumen. The course will begin by defining and explaining the complementary nature of exegesis, biblical theology, and systematic theology,

and offering a theoretical account of how these disciplines would function in sermon preparation. The principles will be illustrated by a study
of several selected sermons from the history of preaching. Finally, the
students will incorporate these theoretical insights into sermons that they
will write and present to the class.

As to academic justification, that question did not arise, at least, to
the students, who were somewhat dazed by the insights brought to bear
from theology (Highfield is a systematic theologian) and biblical
theology, as well as from concrete sermons in history. One of the
matters discussed was discourse genre in order to help the students, as
well as the professors, categorize the 30 sermons taken up, which had
been delivered by great preachers, beginning with Bernard of Clairvaux.

In addition to setting forth my insights on the relationship of biblical
theology to hermeneutics, and therefore to sermonizing, I set out for the
first time to discuss systematically the genres located in biblical
materials. I suggested that these genres might inform priorities in
preaching, as well as furnish insights into rhetorical approaches of
diverse materials. I noted that much material in Scripture is narrative,
including some oral discourses. However, other materials, such as laws
and proverbs, are itemizational, while others, including oral discourses,
are topical or argumentative. Then there are the less frequently
employed genres identified by biblical scholars over the long course of
scholarly analysis such as parables, proverbs, psalms, allegories,
apocalypses, epistles, gospels, and so on. We were then able to note
genre approaches in the 30 noted sermons, as well as in the sermons
presented by the students. The course caused me to think anew about
the genre and analysis of biblical materials, drawing upon the insights
of classical and new rhetorics.

*What, then, do you think to be the relationship between academia and
Church life? It's fairly clear from your answer here that there is a clear
practical connection. What is the theoretical connection also?*

I don't see any *a priori* or foundational connection between academia
and Church life. The fact is, of course, that in the twentieth century
academia has set out to cut itself off from interchange with communities of faith. It's interesting what forces them back together. For
example, 30 years ago the up-and-coming archaeologists rejected the
concept of biblical archaeology, in preference for a form of archaeology

without political or religious agendas. There was considerable support from the scholarly guild. But the archaeologists discovered their funds drying up. So they are back once again interfacing with religious communities.

My personal commitment is first to the Church, or best stated, to him who is the God of the Church, and then to academia. I have therefore sought academic institutions with the same commitment. My personal conviction is that the Church thrives through interfacing with academia. I agree with the declaration of long ago, that the Church advances as much by the ink of scholars as it does by the blood of martyrs. My vision of theological training is that the two must constantly interface. Pragmatically, I find it strange that the scholarly study of religion has set out to cut itself adrift from communities of faith. No one, I think, assumes that the academic study of business is enhanced through scientifically generated objectivity in which the academic community is isolated from the business community. I do, however, think that religion itself is a first order experience, whereas the academic study of religion is a once removed, or second order, experience. Without communities of faith, religion academics have nothing to study. Without academics, religious communities lack sufficient reflective and critical implements for checking out original moorings, coherences and consistencies.

The reason I've titled this interview 'Acting on the Center' is that you are very clear at several points in the text that the end and center of our biblically informed belief system should be the putting of the beliefs into action (one configuration of which might involve the cooperation of academic and religious communities). You stress that this is our example from the Bible: that God first acts and then expects us to follow that example—not in what we say we believe, but in the way we actually manifest it in our lives. So I'm now wondering about the title of the book: since the book is so focused on action, is it ironic that the title calls for 'hearing' (which could be construed as a passive position)? Secondly, what is the status of 'text' in your book, and does it change when you are writing about/theorizing a rhetorical analysis of Scripture? How does a specifically rhetorical consideration of Scripture help elucidate the role of Scripture in the life of one who studies the Word?

I think you are correct that the title, *Hearing God's Voice*, does not identify fairly the focus of the book. I stressed more the concretizing of concepts in Scripture in the life and action of the Church. But one who produces trade books has to quarrel with publishers over titles. Publishers are more interested in titles that sell, established by the dictates of market research. After the publisher rejected my original scholarly title, *Hermeneutics: Autobiographical Reflections*, I proposed *Where God Speaks: Interpreting Scripture in the Church*. But be that as it may, Jesus, in the Sermon on the Mount, eschewed hearing alone, declaring that in the kingdom of God hearing is inevitably accompanied by doing. They are two sides of the same coin, so that in the disciple, hearing incorporates action. On this dipolar basis, perhaps the title is, in fact, descriptive of the thrust of the book.

In regard to the status of the text, in *Hearing God's Voice* most of my readers assign Scripture a privileged position. They perceive the Bible in various ways, but it is privileged because it is the text they read far more than others in the Church, since they assign it an add-on merit, a merit derived from deity. Most accept the designation 'Word of God' as descriptive. But they will vary as to the manner in which it came to be the Word of God. Not many hold the view that God is the author through dictation. The different texts designated as Scripture manifest the traits and vocabulary of their human authors. Nevertheless, God is involved in the final outcome. In the book, therefore, when interpreting Scripture, rather than declaring, 'The Bible is to be interpreted in this manner', I state, for example, that according to Leviticus, 'You are to be holy because I the Lord your God am holy', that Jesus in the Sermon on the Mount declared, 'Be perfect, therefore, as your heavenly father is perfect', and that Paul wrote to the Corinthians, 'Be imitators of me as I am of Christ'. I am, in other words, always author specific. The manner in which the text is breathed by God is therefore always mediated through a human author.

I therefore commence with a text from Scripture as if I am doing author–reader centered criticism. At this stage I am interested in ascertaining what the text meant (to employ the distinction of Krister Stendahl between what the text 'meant' and what it 'means' in his 1962 essay on hermeneutics in *The Interpreter's Dictionary of the Bible* [see n. 4]). I am aware that this distinction has numerous detractors, but I view it as having certain heuristic benefits. Since I believe that all later theology sits under the judgment of biblical theology in its varied manifestations, I therefore believe that what an author meant in the theology of a biblical text must be ascertained before one hurries on to declare a theology for today: which is, the hermeneutical move. In practice, I agree, it is difficult to separate the 'meant' from the 'means'.

So why have I declared another dipolar, that is, author–reader centered criticism? I believe the two should not be separated, unless again for heuristic purposes. As I wrote in *Hearing God's Voice*, in the early 1960s I became convinced that while speaker purpose is always the first motivating factor in determining the subject matter and direction of a discourse, the form it takes as to rhetorical strategies is always dependent upon the audience, that is, if the aims of the speaker are in any sense to be attained. Therefore, I came to embrace a rhetorical criticism which was heavily audience centered. What a text 'meant' must therefore up-front and center assess the perspectives of the reader. The situation of the reader must be ascertained through painstaking historical sleuthing. But assessing the rhetorical strategies may also contribute since these strategies are precisely audience centered. Now when the church corporately makes its hermeneutical move, and I am more interested in the hermeneutical moves of the church than of individuals, in a sense, reader-response interpretation moves to the forefront. The question to be addressed is what this text means to this church in this particular time and setting. But, as I argue in *Hearing God's Voice*, I believe the church is only ready to address the text in this manner *after* it has assessed what the text meant.

I now am ready to comment on the role of scholarly rhetorical criticism. I see rhetorical criticism as contributing to what the text meant. It is concerned with assessing how a rhetorical analysis of 1 Thessalonians, for example, helps determine what the letter meant in its own setting. The rhetorical analysis of texts, for the most part in the scholarly guild, is not concerned with what a text should mean in a confessional body or in a particular congregation. I do think, however, that those who undertake the task of determining in the midst of a congregation what a text means are assisted through being rhetorically informed. They are more aware of the rhetorical features of the text and how these may assist in bestowing power from the discourse upon the contemporary Church.

You are talking here primarily about how the Church and scholars engage in interpretation, but to what extent does rhetoric as theory (methodology) and as discipline conceive of itself as non-hermeneutical? Or, to what extent is rhetoric (not) about interpretation?

Every humanistic discipline is in some sense hermeneutical in that it sets out to interpret an aspect of human existence. For example, psychology sets out to explain or interpret the deep inner recesses of human personality. Sociology takes up humanity from another aspect, that is, social patterning and structuring. Psychological or sociological criticism can therefore be perceived as resulting from certain presuppositions regarding interpretation. In other words they proceed from the foundation of a certain hermeneutical mindset. In this sense rhetoric also commences with certain hermeneutical presuppositions, that is, that all discourse is an inextricable mixture of the aspirations of a speaker/author and the needs of audiences/readers. Rhetoric focuses on the discourse strategies whereby this communicative interaction takes place. It is a discipline in its own right, just as are psychology and sociology, but perhaps more a cognate discipline to hermeneutics than other humanistic disciplines, because the provenance of both hermeneutics and rhetoric is text/discourse.

Yes, but doesn't rhetorical theory believe that somehow it isn't involved in the work of interpretation, or what the text 'means'? How would you express the explicit connection between rhetoric and hermeneutics?

I think that much of the early motivation to apply rhetorical theory to biblical criticism in the last half of this century has been to discover what the text meant. The effort was therefore only indirectly related to what the text means. The hermeneutical move occurs with the conviction that did not seem that strong in some, that a better understanding of what it meant would in turn result in a superior perspective on what it means. In my own case, my main concern is what it means, thus the strong interest in hermeneutics. But, as I have argued here, I am committed to what the Scripture meant always sitting in judgment on what it means. Therefore the what it 'meant'/what it 'means' dichotomy is imperative for heuristic purposes. But in my case, as well, it is imperial because of my theological commitment. The result is a hermeneutic generated from a special set of presuppositions. If, then, rhetorical analysis can better help us understand what the text meant, as I think it can, it is inextricably involved in the critical process. Furthermore, since I think what it means must also be rhetorically informed, rhetoric is crucial for both sides of the equation, and therefore endemic to a legitimate hermeneutics.

I'd like you to elaborate on this passage about hermeneutics from Hearing God's Voice: *'Culture, even our own, influences hermeneutics far more than we realize. We discover cultural influence through examining Christian history as well as that of our own movement'.*[9] *You set out an interesting and thought-provoking argument of cultural reasons for certain aspects of religious practices. Does discovering 'cultural influence' entail getting to a purer level of interpretation, or are we trying to maintain a core while accounting and allowing for cultural changes? If so, how is it that that core, that center, escapes interpretive (and cultural) instability?*

You are right in declaring that I see all hermeneutical commitments as having origins in a culture, or multi-cultures. Enlightenment hermeneutics, for example, do not spring up independently. They are based upon a repositioning and reformulating of several commitments already overt or covert in the Greco-Roman, Christian West. For the most part, I have not been interested in cultural purgation, which entails the peeling back of successive layers of adulterated membranes, so as to arrive at the original pristine nucleus. I have been more interested in identifying cultural influences in order to cure or purge the church of those who contend that their hermeneutics transcend human cultures of all sorts. Wittgenstein set out on a mission of purgation so as to cure philosophers of philosophizing. My mission has not been to purge the Church of either hermeneutics, theologizing or culture. Rather, the purging side of my mission has been to notice the cultural aspects of hermeneutics so as perhaps to discover hermeneutical presuppositions which run counter to or inhibit the identifying of those growing out of biblical visions. Biblical presuppositions are ensconced in culture. All human existence is ensconced in culture. Efforts to purge humanity of culture result in purging humanity itself. In the biblical witness, God did not eschew culture. He embraced it through choosing Israel, a people with a culture, and sending a Son who emptied himself in order fully to embody humanity, culture and all.

Certain biblical presuppositions are transcultural—that is, they cut

9. Olbricht, *Hearing God's Voice*, pp. 441-42.

across different cultures, taking on the nuances of the cultures they embrace—but none can be said to be above culture. For example, Micah declared,

> He has told you, O mortal, what is good;
> and what does the LORD require of you
> but to do justice, and to love kindness,
> and to walk humbly with your God? (Mic. 6.8).

Take justice. It is the effort to see that persons are treated in a caring, equitable way, suitable to their time, place and position. It is informed and, in fact, generated by the God of Israel who exhibits these very characteristics. It is true that 'justice' may seem to transcend culture. It may seem to have an essence as Plato hoped. But what can that be? It can have little to do with humans since humans are always an embodiment of time and place. In fact, the essence of justice for which Plato sought was beyond time and place. But in the biblical vision God himself is not beyond time and place, even though he is beyond human time and place. To me, any effort to set forth a transcendental hermeneutic which in turn can identify a transcendental theological core is like buying petunias from a nursery, carefully purging their roots of all the soil with water, and setting them out in a newly fumigated soil so as to grow pristine petunias. Rather than thriving, petunias treated in this way die. So also do humans purged by a transcendental hermeneutic which in turn claims to have isolated transcendental theology.

I would argue that this assertion of cultural specificity is also linked to material conditions by virtue of its insistence on the physical: 'If God's word is dynamic, if the resurrection of Jesus Christ is the best news of the centuries, and if the story is so important that it is to be told with passion, then a public hermeneutic must ultimately include these oral and physical dimensions... Factors that contribute to a more dynamic personality, therefore, enhance the vocal and bodily interpretation of the Gospel.'[10] Will you elaborate on 'physical dimensions' and 'bodily interpretation'?

What I am arguing for here is a vision of humanness which is holistic. It includes all aspects of what it means to be human. Though I said very little on this in *Hearing God's Voice*, in the 1950s I was greatly

10. Olbricht, *Hearing God's Voice*, pp. 162-63.

influenced by gestalt psychology and in the 1960s by the phenomen-
ology of Merleau-Ponty. In Scripture, a holistic view of humanity is
affirmed in such words as 'heart' in the Old Testament, and 'body' in
the New Testament. My point, then, is that both hermeneutics and
rhetoric must embrace the whole of humanity, not just the senses, the
mind or the emotions. The human in her or his wholeness is also
dynamic, which must also be incorporated into hermeneutics and
rhetoric.

What I meant by bodily interpretation has to do with the Church, the
congregation, that is, the body of Christ. I argued from the start that
hermeneutics is not an individual project which is then foisted upon the
church. Rather, it is a bodily enterprise—that is, that what the
Scriptures mean is to be hammered out by the whole body of believers
in each congregation.

In the last part of Hearing God's Voice, *you talk about the necessity for
churches (interpretive communities) to decide on interpretations. This
seems quite consonant to me with your interest in audience-centered
rhetoric that you discuss in* Hearing God's Voice. *Would you elaborate
on the importance of audience-centered rhetoric? Would you then talk
a little about the ways that a concern for interpretive communities and
for audience-centered rhetoric is different than reader-response criticism (in its viable forms, perhaps; not necessarily its Barthesian/
Fishesque impossibility)?*

I have already noted the compatibility of audience-centered rhetoric
and reader-response criticism. But I see a difference. An audience-
centered rhetoric declares that a speaker or writer can only ignore her
audience or reader at great risk. The discourse may happen, but little, if
any, communication will occur. Such effort is doomed to be abortive
from the start. Reader-response criticism also suggests that the audience
determines the proper interpretation of a text. The difference lies in the
fact that the audience is a new one, located in a different time and
place. It is not the same audience addressed by the original speaker or
writer. Therefore, the interpretation itself may be a new one. New
audiences for ancient texts are inevitable. If it is possible for the
Scriptures to be living discourse from generation to generation, new
readers must bring to bear new insights. To that extent reader-response
criticism is inevitable. But I insist, as I have already explained, that it is

dangerous to turn loose on ancient documents new readers who have not paid their dues in respect of assessing carefully the manner in which the original audience was determinative for the manner in which the speaker or writer proceeded rhetorically. In other words, reader-response criticism needs the initial controls of traditional grammatico-historical criticism. It is only in this manner that the theology of the Scriptures can sit in judgment on the theology of the Church as it proceeds corporately and imaginistically to interpret the Bible.

You have said a couple of times in this interview that you aren't a foundationalist. Would you elaborate on what that position means in its connection to rhetoric, or to your ideas on hermeneutics in Hearing God's Voice*? In what way is community a foundation for interpretation?*

Perhaps if I approach this question autobiographically, at least how I came to turn away from foundationalism, it will be clear. In the early 1950s, I tended to think that a series of propositions could be set forth that provided a sure foundation for all insight and knowledge. These foundations were something to the effect that the Bible is true because evidence can be adduced to establish beyond a doubt that the Bible is historically accurate and contains numerous prophecies that have been fulfilled. This authenticated Bible asserts the existence of God and the deity of Jesus, and therefore establishes their reality beyond a reasonable doubt. Since God exists, he is the creator of the universe. In his creation he incorporated natural laws which when understood provide the certain foundations for explaining every aspect of the universe. With these foundations in tow one can convince every auditor or reader of biblical teachings in regard to baptism, congregational independence, weekly celebration of the Lord's Supper, and the rule of elders and deacons.

In the 1960s through the study of rhetoric, it became more and more obvious to me that in order to persuade a person of something not now embraced, that appeal had to be made not so much to my indubitable conclusions, but to views held by the various persons addressed. I found it was not so simple to prove to a Roman Catholic that congregations should be independent of each other. My Catholic graduate friend asserted that the hierarchical church brought forth and preserved the Bible, and since that church knew nothing of congregational independence this was a concept conceived by Protestants who did not come into existence until 1500 years after the Catholic church was founded. It was clear to me that if I were to convince him, I had do it on grounds other than my certain foundations.

As the 1960s wore on I became convinced that the only foundations of use in argument were those agreed upon by the audience. Aristotle labeled these agreements 'enthymemes'. If this is indeed the case, then there are no universal foundations from which to persuade an audience. Rather than rehearsing certain foundations, one must identify and appeal to presuppositions held by those being addressed. If no common presuppositions are held by all audiences (and such seems to be the case) then foundations are neither certain nor universal. Rather, they are relative only to the audiences holding them. So my rhetorical observations led me to a rhetorically induced relativism. In *Hearing God's Voice* I identified this conclusion as a form of postmodernism which I embraced before postmodernism was identified or popularized. But regardless of declaring a rhetorically informed foundationlessism, I still struggled with the fact that though I could not assume that my auditors accepted or could be persuaded by my certain foundations, I continued to hold that these foundations did in fact exist whether or not any particular set of audience/readers accepted them.

In the 1960s I took up the study of philosophy, theology and biblical theology. I don't have space here to present such details as may be found in *Hearing God's Voice*, but I came to doubt that what I believed could be set out upon certain and cogently related foundations, Cartesian style. I was still intrigued by certain arguments, for example, Descartes's dictum that we cannot doubt that we doubt, or Anselm's ontological argument. Nevertheless, I had come to believe that no universal foundations remain which uphold reality, or from which certain knowledge accrues. I have been influenced in these directions through the work of Stanley Hauerwas and associates, who recently stated the case effectively in *Theology without Foundations*.[11]

But I still believed in starting-points for reality. These, however, rested not in texts or in abstract certainties, but in God—creator and sustainer, and the father of the Lord Jesus Christ. Apart from him no universals exist. Whatever apparent universals are discoverable, he created them. No universals explain his being, activities or commitments. He himself defines himself, his reality, whatever moral and ethical rules

11. S. Hauerwas, N. Murphy and M. Nation (eds.), *Theology without Foundations* (Nashville: Abingdon Press, 1994).

there may be, and other rights and wrongs. No exterior rules define his person or what he must be or do. He himself makes the rules. Abstract reason may insist that God is omnipresent, omniscient and omnipotent. Such reason may go on to insist that God cannot leave himself vulnerable to aberrant love, or abscond omniscience for incomplete knowledge. But such rules cannot be superimposed upon God. What if, in fact, he so loved the world, a world which rejected his Lordship, that he gave his only beloved Son, or that the Son emptied himself of omipresence, omniscience and omnipotence and took on the very being of humanity? That he did this may contradict what it means to be God from certain abstract universals. But if he himself determines what it means to be God, then so be it, even if the foundations crumble. What remains is the community of God in praise, as affirmed in the nineteenth-century hymn: 'We praise thee, O God, for thy Spirit of light, who has shown us our Savior, and scattered our night'. That community knows God in experience and in the discrete. Universal foundations evaporate. I believe that Christians have no other foundation than God alone, as declared in the great hymn, 'The church's one foundation is Jesus Christ her Lord; She is his new creation by water and the word'. He is the one proclaimed. Readers/auditors may concur or defer. Nothing universal or foundational adjudicates this posture in any manner whatever.

If the materiality of the community of the Church is important for the formation and reinforcement of the story and worship, as you clearly demonstrate, what conclusions can we draw about rhetoric and material practices? To what extent is rhetoric still fluid, even when anchored in (and, I would say, anchoring) material/cultural practices?

Rhetoric, I think, is especially related to and changes within material or situational differences. The ancient Greeks already noticed diverse materiality and therefore identified three genres of rhetoric: those of the political assembly, the court room, and the market place (or deliberative, forensic and epideictic genres). Biblical scholars, coming to rhetoric through the eyes of those who are out to preserve the ways of the fathers rather than advancing their insights, have tended to argue that the ancient rhetoricians identified the major situations for all humans in all times and places. This conclusion, one should think, would be questioned immediately, but strangely it has survived. The reason, in part, is that modern rhetorical scholars have not progressed much beyond the ancient constructs in rhetoric. Maintaining such a conclusion is the same as arguing that the Greeks had it right; there are four elements that comprise all nature: earth, water, air and fire. Chemists through the ages have revised these categories, rejected the above and divided the basic elements into 110 and placarded these on atomic charts in science classrooms all over.

Speakers and writers employ many strategies for attaining their ends. These vary considerably, even within the same context, depending on the auditors or readers. Twentieth-century communication scholars have commenced to map an increasing number of these diverse strategies, but it is almost a fledgling discipline. The issues are complex and few are dedicated to the sort of rigor and creativity which characterize Aristotle's heads-up observations. Materiality includes multiform nuances of existence. We should acknowledge multiple diversity, not ignore it.

What is required before much progress can be made in the rhetorical analysis of the Scriptures is the maturing of the discipline of rhetoric itself through observations of endless forms of diversities in rhetorical situations and strategies.

INTERPRETIVE UNICITY:
THE DRIVE TOWARD MONOLOGICAL (MONOTHEISTIC) RHETORIC

J.D.H. Amador

1. *Authorial Unicity*

I was struck by a remark in Joachim Classen's presentation to the 1995 London Conference, wherein he quickly, and perhaps facetiously, referred to and commented upon a number of papers. One remark was directed at the paper Erika Mae Olbricht had presented, 'Dead Authors and Risen Critics: Postmodernism's Rhetoric of Death'. He quipped, 'I was interested to note that as quickly as the author was proclaimed dead, he was raised again'. Setting aside the question of his intention and motivations behind this remark, I simply note that it was quite true.

Which, given my own theoretical preoccupations with attempting to develop a post-humanist rhetorics, I found quite disturbing. Because, I think, Olbricht has pinpointed something important for us here to consider: what is the function that we ascribe to the author of a given biblical text? Now, indeed, with respect to the Bible, it could be said that critics make use of a variety of 'authors' in their interpretations: for, in spite of the certain anonymity of some texts, the questionability of the ascription of a given author to other texts, and the known pseudonymity of still more texts, critics continue to produce works that ascribe a certain intentionality to a text, a singularity of purpose, a consistency of message, a coherence in (theological and ideological) perspective, to which they ascribe a given name (Paul, Mark, John, Moses, etc.) or personified title (the Chronicler, the Deuteronomic historian, etc.). I think what is behind this is not just simply or predominantly a conservative preservation of methodologies and their roots in modernity, but a monotheistic ideology governing our critical analyses: god as author, god as text/word.

This ideology affects our work in several different ways: in the function of authorial 'intentionality' as the critical goal of our analyses (analogous to discerning the 'will of god' in the Scriptures), and in the function of authorial unicity. I will touch upon the former function later in this essay. It is the latter function which interests me at this moment.

What do I mean by authorial unicity? I mean the assumption that a singular governing theme, a singular intentionality or purpose, governs the direction and goal of the text. It is what we mean when we refer to *the* point, *the* main argument of a book or letter. It is what we use as the impetus to iron out inconsistencies or confusion in the text by means of our analyses. It is what is behind our attempts at biography, or at understanding the situation (historical, social, cultural) that surrounds the production of the text and gives it meaning. It is at work when we speak of the 'theology' of a particular text, author or tradition. It infuses our critical practice through and through.

In this essay I want to (1) show how it dominates our work, (2) offer an analysis which simply refuses to ascribe such unicity in a critical reading of a text, (3) suggest theoretical clarification regarding 'intentionality', which might help us methodologically to avoid the trap of unicity in our critical efforts and bring us nearer to a post-humanist critical direction to our work, and (4) offer some potential implications for our work if we adopt, at the very least, a less monological understanding of authorial unicity and 'intentionality'.

2. *Examples*

I would like to take the case of Paul, someone whose life and message has been the object of innumerable studies. At stake here is the fact of a 'real' author behind at least some of the letters written in his name, an author whose message and ministry we believe we can reconstruct with some certainty after careful study. Here it is very tempting to ascribe a unicity to his message, since it is 'obvious' that the 'same' individual is writing these (authentic) letters. At the very least, we should be able to find coherence in any given letter. Surely it cannot be too surprising to find a singularity of intention, a coherence in argumentation, a consistency in his advice and explanations when he sits down to address the circumstances of a particular community under his care.

I believe I can quickly cite some of the more 'obvious' drives toward unicity in our own interpretive efforts of Paul's letters. I can do so by limiting my references to the work done by this conference: examples are ready to hand, even if we limit our gaze to several of last year's excellent presentations.

One of the more 'obvious' examples of the drive for unicity can be found in attempts, through appeal to rhetorical arrangement, to 'prove' the coherence of a letter whose unity has been called into question by earlier methodological means such as source- (and form-) criticism. Duane Watson's work is a good example of what I mean,[1] where he combines insights both of traditional epistolographic structures and rhetorical arrangement in order to argue for the literary unity and argumentative coherence of Philippians. The difficulty with this approach is the notorious inability of critics to agree upon the features of arrangement when confronted with the kind of hybrid documents we have in the Pauline epistles, which conform to no explicit tradition of composition in the ancient world. As Stanley Porter has indicated, let us not confuse our creative ability to combine epistolography and rhetoric with the ancients', who, after all, seem not only to have made no such connection between these fields in their *paideia*, but also never seem to have engaged in the kind of rhetoric-critical analyses which we take for granted.[2] The unicity of these documents confronts us as a fact in the canon; it is the burden of those who wish to seek out sources and to partition a given letter into a series of correspondence to show that the kinds of 'seams' and 'trajectories' they use to prove their case can overcome the objections which we, as rhetoricians, can raise with respect to shifts in argumentative situations being typical features of argumentative praxis. We need not and should not turn to formalistic analysis of argumentative arrangement as a means of providing structural unicity and argumentative coherence to these texts. Such classifications are notoriously problematic, and may undermine analytical attention to shifting argumentative strategies.

On the other hand, the drive toward unicity can be found in the analytic attempt to discern an overarching framework in order to provide

1. D.F. Watson, 'The Integration of Epistolary and Rhetorical Analysis of Philippians', in S.E. Porter and T.H. Olbricht (eds.), *The Rhetorical Analysis of Scripture: Essays from the 1995 London Conference* (JSNTSup, 146; Sheffield: Sheffield Academic Press, 1997), pp. 398-426.

2. S.E. Porter, 'The Theoretical Justification for Application of Rhetorical Categories to Pauline Epistolary Literature', in S.E. Porter and T.H. Olbricht (eds.), *Rhetoric and the New Testament: Essays from the 1992 Heidelberg Conference* (JSNTSup, 90; Sheffield: JSOT Press, 1993), pp. 100-122.

argumentative coherence. This is seen when a critic reduces complex argumentative trajectories to a single hypothesis, stasis, genre or rhetorical situation. It is a critical move which provides the author with a presumption of coherence which may, in 'fact', not be there. To reduce the rather complex and changing argumentative situation of the Corinthian correspondence, for example, to that of any single genre (Mitchell, Schüssler Fiorenza),[3] to emphasize a 'fundamental' and coherent theological system which undergirds the variety of argumentative strategies in the letter (Wire),[4] is to do a great disservice to the evidence. And while I find Ira Jolivet's conclusion enticing and thought-provoking,[5] the identification of the letter to the Romans as a single *stasis* of 'an argument from the letter and intent of the law' directed at a controversy between Jewish and Gentile Christians provokes the question of whether Romans 11 and 12 do enough to reconcile what must have been (by this point in the argument) a thoroughly disenchanted Jewish sector of the community. If Jolivet is right, then has not Paul stirred up a controversy in a community he has had no prior relation to, and from whom he seems to require a great deal? But if this seems counterintuitive, then perhaps the situation is more complex than *stasis* theory can admit. *Stasis* theory was an important inventional strategy for the ancients in certain rhetorical situations, and can be a useful heuristic tool for our analyses. But it is reductionistic as an analytical tool, especially given the highly complex argumentative situations and strategic ends encountered in Paul's epistles.

The flip-side to the drive to 'prove' argumentative unicity or coherence of a given Pauline epistle is that which seeks to splinter it apart under the assumption that coherent and complete argumentative structures are signs of source documents behind the supposed compilation of the canonical text. Thus, Frank Hughes's continued interest in pursuing rhetorical analyses of source fragments in the Corinthian

---

3.   M.M. Mitchell, *Paul and the Rhetoric of Reconciliation: An Exegetical Investigation of the Language and Composition of 1 Corinthians* (Louisville, KY: Westminster/John Knox Press, 1993); E. Schüssler Fiorenza, 'The Ethics of Interpretation: De-Centering Biblical Scholarship', *JBL* 104 (1988), pp. 3-17.

4.   A. Wire, *Corinthian Women Prophets* (Minneapolis: Fortress Press, 1990).

5.   I. Jolivet, Jr, 'An Argument from the Letter and Intent of the Law as the Primary Argumentative Strategy in Romans', in Porter and Olbricht (eds.), *The Rhetorical Analysis of Scripture*, pp. 309-35.

correspondence,[6] as though individuals cannot compose more than a single argumentative strategy, or cannot have more than one argumentative intention or pragmatic response to complex situations or circumstances. His efforts simply beg the question of the validity of the partition theories, accepting their results and applying his own powerful critical acumen upon the literary fragments that remain. Here is a drive to eliminate ambiguity, to supply Paul with a singularity of and consistency in purpose and argumentative composition, each fragment indicating a new document in a 'logical' progression of the changing relationship of the communities to Paul, rather than shedding light on the complexity of argumentative and rhetorical situations confronting Paul in relationship to the community in these letters, especially 2 Corinthians.

Gary Selby[7] describes a coherent, if complex, Bitzerian rhetorical situation to which Paul's apology in 1 Corinthians 1–4 is addressed. By the end of his analysis, the *persona* which Paul adopts (an apocalyptic seer) is the one 'best suited' to the constraints which have entered into the argumentative picture. Here is a new, but related, aspect of the drive for unicity at work in our critical efforts: the assumption that Paul's analytical abilities are exceptional enough to help him create the most 'fitting' response to the situation confronting him. As historians, this is an important assumption, since it helps us to come that one step closer to understanding the circumstances which we want to describe: the early Christian community. If we can take for granted Paul's analytical acumen, assume his argumentative strategies were not only 'the best', but effective, then through his rhetoric we can reconstruct not only the situation he was addressing, but even the relationship between himself and the community (the struggles, the position each ascribes to the other, the self-understanding of each with respect to the new *paideia* being generated by them both, etc.). It adds one more piece of the puzzle to understanding Paul's ministry, and the Hellenistic missionary movements, in ever greater detail.

In other words, the drive behind keeping the author intact, to making him the focus of our work and the limit of our analyses, is also the

6.	F.W. Hughes, 'Rhetorical Criticism and the Corinthian Correspondence', in Porter and Olbricht (eds.), *The Rhetorical Analysis of Scripture*, pp. 336-50, especially nn. 2 and 3.

7.	G. Selby, 'Paul the Seer: The Rhetorical *Persona* in 1 Corinthians 2.1-16', in Porter and Olbricht (eds.), *The Rhetorical Analysis of Scripture*, pp. 351-73.

drive that gives impetus to our assuming for him a strength to his work. We see this drive at work in Glen Holland's analysis of Paul's use of irony in 1 Corinthians, an analysis which strikes me as counterintuitive. It is worth quoting in full the length to which 'we' go to assume the best intentions, abilities, critical understanding and rhetorical power of Paul:

> Paul's use of irony as a rhetorical technique made sense in terms of both his audience and his goals in the Corinthian correspondence... [It] was [also] well-suited to his desire to end the divisions among the Corinthians by reaffirming the normative values he had taught them during his Corinthian ministry... The complicity between Paul as an ironic rhetor and the 'wolves' among the members of his audience evoked both sympathy for his position and esteem for Paul as an apostle who suffered for the sake of the gospel and his congregations.
>
> Such complicity also served another of Paul's purposes: he wanted to strengthen the personal bond between the Corinthians and himself. This was a particularly delicate task... His irony...served his purposes admirably.[8]

Now, I will admit this might be an anachronistic conclusion on my part (Socrates notwithstanding), but I would suggest that one of the *worst* means by which to secure complicity and to strengthen personal bonds between an orator and an audience is through irony: at least three-quarters of the audience (Holland's 'sheep confederates', 'wolf victims' and 'sheep victims')[9] are the potential objects of rebuff or confusion. Indeed, I would suggest that the most consistent response to an ironic orator is not affection, but annoyance, if not hatred. Assuming success on Paul's part ('Paul's use of irony as a rhetorical technique made sense in terms of both his audience and his goals in the Corinthian correspondence')[10] leads us again and again to the conclusion, 'Paul's use of irony when it was most likely to produce the result he sought offers additional evidence of Paul's rhetorical expertise'.[11]

We find a similar inclination in the work on Romans 5–8 by Jean-Noël Aletti:

---

8. G. Holland, 'Paul's Use of Irony as a Rhetorical Technique', in Porter and Olbricht (eds.), *The Rhetorical Analysis of Scripture*, pp. 234-48 (246-47).

9. Holland, 'Paul's Use of Irony', pp. 236-37.

10. Holland, 'Paul's Use of Irony', p. 246.

11. Holland, 'Paul's Use of Irony', p. 247.

> This assembling of *propositiones* and of *partitiones* obviously shows
> that Paul is more skilful in the art of arranging his proofs (*pisteis*) than
> we normally think. While giving the impression of going off the track
> from time to time, even to the extent of making those who are less famil-
> iar with the rules of rhetoric wonder, one has to admit that his argumen-
> tation always remains solid. [12]

I'm not sure why we cannot simply accuse Paul of, in fact, wander-
ing off the track, that in Romans, as in Corinthians, Galatians and
Philippians, his argumentation in fact does *not* remain solid.

Finally, I would suggest that the drive toward authorial unicity can
also be seen in efforts that emphasize the 'unique' character of a given
author's work(s). This is the case in Joachim Classen's analysis,[13]
which, through a close reading of the letter to Titus, continually
attempts to elaborate important rhetorical implications for 'unique'
syntactical or lexigraphical features of the letter. Such 'unique' qualities are ascribed to an intentionality which governs 'a carefully considered structure'.[14] I cannot suggest conclusively otherwise, but the point
I could draw is this: is the structure carefully considered because of
his/our careful reading and the motive to find it so? Just how much
importance should we ascribe to vocabulary or syntactical features of
the text which may be considered 'unique' when limiting ourselves to
the Pauline corpus, the epistolographic literature, the New Testament,
or even extending it to include the entire Greek corpus from antiquity,
but which may not be 'unique' at all when we linguistically ponder the
fact that such changes occur in everyday speech and writing all the
time? We make such careful, comparative lexigraphical and syntactical
analysis and ascribe importance to any 'unique' qualities we might
thereby uncover because this is, after all, the word of god, or at least of
one of his more important functionaries, and hence each word, each
nuance, is ripe with import, whether that import be theological or
rhetorical. But this critique is not meant to dismiss either his work or
its conclusions (both of which are exemplary), only to point up an
additional perspective on the 'intentionalities' at work in any effort of

12. J.-N. Aletti, 'The Rhetoric of Romans 5–8', in Porter and Olbricht (eds.),
The Rhetorical Analysis of Scripture, pp. 294-308 (300).

13. C.J. Classen, 'A Rhetorical Reading of the Epistle to Titus', in Porter and
Olbricht (eds.), *The Rhetorical Analysis of Scripture*, pp. 427-44.

14. Classen, 'Rhetorical Reading', p. 444.

interpretation, reading or reception: *we* may be an important contributor of 'intention', 'structure' and 'excellence'/'importance'.

3. *Alternatives*

Leaving aside the question of 'authorship' as a governing construct per se, and addressing solely the issue of unicity, I would like to reflect a bit upon rhetorical-critical practice as it is currently performed by posing this simple question: how often has anyone ever run into a rhetorical-critical analysis of a biblical text which came to the analytical conclusion, 'What a mess!'? I suggest very infrequently, perhaps even never. I will set aside here the issues raised by feminist critics, since their ethical judgment is not what I am talking about: even Schüssler Fiorenza and Wire assume Paul's writings are rhetorically apt or fit, in spite of their condemnation of his argumentative intent.[15] What I am speaking of is the presumption brought to the letters by his interpreters that he is a competent, capable rhetor. In all the literature I have read, I do not believe I have run into one truly *critical* approach to Paul's rhetoric.

It is this lacuna which I would hereby like to begin addressing. I do so by reference to 1 Cor. 11.3-11, and will assume, in part, the methodological procedures standard in the disciplinary discourse of our field. In other words, while I will adopt the figure of 'author' for argument's sake, I will not assume the implications of unicity shared by my colleagues.

To begin, the argument concerns the issue of womyn's head-covering during prophetic speech. It begins with an argument from the rule of justice, that is, similar people under similar circumstances are to be treated similarly, or 'Any man who prays or prophesies with something on his head disgraces his head, but any womon who prays or prophesies with her head unveiled disgraces her head' (11.4-5). Its purpose is to establish analogous concepts of 'shame' (11.3-7) between men and womyn, but is based upon a threefold hierarchical definition of 'head'. Even this much is highly complex and convoluted.

A definition of subordination in 11.3 ('But I want you to understand that Christ is the head of every man, and the man is the head of the womon, and God is the head of Christ') serves to act as example, to establish a concept of reality. This indicates that although the example

15. See works cited in nn. 3 and 4, above.

is agreed upon (that is, perhaps the figures are understood, a relationship among them is somehow expected and so on), the meaning of the example is not agreed upon (in this case, hierarchy and subordination). As definition, however, there is no room left for discussion, for it serves as the basis upon which relationships must logically be based (11.7: 'for a man ought not to have his head veiled, since he is the image and glory of God; but womon is the glory of man'). By the rule of justice, then, certain actions of members represented or affected by this definition/example must be treated appropriately, that is, within this argumentative framework. Therefore, concepts of shame/dishonor are argued for with respect to both men and womyn, but within this hierarchy: men cannot pray or prophesy with their head covered, for this shames them, for they are the image of and glory of god; womon, however, cannot pray or prophesy without a covering, for she is the glory of man.

As you can see, however, 'head' has come to mean something else/ more: 'glory'. This explains the next, quasi-logical appeal based upon 'reality': for a womon to pray without a covering would dishonor her head as though she had cut off her hair (11.6). If it were all right to cut off her hair, then none of this discussion would matter. Realistically, however, it is not all right. Here, 'head', 'hair', 'position', 'glory' and perhaps 'husband' (to dishonor her 'head', after equating 'head' with 'man', is it implied that when a womon shaves, she is publicly dishonoring her husband?) all come to function rhetorically the same way. Finally, all of these arguments assume a desire to disassociate the audience from shameful behavior, and perhaps even to disassociate private from public behavior.

There is a quick concession, however, that this distinction between man and womon is not all that great (11.11-12), since womon came from man (authoritative reference to Gen. 2), and man now comes from womon (appeal to structure of reality); and all things are from God (another hierarchical definition). But that 'head' and 'glory' continue to be made equivalent is seen in the next, rather cryptic argument from justice (cf. 11.7: 'ought') concerning covering on account of the angels: the womon's glory, as that which is the glory of man, must be further disassociated from the divine (angels), since man is in the ambiguous position of being both in the image of the divine, and yet human.

Next appears a new argumentative tact: the introduction of an argument from 'nature', picking up on the previous discussion of womyn's shorn hair, applied by means of an argument of justice: since womyn don't cut their hair, but men do, and since long hair is degrading to men, and not to womyn, then long hair is their covering (cf. 11.6). *Only now, womyn's hair is equated with covering, thus undermining any reason for a veil.*

Finally, all previous attempts at reasoning for veiling are overthrown by a blatant argument from authority: neither the missionary community (around Paul?) allows a practice of womyn prophesying without a covering, nor do any of 'the other churches of God' (11.16).

This is an excellent example of how amplitude and accumulation in argumentation weaken or crucially undermine the point being made.[16] The argumentation broached at the end of the argument leads to a conclusion contrary to the explicitly stated conclusion aimed at—that is, if womyn's hair is their covering, why do they need a covering to pray or prophesy? In the face of this rhetorical incompatibility, there is no attempt at reconsideration of the conclusion, nor new argumentative tact. Instead, there appears from out of nowhere (note its incompatibility with 'judge for yourselves' in 11.13) an argument to silence based on implicit censure: 'We have no such custom, nor do the churches of god' (11.16). The call to silence and censure is the end of rhetoric, an ethically self-contractory appeal meant to stifle all further discussion. It is a power move, pure and simple; the last resort of a weak argument.

But, more importantly, I shall use this argument as an entry into a thesis I would like to explore, but cannot do so here with any depth. Positing for the moment an 'authorial' figure behind these texts, a figure as a governing critical construct, we can at least posit a much greater complexity than we have currently ascribed to him in our analyses. Indeed, I would suggest the following critical assumption: it is not necessarily the case that Paul's argumentation is lucid, his stratagems effective, his rhetoric 'handbook'-perfect and 'fit', his argumentative trajectories consistent, his conclusions persuasive. 1 Corinthians, it seems to me, offers a number of examples of very confusing arguments, but does not have a monopoly on what may be considered at the very least 'difficult', 'obscure' or 'complex' argumentation: consider the bewildering variety of argumentative trajectories, the multiple (and problematic) exegetical proofs and the unanticipated interjection of the

---

16. C. Perelman and L. Olbrechts-Tyteca, *The New Rhetoric: A Treatise on Argumentation* (trans. J. Wilkinson and P. Weaver; Notre Dame: University of Notre Dame Press, 1969), pp. 479-85.

issue of circumcision in Galatians 3–5. And, in spite of Aletti's helpful elucidation of the *dispositio* of Romans 5–8, and admitting that the argument finally does manage to bring itself together, I have a difficult time as a rhetorical critic agreeing that this section displays an argumentative 'skill' or 'solidity'. I might also suggest that the apparent argumentative break in Phil. 3.1 is also rather awkward. And, partition theory notwithstanding, one might admit that 2 Corinthians does seem to wander a bit; its changing argumentative situations are not tightly woven together.

If I can, by means of a hyperbolic synecdoche, present my thesis pointedly: Paul is no rhetor; he is a pastor.[17] He is no systematic theologian; he is a pragmatic worker striving to confront issues he could never have anticipated. I do not mean to suggest that a pastor, by definition, cannot be rhetorically powerful, nor that a pragmatic worker cannot elucidate his theoretical foundations from which he works. I simply mean to shift our analytical assumptions a bit, in order to free ourselves from the hegemony of the 'canonical' and 'orthodox' authority of Paul in order to make room for the possibility of criticism in our work.

If we use 1 Cor. 11.3-11 as a heuristic 'test case' for this thesis, and take a close look around at the Pauline corpus, perhaps we might begin to see not only the 'genius' of Paul, but also the mediocrity. Perhaps we can begin to note where argumentation breaks down, where argumentative situations once presumed secure have shifted beneath the feet of the rhetor. Perhaps we can note the function and prominence of argumentative appeals to character and authority which Paul makes as a 'last' resort in the face of (active or anticipated) objections, a shift which, ultimately, is a call to silence and a stifling of rhetorical engagement. Perhaps we can begin to become sensitive to the potential that argumentative depictions of the situations (in *narratio,* but also elsewhere) are just that: argumentative, with the selection of data taking place, the choice of depictions, and so on, serving a function driven, perhaps, by the rhetor's own attempts to define, not describe, the circumstances. Perhaps we can become *critics* and begin to *judge* Paul.

This leads to a second thesis I think is in need of pondering, but,

---

17. W. Wuellner, 'Paul as Pastor: The Function of Rhetorical Questions in First Corinthians', in A. Vanhoye (ed.), *L'Apôtre Paul: Personnalité, style et conception du ministère* (Leuven: Leuven University Press, 1983), pp. 49-77.

again, one that I cannot here develop thoroughly: the issues confronted by Paul in his correspondence may not necessarily be the result of outside influences or agitators, nor are Paul's arguments developed to respond conservatively to earlier or 'more authentic' pneumatic freedom preaching of a 'discipleship of equals', and so on. Instead, I suggest they may arise because Paul's preaching Christ's death (and resurrection) is simply so broad as to allow a wide range of interpretation and understanding. The Thessalonians, in the face of Paul's (or their own) persecution, and in the light of the deaths of recent members, wonder just what the promise of the resurrection means, when it is to come, how long they must wait and what will it look like. Galatian churches have raised a plethora of issues, including some congregations deciding that Christ's death has not abrogated certain social practices and obligations which serve to identify them with the Jewish faith and tradition. The Corinthians assert in their lives the freedom which this gospel message explicitly develops: strength in wisdom through the resurrection gives them freedom from worry over food to idols, gives womyn autonomy over their lives to leave their pagan husbands, slaves can leave their masters, and so forth. All of these responses, it seems to me, are quite valid (or at least possible) in light of the vagueness and breadth of Paul's gospel each time he attempts to clarify it. This is one of the dangers of 'universal' values, that we might all think we agree upon them, but when we come to put them into practice, or to give them specific shape and function, we find ourselves in disarray and disagreement.

In other words, I suggest that he is, at least in part, arguing *against himself* as a result of the reasonable, but for him unexpected, pragmatic applications and implications of his message. He is attempting to clarify *first*, and only later (if at all) systematize, or, better, *justify*. The issues he confronts are not philosophical or theological; they are pragmatic. And in addressing the everyday problems or actions of these communities from far away, he is in the rather difficult position of responding, not just to them, but to *himself*.

This could explain, at least, prominence of arguments for *mimesis*, the frequent use of digression, the persistent need for clarification on specific issues, the prominence of *epideictic* features of argumentation, even the breaks and seemingly disparate collection of arguments and issues: it is the nature of dissociative and disassociative argumentation ('No, I didn't mean that, but this...') that it is essentially reactive, addressing various misunderstandings as they unexpectedly arise, continually forcing the rhetor to clarify and reclarify foundational justifications as they are related to the issues at hand.

Among the varieties of issues we must be cognizant of when embarking upon rhetorical criticism of texts is that, for a variety of reasons (entropy in the communication system,[18] deep-seated motivations working against linguistic expression,[19] power systems and ideological influences,[20] etc.), an intended effect simply fails not only because the recipient 'does not understand', but because the expression itself is unclear or broad and vague, or the author/composer/impetus itself has simply communicated and argued poorly.

4. *Invitations*

Theoretically, what is at stake? The loss of our monotheistic ideology of author worship. We assume a monological intentionality behind every work, a belief that a single individual is at work guiding the production of a given text, and discerning and understanding this individual's intentions are the purposes of critical analysis. But, as some of us here have time and again pleaded, there are more 'intentionalities' at work in every effort of communication, which include at least:

1. The 'intentionality' of an author and the 'intentionality' of his/her (Lacanian) desires which work against any linguistic expression she or he produces;
2. the 'intentionality' of the materiality of communication, the effect of which we can see, for example, in 'canonical criticism', that is, as a single communicative product, impacted by its medium and described as having a 'unified' form, or purpose;
3. the 'intentionality' of the 'starting-points and frameworks of argumentation', the systems and structures at work which

18. J.D. Hester, 'A Flash in the Dark: Kennedy, Energy and the Power of Argumentation' (unpublished paper; London Rhetoric Conference, 1995).

19. J. Lacan, *Ecris: A Selection* (trans. A. Sheridan; New York: W.W. Norton, 1977). See also the issue of *Pre/Text: A Journal of Rhetorical Theory* 15.1–2 (1994) entitled, 'Lacan and the Question of Rhetoric'; cf. esp. the excellent article, T. Dean, 'Bodies that Mutter: Rhetoric and Sexuality', pp. 81-117.

20. M. Foucault, *Power/Knowledge: Selected Interviews and Other Writings 1972–1977* (ed. C. Gordon; New York: Pantheon Books, 1980).

authorize texts and methods as canonical and legitimate, which give various forms of sanction and opportunities to perpetuate their function and relationship to these systems; and

4. the 'intentionality' of the critic and critical analytics of the text, both of which may serve the purposes of upholding traditional interpretations and power relations, and are themselves supported or thwarted by institutional and systemic means, including academic, ecclesial, but also systems of publication.

In other words, we must embrace, as recent theories of psychoanalysis have embraced, the concept that the Self (like Nietzsche's god) is dead.[21] This will open up new horizons of critical interpretive targets, methodological developments and interpretive purposes/goals to our rhetorical analytical efforts (something I, personally, am more interested in pursuing).

But leaving this aside as something quite unlikely to be adopted by many people in our discipline, at the very least I suggest we must give up the idea of Paul as genius theologian and rhetor. Perhaps he was, but perhaps he wasn't. I would suggest that while one can describe what one finds as ingenious in his argumentation, especially in light of the need to meet with the confusions and difficulties raised by communities far away from him, one can also note his tendentious and problematic passages. In this way, we are giving ourselves the chance to approach his letters as the truly human documents they are, to consider the issues he addresses from another perspective, to note and appreciate where his real genius and insight shine through by comparison to where it notably fails to achieve results.

In turn, we will no longer allow ourselves the role of interpreter as conservative retainer of Paul's canonical status and reputation. Such a role, both theoretically and also pragmatically, has meant that we abrogate our obligation to fulfill our role as rhetorical *critics*—we must become something more than rhetorical 'yes-men' and 'yes-womyn', and take a cue from our feminist and liberationist sisters and brothers: not everything that goes on in our biblical texts is worthy of emulation;

21. C. Zweig, 'The Death of the Self in a Postmodern World', in W. Anderson (ed.), *The Truth about the Truth: De-confusing and Re-constructing the Postmodern World* (New York: Putnam's Sons, 1995), pp. 145-50.

but, by default, by sheer assumption, our critical acumen has been used to preserve and defend just such a conclusion. It is time we take on the assumption and ponder the hitherto unponderable: Paul often is, as noted even in the canon (2 Pet. 3.15), pretty darn tough to understand; and that might, at times, be *his* fault, not ours.

RHETORIC AND IDEOLOGY: A DEBATE WITHIN BIBLICAL SCHOLARSHIP OVER THE IMPORT OF PERSUASION[*]

Dale Patrick with Allen Scult

Rhetoric has historically labored under the suspicion that it is the art or technique of manipulating audiences into believing what the speaker wants them to believe. Some of its foremost practitioners have even suggested that the orator's task is to render a point of view plausible and compelling, irrespective of its truth value. According to Quintilian, for example, the speaker in a court of law should endeavor to persuade 'the judge [to] believe what we say whether or not it is true'.[1] While Quintilian obviously means for this prescription to apply only to judicial rhetoric, in order to ensure that every defendant will be represented by the best possible case made on his behalf, this capacity of the rhetorician to make an equally strong case on any and all sides of a question has cast the entire discipline into disrepute.

Aristotle's classic definition of rhetoric as the 'discovery in the

---

[*]   Allen Scult and I composed this essay in the summers of 1993 and 1994. I had the original perception that ideology critique is a species of rhetorical analysis; it was also my idea to treat the book by the Cootes as a specimen of this hermeneutical strategy (R. Coote and M. Coote, *Power, Politics and the Making of the Bible: An Introduction* [Minneapolis: Fortress Press, 1990]). Scult brought in Aristotle and Perelman and nuanced many points. The text was composed dialogically, each of us revising the essay in turn until we were satisfied with the result. By the time we had finished, the piece had grown too long, and the critique of the Cootes' application of ideology critique to Old Testament writings had become ancillary to the main argument. I volunteered to cut it for submission to a journal and Allen signed off on the result. I have since adapted it several times on my own for presentation to different audiences.

1.   Quintilian, 4.2.34 (LCL); cited by J.D. O'Banion, 'Narration and Argumentation: Quintilian on *Narratio* as the Heart of Rhetorical Thinking', *Rhetorica* 5 (1987), pp. 325-51 (345).

particular case what are the available means of persuasion'[2] seems to support this notion of rhetoric's duplicity by suggesting that merely *discovering* the most persuasive arguments constitutes the objective of rhetorical activity. The rhetor then has the resources to make a strategic decision about which argument to employ. Its truth or falsehood does not necessarily bear on his decision. The quest for truth, on this view, properly belongs to philosophy, where opinion is subjected to the rigorous scrutiny of dispassionate reason.[3]

This perception does not bode well for a scholarly program devoted to understanding ancient sacred texts as rhetoric. For whenever we elucidate the means by which an author sought to persuade his or her audience of something, our colleagues will be inclined to interpret this as the uncovering of 'a dirty little secret'. We will be disclosing a stratagem of deception—an argument whose purpose it is to say whatever needs to be said to give the *appearance* of truth, and thus to be persuasive.

An examination of how the argument gives an appearance of truth leads naturally to questions of motive and purpose. Aristotle's formulation leaves that question open because he considered rhetoric to be the means of attaining practical ends, ends largely determined by the situation and the exigency of the speaker. In the case of judicial rhetoric, for example, the end is a favorable decision of a court; in a deliberative situation, speakers seek to persuade decision-makers of policies which they believe to be favorable to the interests of the body politic. Aristotle did not recognize the rhetorical in historiography, law codes, epic and dramatic poetry, or philosophical dialogs—the sorts of discourse that were reduced to written texts and designed for general audiences. Scholars who seek to apply his rhetoric to textual material must extrapolate his principles and apply them analogically. Texts may derive from situations as specific as oral discourse, but not normally; and even when a text was designed for a specific situation it can be reused in new ones. This renders the question of motive and purpose particularly tricky.

One contemporary version of rhetorical analysis finds evidence of the same strategic motive lying behind most, if not all, persuasive texts—

2.   Aristotle, *Rhet.* 1355b.
3.   Cf. O'Banion, 'Narration and Argumentation', p. 346. While all sorts of questions can be raised against this traditional dichotomy of logic and rhetoric, it is a tenacious conviction that still shapes the university curriculum.

namely, the justification of domination and privilege. The task of this sort of analysis, which often goes by the name of 'ideology critique', is to uncover the particular power interests being served by a text and the class interests of the audience to which the text pitches its appeal.

Ideology critique is hardly the only option open to the student of textual rhetoric. One can entertain the possibility that a text's persuasive power is indicative not just of its capacity to give the appearance of truth, but of its articulation of truth.[4] Perhaps the creators of the text aspired not to manipulate their audiences for whatever ulterior motive, but to bring the truth to their audiences in appropriate language. Aristotle's original formulation suggests this possibility as well, when he says that 'truth and likeness to truth are discerned by one and the same faculty'.[5] If we relate this passage back to his definition, we see that 'discovering the available means of persuasion in a given case' can lead to arguments which persuade because they indeed *are* true, as well as to arguments strategically conceived to persuade by giving the *appearance* of truth; and what is more, the same artistic faculty is capable of producing both. How do we know which possibility obtains in a given case? In the very next paragraph, Aristotle affirms his trust in the nature of language not to lead us astray: 'Truth and justice are by nature more powerful than their opposites'.[6] That is, a competent and well-meaning audience seriously engaged in the quest for truth can ultimately make a well-founded judgment regarding the truth of a given suasive argument. Surely the community of scholars aspires to be such an audience. This need not be taken to imply that all debates over truth can be resolved, but rather only that the persuasive power of a speech or text may be

---

4.   The reader may wonder how the word 'truth' is being used. It is predicated of the point to which the author argues, e.g. that John is indeed innocent of killing Joe. Since the truth of the point can be judged only by the arguments and other suasive factors—e.g. imaginative associations and affective appeal—that can be enlisted in support of it, its truth depends on 'rhetorical power'. Of course, an author may fail to make the strongest case possible for the one he or she is advocating. But given a text which is persuasive, one has to judge whether the means of persuasion are offered in good faith. It is my position that the interpreter should assume that the text seeks to persuade an intellectually, emotionally and morally competent audience, and judge as best one can whether it succeeds in doing so.

5.   Aristotle, *Rhet.* 1355a.

6.   Aristotle, *Rhet.* 1355a.

evidence of its truth.[7] This is sufficient to support our interpretive strategy.

This 'optimistic' version of the rhetorical approach aligns itself with what Paul Ricoeur called the 'hermeneutics of affirmation', and takes its stand firmly against ideology critique, which fits what Ricoeur termed the 'hermeneutics of suspicion'.[8] Rather than seeing a text's claims to truth as a stratagem of domination, the hermeneutics of affirmation is willing to take the text's power as a possible indication of its truth. It is willing to assume that truth can be expressed with suasive power, and indeed that it generates such power. In order to experience the possible truth of a rhetorically powerful text, the interpreter must be willing to grant that a text's rhetorical power might indeed be a reflection of the validity of its truth-claims. If, however, one presumes, as does ideology critique, that a text's persuasive appeal represents the power interests of its authors masquerading as truth-claims, then in order to examine the rhetorical dynamics of a text, critics must necessarily distance themselves from these truth-claims. In its zeal not to be 'taken in' by the text's rhetoric, ideology critique becomes too one-sided—too fixed on the deceptive capacity of rhetoric to give the appearance of truth and therefore blinded to its concurrent capacity to indeed represent the truth.

Rhetorical analysis can and should be both an explanation of how a text might have persuaded audiences of its truth and a means by which interpreters can experience that truth for themselves. Indeed, the latter goal becomes an essential tool in the realization of the former. Additionally, this affirmative version of the rhetorical approach can serve to integrate the interpreter into the mainstream of the text's readership, which also most likely read the text as discourse which genuinely aspired to speak the truth. By contrast, the essentially suspicious atti-

7.   Aristotle is probably optimistic that reason can arrive at the true judgment between competing claims. I do not hold such an optimistic rationalism. Not only are the human mind and heart capable of fundamental self-deception, but ultimate questions cannot be answered by reason. I do believe, however, that the free exchange of ideas among competent interpreters can result in good judgments regarding conscious deception and most cases of self-deception. Even with contested first principles, discussion and debate among interpreters can clarify and focus the issues.

8.   A recurring theme in his writings; consult, e.g., D. Ihde (ed.), *The Conflict of Interpretations: Essays in Hermeneutics* (Evanston, IL: Northwestern University Press, 1974), pp. 287-334.

tude of ideology critique would seem to isolate the critic from the lifeblood of the text's interpretive tradition.

That is the gist of the argument of this essay; the rest is amplification. Let us begin with the train of thought that supports ideology critique and then examine an example. My reply will be formulated as an argument for the 'hermeneutics of affirmation'.

1. *The Suspicious Hermeneutics of Ideology Critique*

Ideology critique is a species of rhetorical analysis broadly defined. It would not fit those modes of rhetorical analysis which take rhetoric as an oral and, by extension, literary genre or set of genres,[9] or as the craft of composing discourse to communicate effectively and eloquently.[10] Its practitioners seek to reconstruct the motives and purposes of the author by matching the content and appeal of a text with its historical— including its institutional, socio-economic and politico-cultural—setting.[11] The text is presumed to be a justification of the interests of the

9. For examples of this generic view of rhetoric, see G. Kennedy, *New Testament Interpretation through Rhetorical Criticism* (Chapel Hill, NC: University of North Carolina Press, 1984); the position is defended in a rigorous fashion by M.M. Mitchell, *Paul and the Rhetoric of Reconciliation: An Exegetical Investigation of the Language and Composition of 1 Corinthians* (Louisville, KY: Westminster/ John Knox Press, 1993), a student of H.D. Betz (whose commentary, *Galatians: A Commentary on Paul's Letter to the Churches in Galatia* [Hermeneia; Philadelphia: Fortress Press, 1979], gave rhetorical analysis much imputus); one finds many other studies following the same general strategy in S.E. Porter and T.H. Olbricht (eds.), *Rhetoric and the New Testament: Essays from the 1992 Heidelberg Conference* (JSNTSup, 90; Sheffield: JSOT Press, 1993); and D.F. Watson (ed.), *Persuasive Artistry: Studies in New Testament Rhetoric in Honor of George A. Kennedy* (JSNTSup, 50; Sheffield: JSOT Press, 1991). There are many scholars stradling the fence, so to speak, by identifying rhetorical tropes and figures in Gospel narratives. B. Mack and V. Robbins, *Patterns of Persuasion in the Gospels* (Sonoma, CA: Polebridge Press, 1989), and B. Mack, *Rhetoric and the New Testament* (Minneapolis: Fortress Press, 1990), start with the classical view of rhetoric, but move in the direction of social science (anthropology).

10. See P. Trible, *Rhetorical Criticism: Context, Method, and the Book of Jonah* (Guides to Biblical Scholarship, Old Testament Series; Minneapolis: Fortress Press, 1994), pp. 36-40, and Part 2. This conception of the task of rhetorical analysis goes back to James Muilenburg; see his influential 'Form Criticism and Beyond', *JBL* 88 (1969), pp. 1-18.

11. From experience, I would say that they do not expend much effort seeking

68   *The Rhetorical Interpretation of Scripture*

author and audience. Let us review the train of reasoning that leads to their practice ('praxis').

They start with the commonplace in contemporary hermeneutics that authors and their audiences, and contemporary interpreters as well, are always *situated*. That is, the author is situated in a particular society and culture, sharing its language, concepts, principles, beliefs, attitudes, institutions, practices and even moods. This shared 'horizon' provides a bridge to the author's contemporaries, but separates the text from audiences of different eras and cultures, which have different 'horizons'.[12] The emergence of modern science brought this problem to the fore in biblical interpretation; to a lesser degree, the debate over slavery in the United States did so as well. Much of the effort of modern biblical hermeneutics, and secular hermeneutics as well, is devoted to rebuilding the bridge which the processes of time have made impassable.[13]

Ideology critique emphasizes an element of situatedness often overlooked or down-played by other hermeneutics: the author's and original audience's situatedness is not neutral, but involves interests that must be defended.[14] An author is not a disinterested questor for truth, but a participant in a power structure who seeks to maintain and enhance the power and privileges he or she enjoys. That which keeps authors from attaining a universal truth is not only—to use a classical theological

to discover how a text appeals to its audience, and in that sense fall short of the task I set for reading a text for its rhetorical appeal. However, there is nothing which would preclude them from doing so.

12. H.-G. Gadamer introduced the term 'horizon' into the discussion of the differences between cultures; see his *Truth and Method* (New York: Seabury, 1975), pp. 269-74, 337-41.

13. Gadamer introduced the metaphor of 'fusing horizons'; see *Truth and Method*, p. 358.

14. J. Habermas, *Zur Logik der Socialwissenschaften* (Frankfurt: Suhrkamp, 1970), offered a critique of Gadamer; available in English as 'A Review of Gadamer's *Truth and Method*', in F. Dallmayr and T. McCarthy (eds.), *Understanding and Social Inquiry* (Notre Dame: Notre Dame University Press, 1977). Gadamer responded in an essay entitled, 'Rhetorik, Hermeneutik und Ideologiekritik: Metakritische Erörterungen zu *Wahrheit und Methode*', in K.O. Apel *et al.* (eds.), *Hermeneutik und Ideologiekritik* (Frankfurt: Suhrkamp, 1977). For a review of this debate, see G. Warnke, *Gadamer: Hermeneutics, Tradition and Reason* (Stanford: Stanford University Press, 1987), pp. 107-38. The debate has continued since this first confrontation; the present essay intends to join it.

typology—ignorance due to finitude, but to sinful self-aggrandise-ment.[15]

The situatedness of an author, and hence an author's text, occurs at two levels. The author has his or her own interests to maintain and enhance within the community he or she seeks to persuade. There are also what we might call the 'class' interests of the audience. The writing culture of the ancient world was restricted to upper socio-economic classes; to persuade an audience by writing, the author would have to identify his or her interests with the interests of the upper classes.

The rhetorical exchange is regarded as a manipulation of the opinions and attitudes of an audience so that they will adopt the desired viewpoint, render the desired decision or choose the desired policy. In other words, the text's rhetoric is seen as being driven decisively by the exigencies of persuading the particular audience. Truth-seeking is taken as a ploy, not as an objective shared by rhetor, audience and interpreter. What matters is the *appearance* of truth, used as a strategy to persuade particular audiences.

Rectitude, too, can be seen as a matter of appearances. The audience is susceptible to the image of acting with nobility and justice. The rhetor cultivates the collective sense of moral dignity and aligns the decision he or she is advocating with it. Thus, even a rhetoric that seems to address the 'better self' is a manipulation of the ego-needs of the audience in the service of self-interest and the will to dominate.

Discourse is a 'cultural product', as ideology critics put it to underline their viewpoint by metaphor; it is designed to maintain the legitimacy of the power structure or to gain access to it. The object of ideology critique is not only to discover how a rhetor manipulates his or her audience, but also to discover the class interests the discourse serves. Since the power structure controls the flow of discourse in the society, only the power elite has access to the podium or pen; a maverick may speak out for the voiceless from time to time, but the power elite will countenance such activity only if the discourse can be neutralized and/or made to serve their interests.

Feminist and gay liberationist interpreters have expanded the idea of class interest to include gender interests. These cut across socio-economic classes, because assumptions and beliefs about what is 'natural'

---

15. Reinhold Niebuhr worked with this dicotomy, and in fact articulated much of the reasoning that goes into ideology critique; see R. Niebuhr, *The Nature and Destiny of Man*, I (New York: Charles Scribner's Sons, 1941), pp. 150-240 *passim*.

and honorable for males and females usually are not restricted to a particular elite. Since gender assumptions are seldom contested[16] in the ways sociopolitical power is, a critique of their influence on rhetoric is more in terms of taken-for-granted attitudes than overt justifications.

There is an ironic twist to the force of persuasive texts which fuels the ideological critic's sense of calling. If the appeal of an ancient author to his or her audience's class interests were simply a historical determinant of what a text says, the interpreter could treat it like the views of ancient cosmology. However, the arguments that appeal to the beliefs, values, attitudes and practices of a given class, or perhaps all classes of a given era or culture, re-enforce them and pass them on to audiences with different class interests and culture.

The fact that texts are passed on and used in new historical settings would seem to be an embarrassment to ideology critique. In later situations within a culture and in different cultures, the ideological interests of the author and the audience are no longer operative in their suasive power. The ideology critic must regard the reuse of texts as itself serving ideological purposes. The modern use of the Bible comes under the same skeptical eye as its origin, redaction and canonization.

The ideology critique of texts is intrinsically polemical: namely, the unmasking of a text's pretensions to disinterested truth. For many practitioners, the deconstruction of 'canonical' texts thus serves the powerless and the marginalized in their struggle against those who exploit their gullibility to legitimize their domination.[17] Stripped of their legitimation, the powerful lose the aura of authority and majesty that keeps the masses subjugated. We might say that ideology critics aspire to be revolutionaries in academic garb.[18]

A Case in Point
There are an increasing number of ideology critiques of biblical literature appearing in scholarly journals and books, and any one of them could serve as an example of the interpretive strategy. While each case rests upon the strength of its own argumentation, the issue in dispute is whether interpretation should proceed from a position of suspicion or

16. Though we do speak of a 'war between the sexes'.
17. This motive fits the Marxian tradition more than the Nietzchean.
18. We might also compare them, less glamorously, to contemporary journalists who reduce the policies and speeches of politicians to public relations in order to manipulate the constituencies the politicians are seeking to appease or recruit.

from the conviction that truth has the power to generate a persuasive articulation.

Robert and Mary Coote have published what amounts to an ideology critique of the entire Old and New Testaments under the title, *Power, Politics and the Making of the Bible*. The very comprehensiveness of this volume makes it attractive as a case study. It is a kind of programmatic essay showing the blueprints of the building Robert has been constructing and continues to construct for Old Testament literature.[19]

Before actually offering an ideology critique of any Old Testament writing, the Cootes[20] set out a socio-economic description of the polity which produced the literature.[21] They start with the people of a village engaged in agriculture, and then work up the socio-economic ladder to the power elite. Each is said to have its own cult. Only the cult of the rich, however, produced texts, and it is from these elitist texts that the Old Testament is descended. Thus, in the authors' approach, the ideological interests of the Old Testament writings in general are settled before any particular text is examined.

While the Cootes are probably right that writing and reading were a mode of communication restricted to socio-economic elites, it is not that certain that each socio-economic class had its own cult and religious tradition. There are various provisions in the law codes[22] and indications of royal actions suggesting a priestly tribe or class governed the performances at Yahwistic altars;[23] and there are provisions for common festivals[24] and rules for altars devoted to YHWH.[25] Of course, one may raise doubts about such evidence, but there is at least the pos-

---

19. Among them are: R. Coote, *Amos among the Prophets: Composition and Theology* (Philadelphia: Fortress Press, 1981); in collaboration with K.W. Whitelaw, *The Emergence of Early Israel in Historical Perspective* (Sheffield: Almond Press, 1987); *Early Israel: A New Horizon* (Minneapolis: Fortress Press, 1990); and, in collaboration with D.R. Ord, *The Bible's First History* (Minneapolis: Fortress Press, 1989).

20. While Robert was primarily responsible for the Old Testament and Mary for the New Testament, the book is published as a collaborative effort, and I will honor that decision by ascribing authorship to both.

21. Coote and Coote, *Power, Politics and the Making of the Bible*, pp. 12-18.

22. Deut. 18.1-8, *passim*; cf., e.g., Exod. 28.1-5; 32.25-29; and Deut. 33.8-11.

23. 1 Kgs 12.31 sounds as though Jeroboam deviated from a norm of Levitical membership for priests.

24. E.g. Exod. 23.10-19.

25. E.g. Exod. 20.23-26.

sibility that the reports are well founded. Moreover, it is not certain whether writing culture was significantly different from oral culture, or when writing expressed the interests and perspectives of socio-economic elites and when those of the common people.[26]

King David, according to the Cootes, inaugurated the writing of biblical literature. Their characterization of one of the documents commissioned by him is sufficient for our purposes:

> The first requirement of royal propaganda was an apologia, or justification of David's actions in establishing his rule. Accordingly David commissioned the kernel of the Prophets, an account of his overthrow of the house of Saul, which appears in 1 Samuel 15 to 2 Samuel 5, asserting David's loyalty to Saul and acquitting him of any implication in the deaths of Saul, Ishbaal, or Abner. David's success is attributed solely to the solicitude of YHWH. Further to allay suspicion among Saul's supporters among the Israelite sheikhs, what became 2 Samuel 21.1-14 and 2 Samuel 9 demonstrated the purity of David's motives—he was only acting on divine command—in executing seven members of the house of Saul. The account in 2 Samuel 13–20 is addressed to Judahite supporters of Abishalom, depicting the rebellion as a private affair, an individual adventure that caused David much personal grief.[27]

I selected this example because there is sufficient agreement between us to avoid scholarly arguments on subsidiary or side issues. The accounts the Cootes identify do appear to be composed by authors commissioned by David to legitimate his kingship. The very specific events and relationships they recount would be of greatest concern to the people of that era: who would have cared about the legitimacy of Saul once Jeroboam had established his rule over the northern tribes? Who would have cared about the tragic course of events within the Davidic household after Rehoboam had succeeded his father Solomon in Judah?

It is, of course, possible that these events and relationships were simply told to make the story interesting and powerful; they could be folklore or fictional motifs.[28] However, if the works are historical, as they purport to be, the most likely rhetorical setting for the narrative

---

26. The Elisha traditions in 2 Kings surely represent the perspectives of prophetic guilds at rural northern sanctuaries, and hence the views of the common people of the hill country of the northern kingdom.

27. Coote and Coote, *Power, Politics and the Making of the Bible*, pp. 25-26.

28. So D. Gunn, *The Story of King David: Genre and Interpretation* (JSOTSup, 6; Sheffield: JSOT Press, 1978), pp. 35-62.

would be a time when the legitimacy of David's kingship was a live issue. The story of David's rise to power can be most fruitfully interpreted as an account of a course of events whose purpose it is to demonstrate David's innocence and thus legitimize his rule.[29]

I think that the narrator explicitly divulges his rhetorical objective in 2 Sam. 3.36-37:

> And all the people took notice of it, and it pleased them, as everything the king did pleased all the people. So all the people and all Israel understood that day that it had not been the king's will to slay Abner ben Ner.

This is not only the view of the people of the time, but the view the writer wants the reader to adopt. Indeed, the narrative in 1 Samuel 16 through 2 Samuel 6 seems designed to show that David was not at fault in his rupture with Saul, that he did not actually commit treason when he entered into alliance with Achish of Gath, that he did not cause, or even desire, the death of Saul, Jonathan or Abner, and that he did not engineer Ishbaal's assassination.

Wherein, then, do I want to locate the disagreement? It is not over the 'facts', but over how those facts are viewed. Note the following characteristics of the Cootes' rhetoric. First, the texts are described totally within an ideological frame. Secondly, each writing is provided with a transparent, simple, ideological motive, and various details in the story are traced directly to specific Davidic policies. The content and theological framework of each writing is ascribed fully to David's intent to assure his subjects of his legitimacy; no allowance is made for the severe constraints of public opinion, oral traditions and popular institutions. Thirdly, the narrative is dubbed 'propaganda'.

Regarding the first characteristic, the Cootes do not describe these documents in terms of what they say or how they appealed to the original audience. The biblical text comes 'packaged', as it were, in the perspective the authors want us to adopt. This may have been necessitated by their need for economy; perhaps they expect the reader to know the narrative and judge their description accordingly. Perhaps, though, the implied message is that any sophisticated reader would immediately

---

29. D. Patrick and A. Scult, 'Forensic Narration in Biblical Narrative', in *idem, Rhetoric and Biblical Interpretation* (JSOTSup, 82; Sheffield: Almond Press, 1990), pp. 57-79.

recognize the tendentiousness of the narrative. In any case, the effect is unfortunate, leaving no space in their text to weigh the evidence.

As to the second characteristic, not only do they purport to know the overall motive and purpose of the narratives, they ascribe particular details in them to David's cover-up and policy needs. Since no effort is made to consider what the audience knew and how the text is designed to persuade them, the assertions come across as oracles. The reader is left wondering whether the authors are privy to secret knowledge of what went on behind closed doors. Are the motives and purposes of the history of David's rise and reign so easily decipherable? There have been major disagreements over the import of these narratives.[30] Is it just that we have lacked the interpretive key, or is the text a bit more dense and subtle than ideology critique will allow?

This leads to the main point of contention, the third characteristic: is apologia necessarily propaganda? The word propaganda connotes the most blatant manipulation of information and attitudes to recruit support for a cause or a party. The purpose of propaganda is to tell people what to think in order that the propagandist might control them.[31] If the discourse represents an honest attempt to argue for an idea which the maker of the discourse believes to be true, it ceases to be propaganda. If the discourse also shows a respect for the audience by arguing in a way which appeals to its judgment, it moves still further from the realm of propaganda.

The term apologia suggests a considered defense of a person, institution or cause which argues its case to an audience on the basis of evidence and reasonable inference as well as the reasons of the heart. Historical narrative can be an apologia when it is designed to demonstrate the guilt or innocence of some person or group, or to elicit praise or blame for their actions. There is something intrinsically trustworthy about an apologetic in which the audience is encouraged to join in the

---

30. See Gunn's survey in *The Story of King David*, pp. 17-34.

31. There is some debate among rhetorical theorists regarding the demarcation between argumentation and propaganda: cf. C. Perelman and L. Olbrechts-Tyteca, *The New Rhetoric: A Treatise on Argumentation* (trans. J. Wilkinson and P. Weaver; Notre Dame: University of Notre Dame Press, 1969), pp. 51-54; this evaluative definition is informed by J. Ellul, *Propaganda: The Formation of Men's Attitudes* (trans. K. Kellen and J. Lerner; New York: Knopf, 1965), though his conception links propaganda specifically to modern technology and power-legitimation.

completion of the argument or story and to make a judgment for themselves.

Scult and I have argued elsewhere that the narrative of David's rise to power is a 'quasi-forensic narration'[32] because it recounts events in a way that appeals to the audience to make a judgment regarding innocence and guilt. The audience is aware that other accounts can be given, so they must judge the veracity of a specific version.[33] The rhetorical design of this text does not guarantee its veracity, but we have no reason to judge it as ideologically driven and distorted simply because its apparent intention is to persuade the audience of David's innocence and right to royal office. The narrative does not present us with cardboard characters; David is not simply a hero, Saul a villain. The flaws in David's character are readily discernible, and the narrative which follows (2 Sam. 9–20, 1 Kgs 1–2) makes no secret of his sins and failures. The subtlety of the narrative deserves some attention in 'reading' the intent behind it and the effect it produced on audiences. Here we can discern a rhetoric that cultivates a complex view of human character and appeals to the audience to take that complexity into account as it judges David. Such training in judgment imparts a profound understanding of human character and action whether or not the narrative is historically accurate.

Most of the points at issue between the Cootes' ideology critique and a rhetoric under the hermeneutics of affirmation sound as though they have to do with scholarly rhetoric. If one takes rhetoric in the broad sense of the mode and end of an argument, yes, it is a matter of rhetoric. It is not that the Cootes' description of the Davidic histories is wrong, but that it shapes a reading of the biblical text which is more concerned to avoid being deceived than to learn the truth the text may have to divulge. It was not my objective to refute their position, but to show that there is a reasonable alternative to it.

32. For this rhetorical category of narrative, see Patrick and Scult, *Rhetoric and Biblical Interpretation*, pp. 57-79.

33. How do we know that the audience knew that other versions are possible? The accounts of the rather delicate, ambiguous actions and alliances of David can best be understood as 'replies' to doubts the audience had, perhaps even rumors in circulation. 1 Chronicles cuts most of these accounts out and thereby gives a much more idealistic picture of the king; neither the author of Chronicles nor its contemporary audience desired the ambiguity of 1–2 Samuel and 1 Kgs 1–2.

2. *The Hermeneutics of Affirmation*

Before explaining and attempting to justify an understanding of textual rhetoric guided by its possible truth, it might be worthwhile considering and setting aside the classical theological answer to the type of skepticism found in ideology critique. The doctrine of the divine inspiration of Scripture holds that God preserves the writing of the Scriptures from the corruption of sin and the limitations of finitude. The strongest versions of this doctrine, of course, would hardly acknowledge the effect of human instrumentality at all, but there are expositions of the doctrine which recognize the manifest individualities of style, emphasis and perspective. There is ambivalence over whether any writings were actually expressions of sin, but if the Lord can make Assyria an instrument of his anger (Isa. 10.5), it would theoretically be possible to make a sinful writing a redemptive word.

Why not adopt this theological answer to ideology criticism? The critical scholarly enterprise is not about to accept recourse to divine miracle to guarantee the trustworthiness of the Bible. The interpreters who appeal to divine inspiration to solve general hermeneutical problems isolate themselves from the community of scholars.[34] Any case for the trustworthiness of biblical rhetoric must be applicable to non-biblical texts as well, though nothing precludes taking particular personal and cultural factors into account when judging the trustworthiness of a particular text.

This leaves us with the question: is there a sound humanistic reason to trust the rhetoric of the text one is interpreting? Should the texts of the Western literary canon, the classics, be privileged in this respect because they have exhibited rhetorical power in a great diversity of historical settings? Or should greater caution be exercised toward 'cultural icons'? How should trust and criticism play themselves out in interpretation?

There is at least one good humanistic reason to trust that authors are bargaining in good faith with their audiences: in approaching texts in this way the interpreter exemplifies, and thereby justifies, a view of

---

34. Perhaps it would also come under the strictures of what Dietrich Bonhoeffer said about the 'God of the gaps' (D. Bonhoeffer, *Letters and Papers from Prison* [ed. E. Bethge; trans. R. Fuller; New York: Macmillan, rev. edn, 1967 [1953]), pp. 174-75).

human existence in which the knowing subject is open to being taught by others. The interpreter can only *receive* truth from a text if he or she is willing to entertain the possibility of its being true. Those who are on guard against deception curtail this openness to others.[35]

Let us call this the rhetoric of the *hermeneutics of affirmation*. It accords a text the initial presumption that its power to persuade is a concomitant of the truth it has to divulge. The interpreter also assumes that the rhetorical manipulations underlying that power are for the purpose of leading the audience to good judgment. Though the author seeks to present a compelling case, the discourse is designed to allow the audience space to re-enact the author's train of thought so that it can discover the truths the text has to convey.

Even after having decided to risk the hermeneutics of affirmation, however, the rhetorical analyst is still left with difficult questions of motive and purpose, for these are rarely simple and unmixed. Let us say, for example, that the analyst finds a particular text to be honestly and wholeheartedly devoted to conveying an idea the author believes to be true. Even in this simple case, however, the rhetor may also be involved in community-building, self-promotion or even the maintenance of the political supremacy or prestige of a particular class. These may be congruent with or extraneous to the main objective of the discourse. The rhetorical analyst must discern these subsidiary rhetorical purposes, and judge whether they enhance, undermine or are irrelevant to the primary objective.

a. *Audience*

Another set of decisions comes into play when the rhetorical analyst takes account of the audience for whom a communication was designed. The rhetor had a concept of the audience he or she was addressing[36] and shaped what was said in order to have the desired effect on that audience. For purposes of experiencing the text from the perspective of this intended audience, the rhetorical analyst reconstructs what might be termed the text's 'ideal audience'. Other rhetoricians call the audience as projected by the discourse the 'implied audience'.[37]

---

35. Classics, in my opinion, deserve the presumption of trustworthiness not only to exemplify openness to textual communication, but also to the judgment of others.

36. Perelman and Olbrechts-Tyteca, *The New Rhetoric*, pp. 19-23, 31-34.

37. See A. Culpepper, *Anatomy of the Fourth Gospel: A Study in Literary*

An example may clarify how these definitions of audience operate. A racist speaker (or writer) must judge the attitudes of his audience and select those images, beliefs and attitudes which would arouse its racist sentiments and lead it to support, say, the separation of the races and protection of the privileges of the dominate race. The speaker 'constructs' a racist audience from the mixture of ideas, attitudes, experiences and social pressures to which the audience is subject. The 'ideal audience' for the racist's discourse would be an audience that responds predictably to the appeal and supports the speaker's objective. An anti-racist speaker could address the same audience with the purpose of persuading it to support equal justice for all and fraternity among the races. Her discourse would have to appeal to different attitudes, images, beliefs and experiences, constructing a non-racist audience.[38]

Chaim Perelman calls attention to another dimension of the audience by coining the term 'universal audience'. The universal audience is composed of those most competent to judge the truth-claims of the argument.[39] In a judicial case, this would be an audience that knows the facts and the law, and who is intellectually and morally capable of an impartial and merciful decision. In respect to the rhetoric of the racist, the universal audience would consist of those with no interests in maintaining their own power and privileges, and no fear of others, and who accept the norms of justice and fraternity for all members of a community. Actually, this description is *my* conception of the universal; the racist would *probably* deny that a universal morality exists, but he *might* envisage a universal congenial to his objectives.

The anti-racist speaker would be talking to her actual audience with approximately my idea of the 'universal audience' in her mind. She cannot address the actual audience, with its mixed motives and attitudes, as if it were the universal audience; rather, she must carefully calibrate her discourse to construct an approximation of the universal

Design (Philadelphia: Fortress Press, 1983), pp. 205-27; he draws upon the work of Wayne Booth, particularly his *Rhetoric of Fiction* (Chicago: University of Chicago Press, 1974), and P. Rabinowitz, 'Truth in Fiction: Reexamination of Audiences', *Critical Inquiry* 4 (1977), pp. 121-41.

38. A classic image of an audience responding positively to rhetors on the opposite side of the same question is found in Shakespeare's depiction of the funeral orations over Julius Caesar by Brutus and Anthony (*Julius Caesar*, Act III, Scene 2).

39. Perelman and Olbrechts-Tyteca, *The New Rhetoric*, pp. 31-35.

audience. There will be compromises with the prejudices and fears of the actual audience, some of which she herself may not recognize as questionable.[40] She is, nevertheless, appealing to the universal audience and subjecting her rhetoric to its good judgment.

Understanding an ancient sacred text such as the Bible would seem to require a hermeneutic which affirms the author's desire to, and ultimate success at, appeal to 'both' audiences, or the double aspect of the audience. By examining the text's argument from the perspective of both the historical audiences which it has actually affected and the universal audience to which its truth-claims aspire, the rhetorical analyst is in a position to better understand the text's truth-claims, its rhetorical power, and the interaction between the two.

As just outlined, rhetorical analysis is a bridge between exegesis and hermeneutics. Rather than assuming the affirmative stance of hermeneutics to be at odds with an objective analysis of the text, it sees a reading of the text in 'its possible rightness or truth' as the key to grasping its rhetorical power. Such a reading tries simultaneously to understand the text as both expressing the truth to a universal audience and bringing that truth to audiences in particular historical times and places. The sort of analysis we are proposing thus enables the interpreter to use the rhetorical shape of a text and the transactions between text and audience that shape the truth the text has to tell in both its epistemological and historical dimensions. If the interpreter plays the audience the text invites, he or she should be able to fathom the most profound level of the text's power to persuade.[41]

b. *God as Universal Audience*
In his discussion of the ambiguities of rhetoric, Plato offers the idea that the rhetor who is genuinely interested in truth 'must make this toilsome effort not for the sake of his speech and his conduct in relation to men: it is the gods he must think of'.[42] Whether Plato says this seriously or in jest, it is certainly an idea worth thinking about for religious texts like the Bible. Would not an author whose piety is shown in

40. It is discomforting to read some of Abraham Lincoln's addresses today because he was not entirely free from the racism of his time. One would still want to grant that he intended his discourse for the judgment of the universal audience.

41. This position is set forth more fully in Patrick and Scult, *Rhetoric and Biblical Interpretation*, pp. 21-24.

42. Plato, *Phaedrus* 273b.

the content and purpose of his or her discourse be conscious of the effect of what is being said on the God who had called him or her to speak?

The apostle Paul expresses such a consciousness in a number of his letters. 1 Thessalonians 2.3-6 exemplifies his view well:

> For our appeal does not spring from error or uncleanness, nor is it made with guile; but just as we have been approved by God to be entrusted with the gospel, so we speak, not to please men, but to please God who tests our hearts. For we never used either words of flattery, as you know, or a cloak for greed, as God is witness; nor did we seek glory from men.

Similar claims are made in 2 Cor. 2.17, 12.19, and Gal. 1.10.[43] The authority by which the apostle speaks is also the audience to which he is responsible. Of course, Paul is not really trying to persuade God, but rather in his efforts to persuade humans he does not want to 'misrepresent God' (1 Cor. 15.15).

While we do not find such explicit asseverations in the narratives of the Hebrew Bible, we do find approximations in the prophets. The prophets of the Old Testament understood themselves to be called to speak for God (e.g. Isa. 6.9-10; Jer. 1.9-10; Ezek. 2.1–3.11); hence, they could reply to objections to their message that they were simply relaying what they had been told (cf. Isa. 8.16-20; Jer. 26.12-15; Amos 7.14-15). One of the charges these prophets leveled against their opponents was that the latter sought to please their human audience (cf. 1 Kgs 22.5-28; Jer. 23.14, 16-17; 28.15; Ezek. 13.10-12; Mic. 2.11; 3.5).

The intention of pleasing God and communicating effectively with those aligned with him should guarantee that the narrators and prophets did not consciously manipulate information and emotions to win their audience. They could not be 'base rhetors' in the presence of the universal audience.

c. *Are There Interests Generated by Beliefs?*
Ideology critics typically hold the view that humans are driven by their 'material interests'—economic privileges, political control, social pres-

---

43. Betz, *Galatians*, p. 44, translates 1.10: 'For am I now persuading men or God? Or am I seeking to please men? If I were still pleasing men, I would not be Christ's slave.' He rejects the idea that the answer to the first question is 'God'. The parallels would suggest that Paul would at least say that he seeks to 'please' God, if not 'persuade' him.

tige. About as 'spiritual' as they will get is authority to determine the use of the society's symbolic 'superstructure'. This is, of course, standard Marxist reductionism. I bring it up here because their view of what constitutes an effective 'interest', one which has significant force in human motivation, would not include 'ideas' and 'beliefs'. This means that they could not acknowledge that authors' consciousness of having God as an audience would effect any significant transcendence of their material interests.

Is it not possible that an 'idea' or religious tradition can attain a high degree of independence from the power structure of a society and articulate a vision which generates its own 'interests'? Let us examine ideology critique itself, for it too appears to be an ideology driven by intellectual and spiritual concerns. If ideology critics were right that all cultural 'products' arise from material interests, they would be vulnerable to the application of their critique to themselves. There is no reason to believe that this cadre of scholars has discovered a way to transcend the self-interest and manipulative techniques which have, according to their own analysis, been the underlying dynamic of virtually all human discourse. By their own claim, these very critiques should be read with a suspicious eye towards the power interests they serve, rather than for the apparent truth of their analysis.

Would it not, however, be more fruitful to read ideology critics not as legitimating their 'material' interests, but rather as being driven by a passion for a certain kind of truth? That passion, reflected in the urgency of ideology critics to conform every cultural product to their prescribed interpretive scheme, is often the most salient characteristic of their writings. The fact that they frequently dispute among themselves over details of their own ideology suggests that their primary interest is to maintain a system of 'true doctrine'. Their political agenda is not the legitimating of their class interests, but the liberation of those who have been oppressed by the power structures that depend upon these texts for legitimation.

Thus their own writings would seem to point up the fact that humans are not only driven by the desire for economic, social and political power; they are also driven by a thirst for truth. Aside from whatever political or economic interests it might serve, a religion or philosophy can generate an interest which supersedes all others—a truth to which believers would sacrifice everything else. The resolution of doubt and the recruitment of devotees to this truth can become the dominant motivating force in their rhetoric.

Meir Sternberg characterizes biblical narrative as 'ideological literature', by which he means a literature designed to inculcate a particular belief system.[44] This is not 'ideology' in the same sense as the Cootes use the term, because YHWH does not have 'interests' in the same sense as does a social class or institution. Rather, it is an 'idea' (actually a *persona*) that has generated its own interests, created or modified institutions and social class structures, and produced a literature designed to establish and maintain conviction. 'Ideology' in this sense is not an epiphenomenon of material interests, but the rhetorical force of conviction given to an idea.

That the authors of biblical texts sought to please God—to answer to this representative of the universal audience—does not guarantee that what they wrote is not conditioned by their socio-economic and political interests, but it does virtually guarantee that they intended to negotiate with their audience in good faith. Moreover, since the God of Israel could generate interests distinct from and superseding material interests, this 'idea' could also become a source of ideological distortion. In the heat of debate, political crisis or messianic passion, the heart does strange things. Job's three companions, for example, are so offended by Job's bitter lamentation that they end up, according to Job, 'making dishonest assertions on God's behalf' (13.7). The author of Job knew that the desire to please God does not guarantee the truth of what one says. God will call Job's companions to account if they 'continue to secretly judge unfairly' (13.10). The interpreter of the Bible can never be certain that the text speaks the truth it claims to speak; like the original audience, one must depend upon one's capacity to exercise good judgment.

3. Conclusion

There is a sound humanistic reason to accord the texts we interpret the presumption that their rhetoric is bargaining in good faith with the audience. A text which has been perceived as true by generations of

---

44. M. Sternberg, *The Poetics of Biblical Narrative: Ideological Literature and the Drama of Reading* (Bloomington: Indiana University Press, 1985), pp. 84-128, *passim.* Sternberg was hardly the first to characterize biblical literature as ideological; he is simply a noteworthy rhetorically conscious exponent.

believers should be respected until it shows that it merits deconstruction and critique. Only by initially granting the text this respect might the dimension of its rhetoric, which is powerful because it is true, be recognized and understood.

One does incur the risk of being duped by a text which insidiously employs the appearance of truth in order to further its own material or spiritual interests. A reader granting the text the possibility of being true might simply be fooled in the same way the author might have been fooled by the rhetorical power of his or her own language to 'sound' true. But this risk is a necessary part of reading the text along with the audiences it has most profoundly affected, for we may surmise that they only arrived at an experience of the text's message by means of this risk. The acceptance of this risk can thus be seen as an entrance way into the hermeneutical circle which can reveal both the truth the text has to tell and the *organon* of its rhetorical power. As one proceeds along the circle, risk and judgment, in dialectical interplay, help one steer the course.

A humanistic hermeneutics of affirmation does not claim to guarantee that the power of a text's rhetoric is an indication of its truth, only of its possible truth. For the religious reader of the Bible, the possible becomes actual through the testimony of the Spirit engendering faith and obedience. Divine inspiration has a very definite role in the rhetorical transaction after all.

HALLIDAYAN FUNCTIONAL GRAMMAR AS HEIR
TO NEW TESTAMENT RHETORICAL CRITICISM

Gustavo Martín-Asensio

This essay is a study in method. My aim, first, is to argue that although the fundamental goals of rhetorical criticism of the New Testament seem both worthwhile and attainable, the approach in its most prevalent form has shown itself incapable of reaching them. Secondly, I wish to present Michael Halliday's 'functional grammar' as a sounder, better informed and more capable method of reaching these goals.

1. *Rhetoric and the New Testament*

The recently published collection of essays, *Rhetoric and the New Testament*,[1] affords a rather complete view of the current *état du jeu* of New Testament rhetorical criticism, and provides sufficient evidence for an evaluation of that 'near volcanic eruption of rhetoric'[2] that New Testament scholarship has witnessed in recent years.

Even a cursory reading of this volume reveals that although the various contributors share similar aims and use analogous terms to describe them, the actual methods employed by these writers are diverse, often seem incompatible, and reveal a field of study that is far from unified. This diversity becomes particularly evident in the many uses and understandings of the word 'rhetoric'. While for several contributors to this volume, rhetoric is generally limited to the discipline taught in certain classical Graeco-Roman manuals such as Cicero's *De Inventione*

---

1. S.E. Porter and T.H. Olbricht (eds.), *Rhetoric and the New Testament: Essays from the 1992 Heidelberg Conference* (JSNTSup, 90; Sheffield: JSOT Press, 1993).
2. W. Wuellner, 'Biblical Exegesis in the Light of the History and Historicity of Rhetoric and the Nature of the Rhetoric of Religion', in Porter and Olbricht (eds.), *Rhetoric and the New Testament*, pp. 492-513 (493).

or Quintilian's *Institutio Oratoria*,[3] for other writers the same word or its cognates are understood in far more generic terms. Thus, Vorster prefers to define rhetoric in terms of social interaction;[4] Reed understands the term as the study and application of argumentation,[5] and speaks of 'persuasive units' rather than Watson's 'rhetorical units';[6] Marshall seems to use 'persuasive power' as synonymous with rhetoric;[7] Berger argues that 'everything that leads the reader's psyche towards a goal has to be regarded as a rhetorical element';[8] in addressing the meaning of 'rhetorical' Lategan prefers 'the broader sense of the word', which for him means 'pragmatic intent';[9] Thurén, in short, concludes that rhetoric 'is not a value-free term'.[10]

This heterogeneous understanding of the term 'rhetoric', and particularly the degree of dependence of the various writers upon the rhetorical manuals of Graeco-Roman antiquity, seem to reveal three

3. From Porter and Olbricht (eds.), *Rhetoric and the New Testament*: F.W. Hughes, 'The Parable of the Rich Man and Lazarus (Luke 16.19-31) and Graeco-Roman Rhetoric', pp. 29-41; F. Siegert, 'Mass Communication and Prose Rhythm in Luke–Acts', pp. 42-58; J.I.H. McDonald, 'Rhetorical Issue and Rhetorical Strategy in Luke 10.25-37 and Acts 10.1–11.18', pp. 59-73; D. Marguerat, 'The End of Acts (28.16-31) and the Rhetoric of Silence', pp. 74-89; D. Hellholm, 'Amplificatio in the Macro-Structure of Romans', pp. 123-51; M. Schoeni, 'The Hyperbolic Sublime as a Master Trope in Romans', pp. 171-92; J. Smit, 'Argument and Genre of 1 Corinthians 12–14', pp. 211-30; D.F. Watson, 'Paul's Rhetorical Strategy in 1 Corinthians 15', pp. 231-49; J. Marshall, 'Paul's Ethical Appeal in Philippians', pp. 357-74.

4. J.N. Vorster, 'Strategies of Persuasion in Romans 1.16-17', in Porter and Olbricht (eds.), *Rhetoric and the New Testament*, pp. 152-70 (155, 167).

5. J.T. Reed, 'Using Ancient Rhetorical Categories to Interpret Paul's Letters: A Question of Genre', in Porter and Olbricht (eds.), *Rhetoric and the New Testament*, pp. 292-324 (295, 297). Lauri Thurén, 'On Studying Ethical Argumentation and Persuasion in the New Testament', in Porter and Olbricht (eds.), *Rhetoric and the New Testament*, pp. 464-78 (466), however, points out that the term 'argumentation' is also subject to a variety of interpretations and uses!

6. Reed, 'Using Ancient Rhetorical Categories', p. 319.

7. Marshall, 'Paul's Ethical Appeal', pp. 357, 371, though Marshall also relies on classical rhetoric as his 'guiding theory', p. 357.

8. K. Berger, 'Rhetorical Criticism, New Form Criticism and New Testament Hermeneutics', in Porter and Olbricht (eds.), *Rhetoric and the New Testament*, pp. 390-96 (393).

9. B. Lategan, 'Textual Space as Rhetorical Device', in Porter and Olbricht (eds.), *Rhetoric and the New Testament*, pp. 397-408 (397).

10. Thurén, 'Ethical Argumentation', p. 467.

distinguishable groups of scholars in this volume. The first group
('group A'), generally following the seminal works of G. Kennedy and
H.D. Betz,[11] sees New Testament rhetorical criticism as the interpretation of the various New Testament documents in light of the conventions and rules of the classical rhetorical texts. The second group
('group B') sees some value in studying the Graeco-Roman manuals,
while at the same time issuing words of caution in regard to a mechani-
cal or slavish application of the classical rhetorical categories to the
books of the New Testament. The third group ('group C') is highly
critical of the Kennedy–Betz approach,[12] and argues for a much more
inclusive notion of rhetoric that incorporates ancient as well as modern
insights into human communication. A more detailed discussion of
each group will clarify these differences.

a. *Group A*
One of the fundamental tenets of the exponents of this approach is the
conviction that many of the writers of the New Testament were familiar
with the categories and concepts of the classical rhetorical manuals.
Whether Luke, for example, had been to rhetorical school,[13] or, more
commonly, Paul and other New Testament writers 'picked up' these
categories merely from living in a rhetoric-saturated culture,[14] the

11. H.D. Betz, *Galatians: A Commentary on Paul's Letter to the Churches in
Galatia* (Hermeneia; Philadelphia: Fortress Press, 1979); G. Kennedy, *New Testa-
ment Interpretation through Rhetorical Criticism* (Chapel Hill, NC: University of
North Carolina Press, 1984).

12. Kennedy disagrees with Betz at significant points (see Kennedy, *New
Testament Interpretation*, pp. 144-48), yet due to their shared understanding of the
significance of the classical manuals for the study of the New Testament, and the
influence that both scholars have had on subsequent New Testament rhetorical
critics, I am arguing that they together are representative of my 'group A' type of
rhetorical criticism.

13. An idea taken for granted by Hughes, 'The Parable', pp. 37-38, who writes,
'If indeed a rather well educated writer, like the writer of Luke–Acts, had been
assigned to make declamations in a genre of Rich Man versus Poor Man *when* he
was in rhetorical school...'(emphasis mine); Hughes adds later, 'Yet given some
ability in *ethopoiïa*, which rhetorical instruction and practice would likely have
developed in a person as well educated as the writer of Luke–Acts...' (p. 38).

14. Thus, for example, Smit, 'Argument and Genre', p. 212, writes: 'these
schoolish handbooks provide a good impression of the rhetoric that was generally
practised in Paul's time and surroundings'; Siegert, 'Mass Communication', pp. 48-
49, argues that anyone addressing an ancient audience 'as spoiled as that of the big

scholars in 'group A' believe that the New Testament writers knew and applied at least the three main rhetorical genera of judicial, epideictic and deliberative. Such confidence leads to statements like Hellholm's, who describes his interpretation of Romans as 'a *decoding* rhetorical process',[15] or Smit's, who argues that 1 Cor. 14.33b-36 is a non-Pauline addition, because it 'runs counter to the rhetorical rules concerning the completeness of the *partitio*'.[16] Unfortunately, however, these writers often end up disagreeing as to what exactly is epideictic or deliberative, and cite ancient authorities such as Quintilian or Seneca against each other, a practice that seems to question the plausibility of the entire approach.[17]

assemblies in the theatres and basilicas' had to employ the particular rhythms taught by Quintilian *et al*. Though he approaches the issue critically, and I have consequently placed him in 'group B', C.J. Classen, 'St Paul's Epistles and Ancient Greek and Roman Rhetoric', in Porter and Olbricht (eds.), *Rhetoric and the New Testament*, pp. 265-91 (269), argues in a similar manner: 'Anyone who could write Greek as effectively as St Paul did, must have read a good deal of works written in Greek and thus imbibed applied rhetoric from others'.

    15. Hellholm, 'Amplificatio', p. 126, emphasis mine.

    16. Smit, 'Argument and Genre', p. 219. The author offers no *textual* backing for this assertion.

    17. Thus Watson, 'Rhetorical Strategy', p. 232, like M. Bünker, is by his own admission 'heavily dependent upon the rhetorical handbooks', yet believes, unlike Bünker, that 1 Cor. 15 is deliberative, not judicial. The debate between Kennedy and Betz is perhaps the best known. Kennedy, *New Testament Interpretation*, pp. 144, 148, argues that Betz's commentary is 'misleading in important respects', because it sees the epistle as apologetic-judicial, rather than (with Kennedy) as deliberative. Kennedy cites Quintilian, 3.4.9 in support of his view. The late Angelico-Salvatore Di Marco ('Rhetoric and Hermeneutic—On a Rhetorical Pattern: Chiasmus and Circularity', in Porter and Olbricht [eds.], *Rhetoric and the New Testament*, pp. 479-91 [479]) seems to have been on target when he wrote, 'Indeed, in rhetoric, scholars do not agree how to name a phenomenon'. The difficulties inherent in making clear-cut distinctions between deliberative and epideictic are evident in statements by McDonald, 'Rhetorical Issue', p. 68, who writes that Peter's speech in Acts 10 'exemplifies *deliberative* rhetoric...but *it also has epideictic* features' (emphasis mine); or Marshall, 'Paul's Ethical Appeal', p. 363, who argues that passages in Phil. 2 and 3 'may be characterized as epideictic, [but] their ultimate purpose is deliberative'; or T.H. Olbricht, 'Hebrews as Amplifaction', in Porter and Olbricht (eds.), *Rhetoric and the New Testament*, pp. 375-87 (378), who believes that Hebrews conforms to the epideictic genre in its superstructure, but 'the body of the argument may be conceived as deliberative'.

b. *Group B*

The writers I place in this group believe that classical rhetorical theory may render service for interpreting the New Testament,[18] but are much less enthusiastic about the applicability of specific categories and structures. For Classen, for example, Philip Melanchthon was a model rhetorical critic of the New Testament (though Kennedy ignores him entirely and Betz relegates him to one footnote), insofar as he made abundant use of the classical manuals when appropriate, while at the same time feeling free to alter and add to their categories and structures.[19] Basevi and Chapa follow Kennedy's method to a large extent, yet warn against applying rhetorical patterns, 'sometimes rather stereotyped, to texts that do not fit a particular Graeco-Roman model'.[20]

c. *Group C*

The critique offered by the writers in this group has done, I wish to argue, irreparable damage to the Kennedy–Betz approach to rhetorical criticism. It is interesting to note that all the essays in Part 2 of this volume ('Rhetoric and Questions of Method') approach the issue from this critical angle. It is the aim of these writers, first, to demonstrate the inadequacy of the narrow, 'group A' understanding of rhetoric. The social contexts of ancient rhetoric and biblical rhetoric, it is argued, were rather different.[21] The rhetorical manuals were addressing not epistolary literature but various types of speeches.[22] Finally, it cannot

18. Classen, 'St Paul's Epistles', p. 289; A.H. Snyman, 'Persuasion in Philippians 4.1-20', in Porter and Olbricht (eds.), *Rhetoric and the New Testament*, pp. 325-37; C. Basevi and J. Chapa, 'Philippians 2.6-11: The Rhetorical Function of a Pauline "Hymn" ', in Porter and Olbricht (eds.), *Rhetoric and the New Testament*, pp. 338-56; Olbricht, 'Hebrews as Amplification', p. 377.

19. Classen, 'St Paul's Epistles', pp. 271-78.

20. Basevi and Chapa, 'Philippians 2.6-11', p. 350. These two writers later add, 'we think it is necessary to underline the flexibility of the three genera' (p. 352).

21. Thurén, 'Ethical Argumentation', p. 470; Similarly Vorster, 'Strategies of Persuasion', p. 153: 'Classical rhetorical categories are inextricably linked to the social situation'. See also Wuellner, 'Biblical Exegesis', p. 503.

22. This seems to be the most devastating criticism of the Kennedy–Betz school and its followers in this volume. S.E. Porter, 'The Theoretical Justification for Application of Rhetorical Categories to Pauline Epistolary Literature', in Porter and Olbricht (eds.), *Rhetoric and the New Testament*, pp. 100-122, deals with this issue in detail. Depending on the previous work of A.J. Malherbe (*Ancient Epistolary Theorists* [SBLSBS, 19; Atlanta: Scholars Press, 1988]), Porter shows that there was in fact a clear line of demarcation between written letters and anything oral.

be demonstrated that the writers of the New Testament were familiar with and adopted (whether consciously or not) the complex structures taught in the rhetorical manuals.[23] The 'group C' writers also 'plead for methodological expansion',[24] arguing that the term 'rhetoric' encompasses much more than Aristotle, Quintilian or Seneca ever envisioned. Thus, Wuellner wants to see rhetoric 'unrestrained', because:

> So long as biblical scholars remain blind to the reality that there is more rhetoric to be experienced in one hour in the marketplace (or even in the nursery) than in one day in the academy, scholarship devoted to biblical rhetoric will remain in a quandary—in a prison self-made and self-imposed.[25]

In light of the above discussion, it seems fair to say that the Kennedy–Betz approach to rhetorical criticism has run its course. While Kennedy expressed his aims in terms similar to those Berger, Crafton and others have used in the present volume,[26] his rigid dependence on Graeco-

---

Secondly, the sporadic discussion of letter writing was only a late addition to the study of ancient rhetoric (Julius Victor's *Ars Rhetorica* [fourth century CE]), and was limited to matters of style; similarly Classen, 'St Paul's Epistles', p. 269, writes: 'Most ancient handbooks of rhetoric do not deal with letters, and where they do, they are content with a few remarks mostly on matters of style'; see also Reed, 'Using Ancient Rhetorical Categories', pp. 309-11; and Lategan, 'Textual Space', p. 397. If indeed it is the case that all the insights New Testament interpreters may draw from Graeco-Roman rhetoric are limited to stylistic matters, Kennedy's approach may, by his own admission, be said to have failed. Thus, at the outset of his highly influential work, Kennedy states: 'To many biblical scholars rhetoric probably means style, and they may envision in these pages discussion of figures of speech and metaphors not unlike that already to be found in many literary studies of the Scriptures. The identification of rhetoric with style—a feature of what I have elsewhere called letteratirizzazione—is a common phenomenon in the history of the study of rhetoric, but represents a limitation and to a certain extent a distortion of the discipline of rhetoric as understood and taught in antiquity' (*New Testament Interpretation*, p. 1).

23. Thurén, 'Ethical Argumentation', p. 470: 'However, a close identification of ancient techniques is meaningful only if we can reasonably assume that the authors had learnt those techniques by name at school'; see also Porter, 'Theoretical Justification', p. 105.

24. Vorster, 'Strategies of Persuasion', p. 153.

25. Wuellner, 'Biblical Exegesis', p. 500.

26. Kennedy, *New Testament Interpretation*, p. 12: 'The ultimate goal of rhetorical analysis, briefly put, is the discovery of the author's intent and of how that is transmitted through a text to an audience'; 'The primary aim of rhetorical

Roman manuals, together with the concomitant narrow understanding of the term 'rhetoric', has kept him and his followers from reaching these aims. Of the many important questions that *Rhetoric and the New Testament* has raised, perhaps the most fundamental is simply: what is rhetoric? If indeed rhetorical language is that language which is functional or purposeful, is it not the case that all human communication is rhetorical *in this sense*?[27] Does the usefulness of the word 'rhetoric' outweigh the problems arising from its traditional association with the Graeco-Roman manuals?

A feature common to many of the essays in all three groups is an emphasis on the *function* of texts in their social contexts as central to rhetorical study. The writers in 'group A' normally express this idea in terms of rhetorical situation (corresponding to the *Sitz im Leben* of form criticism), exigence (the need or problem arising from that situation and

criticism is to understand the effect of the text' (p. 33); '[the Bible is] rhetorical, again not in the sense of "false" or "deceitful", but in the sense of "purposeful"' (p. 158).

27. M. Gregory and S. Carroll, *Language and Situation: Language Varieties and their Social Context* (London: Routledge & Kegan Paul, 1978), p. 94: 'prescriptions for how to use language well and effectively...is what is meant here by a "rhetoric"'. Berger, 'Rhetorical Criticism', p. 395: 'Hermeneutics is based on rhetoric, because application does not merely rely on theoretical comprehension... but mainly on the pragmatic effect (function)'. Thus also G. Leech, *Principles of Pragmatics* (London: Longman, 1983), p. 15: 'The point about the term rhetoric, in this context, is the focus it places on a goal-oriented speech situation, in which speaker uses language in order to produce a particular effect in the mind of hearer. I shall also use the term rhetoric as a countable noun, for a set of conversational principles, which are related by their functions.' In this regard, R. Hasan, 'Rhyme and Reason in Literature', in S. Chatman (ed.), *Literary Style: A Symposium* (London: Oxford University Press, 1971), pp. 287-99 (299), writes: 'the sharp division of rhetoric and grammar is itself a fairly recent phenomenon in the long history of the study of language and literature'. See also M. Halliday, *An Introduction to Functional Grammar* (London: Edward Arnold, 1985), pp. xxiii, xxviii; speaking of the limited scope of linguistic theory, A. Van Dijk, *Text and Context: Explorations in the Semantics and Pragmatics of Discourse* (London: Longman, 1977), p. 4, writes that 'rhetorical function [is] related to the EFFECT of the utterance on the hearer' (emphasis original), adding that 'we do not want to treat such structures within a linguistic theory of discourse because they are restricted to certain types of discourse or certain STYLISTIC USES of language, and because they cannot be accounted for in terms of a grammatical form-meaning-action rule system'. We must ask, however, what type of discourse or what stylistic use of language can be said to have no effect on the hearer?

capable of being addressed or removed by discourse), and rhetorical strategy (the function intended for the text, in the form of Graeco-Roman deliberative, epideictic or judicial structures).[28] On the other hand, the contributors in 'group B' and 'group C' generally insist that New Testament texts, their functions and contexts, be studied in light of 'general human communication, and...be analysed with the best means available, whether ancient or modern'.[29] Dennis Stamps excepted,[30] the writers in this volume share a certain degree of optimism as to the possibility that the careful, systematic analysis of a text (whether by means of classical or Burkean rhetoric, pragmatics or neo-form criticism) will yield insights into its intended function(s) and the situation it is designed to address, that is, 'what kind of effect was it intended to

28. McDonald, 'Rhetorical Issue', pp. 60-70; Watson, 'Rhetorical Strategy', pp. 233-35.

29. Thurén, 'Ethical Argumentation', p. 471.

30. See his 'Rethinking the Rhetorical Situation: The Entextualization of the Situation in New Testament Epistles', in Porter and Olbricht (eds.), *Rhetoric and the New Testament*, pp. 193-210. Stamps is very critical of Bitzer and Kennedy's understanding of the concept of rhetorical situation, and denies a direct correspondence between rhetorical forms in the text and the actual historical context. His caveat seems reasonable enough. Stamps is right in pointing to the subjective nature of the rhetorical situation as 'inscribed in the text', since it necessarily reflects the author's perspective on the historical events that motivate his text, rather than those events pure and simple (p. 199). One may even agree that the author's representation of the rhetorical situation in his text is in fact part and parcel of his rhetorical strategy. Yet, Stamps also recognizes that 'it may be granted that any text, and an ancient New Testament epistle in particular, stems from certain historical and social contingencies' (p. 199); and that, regarding 1 Corinthians, 'the sender must present the entextualized situation in such a manner that elicits correspondence with some, if not most of the audience' (p. 200). Thus, though it is certainly true that 'any textual presentation of historical reality represents a process which involves interpretation and narrativization' (p. 199), this is equally true of any presentation of history, textual or non, and the selection and arrangement that this involves does not necessarily falsify or distort history. If true communication (in the widest sense of the word) is to take place between writer and reader/hearers, he must make reference to facts and ideas about the world that are commonly known and accepted. Though Stamps claims not to have slipped into formalism (p. 199 n. 17) his concluding statement seems to indicate otherwise: 'In more literary terms, the textuality of the rhetorical situation means that the speaker and audience as literary constructions themselves only meet in the "world-of-the-text". One aspect of the world-of-the-text which the text constructs is the rhetorical situation' (p. 210).

achieve and what does this tell us about the situation?'[31]

I wish to argue that rhetorical criticism in all its forms has done much to highlight the importance of *function in context* in our study of the New Testament documents. In addition, its emphasis on the analysis of the various letters and books *prout extant* is a welcome corrective to the recurrent speculation of some of the older critical methods. Yet, for these fundamental insights to be truly fruitful a more 'productive match' must be sought between the biblical texts and a critical method. Such a method must, in the words of Crafton in this volume, 'develop categories of genre which reveal authors' tactics for handling circumstances, thereby connecting literature to real life'.[32] Such a method, in short, must be aimed at the study of language as a means, indeed the primary means, of social interaction. It is my contention that this method exists, and may be used with profit in the study of the New Testament. Throughout the remainder of the present essay I shall introduce Michael Halliday's 'functional grammar' as an ideally suited method for achieving the aims of rhetorical criticism as expressed by Crafton above.

2. *Background to Hallidayan Functional Grammar*

[W]hen a savage learns to understand the meaning of a word, this process is not accomplished by explanations, by a series of acts of apperception, but by learning to handle it. A word means to a native the proper use of the thing for which it stands, exactly as an implement means something when it can be handled and means nothing when no active experience of it is at hand. The word therefore has a power of its own, it is a means of bringing things about, it is a handle to acts and objects and not a definition of them.[33]

31. Berger, 'Rhetorical Critisim', p. 392. Similarly J.A. Crafton, 'The Dancing of an Attitude: Burkean Rhetorical Criticism and the Biblical Interpreter', in Porter and Olbricht (eds.), *Rhetoric and the New Testament*, pp. 429-42 (435), writes: 'Burke's concern with rhetorical strategy leads to a fascination with how people deal with life through language, how they attempt to "encompass" situations. Burke proposes that these ventures may be explored through a "sociological criticism of literature". Such a method would develop categories of genre which reveal authors' tactics for handling circumstances, thereby connecting literature to real life.'

32. Crafton, 'Dancing of an Attitude', p. 435. See definition of 'register' below.

33. Malinowski, 'The Problem of Meaning', cited in T. Langendoen, *The London School of Linguistics: A Study of the Linguistic Theories of B. Malinowski and J.R. Firth* (Research Monograph, 46; Cambridge, MA: MIT Press, 1968),

Statements on language and culture (such as the one above in the ethnographic papers of Bronislaw Malinowski) represent the earliest expression of what has come to be known as functional grammar. Though the focus of Malinowski's study of the Trobriand culture in the 1920s was primarily anthropological, four of his treatises and articles from the period[34] include significant discussions of language as the primary means of cultural behaviour.

Malinowski's early discovery of the raw instrumentality of much of the natives' language is summarized in some detail in 'Classificatory Particles'. In seeking to understand the meaning of certain words and formatives in the culture of Kiriwina, it was discovered that constant reference to ethnographic data was unavoidable. Thus the use of bare numeral stems without classificatory particle is reserved for the counting of baskets of yams, which in the local culture is felt to be 'counting *par excellence*'.[35] Several similar examples led Malinowski to issue a call for a semantic theory that would account for lexico-grammatical facts in light of the cultural constraints that motivate them.[36] Two years after the publication of 'Classificatory Particles', Malinowski's first substantial ethnographic treatise appeared under the title *Argonauts of the Western Pacific*. Particularly significant in this work is the final chapter entitled 'The Power of Words in Magic', in which the author argues that 'magical style' in its pure instrumentality is different from ordinary narrative. Each word or formula is wielded as a tool or weapon to bring about specific effects in the world.

With 'The Problem of Meaning' we see a major shift in the sociolinguistic thought of Malinowski. In an attempt to spell out his

p. 23. Langendoen's monograph is a revision of his doctoral dissertation produced at MIT under Noam Chomsky in 1964.

34. 'Classificatory Particles in the Language or Kiriwina', *BSO(A)S* 1.4 (1920), pp. 37-78; *Argonauts of the Western Pacific* (London: Routledge, 1922); 'The Problem of Meaning in Primitive Languages', in O.K. Ogden and I.A. Richards, *The Meaning of Meaning* (New York: Harcourt, 10th edn, 1923), pp. 296-336; and *Coral Gardens and their Magic* (New York: American Book, 1935), the last being Malinowski's final word on his semantic theory. Key ideas from this work were soon taken over by J.R. Firth, who was by this time interacting with Malinowski in seminars led by the latter at the University of London.

35. See Langendoen, *The London School*, p. 11.

36. Thus, in 'Classificatory Particles', cited in Langendoen, *The London School*, p. 11, Malinowski writes of the need 'to show how necessary it is to give some ethnographic information if grammatical relations are to be fully understood'.

ethnographic semantic theory, he concludes that words derive their meaning not from the physical qualities of their referents, but from the socio-cultural context in which they are uttered, from the function they are made to serve.[37] In this regard, Malinowski is forced to conclude that 'magical style', rather than being an exception is in fact the rule (other types of language such as a scientific treatise being derivative and secondary). His argument in support of this assertion is twofold. First, in primitive societies, where there is no written language, the only type of communication possible is that of the purely functional sort,[38] in which each utterance is inseparably tied to the context of situation. Secondly, language acquisition by infants develops along strictly functional lines, indeed, '[t]he child *acts* by sound at this stage'.[39]

Malinowski's work, *Coral Gardens and their Magic*, has been by far the most influential, and represents the apex of his sociosemantic theory. In *Coral Gardens* Malinowski pursues his insights into language as a mode of cultural behaviour to their logical conclusions:

> The sentence is at times a self-contained linguistic unit, but not even a sentence can be regarded as a full linguistic datum. To us, the real linguistic fact is the full utterance within its context of situation.[40]

By 1935, the isolated and germinal insights of 'Classificatory Particles' had been integrated into a fairly detailed theory of language as a mode of (societal) action, already including several of the essential tenets of functional grammar. By this time, Malinowski and John Firth were interacting regularly at University College, London, and the influences were mutual. It was Firth's vision to shape Malinowski's ideas about language in society, and that of context of situation in particular, into a consistently linguistic theory. While Malinowski had

37. Though he seems to have contradicted himself at other points of this same essay. See Langendoen, *The London School*, p. 19.

38. Thus also O. Uribe-Villegas, 'On the Social in Language and the Linguistic in Society', in O. Uribe-Villegas (ed.), *Issues in Sociolinguistics* (The Hague: Mouton, 1977), pp. 57-111, esp. p. 85: 'Among primitive peoples, language is purely an instrument'.

39. Cited in Langendoen, *The London School*, p. 17 (emphasis in original). M. Halliday, *Learning How to Mean: Explorations in the Development of Language* (London: Edward Arnold, 1975), is a thorough investigation of this idea.

40. Cited in Langendoen, *The London School*, p. 31. Not surprisingly, Langendoen is highly critical of this development in Malinowski's thought. See n. 33, above.

defined context of situation in rather concrete language, Firth came to realize that for the notion to become a truly valuable one, and capable of sufficiently wide application, it needed to be expressed in more abstract terms.[41] Thus, Firth suggests the following 'categories of context of situation': relevant features of participants, their verbal and non-verbal actions, relevant objects, and the effect of the verbal action. In addition, the notion of 'typical' context of situation was introduced to account for the limited variety of social situations an individual encounters throughout his or her life. Once a patient, for example, begins to converse with his doctor on the nature of his ailment, the doctor is, in his response, bound by the social-linguistic conventions proper to the context of 'doctor–patient interviews', a context type familiar to most members of modern society. From this follows that as there is a limited number of recognizable context types, there is in each case a context-specific language variety: 'The multiplicity of social roles we have to play...involves also a certain degree of linguistic specialization. Unity is the last concept that should be applied to language.'[42] Such variety of language according to use or function has come to be known as 'register'.[43]

It is Firth's somewhat *sui generis* understanding of 'meaning' that has earned him (and many of his followers) the greatest criticism from several sources. Although Firth's use of the word 'meaning' may be

41. Firth, cited in C. Butler, *Systemic Linguistics: Theory and Applications* (London: Batsford, 1985), pp. 4-5: '[context of situation is] a group of related categories at a different level from grammatical categories but rather of the same abstract nature'.

42. Firth cited in Langendoen, *The London School*, p. 46.

43. See Butler, *Systemic Linguistics*, p. 67; M. Halliday, *Language as Social Semiotic: The Social Interpretation of Language and Meaning* (London: Edward Arnold, 2nd edn, 1979), pp. 31-35, 60-74; Halliday, *Learning How to Mean*, p. 126; M. Berry, *Introduction to Systemic Linguistics*. I. *Structures and Systems* (London: Batsford, 1977), pp. 2, 87-89; J. Ure and J. Ellis, 'Register in Descriptive Linguistics and Linguistic Sociology', in Uribe-Villegas (ed.), *Issues in Sociolinguistics*, pp. 197-240; Gregory and Carroll, *Language and Situation*, pp. 27-74; M. Ghadessy (ed.), *Register Analysis: Theory and Practice* (London: Pinter, 1993); for a collection of essays on register in English see M. Ghadessy (ed.), *Registers of Written English* (London: Pinter, 1988); for an application of the notion of register to the Greek of Mark's Gospel, see S.E. Porter, 'Dialect and Register in the Greek of the New Testament: Theory', in M.D. Carroll R. (ed.), *Rethinking Context, Rereading Texts: Contributions from the Social Sciences to Biblical Interpretation* (Sheffield: Sheffield Academic Press, forthcoming).

'highly idiosyncratic',[44] it cannot be branded as inconsistent within his own theory of function in context. Firth's assertion (after Malinowski) that 'meaning is function in context' amounts to a recognition of the impossibility of establishing a clear-cut distinction between sense and reference,[45] semantics and pragmatics,[46] linguistic knowledge and knowledge of the world. Katz and Fodor notwithstanding, it seems impossible to construct a semantic theory devoid of any reference to the contextual elements of words or sentences.[47] Instead, Firth proposed that meaning ought to be understood in terms of a multi-layered context theory, in which there are contexts of situation as well as grammatical and phonological contexts. The function, and consequently the meaning, of each linguistic element is understood in terms of their relationships with the other elements in their environment.

Last, Firth's maxim known by him as 'renewal of connection', insofar as it is followed, ensures that the entire model will remain firmly based on the data of real language in use. In the words of Monaghan: 'renewal of connection with language in situations requires a relativization of the linguist's metalanguage. It is not the theory that gives validity to the description, but rather the description has to be always tested against real language in use.'[48]

It may well be that Firth's theory of context had some serious limitations and was of a merely programmatic nature, yet,

44. These are Butler's words. It seems clear, however, that much of what Firth means by 'meaning', is already present in Saussure's *Course*. Saussure's 'values' are perhaps the best example.

45. See F.R. Palmer, *Semantics, a New Outline* (Cambridge: Cambridge University Press, 1976), pp. 30-34.

46. See S. Levinson, 'Defining Pragmatics', in *idem, Pragmatics* (Cambridge: Cambridge University Press, 1983), pp. 5-35; G.N. Leech, *Principles of Pragmatics* (London: Longman, 1983), argues for the strong interdepencence of both disciplines, thus also J. Lyons, *Language, Meaning and Context* (London: Fontana [Collins], 1981), pp. 71, 72, who warns against drawing this distinction too sharply.

47. Deictic markers such as 'he', 'then' or 'there' are perhaps the best example of this. 'The single most obvious way in which the relationship between language and context is reflected in the structures of languages themselves is through the phenomenon of deixis' (Levinson, *Pragmatics*, p. 54).

48. J. Monaghan, *The Neo-Firthian Tradition and its Contribution to General Linguistics* (Linguistische Arbeiten, 73; Tübingen: Max Niemeyer, 1979), p. 185; see also pp. 36-40.

If we cannot get very far with context of situation this is perhaps no more than a reflection of the difficulty of saying anything about semantics, and it is surely better to say a little than to say nothing at all ... The proper conclusion, perhaps, should be that we need far more sophisticated techniques for context of situation than have yet been developed.[49]

3. *Hallidayan Functional Grammar*

The openly acknowledged indebtedness of Michael Halliday to John Firth, his teacher at University College, London, becomes particularly evident in statements such as the following: 'Text is meaning and meaning is choice, an ongoing current of selections each in its paradigmatic environment of what might have been meant (but was not)'.[50]

As I pointed out above, Malinowski coined the term 'context of situation' to account for the typical environments in which members of a society behave linguistically. Firth, in turn, attempted to convert what was essentially the latter's sporadic collection of primarily anthropological insights into a coherent socio-linguistic theory. Firth's success was, however, only partial, and his theory has often been described as merely 'programmatic'.[51] Standing firmly in the tradition of his two predecessors of the London school, Halliday set out to investigate and expound 'the functional basis of language'. For Halliday, language is the primary attribute of social man ('homo grammaticus'), and the behavioural potential of a society (i.e. what it 'can do') is primarily realized by its linguistic potential ('can mean', sociosemantics), which is itself realized in the lexico-grammar ('can say').[52] Language, then, is fundamentally functional, indeed, it is our most effective means of 'doing'. This functional nature of language has in large measure—argues Halliday—determined its current form, and is reflected in its three major functional components or 'meta-functions': the ideational, the interpersonal and the textual.[53] Halliday's chief hypothesis in regard

49. Palmer, *Semantics*, p. 51.

50. Halliday, *Language as Social Semiotic*, p. 137.

51. Butler, *Systemic Linguistics*, p. 13.

52. See Halliday, 'Language in a Social Perspective', in *idem*, *Explorations in the Function of Language* (London: Edward Arnold, 1976), p. 51.

53. The independence and validity of Halliday's three functional components have been questioned by Fawcett, among others, who proposes a much greater number of these; see R.P. Fawcett, *Cognitive Linguistics and Social Interaction: Towards an Integrated Model of a Systemic Functional Grammer and the Other*

to these 'meta-functions' is that each tends to be determined and con-
strained by one element of the context of situation (see Fig. 1). Thus,
the 'field' (i.e. 'what is going on'—for example, a game of poker) tends
to constrain the choices arising from the ideational meta-function. The
element of 'tenor' (i.e. the participants), similarly, tends to constrain the
interpersonal choices, while the 'mode' (the function of language in the
situation, e.g. to warn) constrains the textual choices.[54]

Elements of Situation	'tends to determine…'	Meta-Functions	Functional Roles	Realizations in Text
Field ('what is going on')		Ideational>	Transitivity	
Tenor (participants)	>REGISTER> A context-specific, function-based language variety.	Interpersonal>	Mood, Modality	
Mode (medium and function)		Textual>	Theme/Rheme, Information	
'Can mean' (semantics)				'Can say' (lexico-grammar)

Figure 1. The Hallidayan System of Register

Hallidayan functional grammar can be approached from several
angles. Given my present aim—namely, to demonstrate its methodological suitability for the rhetorical/functional study of the New
Testament documents—I wish to emphasize the following points:

1. Its focus is on language as an 'inter-organism' phenomenon. This

---

Components of a Communicating Mind (Heidelberg: Julius Groos Verlag, 1980).

54. Halliday, *Language as Social Semiotic*, is unclear as to the degree of determination of meta-functions by elements of situation, thus, his descriptions of this
relation range from 'a general tendency' (p. 68); to 'A systematic correspondence'
(p. 116); 'tends to determine' (p. 117); 'activates', 'determines' (p. 125); 'rule'
(p. 142). For more on this problem, see Butler, *Systemic Linguistics*, p. 88.
Compare Kennedy, *New Testament Interpretation*, p. 34: 'The situation controls the
rhetorical response in the same sense that the question controls the answer and the
problem controls the solution'.

is perhaps one of Halliday's favourite terms, used often to contrast his linguistic approach with that of Noam Chomsky, who favoured an 'intra-organism' perspective. In other words, Halliday's theory is decidedly socio-linguistic[55] rather than psycho-linguistic. It focuses on language as the primary means of social behaviour, rather than as 'competence' stored in people's brains. Given the above-mentioned sociological focus, it is not surprising that the emphasis of linguistic analysis is placed on system and choice, that is, on the paradigmatic rather than the syntagmatic axis (see the Halliday quotation at the beginning of this section [p. 97]). In connection with this, Halliday argues that the failure of many text-descriptive theories is rooted in an inability or unwillingness to account properly for paradigmatic relations. If we are to relate a text to 'higher orders of meaning, whether social, literary or of some other semiotic universe',[56] we must—argues Halliday—move beyond the mere description of syntax to an account of the contextually determined networks of options from which particular textual choices emanate. Our knowledge of the language system(s) (e.g. the transitivity network in English) allows us to explain the various lexico-grammatical structures in a text as purposeful choices, indeed, as part and parcel of a larger rhetorical strategy.

2. Its aim is the study of texts,[57] 'which may be regarded as the basic unit of semantic structure'.[58] This is demonstrated in Halliday's analysis of William Golding's *The Inheritors*,[59] in which various linguistic

55. Besides acknowledging his debt to Malinowski, Halliday has affirmed his dependence on the sociological theory of Basil Bernstein. See 'The Significance of Bernstein's Work for Sociolinguistic Theory', in Halliday, *Language as Social Semiotic*, pp. 101-107. For a discussion of the origin and significance of socio-linguistics, see O. Uribe-Villegas, 'Introduction: Sociolinguistics in Search of a Place among the Academic Disciplines and Political Practices', in Uribe-Villegas (ed.), *Issues in Sociolinguistics*, pp. 9-44, esp. p. 22.

56. Halliday, *Language as Social Semiotic*, p. 137.

57. Halliday, *Language as Social Semiotic*, pp. 56-57: 'We are interested in what a particular writer has written, against the background of what he might have written…in what it is about the language of a particular work of literature that has its effect on us as readers'; see also Butler, *Systemic Linguistics*, pp. 193-201; Berry, *Systemic Linguistics*, p. 25.

58. Halliday, *Language as Social Semiotic*, p. 60.

59. M.A.K. Halliday, 'Linguistic Function and Literary Style: An Inquiry into the Language of William Golding's *The Inheritors*', in Halliday, *Explorations in the Function of Language*, pp. 103-35.

means of foregrounding are discussed in light of the overall theme of the narrative. In a similar study, Halliday uses the text of James Thurber's fable, *The Lover and his Lass*, to illustrate the concept of situation in written narrative, as well as the links 'between the semantic configurations of the text and the situational description'.[60] R. Hasan has produced similar analyses, using as sample texts a poem, Les Murray's 'Widower in the Country', and a short story, Angus Wilson's *Necessity's Child*.[61] In the analysis of texts, Halliday argues, there are two possible levels of achievement. The first may be described as a contribution to the understanding of the text and is reached by the study of lexis and grammar. This first level of analysis may help to answer the question of why a text means what it does. The second level represents a significantly higher achievement, and focuses on whether or not the text in question is effective in encompassing the situation it is designed to address. It is the second level of achievement that Halliday's functional grammar aims for. Such an agenda seems rather well suited for the fulfilment of the aims of rhetorical criticism as expressed above. If rhetoric is the study of effective communication (*ars bene dicendi*), a text may be considered rhetorically successful insofar as it is shown to be *functionally appropriate to the situation* that motivated it. It follows, then, that rhetorical theory must be equipped to encompass the fundamental elements of situation, the text and the reciprocal relations between them. This leads to the third and final point I wish to make.

3. Perhaps most importantly, the aim of Hallidayan functional grammar is to expose and exploit the links between text and its context of situation:

> [A] text is an instance of social meaning in a particular context of situation. We shall therefore expect to find the situation embodied or enshrined in the text, not piecemeal, but in a way which reflects the systematic relation between the semantic structure and the social environment.[62]

This is, I wish to argue, the facet of functional grammar that is most valuable for our task of interpreting the New Testament documents. In

---

60. M.A.K. Halliday, 'The Sociosemantic Nature of Discourse', in *idem*, *Language as Social Semiotic*, pp. 128-50.

61. R. Hasan, *Linguistics, Language and Verbal Art* (Oxford: Oxford University Press, 1985).

62. Halliday, *Language as Social Semiotic*, p. 141.

ancient texts such as these, where the context of situation is at best only partially understood, a functional analysis of their language may yield important clues for the recovery of that context.[63] An example offered by Halliday serves to illustrate this. In his analysis of *The Lover and his Lass*, mentioned above, Halliday finds that the three roles the writer wishes to adopt in relation to his readers (recounter, humorist and moralist) are embodied respectively in his choices of mood (every clause in the narrative section of the story is declarative), 'vocabulary as attitude' (e.g. the expression inamoratus), and the 'special mood structure' characteristic of proverbial literature.[64] These are choices in the interpersonal network and relate to the situational element of tenor.

Within the framework of his functional grammar, Halliday's register[65] theory best illustrates the above-mentioned aims. Like Kennedy and Betz, Halliday is concerned with 'language varieties according to use', yet, unlike these two scholars and their followers, he seems to have succeeded in constructing a model capable of wide application across temporal and geographical boundaries.[66] Starting from the

63. R. Hasan, cited in M. Ghadessy, 'The Language in Written Sports Commentary: Soccer—A Description', in Ghadessy (ed.), *Registers of Written English*, pp. 19-24 (21), writes, 'the relationship between text and context is two-fold for the acculturated reader: if we have access to the context, we can predict the essentials of the text; if we have access to the text, then we can infer the context from it'. Similarly, G. Brown and G. Yule, *Discourse Analysis* (Cambridge: Cambridge University Press, 1983), pp. 49-50, affirm that 'Even in the absence of information about place and time of original utterance, even in the absence of information about the speaker/writer and his intended recipient, it is often possible to reconstruct at least some part of the physical context and to arrive at some interpretation of the text. The more co-text there is, in general, the more secure the interpretation is.' See also Halliday, *Language as Social Semiotic*, p. 62; Porter, 'Dialect and Register'.

64. Halliday, *Language as Social Semiotic*, p. 148.

65. The term was first used by T.B.W. Reid, 'Linguistics, Structuralism and Philology', *Archivum Linguisticum* 8.2 (1956), p. 134, in the context of a discussion of bilingualism.

66. Unlike the culturally bound categories of epideictic, judicial and deliberative genera, the notion of register (including that of the three meta-functions which constrain it) is flexible and sensitive enough to permit its widest application. Thus Halliday, *Functional Grammar*, p. xxxiv: 'it is postulated that in all languages the content systems are organized into ideational, interpersonal and textual components. This is presented as a universal feature of language. But the descriptive categories are treated as particular. So, while all languages are assumed to have a

Malinowskian insight that 'the language we speak or write varies according to the type of situation',[67] Halliday seeks to establish what elements of situation determine what linguistic features in the text. As was briefly mentioned above, the element of field ('that which is going on', e.g. a game of poker), for example, determines choices arising from the ideational component of language, realized in structures such as types of process, participant structures, and so on. The sum total of the discernible lexico-grammatical and entonational (if dealing with a spoken text) features deriving from field, tenor and mode constitutes a context-specific variety of language: it constitutes a register. While the usefulness of the notion is widely acknowledged, recent scholarly dis-cussion of register analysis has raised several questions of importance. Robert de Beaugrande, for example, objects to 'making "social" cate-gories [i.e. field, tenor, and mode] correspond to language forms',[68] and prefers to define register in essentially psychological terms. Whether register must ultimately be understood socio-semantically or lexico-grammatically may well be merely a matter of point of view. I for one wish to argue with Matthiesen that lexico-grammatical analysis may be used with profit, at least as a point of entry into the study of registers, and that at least from this angle 'registers can be described in the same way as languages'.[69]

4. *Foregrounding as a Point of Entry into New Testament Greek Register Analysis*

The complexity of some of the issues involved in recent discussion of register, together with the preliminary and pioneering nature of the

"textual" component, whereby discourse achieves a texture that relates it to its environment, it is not assumed that in any given language one of the ways of achieving texture will be by means of a thematic system.' See also Ure and Ellis, 'Register in Descriptive Linguistics', p. 201.

67. Halliday, *Language as Social Semiotic*, p. 32.

68. R. de Beaugrande, '"Register" in Discourse Studies: A Concept in Search of a Theory', in Ghadessy (ed.), *Register Analysis*, pp. 7-26 (13). But see C. Matthiesen, 'Register in the Round: Diversity in a Unified Theory of Register Analysis', in Ghadessy (ed.), *Register Analysis*, pp. 221-92, esp. p. 236, who clarifies the matter by stating that while 'the semantic system is realized by the lexico-grammatical one…context of situation is realized not directly by the linguis-tic system but by *variation in* the linguistic system' (his emphasis).

69. Matthiesen, 'Register in the Round', p. 275.

conclusions thus far, must not be allowed to create too negative an impression of its real potential. The fruitful and insightful analyses of texts carried out by Halliday and Hasan among others are fair indicators of the results that further research along these lines may yield. Secondly, it must be noted that in New Testament studies, given the limited corpus of texts at our disposal, I will not be concerned with several of the issues that most often occupy and divide register analysts, namely, register as a means of investigating idiolects (the sum total of the registers an individual controls) or sociolect (the sum total of registers discernible in a given society). The scantiness of our data clearly precludes such ambitious aims.

Discussing the complexity of register analysis in English, Matthiesen proposes that analysts must first 'be able to make principled selections' from all the evidence available, and secondly, 'use such selections as a way into a comprehensive account'.[70] I wish to suggest that, in applying register analysis to the Greek of the New Testament, the study of patterns of *foregrounding*[71] may be chosen with profit as that initial

---

70. Matthiesen, 'Register in the Round', p. 275.

71. The key works on the subject of foregrounding are: J. Mukarovsky, 'Standard Language and Poetic Language', in P.R. Garvin, *A Prague School Reader on Esthetic, Literary Structure and Style* (Washington, DC: Georgetown University Press, 1964), pp. 17-30; R. Jakobson, 'Linguistics and Poetics', in T.A. Sebeok (ed.), *Style in Language* (Cambridge, MA: MIT Press, 1960), pp. 350-68; G.N. Leech, 'Linguistics and the Figures of Rhetoric', in R. Fowler (ed.), *Essays on Style and Language: Linguistic and Critical Approaches to Literary Style* (London: Routledge & Kegan Paul, 1970), pp. 135-56; Halliday, 'Linguistic Function and Literary Style'. See also G.N. Leech, 'Foregrounding and Interpretation', Chapter 4 of his *A Linguistic Guide to English Poetry* (London: Longman, 1969); S. Wallace, 'Figure and Ground: The Interrelationships of Linguistic Categories', in P.J. Hopper (ed.), *Tense–Aspect: Between Semantics and Pragmatics* (Amsterdam: John Benjamins, 1982), pp. 201-23; S. Fleischman, 'Discourse Functions of Tense-Aspect Oppositions in Narrative: Toward a Theory of Grounding', *Linguistics* 23.6 (1985), pp. 851-82; S. Fleischmann, *Tense and Narrativity* (Austin: University of Texas Press, 1990); S. Fleischmann and L. Waugh (eds.), *Discourse Pragmatics and the Verb* (London: Routledge, 1991) (the last four works focus on tense-aspect); W. van Peer, *Stylistics and Psychology, Investigations of Foregrounding* (Croom Helm Linguistics Series; London: Croom Helm, 1986), esp. Chapter 1; Hasan, *Linguistics, Language and Verbal Art*, esp. pp. 29-106; H. Dry, 'Foregrounding: An Assessment', in S.J.J. Hwang and W.R. Merrifield (eds.), *Language in Context: Essays for Robert E. Longacre* (Dallas: Summer Institute of

selection, with a view to an eventual comprehensive analysis of register. The need of writers to mark varying degrees of saliency in narrative
seems to be a universal one. By investing the text with diverse view-
points on the action, highlighting key elements or episodes through
lexico-grammatical means, the skilled narrator is able to impose an
'evaluative superstructure' upon the text, aimed at effecting the desired
response(s) in the reader. The textual function of language, of which
foregrounding strategies are a realization, enables the writer to organize
his text into a coherent and cohesive whole, so that what he writes is
appropriate to the context and fulfils its intended function.

A recent study by this writer of the present and aorist tense forms in
Ephesians[72] confirms that aspect is a common means of foregrounding
in the Greek of the New Testament.[73] In Ephesians 5, for example, we
find 55 present forms and 8 aorist forms, the latter being used to
express the acts of Christ in every instance except one,[74] while the
former convey instructions, commands or statements pertaining to the
immediate experience of the readers or hearers. I found the latter usage
to be consistent throughout the epistle, and proposed the conceptual
features of (+immediacy) for the present tense forms and (+immediacy)
for the aorist, concluding that the present tense forms are consistently
foregrounded (reckoned as prominent) in virtue of *both* the feature of
(+immediacy) discernible in them, and their contrast with the aorist
tenses which are unmarked as to that same feature. The present tense
forms in Ephesians are used consistently by the author to communicate
the verbal ideas that are most central to his purpose, or those related to
the immediate experience or the behaviour of his audience. In contrast
to this, the aorist tense form is used when the author does not intend to
signal immediacy or closeness to the experience of the audience, and is
instead relating, for example, the acts of God or Christ on their behalf
without a hortatory or paraenetic (exhortative) emphasis.

Linguistics, 1992), pp. 435-50. For a complete bibliography, see van Peer, *Stylistics and Psychology*, Chapter 1.

72. G. Martín-Asensio, 'An Assessment of Markedness Theory as Applied to Greek Verbal Aspect by Buist Fanning and Stanley Porter, with Reference to Ephesians' (MCS thesis; Regent College, Vancouver, BC, Canada, 1995).

73. See S.E. Porter, *Verbal Aspect in the Greek of the New Testament, with Reference to Tense and Mood* (New York: Peter Lang, 1993), p. 92, on 'planes of discourse'.

74. The proverbial saying οὐδεὶς γάρ ποτε τὴν ἑαυτοῦ σάρκα ἐμίσησεν (Eph. 5.29).

In another recent essay by this writer,[75] transitivity patterns were found to play a central role in the foregrounding scheme employed by the author in the shipwreck narrative of Acts 27. The central thesis of this essay is that the theme of divine sovereignty and the futility of human opposition to the divine will is embodied in the author's foregrounding scheme in the shipwreck narrative. In a seminal work on transitivity in a large number of the world's languages, Hopper and Thompson noted that narrative story-lines are usually carried by people who intentionally initiate events.[76] In Halliday's terms, it is agents who are represented as bringing about events in ergative clauses, while their absence in non-ergative clauses[77] leaves the question of causation unanswered. In the shipwreck story, against the background of the non-agentive participants ('we', Paul and 23 inanimate participants), the author foregrounds the highly dynamic 'they' agent (sailors, soldiers or both, often referred to simply as 'they') who appears to be actively involved in the shaping of events. The resolve of the ship's crew and captain to sail is strong enough to sway Julius the centurion, who from that point until the end of the narrative fades into the background. As the story progresses, however, the utter futility of the sailors' efforts is revealed, as the ship begins to drift, helplessly carried by wind and waves. The conclusion of the narrative sees the safe rescue of all the ship's passengers and crew at the expense of the ship and its cargo, in strict fulfilment of the divine message conveyed to Paul in vv. 21-26.

Besides tense-aspect morphology and transitivity patterns, attention must also be paid to clause structure,[78] 'given' and 'new'[79] elements, and, closely related to the latter, 'frames' or 'scripts'[80] in our search for indicators of *relevant* prominence in the New Testament texts. The

75. G. Martín-Asensio, 'Foregrounding and its Relevance for Interpretation and Translation, with Acts 27 as a Case Study', in S.E. Porter and R.S. Hess (eds.), *Translating the Bible: Problems and Prospects* (JSNTSup, 173; Sheffield: Sheffield Academic Press, 1999), pp. 189-223.

76. P.J. Hopper and S.A. Thompson, 'Transitivity in Grammar and Discourse', *Language* 56.2 (1980), pp. 251-99, esp. p. 286.

77. See Halliday, *Functional Grammar*, pp. 144-57.

78. See S.E. Porter, 'Word Order and Clause Structure in New Testament Greek', *Filología Neotestamentaria* 4 (1993), pp. 177-205, for an analysis of 'marked' and 'unmarked' clause structures in New Testament Greek.

79. See Brown and Yule, *Discourse Analysis*, pp. 169-76, 179-82; Halliday, *Language as Social Semiotic*, p. 148.

80. Brown and Yule, *Discourse Analysis*, p. 238.

analysis of frames is of particular interest, as these may be understood as micro-registers within a larger work. The question may be asked, for example, what is the typical or standard way (i.e. a 'frame') of introducing a character or a new episode in Paul's travels in Luke–Acts? In that light, what kind of unexpected variation may be considered frame-breaking, and is that variation intentional and purposeful in light of the overall theme?[81] The phenomenon of foregrounding in its various forms, part of the textual functional component[82] of language, represents an important key to the author's intention and consequently to the situation his text is intended to impact.

5. *Conclusion*

In his contribution to *Rhetoric and the New Testament*, Jeffrey Reed acknowledges the existence of a *functional* correspondence between the writings of St Paul and the rhetorical manuals, while at the same time denying any significant *formal* correspondence between the two.[83] In fundamental agreement with Reed at this point, my argument in this paper has been that the inability of the writers in 'group A' to make this important distinction has rendered their approach largely ineffective, clearly illustrating that 'labels [such as "rhetorical"] can obstruct, and not only help'.[84]

---

81. Though he does so in the context of given/new elements, Porter, 'Dialect and Register', has discussed the same concept in his analysis of register in Mark's Gospel: 'Within individual sub-units, the apparently *normal narrative pattern* is to establish the location, time and characters in the first one or two verses of the episode, before elaborating it' (emphasis mine).

82. A distinction must be made here between the patterns that are foregrounded and the phenomenon of foregrounding itself. Though foregrounded patterns such as certain types of verbal groups and clauses are choices arising from the transitivity network, and therefore the ideational meta-function, foregrounding itself in its various forms is something consistent throughout the text, contributing to its 'texture', and belongs in the textual meta-function. On this point, see E.A. Nida, J.P. Louw, A.H. Snyman and J.V.W. Cronje (eds.), *Style and Discourse* (Cape Town: Bible Society of South Africa, 1983), p. 46; and Fleischman, *Tense and Narrativity*, p. 168.

83. Reed, 'Using Ancient Rhetorical Categories', pp. 300, 301, 307, 308, 317, 321-24.

84. N.E. Enkvist, 'Text and Discourse Linguistics, Rhetoric, and Stylistics', in T.A. Van Dijk (ed.), *Discourse and Literature* (Amsterdam: John Benjamins, 1985), p. 11.

In suggesting that Michael Halliday's functional grammar is an ideally suited method for achieving the aims of rhetorical criticism as expressed by Crafton and others in this volume, I do not wish to preclude other approaches to the same problem. I do, however, wish to argue with Hasan that if analyses of literary texts (be they ancient or modern) are to lead to something more than statements of personal preference they must be linguistically informed, for

> To arrive at the truth—the theme(s) of a literature text—we must go through the time-demanding exercise of meticulous linguistic analysis; it is this alone that can show what is being achieved in the work and how. And until we can do this, it is meaningless to talk of evaluation, for what we are evaluating in the absence of such careful analysis is more likely to be our inexplicit impressions against our equally accidental preconceptions of what an artist should or should not do.[85]

85. Hasan, *Linguistics, Language, and Verbal Art*, p. 106; See also R. Hasan, 'Linguistics and the Study of Literary Texts', *Etudes de linguistique appliquée* 5 (1967), pp. 106-109.

CLASSICAL RHETORICAL CRITICISM AND
HISTORICAL RECONSTRUCTIONS: A CRITIQUE

Thomas H. Olbricht

One of the achievements claimed for rhetorical analysis of the Scriptures in the last two decades is assistance in reconstructing the historical setting of the text. This, I suggest, is a relatively new development.

The Greco-Roman rhetoricians set out not so much to master rhetorical criticism, but to provide insight and practical guidelines for those engaged in speaking and writing.[1] In the twentieth century, discourse—biblical or otherwise—is constantly being subjected to rhetorical analysis.[2] The foundation for this critique begins with classical rhetoric and extends to modern discourse analysis and rhetorics of various sorts.[3] Through medieval times, rhetorical analysis chiefly assessed style, including tropes and figures. In the eighteenth century, rhetorical critics turned to speakers and audiences.[4] In America in the twentieth century,

1. G.A. Kennedy, *The Art of Persuasion in Greece* (Princeton, NJ: Princeton University Press, 1963); *idem, The Art of Rhetoric in the Roman World* (Princeton, NJ: Princeton University Press, 1972); H. Lausberg, *Handbuch der Literarischen Rhetorik: Eine Grundlegung der Literaturwissenschaft* (2 vols.; Munich: Heuber, 1960).

2. R.H. Roberts and J.M.M. Good (eds.), *The Recovery of Rhetoric: Persuasive Discourse and Disciplinarity in the Human Sciences* (Charlottesville: University of Virginia Press, 1993).

3. R.J. Conners, L.S. Ede and A.A. Lunsford (eds.), *Essays on Classical Rhetoric and Modern Discourse* (Carbondale: Southern Illinois University Press, 1984). See also V.K. Robbins, 'The Present and Future of Rhetorical Analysis', and T.H. Olbricht, 'The Flowering of Rhetorical Criticism in America', in S.E. Porter and T.H. Olbricht (eds.), *The Rhetorical Analysis of Scripture: Essays from the 1995 London Conference* (JSNTSup, 146; Sheffield: Sheffield Academic Press, 1997), pp. 24-52, 79-102 respectively. For the Old Testament see the insightful comments of L.G. Perdue, *The Collapse of History: Reconstructing Old Testament Theology* (Minneapolis: Fortress Press, 1994).

4. G. Campbell, *The Philosophy of Rhetoric* (ed. L.F. Bitzer; Carbondale:

rhetoricians who teach speech and composition have stressed invention and rhetorical proofs.[5] Beginning with Muilenburg, biblical scholars approaching the Scriptures rhetorically have focused chiefly on structure (*taxis*), that is, arrangement.[6]

James Muilenburg is accredited with the resurgence of rhetorical analysis of Scripture. In a 1968 Society of Biblical Literature presidential address, he stated:

> What I am interested in, above all, is in understanding the nature of Hebrew literary composition, in exhibiting the structural patterns that are employed for the fashioning of a literary unit, whether in poetry or prose, and in discerning the many and various devices by which the predications are formulated and ordered into a unified whole. Such an enterprise I should describe as rhetoric and the methodology as rhetorical criticism.[7]

The second person who contributed to the new interest in rhetorical criticism was George Kennedy, Professor of Classics at the University of North Carolina. Kennedy proposed a more comprehensive enterprise in that he stressed invention, arrangement and style. In setting out a methodology, Kennedy offered five steps.[8] But in practice he focused

Southern Illinois University Press, 1963). Those interested in narrative are familiar with W.R. Fisher, *Human Communication as Narration: Toward a Philosophy of Reason, Value, and Action* (Columbia: University of South Carolina Press, 1987).

5. L. Thonssen, *Selected Readings in Rhetoric and Public Speaking* (New York: H.W. Wilson, 1942); L. Thonssen and A.C. Baird, *Speech Criticism: The Development of Standards for Rhetorical Appraisal* (New York: Ronald Press, 1948); A.C. Baird, *Rhetoric: A Philosophical Inquiry* (New York: Ronald Press, 1965); see my review of this book in *The Journal of Communication* 16 (1966), pp. 229-33. At the same time I reviewed M. Natanson and H.W. Johnstone, Jr, *Philosophy, Rhetoric, and Argumentation* (University Park: Pennsylvania State University Press, 1965).

6. For extensive bibliography, see D.F. Watson and A.J. Hauser, *Rhetorical Criticism of the Bible: Bibliography and Methodology* (Leiden: E.J. Brill, 1993). This work includes both the Old and New Testaments.

7. J. Muilenburg, 'Form Criticism and Beyond', *JBL* 88 (1969), pp. 1-18 (8). But also Amos Wilder must be recognized: A.N. Wilder, *The Language of the Gospel: Early Christian Rhetoric* (New York: Harper & Row, 1964). See also his Society of Biblical Literature presidential address for 1955, 'Scholars, Theologians and Ancient Rhetoric', *JBL* 75 (1956), pp. 1-11, in which interestingly he does not cite or refer to by name any ancient rhetorician; and J.D. Crossan, *A Fragile Craft: The Work of Amos Niven Wilder* (Chico, CA: Scholars Press, 1981).

8. G.A. Kennedy, *New Testament Interpretation through Rhetorical Criticism*

for the most part on structure or arrangement. In Kennedy's second step—that is, 'determining the rhetorical situation'—he laid the groundwork for employing rhetoric to assess the historical situation, but he did not himself proceed to do so to any extent.[9] A third person who sparked great interest in rhetoric was Wilhelm Wuellner. In a major publication, Wuellner commented on the manner in which arguments unfolded in Romans, or again basically on the structure.[10]

While one may discover occasional remarks on rhetorical criticism as an aid to reconstructing audiences in various books and periodicals, I should now like to turn to three works in which the authors explicitly argue that attention to rhetoric is an important means by which to reconstruct the situation of a document.[11]

(Chapel Hill, NC: University of North Carolina Press, 1984), pp. 33-38.

9. See, for example, his comments on Galatians (Kennedy, *New Testament Interpretation*, pp. 144-52).

10. W. Wuellner, 'Paul's Rhetoric of Argumentation in Romans: An Alternative to the Donfried–Karris Debate over Romans', *CBQ* 38 (1976), pp. 330-51 (reprinted in Karl Donfried [ed.], *The Romans Debate* [Minneapolis: Augsburg, 1977]). Also W. Wuellner, 'Where Is Rhetorical Criticism Taking Us?', *CBQ* 49 (1987), pp. 448-63; *idem*, 'Biblical Exegesis in the Light of the History and Historicity of Rhetoric and the Nature of the Rhetoric of Religion', in S.E. Porter and T.H. Olbricht (eds.), *Rhetoric and the New Testament: Essays from the 1992 Heidelberg Conference* (JSNTSup, 90; Sheffield: JSOT Press, 1993), pp. 492-513. See also B.L. Mack, *Rhetoric and the New Testament* (Minneapolis: Fortress Press, 1990).

11. Other works include: D.F. Watson, *Invention, Arrangement, and Style: Rhetorical Criticism of Jude and 2 Peter* (Atlanta: Scholars Press, 1988); W.G. Überlacker, *Der Hebräerbrief als Appell. I. Untersuchungen zu exordium, narratio und postscriptum (Hebr 1-2 und 13, 22-25)* (Lund: Almqvist & Wiksell, 1989); L. Thurén, *The Rhetorical Strategy of 1 Peter with Special Regard to Ambiguous Expressions* (Åbo: Åbo Academy Press, 1990); A.C. Wire, *The Corinthian Women Prophets: A Reconstruction through Paul's Rhetoric* (Minneapolis: Fortress Press, 1990); M.M. Mitchell, *Paul and the Rhetoric of Reconciliation: An Exegetical Investigation of the Language and Composition of 1 Corinthians* (Louisville, KY: Westminster/John Knox Press, 1993); B. Witherington III, *Conflict and Community in Corinth: A Socio-Rhetorical Commentary on 1 and 2 Corinthians* (Grand Rapids: Eerdmans, 1995); M.L. Reid, *Augustinian and Pauline Rhetoric in Romans Five: A Study of Early Christian Rhetoric* (Lewiston, NY: Edwin Mellen Press, 1996).

1. *Hans Dieter Betz:* Galatians

The first major effort in the second half of the twentieth century to employ rhetorical insight so as to reflect upon the historical setting of a text is that of Hans Dieter Betz in his commentary on Galatians, published in 1979.[12] Betz believed specifically that some flavor of the historical Paul could be recovered through a rhetorical analysis of his works, and especially the Paul who wrote Galatians. So he observed:

> The belief that Paul was a psychopath is often unconsciously behind the endless variety of notions implying that he was strangely 'Jewish', had an 'oriental temper' and was notoriously incompatible with Greco-Roman culture, of which we are of course the heirs... Having been brought up in Judaism and as a member of the Pharisaic sect, his language, style, and thought must be that of a barbarian.[13]

Paul and his audience, however, according to Betz, can best be understood in the context of the first-century classical world:

> The fact that Paul wrote his well-composed and, both rhetorically and theologically, sophisticated 'apology' forces us to assume that he founded the Galatian churches not among the poor and uneducated but among the Hellenized and Romanized city population.[14]

The clear proof, according to Betz, is that Galatians is 'composed in accordance with the conventions of Greco-Roman rhetoric and epistolography'.[15] This is the case not only in respect to the recipients of Paul's letter but also in regard to his opponents in Galatia: 'Paul's references must be interpreted in terms of their rhetorical origin and function before they can be used as the basis for conclusions about the opponents'.[16]

12. H.D. Betz, *Galatians: A Commentary on Paul's Letter to the Churches in Galatia* (Hermeneia; Philadelphia: Fortress Press, 1979). For other rhetorical reflections on Galatians, see J.D. Hester, 'Placing the Blame: The Presence of Epideictic in Galatians 1 and 2', in D.F. Watson (ed.), *Persuasive Artistry: Studies in New Testament Rhetoric in Honor of George A. Kennedy* (JSNTSup, 50; Sheffield: JSOT Press, 1991), pp. 281-307; D.F. Watson, 'The Rhetorical Structure of Galatians 1.11–2.14', *JBL* 103 (1984), pp. 223-33; and *idem*, 'The Use and Influence of Rhetoric in Galatians 2.1-14', *TZ* 42 (1986), pp. 386-408.

13. Betz, *Galatians*, p. xiv.

14. Betz, *Galatians*, p. 2.

15. Betz, *Galatians*, p. xiv.

16. Betz, *Galatians*, p. 6.

Betz believed that sizing up the rhetorical strategies in Galatians was crucial for determining the outlook of the opponents. In the case of Galatians, according to Betz, the best place at which to begin is the *peroratio* (6.12-17).[17] Betz did not propose this as a general rule. In fact, in other epistles, for example Colossians, whether or not Pauline, no clues may be found in the *peroratio* as to who the opponents are. Most of the clues, are, in fact, in the main argument in Colossians 1 and 2. But in the case of Galatians, Betz is, I think, correct that the attack is the most resolute in the *peroratio*. Betz set out the reason for the significance of the *peroratio* as follows:

> The general purpose of the peroratio is twofold: it serves as a last chance
> to remind the judge or the audience of the case, and it tries to make a
> strong emotional impression upon them.[18]

From the *peroratio* Betz concluded that the enemies had pressured the Galatians into accepting the Torah and circumcision. But exactly what their motives were, according to Betz, is less clear. Why did they want to escape persecution? What is meant when they are charged with not keeping the Torah themselves? At that point Betz turned to scattered materials in Galatians from which he concluded that the opponents offered the Torah and circumcision as a means of addressing the problems of the flesh which had become problematic in their effort to live in the Spirit.[19]

So how did rhetoric help Betz better discern the nature and views of the opponents? It is clear that he did not claim that rhetoric resolved all the traditional conundrums. But through the discovery that Galatians showed definite signs of the influence of classical rhetoric, Betz established, in his judgment, that Paul, his readers and his opponents were at minimum quasi-literate city dwellers. Furthermore, rhetorical structure helped pinpoint the places at which one might expect the characteristics of Paul's opponents to be most clearly articulated. It is only in these two ways that Betz claimed rhetoric helped in determining the Galatian audience for his letter. The chief contribution of rhetorical analysis for Betz was to ascertain the structure of Galatians, and in that manner track the function of the various parts of the letter. In the end, rhetoric provided more insight into the composition of Galatians than into the

17. Betz, *Galatians*, p. 6.
18. Betz, *Galatians*, p. 313.
19. Betz, *Galatians*, p. 8.

situation of audience and the enemies of the gospel.

Betz is justified, I think, in arguing that a larger view of an audience may be determined by the sophistication of the rhetoric. In other words, because of the character of Paul's rhetoric, he was not just writing for those on the lower end of the socio-economic scale. For example, it became clear to me—to my surprise—that the structure of Hebrews conformed to standard eulogistic and funeral sermons.[20] From this one can infer that Hebrews, both in terms of author and audience, represents a degree of rhetorical sophistication. Furthermore, I think Betz was correct in his argument that the *peroratio* in Galatians is a key to the agenda of the opponents. Unfortunately, however, this is not the case in many of Paul's letters, so that it only applies irregularly. But one of the perils of claiming assured results from rhetorical analysis is that often the major addresses of the ancient Greeks—for example, Demosthenes's famous oration 'On the Crown'—did not conform to many Aristotelian conventions.

2. *Robert Jewett:* The Thessalonian Correspondence

It was Robert Jewett six years later, in his book *The Thessalonian Correspondence: Pauline Rhetoric and Millenarian Piety*, who argued the most resolutely up to that time that a major contribution can be made to reconstructing an audience through rhetorical analysis.[21] His reflections on the Betz commentary make clear his intention of employing rhetoric for this expanded purpose:

> The tendency to construe rhetoric largely in terms of the invention and arrangement of the argument, using the sophisticated categories developed by Greek and Latin rhetoricians, is characteristic of the important recent work of Hans Dieter Betz. He has identified the rhetorical genre of the letter and letter fragments he has analyzed, and has provided well-grounded analyses of the literary structural form of the arguments. But his orientation to classical rhetoric and traditional form and literary criticism predisposes him to overlook the potential of rhetoric to aid in the reconstruction of the audience situation and the external circumstances related to the writing.[22]

20. T.H. Olbricht, 'Hebrews as Amplification', in Porter and Olbricht (eds.), *Rhetoric and the New Testament*, pp. 375-87.

21. R. Jewett, *The Thessalonian Correspondence: Pauline Rhetoric and Millenarian Piety* (Philadelphia: Fortress Press, 1986).

22. Jewett, *The Thessalonian Correspondence*, p. 64.

As to the sort of rhetoric that was helpful, Jewett mentioned classical Greco-Roman, but then featured the new rhetoric, which in turn was to be supplemented by an ample selection of cognate disciplines:

> While I wish to make extensive use of the resources of classical rhetoric, since it offers the clearest access to the way material was formed in the Greco-Roman world, I believe that the New Rhetoric and closely associated linguistic theories offer a more comprehensive grasp of epistolary communication. The various theorists associated with the New Rhetoric '...share a rejection of the speaker orientation of the traditional perspective'. They draw attention to the social context of human communication, thereby placing the insights and tools of classical rhetoric within a larger framework accessible to modern social sciences.[23]

The archetype new rhetoric for Jewett is that of Perelman and Olbrechts-Tyteca.[24] As to the cognate methodologies, Jewett commends those identified by David Hellholm who 'has provided the most extensive synthesis of a wide range of hermeneutical, linguistic, and semiotic theories that I have found, stressing the decisive significance of the "communication situation"'.[25] Despite what Jewett declared of merit, there is little evidence in *The Thessalonian Correspondence* that he utilized insights other than those from classical rhetoric.[26]

In the introduction to his book, Jewett proposed that at stake in the Thessalonian correspondence was millenarian piety. He did not at that stage indicate how rhetoric might help arrive at that conclusion. His

---

23. Jewett, *The Thessalonian Correspondence*, p. 64.

24. C. Perelman and L. Olbrechts-Tyteca, *The New Rhetoric: A Treatise on Argumentation* (trans. J. Wilkinson and P. Weaver; Notre Dame: University of Notre Dame Press, 1969).

25. Perelman and Olbrechts-Tyteca, *The New Rhetoric*, p. 65; D. Hellholm, *Das Visionenbuch des Hermas als Apokalypse: Formgeschichtliche und texttheoretische Studien zu einer literarischen Gattung. I. Methodologische Vorüberlegungen und makrostrukturelle Textanalyse* (Lund: C.W.K. Gleerup, 1980).

26. Other rhetorical analyses of the Thessalonian correspondence include: F.W. Hughes, *Early Christian Rhetoric and 2 Thessalonians* (JSNTSup, 30; Sheffield: JSOT Press, 1989); B.C. Johanson, *To All the Brethren: A Text-Linguistic and Rhetorical Approach to I Thessalonians* (Stockholm: Almqvist & Wiksell, 1987); T.H. Olbricht, 'An Aristotelian Rhetorical Analysis of 1 Thessalonians', in D.L. Balch, E. Ferguson and W.A. Meeks (eds.), *Greeks, Romans, and Christians: Essays in Honor of Abraham J. Malherbe* (Philadelphia: Fortress Press, 1990), pp. 216-36; W. Wuellner, 'The Argumentative Structure of 1 Thessalonians as a Paradoxical Encomium', in R.F. Collins (ed.), *The Thessalonian Correspondence* (BETL, 87; Leuven: Leuven University Press, 1990), pp. 117-36.

first task was to determine whether 2 Thessalonians was authentically Pauline. He concluded that it is probably Pauline based on its rhetorical features: 'The marks of authentic use of Pauline vocabulary, style and argumentative form are sufficiently extensive that any forgery hypothesis is hard to sustain'.[27]

As to the sequence of the letters, Jewett argued that the traditional sequence is supported by the rhetoric of the letters and the historical details. The rhetorical contribution has to do with the arguments. In the first letter Paul set out the apocalyptic significance of suffering; in the second he declared that suffering authenticated the believer's faith and that in the end time the persecutors would be punished.[28] The setting forth of the connection between suffering and the coming end in 1 Thessalonians therefore of necessity preceded the second letter. Furthermore, in epistolary rhetoric, according to Jewett, the references to the early beginnings of the church also sustain the canonical sequence. The founding of the Thessalonian mission is mentioned in the first letter; the second letter declared only what happened after the first letter was written.[29] These observations therefore alert us to look out for the changed situation of the readers between the first and second letters. Jewett also argued that these rhetorical observations in regard to beginnings are of help in determining the literary integrity.[30]

By Chapter 5 of *The Thessalonian Correspondence* Jewett took a specific look at the rhetoric of the two letters. He conceded that in ancient letters the mind-set of the audience and the social issues can now only be located chiefly in the letters themselves. Therefore historical reconstruction either precedes or works hand in hand with rhetorical observations.[31] The first question in regard to rhetoric, according to Jewett, is the genre. As to the epistolary genre, Jewett designates 1 Thessalonians a 'thankful' letter after the categories of Pseudo-Libanius. From the standpoint of rhetorical genre Jewett assigned the designation demonstrative, that is, epideictic.[32] 2 Thessalonians, in contrast, Jewett identified as 'reproving', again borrowed from Pseudo-Libanius,

---

27. Jewett, *The Thessalonian Correspondence*, p. 17.
28. Jewett, *The Thessalonian Correspondence*, p. 28.
29. Jewett, *The Thessalonian Correspondence*, p. 29.
30. Jewett, *The Thessalonian Correspondence*, p. 35.
31. Jewett, *The Thessalonian Correspondence*, p. 66.
32. Jewett, *The Thessalonian Correspondence*, p. 71.

but rhetorically, deliberative.[33] The ramifications of these genres for reconstructing the situation and the perspectives of the audience are not set forth specifically, but because, as Jewett believes, the argumentative thread running through the two epistles has to do with apocalyptic confusions, having pinpointed this thread is most crucial in such a reconstruction. If, however, as I think, the focus of 1 Thessalonians is first of all to reconfirm the young congregation on various matters on which it had been taught, and only secondarily in regard to eschatological matters, then the apocalyptic concerns came to the forefront in the time between the two letters.[34]

What, then, are the ramifications of Jewett's rhetorical conclusions for an understanding of the situation of believers in Thessalonica? He argues that clearly, based upon demonstrative (epideictic) rhetoric, the long narratio section 1.6–3.13 is 'in a very real sense the primary argumentative burden of the letter'.[35] He has alluded to this previously, but it is more a pronouncement than a case clearly established by showing from the rhetoricians that narrative sections of epideictic oratory have these characteristics. Jewett further has argued that this section makes clear the relationship between suffering and eschatology which he holds to be the thread running through both letters. Jewett followed his rhetorical observations with much detail typical of standard historical efforts to reconstruct the situation, but none of his points relied specifically upon a rhetorical reading of the text. As Jewett continued to reconstruct the setting, he commended rhetorical analysis of the argument, but he did not relate the argument to insights from any of the rhetoricians or clearly identify the rhetorical aspect.[36]

The challenge at the beginning of Jewett's book for rhetorical analysis to provide new and insightful avenues for reconstructing the situation of the Thessalonians correspondence seemed compelling. Indeed Jewett assembled much valuable data and insight into the setting for these two letters. But the contribution of rhetorical analysis seemed minimal. Rather Jewett was essentially dependent upon a standard grammatico-historical-literary reconstruction. This is not to say that Jewett's work should bring us to despair over the assistance of rhetoric in this task. We might rather conclude that Jewett did not successfully

---

33. Jewett, *The Thessalonian Correspondence*, pp. 81, 82.
34. Olbricht, 'An Aristotelian Rhetorical Analysis', p. 227.
35. Jewett, *The Thessalonian Correspondence*, p. 91.
36. Jewett, *The Thessalonian Correspondence*, pp. 114, 150, 181.

bring to bear the expectations of rhetorical analysis set forth in the early part of his work. Burton Mack in his *Rhetoric and the New Testament* noted the promise of rhetorical analysis for scrutinizing settings, but observed the meagerness of headway:

> The move from rhetorical analysis to the social setting of a text is not yet a dominant feature of this scholarship. It is no doubt too soon to expect elaborate reconstructions of the social implications uncovered in the investigation of a rhetorical situation.[37]

Jewett's projection of the contribution of rhetorical analysis was extremely positive, but the results parsimonious. He did, however, bring significant insight to bear through noticing the sequence of the arguments running from 1 Thessalonians into 2 Thessalonians and assessed with some success the changing situation among believers. Jewett showed that rhetoric can help track beliefs and strains and stresses in respect to these beliefs, especially in cases in which more than one document is available. Nevertheless, aspects of beliefs and challenges must be determined on grounds other than rhetorical sequencing. In addition, Jewett's observation that, because of new developments between 1 and 2 Thessalonians, the genre of the documents changed from epideictic to deliberative, is worthy of consideration. I think Jewett is correct that the tone of the argument changed from the first letter to the second. My problem is that I am not sure in the first instance that much light is cast upon 1 Thessalonians by declaring it demonstrative, that is, epideictic. What one discovers in looking at documents for proofs and arrangement is often helpful. However, not as helpful is identifying concrete strategies in regard to one of the three rhetorical genres over against the other. In some cases one can learn something from identifying genres, but it is my conclusion after trying this on various documents that the results are minimal, especially in regard to the situation of the audience.[38] In this regard I agree with Abraham Smith (see below, p. 118).

Jerry Sumney is of a somewhat different opinion. He published what I consider an important book in 1990, *Identifying Paul's Opponents: The Question of Method in 2 Corinthians*,[39] and for which I gave a

37. Mack, *Rhetoric and the New Testament*, p. 24.

38. Olbricht, 'An Aristotelian Rhetorical Analysis', pp. 224-27.

39. J. Sumney, *Identifying Paul's Opponents: The Question of Method in 2 Corinthians* (JSNTSup, 40; Sheffield: JSOT Press, 1990).

favorable review in *Religious Studies Review*.[40] Sumney developed a systematic approach to identifying opponents in Pauline epistles. In his 1990 publication he paid little attention to rhetoric, but now he has reflected upon rhetoric in a book forthcoming with the tentative title, *Servants of Satan, False Brothers, and Other Pauline Opponents*. I am indebted to him for sending me a statement from his introduction:

> When determining whether a passage is polemical, apologetic, etc. we must take full advantage of the recent advances in rhetorical criticism. Recognizing that a section of text makes up a common rhetorical feature (e.g. a narratio) helps us decide what function it has within the letter as a whole and so whether it is more likely to be polemical, apologetic, etc. Rhetorical criticism can also contribute significantly to our search for opponents if a convincing case can be made that a letter belongs to a particular species (e.g. deliberative). However, some caution is due here because the discovery (or presumption) that opponents form a central part of a letter's occasion (or conversely that they do not) may require us to modify our judgment about a letter's species.

I tend to agree with the first part of this statement more than with the latter part. It is often of help, I agree, to identify the rhetorical nature of a passage, though I think we are wrong to limit the possibilities to the categories of classical rhetoric. I have yet, however, to see much solid information produced by identifying the discourse as one of the three classical genres, because in most cases the identification of the genre itself is problematic. I have read an earlier version of Sumney's chapter on Galatians and while I think he has identified correctly various rhetorical features, it seems to me that he has established little conclusively about the opponents through genre identification. But I am willing to be convinced, and am eager to read his book when it comes out.

3. *Abraham Smith:* Comfort One Another

The most recent effort to reconstruct the audience of a New Testament document through the use of rhetoric is that of Abraham Smith in his book *Comfort One Another: Reconstructing the Rhetoric and Audience of 1 Thessalonians*.[41] As to his methodology Smith stated:

---

40. T.H. Olbricht, review of *Identifying Paul's Opponents*, by J. Sumney, in *Religious Studies Review* 18 (1993), p. 331.

41. A. Smith, *Comfort One Another: Reconstructing the Rhetoric and Audience*

Methodologically, my approach, like that of Jewett and Malherbe, is an audience-oriented approach. That is, I investigate Paul's rhetoric within the literary environment of an alien culture, and like them I seek to gain a sharper, less blurry picture of a Pauline community beyond the obscuring veil of the separating centuries.[42]

This rhetorical analysis, however, must be nuanced and 'one must first determine the function of various types of ancient strategic communication before relating the strategies to specific historical referents in Paul's world'.[43]

In reconstructing Hellenistic rhetoric, Smith offered three cues as especially important. The first is repetitive composition. After characterizing the repetitive features of Greco-Roman rhetoric, Smith noted that variety was endemic in that rhetoric:

Moreover, in accordance with the descriptions and prescriptions of the rhetorical handbooks, even the repetitive patterns were occasionally interrupted by digression or varied with contrapuntal points to alter the pace or shift the focus of a writing without forfeiting a writings' *synthesis* or organic unity.[44]

The second cue is exemplification or comparing and contrasting persons, places and situations with striking examples. By these examples 'Paul and other writers clarified their positions, moralized their writings and shaped the predisposition of their audiences in accordance with the constructed exigency or needs of the rhetorical situation'.[45] The third cue was ethos. Smith set out standard characterizations of ethos from Aristotle, then Cicero. He assigned special significance to character embellishments and typological characterization, that is, stereotypical representations. For Smith certain characteristics Paul assigned to the Thessalonian readers must be understood in the light of standard rhetorical types, for example, the work/toil dichotomy. Smith argued that Paul used this stereotypical contrast to his advantage:

In 2.1-12, Paul's self-description contrasts the deception, cunning wit and flattery of typical marketplace speakers (2.3-5) with the hard work and toil (2.9) of the apostles. By showing that the apostles chose the route of hard work and self-sufficiency, Paul demonstrates the virtue of

of 1 Thessalonians (Louisville, KY: Westminster/John Knox Press, 1995).

42. Smith, *Comfort One Another*, p. 21.
43. Smith, *Comfort One Another*, p. 22.
44. Smith, *Comfort One Another*, p. 30.
45. Smith, *Comfort One Another*, p. 32.

the apostles, for in ancient times toil and self-sufficiency were conventionally regarded as demonstrations of virtuous character.[46]

While the selection of these cues exhibits creativity on Smith's part it is not clear why he selected these and not others. For example, from the Aristotelian proofs triad he selected *ethos* and ignored *logos* and *pathos*. The first two cues seem to throw more light on the discourse itself rather than the audience unless the point is that Paul's readers were apparently familiar with standard rhetorical features in letters. The third cue or insight does suggest that since certain phraseology in arguments is conventional, therefore audience characteristics must be calibrated to take into account the ramifications of these conventions.

Smith, in a chapter on genre, noted that genre studies have focused on formal elements, but that more recently the trend is to determine the *function* of a genre.[47] I think Smith is correct that ancient rhetoricians were interpreted by biblical critics in the 1970s and 1980s as delineating formal functions, but I happen to think that such judgments on the part of these biblical scholars were mistaken.[48] Smith, with justification in my opinion, declared that,

> rhetorical genre studies will not likely prove beneficial in the actual determination of an audience's profile, in part because ancient rhetorical genres functioned as broad stylistic modes into which several literary genres were incorporated, and in part because the general topoi associated with one comprehensive rhetorical genre could readily be subsumed as a smaller strategy within another.[49]

Smith therefore proposed an epistolary genre for 1 Thessalonians, that is, a letter of consolation rather than a rhetorical one. Smith then set forth characteristics of the letter on consolation in the Greco-Roman world.[50] I would argue, however, that as a description of what Paul hoped to accomplish in 1 Thessalonians, 'consolation' seems limited in scope. A more descriptive term, I argue, in terms of Paul's intentions and the audience situation, is reconfirmation.[51] Through looking at the ancient consolatory tradition Smith believed that he discovered a matrix rich enough to reveal insight into all phases of 1 Thessalonians.

46. Smith, *Comfort One Another*, p. 38.
47. Smith, *Comfort One Another*, p. 42
48. Olbricht, 'An Aristotelian Rhetorical Analysis', pp. 224, 225.
49. Smith, *Comfort One Another*, p. 43.
50. Smith, *Comfort One Another*, pp. 48-51.
51. Olbricht, 'An Aristotelian Rhetorical Analysis', p. 227.

Through the consolation genre he implied that characteristics of the audience can then be deduced, though he was not too explicit as to what those characteristics might be:

> Still, the foregoing analysis of a typical social situation reflected in 1 Thessalonians reveals that there are remarkable similarities between Paul's letter and the Hellenistic consolatory tradition—so much so that we can no longer limit Paul's consolatory goal to just one part of Paul's earliest extant letter, namely, 1 Thess. 4:13–18. As we have seen, however, both 1 Thessalonians and the consolatory writings of Paul's contemporaries all share a similar situation, that is, the friendly presentation of consolatory examples and commonplaces to help the auditors overcome one or more experiences of grief.[52]

In the next chapter, titled 'Reconstructing the Rhetoric', Smith set forth details of the letter in respect to consolation. He argued that Paul sought to assuage the grief that resulted from the believer's separation from former relationships. Paul therefore declared a new *philia* through which 'one's power, prestige and security are determined'.[53] His approach is therefore to 'remove false opinions about prestige and security'.[54] This is a useful chapter in terms of understanding the structural aspects and tropographical features of 1 Thessalonians, but it is not too clear just how it reveals new insights into the audience and situation aspects. But some of the ambiguity is reduced in the next chapter in which Smith continues with his view that the rhetorical conventions throw light on the socio-economic status. The believers received the benefits of patronage rather than bestowing it: 'Paul's consolatory writing certainly acknowledges God as a patron. For Paul, God's power is not simply demonstrated in the deity's worship in several regions. It is also shown in God's extension of security to the congregation.'[55] But even then 'the "work" metaphor in 1 Thessalonians was not an indication of a specific social profile; rather, it was a strategic part of Paul's stereotypical construction of the community as independent, wise rustics'.[56] Finally, then, Smith makes more explicit

52. Smith, *Comfort One Another*, pp. 58-59.
53. Smith, *Comfort One Another*, p. 63.
54. Smith, *Comfort One Another*, p. 65.
55. Smith, *Comfort One Another*, p. 100.
56. Smith, *Comfort One Another*, p. 102. For similar arguments, see B.L. Mack and V.K. Robbins, *Patterns of Persuasion in the Gospels* (Sonoma, CA: Polebridge Press, 1989); V.K. Robbins, *Jesus the Teacher: A Socio-Rhetorical Interpretation of Mark* (Minneapolis: Fortress Press, 1992); and L.G. Bloomquist, 'Methodological

the manner in which he thinks rhetorical analysis can help reconstitute the nature of the audience:

> Thus, reconstructing the profile of an ancient audience is a meticulous chore, not merely because language is not transparent, a critical insight offered by many a postmodernist, but also because the critic must recover the sparse notices on the ancient means of persuading audiences, especially those notices on the creation of idealistic images as compensation for a particular audience's momentary plights. Interpretations which overlook these means or strategies thus miss hearing some of the hidden and explicit appeals of ancient texts—a knowledge of which, I think, is necessary for ascertaining an audience profile.[57]

In concluding, Smith offered his work as 'only a first chapter in continuing interpretations about people who have known intense sufferings'.[58]

Smith has indeed envisioned a new manner of employing certain limited features of rhetoric, especially consolation and stereotypical formulas. I perceive this as a new worthwhile development. My reservations about Smith's work are not that these are creative new directions, it is that I think that consolation is too limited a genre to be descriptive of 1 Thessalonians, and while I think the point about the stereotypes may be a brilliant suggestion, at the same time it may well be that these are apt descriptions of the believers in Thessalonica and of Paul himself. For example, in the 1996 New Hampshire primary, the rhetorical strategy of Pat Buchanan was to elicit, through stereotypical charges, the support of blue collar workers. When the results were in, in terms of demographics, the highest percentage of votes Pat secured were persons without college education and blue collar. Paul's use of the clichés therefore may not have been simply stereotypical, they may have reflected the actual situation.

4. *Conclusion*

Although these efforts to reconstruct audience situations through rhetorical criticism do not live up to projections, nevertheless certain proposals are helpful.

Considerations in the Determination of the Social Context of Cynic Rhetorical Practice: Implications for our Present Studies of the Jesus Traditions', in Porter and Olbricht (eds.), *The Rhetorical Analysis of Scripture*, pp. 200-31.
    57. Smith, *Comfort One Another*, pp. 102, 103.
    58. Smith, *Comfort One Another*, p. 106.

Should one wish to recreate an audience employing classical rhetoric, then one should employ the whole classical canon, that is, invention, arrangement, style and delivery. The three works discussed here concentrated on arrangement, style, and, to an extent, invention. Smith examined ethos, but not logos and pathos. There is a sense in which biblical scholars have classically examined the logos of biblical materials in exegetical work, but only in passing ethos and pathos. One can at least project what the author of an epistle perceived as the viable arguments and proof, and the appropriate wellsprings of credibility and emotion. I have recently become convinced that perhaps even the ancient category of memory may contribute more to understanding a discourse and its audience than I earlier perceived.[59] All of the rhetorical features taken together can help in imaging the audience as much as it is possible, and I think the categories of ethos and pathos especially may add insight previously unnoticed by the exegetes.

I think, in addition, there are other contributions rhetorical analysis can make to reconstructing the audience of a biblical document. But I think these can best be based on a perusal of the document itself, rather than through forcing a document into the procrustean bed of ancient rhetorical categories. I have argued that it makes a difference that proof and motivation in classical rhetoric are based upon this-worldly causes, whereas in Scriptures some causes and motivations are transcendental. I have therefore argued that we are permitted to hue out a new genre, for example, 'church rhetoric', and to identify some of its distinctive features.[60] I have also discovered through work on Colossians that in noting that the major proof in this letter is ethos, that it would appear that the perspectives that endanger the believers are still outside the Colossian church rather than within.[61] I have therefore labeled the rhetoric of Colossians 'continuational', whereas Galatians is 'confrontational' and 1 Thessalonians 'reconfirmational'. Another result of rhetorical analysis of Colossians is that the strategy of the author is not to deny what the outsiders embrace, but to declare that whatever the

59. T.H. Olbricht, 'Delivery and Memory', in S.E. Porter (ed.), *Handbook of Classical Rhetoric in the Hellenistic Period 330 B.C.–A.D. 400* (Leiden: E.J. Brill, 1997), pp. 159-67.

60. Olbricht, 'An Aristotelian Rhetorical Analysis', pp. 225-27.

61. T.H. Olbricht, 'The Stoicheia and the Rhetoric of Colossians: Then and Now', in S.E. Porter and T.H. Olbricht (eds.), *Rhetoric, Scripture and Theology: Essays from the 1994 Pretoria Conference* (JSNTSup, 131; Sheffield: Sheffield Academic Press, 1996), pp. 308-28.

powers to which they give deference, they pale in comparison with Jesus Christ in whom the 'fullness of God was pleased to dwell' (Col. 1.19).

I conclude therefore that help from rhetorical analysis so as to reconstruct an audience situation as yet is more a hope than a reality. Rhetorical criticism has become a featured discipline of considerable magnitude. My approach through almost 50 years of academic life has been to learn from the trends, but not to embrace them with closed eyes. That has served me well to this day. It is my conclusion that whatever help rhetorical analysis may be for the reconstructing of audiences, no substitute has yet been discovered for astute historical exploration and analysis.

THE CONTRIBUTIONS AND LIMITATIONS OF GRECO-ROMAN RHETORICAL THEORY FOR CONSTRUCTING THE RHETORICAL AND HISTORICAL SITUATIONS OF A PAULINE EPISTLE

Duane F. Watson

It is usually granted that the historical-critical methodologies used to construct the historical situation of the Pauline epistles are inadequate. Typically the historical situation has been derived from the content of the epistles themselves, with help from what is known of the historical, cultural and social settings of the audiences addressed (mirror-reading). New Testament scholars are becoming aware of the role that rhetorical analysis can play in historical inquiry. They are intrigued by statements like this one from those in the field of rhetoric:

> Every social circle or milieu is distinguishable in terms of its dominant opinions and unquestioned beliefs, of the premises that it takes for granted without hesitation: these views form an integral part of its culture, and an orator wishing to persuade a particular audience must of necessity adapt himself to it. Thus the particular culture of a given audience shows so strongly through the speeches addressed to it that we feel we can rely on them to a considerable extent for our knowledge of the character of past civilizations.[1]

It is the thesis of this essay that Greco-Roman rhetorical theory provides further insight into the historical situation of a Pauline epistle that has not been explored sufficiently.[2] The many facets of the rhetorical situation of a Pauline epistle constructed by rhetorical criticism derive

---

1. C. Perelman and L. Olbrechts-Tyteca, *The New Rhetoric: A Treatise on Argumentation* (trans. J. Wilkinson and P. Weaver; Notre Dame: University of Notre Dame Press, 1969), pp. 20-21.

2. Rhetoric's role in the exegetical and historical enterprise is also being stressed by others. For example, J.N. Vorster ('The Context of the Letter to the Romans: A Critique on the Present State of Research', *Neot* 28 [1994], pp. 127-45) has called for more attention to the rhetorical situation (as entextualized) as providing a way out of the impasse over the context of Paul's letter to the Romans.

from the actual historical communicative situation and allow the interpreter to make inferences about it. Having recognized this contribution, some studies of the epistles have begun to move beyond formal analysis to functional analysis. Questions arise such as: Why did Paul select certain rhetorical features? How was their selection influenced by his audience and the situation addressed? In turn, how are these rhetorical features intended to influence his audience and the situation addressed? There is increasing awareness that the historical situation and the rhetorical response are intertwined and that the latter can help understand the former.

However, systematic treatment of the contributions of Greco-Roman rhetorical criticism to the understanding of the historical situation of the Pauline epistles is wanting. Often such contributions are limited to what the species of rhetoric of a Pauline epistle or portion of a Pauline epistle indicates about its purpose. For example, there is the famous current debate about the species of Galatians, whether judicial (and indicating Paul is defending himself against charges) or deliberative (and indicating Paul is advocating a course of action).[3] This study gathers and assesses what I believe are some of the contributions and limitations of Greco-Roman rhetorical theory for constructing the rhetorical and historical situations of a Pauline epistle (and other New Testament epistles as well).

1. *Justifying the Enterprise:*
The Relationship between the Rhetorical and Historical Situations

We need to clarify the relationship between the rhetorical and historical situations. Fortunately this relationship has been examined closely by those in the field of rhetoric. Lloyd Bitzer's seminal article spawned a considerable debate about the rhetorical situation.[4] Although the debate has not always carefully distinguished the historical situation from the

---

3.   See D.F. Watson, 'Rhetorical Criticism of the Pauline Epistles since 1975', *Currents in Research: Biblical Studies* 3 (1995), pp. 232-34 and literature cited there.

4.   L.F. Bitzer, 'The Rhetorical Situation', *Philosophy and Rhetoric* 1 (1968), pp. 1-14; and refined in his 'Functional Communication: A Situational Perspective', in E.E. White (ed.), *Rhetoric in Transition: Studies in the Nature and Uses of Rhetoric* (University Park, PA: Pennsylvania State University Press, 1980), pp. 21-38.

rhetorical situation (often simply referring to the 'situation'), it does provide direction.

Bitzer gave us the classic definition of the rhetorical situation drawn from his functional approach to communication:

> a complex of persons, events, objects, and relations presenting an actual or potential exigence which can be completely or partially removed if discourse, introduced into the situation, can so constrain human decision or action as to bring about the significant modification of the exigence.[5]

Rhetorical discourses 'obtain their character from the circumstances of the historic context in which they occur'.[6] Such discourse 'participates naturally in the situation, is in many instances necessary to the completion of situational activity, and by means of its participation with situation obtains its meaning and its rhetorical character'.[7] The rhetorical situation 'invites discourse capable of participating with situation and thereby altering its reality'.[8] The rhetorical situation controls the discourse much like 'the question controls the answer and the problem controls the solution'.[9] The rhetorical situation invites a *fitting* response:

> If it makes sense to say that situation invites a 'fitting' response, then situation must somehow prescribe the response which fits. To say that a rhetorical response fits a situation is to say that it meets the requirements established by the situation. A situation which is strong and clear dictates the purpose, theme, matter, and style of the response.[10]

Arthur Miller[11] agrees with Bitzer that an exigence (problem or defect) underlies and gives significance to every rhetorical situation, but argues that the exigence does not determine or specify the rhetorical response, for 'within the limits specified by each exigence, the *ultimate* or *perceived* nature of the exigence depends upon the constraints *of the perceiver*. Thus, the ultimate character of an exigence is a conclusion in the mind of its perceiver.'[12] 'This exigence specifies the limits of the

---

5. Bitzer, 'Rhetorical Situation', p. 6.
6. Bitzer, 'Rhetorical Situation', p. 3.
7. Bitzer, 'Rhetorical Situation', p. 5.
8. Bitzer, 'Rhetorical Situation', p. 6.
9. Bitzer, 'Rhetorical Situation', p. 6.
10. Bitzer, 'Rhetorical Situation', p. 10.
11. A.B. Miller, 'Rhetorical Exigence', *Philosophy and Rhetoric* 5 (1972), pp. 111-18.
12. Miller, 'Rhetorical Exigence', pp. 111-12 (his emphasis).

topic of communication and simultaneously provides opportunities within those limits for adapting to hearers. Rhetors elect given options for communication depending on their own constraints and their judgments of the constraints of their hearers.'[13]

Richard Vatz[14] disagrees with Bitzer that discourse is called into existence or determined by the situation. Meaning is not intrinsic in the situation. It is not 'discovered' but 'created' by the rhetor from the situation as certain facts are given salience and meaning. The rhetorical response controls the situation, not the other way around. Rhetoric is not situational, but situations are rhetorical.

Scott Consigny[15] agrees with Vatz that the rhetorical situation is not determinate of the rhetorical response. The rhetor is creative in formulating an exigence from the facts encountered. The rhetorical situation offers constraints to the rhetor as he or she formulates an exigence and directs its resolution by the audience addressed. Unlike Vatz, Consigny argues that 'the rhetorical situation is not one created solely through the imagination and discourse of the rhetor. It involves particularities of persons, actions, and agencies in a certain place and time; and the rhetor cannot ignore these constraints if he is to function effectively.'[16]

Focusing more on the exigence, Alan Brinton[17] argues that 'being exigent is a property of a set of facts, but it is a *relational property* rather than a purely internal property'.[18] 'The speaker "finds" the situation; it is a set of "givens", he reacts to it evaluatively, his rhetorical acts are part of his response to it and are in that sense grounded in the rhetorical situation.'[19]

David Hunsaker and Craig Smith[20] argue that the rhetorical situation allows certain issues for rhetorical discourse and prevents others from

13. Miller, 'Rhetorical Exigence', p. 118.

14. R.E. Vatz, 'The Myth of the Rhetorical Situation', *Philosophy and Rhetoric* 6 (1973), pp. 154-61.

15. S. Consigny, 'Rhetoric and its Situations', *Philosophy and Rhetoric* 7 (1974), pp. 175-85.

16. Consigny, 'Rhetoric and its Situations', p. 178.

17. A. Brinton, 'Situation in the Theory of Rhetoric', *Philosophy and Rhetoric* 14 (1981), pp. 234-48.

18. Brinton, 'Situation in the Theory of Rhetoric', p. 246 (his emphasis).

19. Brinton, 'Situation in the Theory of Rhetoric', p. 247.

20. D.M. Hunsaker and C.R. Smith, 'The Nature of Issues: A Constructive Approach to Situational Rhetoric', *Western Speech Communication* 40 (1976), pp. 144-56.

arising. Issues are mental constructs whose actualization requires the commonalty of perception of rhetor and audience. 'Normally, issue creation through rhetorical discourse is managed in such a way as to be consistent with and complementary to those issues already perceived by the actual audience.'[21] 'Perceptions between communicators and audiences must have some commonalty in order for communication and conflict to exist. This commonalty is provided by the situation, which both speaker and audience perceive, which generates issues in the minds of both, and which constrains decision and action by both.'[22]

John Patton[23] stresses that the exigence is derived from the historical situation as the perception and judgment of the rhetor and audience and their internal and external constraints such as the facts of the situation, attitudes, beliefs and values. He notes that 'rhetoric is essentially historical...its purpose is to alter real events and experiences'.[24] 'Historical realities remain the focal point for rhetorical activity, although as perceptions and other constraining influences differ responses will vary.'[25]

The rhetorical situation is rooted in the historical situation. The rhetorical situation is an evaluative construction derived from and seeking to change the facts of the historical situation. The historical situation has provided the facts from which the rhetor has interpreted and created an exigence based on personal and audience interest. The rhetor seeks to communicate the exigence to an audience so as to change the historical situation in some way. The exigence specifies the limits of the communication as it is adapted to the audience in light of constraints upon rhetor and audience in the historical situation. One such constraint is the commonalty of the rhetor's and audience's perception of the issues within the historical situation. The rhetorical situation and historical situation are not divorced from one another, only separated by the act of writing and reading.

New Testament scholars have begun to make further refinements to these emerging conceptions. George Kennedy's method of rhetorical criticism, following Bitzer's understanding of the rhetorical situation,

21. Hunsaker and Smith, 'Nature of Issues', p. 153.

22. Hunsaker and Smith, 'Nature of Issues', pp. 155-56.

23. J.H. Patton, 'Causation and Creativity in Rhetorical Situations: Distinctions and Implications', *Quarterly Journal of Speech* 65 (1979), pp. 36-55.

24. Patton, 'Causation and Creativity', p. 44.

25. P.K. Tompkins, J.H. Patton and L.F. Bitzer, 'Tompkins on Patton and Bitzer, Patton on Tompkins, and Bitzer on Tompkins (and Patton)', *Quarterly Journal of Speech* 66 (1980), pp. 85-93 (89).

incorrectly assumes that the rhetorical and historical situations are identical.[26] In essence the historical situation becomes rhetorical with the addition of discourse. Many New Testament scholars rightly understand the rhetorical situation as a textual phenomenon. Wilhelm Wuellner[27] argues that the rhetorical situation is located in the text form and the premises of its argumentation. It is distinct from (although prompted by) the historical situation. Lauri Thurén agrees, stating: 'The rhetorical situation consists of the picture of the audience which the author seems to presuppose, of the audience's premises and expectations, and as a result thereof, of the intended effects of the text'.[28] Elisabeth Schüssler Fiorenza[29] also considers the rhetorical situation to be inscribed in the text, but stresses that it helps us gain access to the actual historical communicative situation which elicits the rhetorical response. Dennis Stamps[30] goes further in proposing that the rhetorical situation is entextualized: 'it is the situation embedded in the text and created by the text which contributes to the rhetorical effect of the text'.[31] It is 'the story of the relationship between the sender and addressees told from the temporal perspective of the time of writing and from the point of view of the sender'.[32] The situation inscribed in the text becomes the basis of its argumentation.

Stephen Pogoloff[33] argues that the rhetorical situation is a narrative construction of the reader which makes sense of the concerns addressed by the author: 'Thus, situational rhetorical criticism offers a mediating position between historical and literary criticism, in which the "world"

26. G. Kennedy, *New Testament Interpretation through Rhetorical Criticism* (Chapel Hill, NC: University of North Carolina Press, 1984), pp. 34-36.

27. W. Wuellner, 'Where Is Rhetorical Criticism Taking Us?', *CBQ* 49 (1987), pp. 448-63 (455-56).

28. L. Thurén, *The Rhetorical Strategy of 1 Peter with Special Regard to Ambiguous Expressions* (Åbo: Åbo Academy Press, 1990), pp. 70-71.

29. E. Schüssler Fiorenza, 'Rhetorical Situation and Historical Reconstruction in 1 Corinthians', *NTS* 33 (1987), pp. 386-403 (esp. pp. 386-89).

30. D.L. Stamps, 'Rethinking the Rhetorical Situation: The Entextualization of the Situation in New Testament Epistles', in S.E. Porter and T.H. Olbricht (eds.), *Rhetoric and the New Testament: Essays from the 1992 Heidelberg Conference* (JSNTSup, 90; Sheffield: JSOT Press, 1993), pp. 193-210.

31. Stamps, 'Rethinking the Rhetorical Situation', p. 199.

32. Stamps, 'Rethinking the Rhetorical Situation', p. 209.

33. S.M. Pogoloff, *Logos and Sophia: The Rhetorical Situation of 1 Corinthians* (SBLDS, 134; Atlanta: Scholars Press, 1992), pp. 75-87.

of the text is neither fiction nor fact, but a value-laden interpretation of a situation shared by reader, implied author, and implied intended reader'.[34] Jan Botha rightly contends that the rhetorical situation is a creation of the rhetor out of the basic facts of the historical situation, but 'this construction cannot be completely at odds with the historical situation if the argument is to be effective'.[35] The textuality and rhetoricity of a text have to be investigated first, but 'an ethically responsible reading of an ancient text inevitably has to deal with historical matters somewhere in the act of interpretation'.[36]

This last step of moving from rhetorical situation to historical situation is the most difficult and least discussed. Elma Cornelius[37] warns us of the dangers of equating the historical and rhetorical situations when trying to use the latter to understand the former. However, if biblical scholars take the above discussion into consideration, this problem can be avoided. The rhetorical situation utilizes only a portion of all the data available from the historical situation, and is itself a construction of the rhetor operating within his or her own constraints. The rhetorical situation is not equated with the historical situation. Portions of the latter are used in the former and it is these that offer some insight into the historical situation. Hypothetical construction of the historical situation based on the rhetor's construction of the rhetorical situation and perception of the audience, not reconstruction of the historical situation, is the end result of the rhetorical study of a text. To the rhetorical situation there needs to be added our knowledge of the historical, cultural and social dimensions of the Greco-Roman world contemporaneous with the Pauline epistles to construct the broader historical situation which makes sense of all the facets of the rhetorical situation.

2. *The Contribution of Greco-Roman Rhetoric*

The following discusses the contribution of Greco-Roman rhetoric to the construction of the rhetorical situations of a Pauline epistle, and

34. Pogoloff, *Logos and Sophia*, p. 87.
35. J. Botha, *Subject to Whose Authority? Multiple Readings of Romans 13* (Emory Studies in Early Christianity; Atlanta: Scholars Press, 1994), pp. 140-50 (150).
36. Botha, *Subject to Whose Authority?*, p. 143.
37. E.M. Cornelius, 'The Relevance of Ancient Rhetoric to Rhetorical Criticism', *Neot* 28 (1994), pp. 457-67 (especially pp. 460-61).

ultimately the historical situation (once the further work just suggested is completed). The discussion will include the audiences and situations suitably addressed by each genre (judicial, deliberative and epideictic); the stasis of the argument(s) as indicative of the nature of the problem addressed; inventional strategies and appropriate contexts for their use; types of argumentation and *topoi* used in invention and what their purpose reveals about the situation and social background of the audience; expressed and unexpressed premises in argumentation (especially in enthymemes) and values extolled and maxims quoted that the author assumes the audience accepts as true and that denote its value system; order of arguments and what they indicate about the relationship between author and audience, whether friendly or strained; the presence or absence of the elements of arrangement or specific features of arrangement; and the style appropriate to specific contexts.[38]

This discussion remains theoretical. Space restraints preclude specific examples of the numerous points. The interpreter of any Pauline epistle must judge the applicability of each point for that epistle. The discussion from the rhetorical handbooks is meant to be as thorough as possible—offering all features of invention, arrangement and style that might be useful for rhetorical and historical construction. However, the discussion could and should be expanded by studies of rhetoric within works of the period to see how it functioned in known historical contexts.

a. *From the Species of Rhetoric*
There are three species of rhetoric: judicial, deliberative and epideictic.[39] Each species is appropriate for particular settings. Judicial or

38. All quotations of the rhetorical handbooks are from the LCL editions. The abbreviations used for the handbooks are as follows: Aristotle, *The 'Art' of Rhetoric* = *Rhet.*; Aristotle, *Topica* = *Top.*; Ps.-Aristotle, *Rhetorica ad Alexandrum* = *Rhet. ad Alex.*; Demetrius, *On Style* = *Eloc.*; Cicero, *De Inventione* = *Inv.*; Cicero, *Topica* = *Top.*; Cicero, *De Oratore* = *De Or.*; Cicero, *De Partiones Oratoriae* = *De Part. Or.*; Cicero, *Orator* = *Or.*; *Rhetorica ad Herennium* = *Rhet. ad Her.*; Quintilian, *Institutio Oratoria* = Quintilian; Longinus, *On the Sublime* = *Subl.*

39. H. Lausberg, *Handbuch der literarischen Rhetorik: Eine Grundlegung der Literaturwissenschaft* (2 vols.; Munich: Hueber, 2nd edn, 1973), I, pp. 51-61, §§53-65; pp. 85-138, §§139-254; J. Martin, *Antike Rhetorik: Technik und Methode* (HbAltW, 2.3; Munich: Beck, 1974), pp. 15-210; G. Kennedy, *The Art of Rhetoric in the Roman World: 300 B.C.–A.D. 300* (Princeton, NJ: Princeton University Press, 1972), pp. 7-23.

forensic rhetoric is concerned with accusation and defense, often in legal settings. Deliberative rhetoric is advice, opinion giving, policy making, and persuasion and dissuasion regarding a particular course of action. Epideictic rhetoric praises and blames. Each species also has a particular goal or end. The end of judicial rhetoric is what is just and unjust. The end of deliberative rhetoric is the possible or impossible, advantageous or harmful, necessary or unnecessary, expedient or inexpedient. Considerations of what is honorable or disgraceful, or just or unjust, are means to these ends. The end of epideictic is the honorable or the dishonorable with a view to increasing or decreasing assent to some value.[40]

All three species of rhetoric relied upon each other, that is, they were mixed as the rhetor saw fit to meet rhetorical objectives and they often share the same ends or goals (*Rhet. ad Alex.* 5.1427b.31ff.; Quintilian, 3.4.15-16). Epideictic rhetoric often comprises extensive parts of judicial and deliberative rhetoric (*Rhet. ad Her.* 3.8.15; Quintilian, 3.4.11). Deliberative and epideictic rhetoric are complementary because what deliberative rhetoric advises and dissuades, epideictic rhetoric praises and blames (Quintilian, 3.7.28).

A Pauline epistle may be a combination of the species of rhetoric, but one will typically predominate. To some extent identification of the species of rhetoric of a Pauline epistle is a partial identification of its purpose. The predominant species indicates the rhetorical situation and purpose(s) of a Pauline epistle. If judicial, Paul may be defending himself against the charges of opponents and/or be leveling his own charges against them. If deliberative, Paul may be advising and dissuading his audience against taking certain courses of action. If epideictic, he is trying to increase audience adherence to values it already holds through praise, or to decrease its adherence to values he disdains through blame. Species of rhetoric used in a supporting role indicate subsidiary issues.

However, the identification of species for construction of the rhetorical situation is not reliable by itself and must be analyzed in light of the epistle's entire use of rhetoric. For example, judicial rhetoric may be used by Paul to argue against a position he does not hold in order to

---

40. Aristotle, *Rhet.* 1.3.1358b.5; *Rhet. ad Alex.* 1.1421b.21ff.; 3.1425b.36-39; 6.1427b.39ff.; Cicero, *Inv.* 2.4.12; 2.51.155-56; *De Part. Or.* 24; *Top.* 24.91; *Rhet. ad Her.* 1.2.2; 3.2.3; 3.6.10; Quintilian, 3.4.15-16; 3.8.1-6, 22-35.

make his own clearer. No real opponents may be involved at all (e.g. the figures of dialogue and diatribe). Argumentation against opposite views where no particular opponent was extant was a key component in rhetorical practice in cultures were literacy was working within a predominantly oral culture.[41]

b. *From the Stasis of the Argument*[42]

The stasis is the basic question at issue arising from a conflict of causes (anything on which two or more opinions can be offered) within any of the three species of rhetoric. The stasis of fact or conjecture involves the question *of whether* something was ever done, or was done by the person accused. The stasis of definition involves admitting the facts while denying they are to be defined as they have been. The stasis of quality admits that something was done, but not that it was wrong. Rather it is claimed that what was done was the best course of action to take under the circumstances. This stasis also inquires into the nature of a thing.[43] Multiple conflicts of issues will result in multiple stases in a work, but one will predominate (Cicero, *Inv.* 1.12.17; Quintilian, 3.6.7-9, 21, 81, 91-103).

In general the main stasis of the argument presented by Paul at any point in an epistle is indicative of the conflict of causes which underlies the argument within the rhetorical situation. The stasis of quality is particularly important because it involves the nature, value and quality of an act, whether just or profitable (Cicero, *Inv.* 1.8.10; 1.9.12). As such it indicates the value system of Paul as well as the audience addressed, whether similar or contrary to that of Paul. The presence of multiple stases indicates other facets of the conflict Paul addresses.

41. Cf. W.J. Ong, *Orality and Literacy: The Technologizing of the Word* (London: Routledge, 1982), pp. 43-45.

42. The need to consider the stases of argumentation and *topoi* in argumentation in order to construct the rhetorical situation of New Testament letters is rightly stressed in J.N. Vorster, 'Toward an Interactional Model for the Analysis of Letters', *Neot* 24 (1990), pp. 107-30.

43. Cicero, *Inv.* 1.8.14; *De Or.* 2.24.104–26.113; *Or.* 14.45; 34.121-22; *De Part. Or.* 9.33–12.43; 18.61–19.67; 29.101-103; *Top.* 21–25; *Rhet. ad Her.* 1.11-17; Quintilian, 3.6.80-104; Lausberg, *Handbuch der literarischen Rhetorik*, I, pp. 64-85, §§79-138; Martin, *Antike Rhetorik*, pp. 28-52.

c. *From Invention*[44]

'Invention is the devising of matter, true or plausible, that would make the case convincing' (*Rhet. ad Her.* 1.2.3). It includes determining the species of rhetoric and the stasis, but mainly involves the devising of proofs. The rhetor selects the types of proof he or she considers to be persuasive in the situation and to the audience involved. Proofs are of two kinds: inartificial or artificial.[45] Inartificial proofs are those not manufactured by the rhetor (witnesses, evidence extracted by torture, informal agreements, contracts, laws, decisions of previous courts, rumors, documents and oaths).[46] Artificial proofs are those constructed from propositions and supporting material gathered from the facts of the case, and include ethos, pathos and logos.[47] Paul's use of inartificial proofs in his epistles, such as the Old Testament and Jewish and Christian traditions, are those that he assumes his audience finds authoritative and that he considers applicable to addressing his exigence.

Ethos is the moral character and conduct, goodwill, goodness and moral uprightness. It is demonstrated throughout the speech by the rhetor.[48] The degree that ethos is used is indicative of Paul's assumptions about the status he does or does not enjoy with the audience. The more he asserts his authority, opinions and assumptions without insinuation or proof, the more he may assume that he is on good terms with the audience and they award him a high status. On the contrary, the more he musters support for his assertions and works to clear his

44. Botha (*Subject to Whose Authority?*, pp. 121-88) offers one of the most complete analyses using the invention and arrangement of a text (Rom. 13.1-7) to construct the rhetorical situation.

45. Lausberg, *Handbuch der literarischen Rhetorik*, I, pp. 190-236, §§348-430; Martin, *Antike Rhetorik*, pp. 97-135.

46. Aristotle, *Rhet.* 1.2.1355b.2; 1.15; *Rhet. ad Alex.* 7.1428a.22-23; 14.1431b. 10–17.1432b.4; Cicero, *De Or.* 2.27.116; *De Part. Or.* 2.5-6; 14.48-51; Quintilian, 5.1-7. Cicero, *De Part. Or.* 2.6 classifies such proofs as either divine or human. Under divine he lists 'oracles, auspices, prophecies, the answers of priests, augurs, and diviners'.

47. Aristotle, *Rhet.* 1.2.1355b.1–1356a.6; *Rhet. ad Alex.* 7.1428a.16ff.; Cicero, *De Or.* 2.27.115-16; *De Part. Or.* 2.5-7; Quintilian, 5.

48. Aristotle, *Rhet.* 1.2.1356a.3-4; 1.8.1366a.6; 2.1.1377b.1–1378a.7; Cicero, *De Or.* 2.43.182-84; *Or.* 37.128; Quintilian, 6.2.8-19; Lausberg, *Handbuch der literarischen Rhetorik*, I, pp. 141-42, §257; Martin, *Antike Rhetorik*, pp. 158-61; G.A. Kennedy, *The Art of Persuasion in Greece* (Princeton, NJ: Princeton University Press, 1963), pp. 91-93.

reputation through insinuation, the more he may assume he is on poor terms with the audience.

Pathos is emotion and is used in proof to influence the audience positively for the rhetor and his cause and negatively for the opposition and its cause.[49] The emotions of the audience as tied to thoughts, judgments and opinions were carefully considered by the rhetor. Cicero wrote that 'in order to explore the feelings of the tribunal, I engage wholeheartedly in a consideration so careful, that I scent out with all possible keenness their thoughts, judgements, anticipations and wishes, and the direction in which they seem likely to be led away most easily by eloquence' (*De Or.* 2.44.186). Emotion is aroused for the rhetor if he or she seems to be working for what the audience deems good and useful (*De Or.* 2.51.206). The emotions tendered by the rhetor are usually amplified beyond the facts of the case, both positively and negatively (Quintilian, 6.2.23-24).

Any construction of the rhetorical situation of a Pauline epistle needs to be aware that the case may be more or less important than arguments from pathos make it seem. However, these arguments are used because Paul believes them to be what the audience deems good and useful and to be effective in arousing the emotion of the audience, whether love, hate, envy, anger, and so on. Thus the nature, perspective and values of the audience and its relation to Paul and the case may be gauged in part by the arguments from pathos.

Proof from logos includes example (induction) and argument (deduction). Proof from example is 'the adducing of some past action real or assumed which may serve to persuade the audience of the truth of the point which we are trying to make'.[50] Examples include those from history, fictions of poets, fables and proverbs when they are abridged fables (which are particularly useful with an uneducated audience), similitudes or comparisons, and judgments. Judgments, *kriseis*, are 'whatever may be regarded as expressing the opinion of nations, peoples, philosophers, distinguished citizens, or illustrious poets' (Quintilian, 5.11.36;

49. Aristotle, *Rhet.* 1.2.1356a.5; 2.1.1378a.8–17.1391b.6; Cicero, *De Or.* 2.42.178; 2.44; 2.51-52; *Or.* 37.128–38.133; Quintilian, 5.12.9-13; 6.2.20-24; cf. 5.8.1-3; Lausberg, *Handbuch der literarischen Rhetorik*, I, pp. 140-41, §257; Martin, *Antike Rhetorik*, pp. 158-62; Kennedy, *The Art of Persuasion*, pp. 93-96.

50. Quintilian, 5.11.6. See Aristotle, *Rhet.* 2.20; *Rhet. ad Alex.* 8; Cicero, *Inv.* 1.30.49; Quintilian, 5.11; Lausberg, *Handbuch der literarischen Rhetorik*, I, pp. 227-35, §§410-26; Martin, *Antike Rhetorik*, pp. 119-24.

cf. Cicero, *Inv.* 1.30.48). They include common sayings, popular beliefs and supernatural oracles.[51] Examples tend to be similar to or the opposite of those under discussion (*Rhet. ad Alex.* 8.1429a.20ff.). The parallel between the example and the point proven can be partial or complete (*Rhet. ad Alex.* 8.1430a.7ff.; Quintilian, 5.11.5-7).

Paul's use of examples is helpful for the construction of the rhetorical situation of an epistle. The examples chosen for argumentation and their types are supposed to be known by the audience, who find parallels drawn from them convincing. The points of comparison drawn from the examples for the argumentation further refine our knowledge of the situation, for they are supposed to be points paralleled in the situation, or opposite those points.

The argument is 'a process of reasoning which provides proof and enables one thing to be inferred from another and confirms facts which are uncertain by reference to facts which are certain' (Quintilian, 5.10.11; see Cicero, *Inv.* 1.34-41). There are three types of argument: syllogism, epicheireme and enthymeme. The syllogism has three parts: the major premise which presents the principle underlying the syllogism; the minor premise which supports the point of the major premise needed for proof; and the conclusion. The major and minor premises themselves may or may not need supporting proof. An epicheireme consists of three parts: the major premise or the subject of inquiry; the minor premise or the proof of the major premise; and the conclusion or the agreeable element of the major and minor premises. The epicheireme only differs from the syllogism in that its statements may be admitted facts or need proof and are often no more than probable, whereas the syllogism deals with statements whose truth is unquestioned.[52] An enthymeme is a proposition with one supporting reason explicitly stated and one reason implicit. The supporting reason may be necessary or only probable.[53]

What are regarded as certainties for use in arguments are things perceived by the senses (e.g. signs), things about which there is general agreement, things established by law or passed into current usage, and

---

51. Aristotle, *Rhet.* 2.23.1398b.12; Cicero, *Inv.* 1.30.48; Quintilian, 5.11.36-44; cf. *Rhet. ad Alex.* 1.1422a.25ff.; Cicero, *De Part. Or.* 2.6.

52. Quintilian, 5.10.1-8; 5.14.5-16; Lausberg, *Handbuch der literarischen Rhetorik*, I, pp. 197-201, §§367-72; Martin, *Antike Rhetorik*, pp. 105-106.

53. Aristotle, *Rhet.* 1.2.1357a.13-15; 2.22-26; 3.17.1418a.6–1418b.17; *Rhet. ad Alex.* 10; Quintilian, 5.10.1-3; 5.14.1-4, 24-26.

what is admitted by either party, what has been proven, or whatever is not disputed by the opposition (Quintilian, 5.10.12-15). These materials indicate the cultural values and the norms of the audience addressed and are particularly noted in the supporting premises of argumentation. For example, maxims quoted were considered to be the general principles of human behavior and the opinion of those addressed and indicative of the moral preference of the speaker (Aristotle, *Rhet*. 2.21.1395b. 15-16). Careful analysis of Paul's argumentation yields both the stated and unstated premises which he assumes his audience will accept and those which he must support because he is uncertain it will accept them. These indicate the cultural and religious values and norms of his audience.

Proofs are formulated using topics or sources of argument.[54] Common topics include the possible/impossible, past fact, future fact, and degree (more/less, greater/lesser). Topics can be common (applicable to all species of rhetoric and things) or specific (applicable to particular species of rhetoric and things). Specific topics for judicial rhetoric include the just/unjust and equity/inequity; for deliberative include happiness/unhappiness, expedience/harm, honor/dishonor, necessary/unnecessary, and good and degrees thereof; and for epideictic include the noble/disgraceful and virtue/vice. What is eulogized is expected to be a shared value (*Rhet. ad Alex*. 35.1440b.14–1441b.13) and the rhetor was urged to consider what the audience considers praiseworthy (Aristotle, *Rhet*. 1.9.1367b.30). Topics are drawn from social intercourse, precedent, tradition, manners and disposition of fellow-countrymen (Cicero, *De Or*. 2.30.131). The situation dictates the topics used (Quintilian, 5.10.100-18): 'arguments are to be drawn from the circumstances of each particular case; especially as the majority of proofs are to be found in the special circumstances of individual cases...we have to discover for ourselves whatever is peculiar to the case which we have in hand' (Quintilian, 5.10.102-103). The common and specific topics within a Pauline epistle were chosen with the situation in mind and were drawn from social intercourse and traditions familiar to the

---

54. Lausberg, *Handbuch der literarischen Rhetorik*, I, pp. 201-20, §§373-99; Martin, *Antike Rhetorik*, pp. 107-19, 155-57, 162-65; J.C. Brunt, 'More on the *Topos* as a New Testament Form', *JBL* 104 (1985), pp. 495-500. For extensive handbook references to *topoi*, see D.F. Watson, *Invention, Arrangement, and Style: Rhetorical Criticism of Jude and 2 Peter* (SBLDS, 104; Atlanta: Scholars Press, 1988), p. 19 n. 180.

audience. These topics were appropriate for specific rhetorical purposes and contexts which are very helpful in delineating Paul's rhetorical and historical contexts.[55]

d. *From Arrangement*
The construction of the rhetorical situation from any element of arrangement must take the content of the entire epistle into consideration for a balanced assessment. Each element has its particular techniques for amplification, exaggeration and misrepresentation.

1. *The Exordium*. The *exordium* is the beginning component of arrangement which aims to make the audience attentive, well disposed and receptive.[56] It is composed with the historical situation and its constituent parts utmost in the mind of the rhetor:

> We must also indicate the easiest method of composing an *exordium*. I would therefore add that he who has a speech to make should consider what he has to say; before whom, in whose defence, against whom, at what time and place, under what circumstances he has to speak; what is the popular opinion on the subject, and what the prepossessions of the judge are likely to be; and finally of what we should express our deprecation or desire. Nature herself will give him the knowledge of what he ought to say first (Quintilian, 4.1.52).

An *exordium* is to be appropriate to the case at hand and not transferable to another (Cicero, *De Or.* 2.78.315, 319; 2.80.325). It must be developed in due proportion to the importance of the case at issue. Thus no *exordium* is needed if the case is petty and the rhetor can launch directly into the case at hand (Cicero, *De Or.* 2.79.320). Simple cases require a short *exordium*, while complicated, suspect or unpopular cases require a longer *exordium* (Quintilian, 4.1.62). The need of the *exordium* to be appropriate to the situation addressed and proportionate to the importance of the case at hand makes it a key element in constructing the rhetorical situation of a Pauline epistle. In general the

55. For the insights that Paul's selection of *topoi* can make for interpretation of his purposes and context, see J.L. Jaquette, *Discerning What Counts: The Function of the* Adiaphora Topos *in Paul's Letters* (SBLDS, 146; Atlanta: Scholars Press, 1995).

56. Aristotle, *Rhet.* 3.14-15; *Rhet. ad Alex.* 29; 35.1440b.5-13; 36.1441b.30–1442b.28; Cicero, *Inv.* 1.15-18; *De Or.* 2.77.315–80.325; *De Part. Or.* 8.28-30; *Rhet. ad Her.* 1.3.4–7.11; Quintilian, 4.1; Lausberg, *Handbuch der literarischen Rhetorik*, I, pp. 150-63, §§263-88; Martin, *Antike Rhetorik*, pp. 60-75.

greater the proportion of an epistle devoted to an *exordium* the more important, complex, or suspect Paul may perceive his case to be to the audience.

Much can be inferred about the rhetorical situation from the approach and content of the *exordium*. If an *exordium* is used, it can be direct or use insinuation.[57] A direct opening can be used with an honorable case and usually is quite minimal since the rhetor already has the goodwill of the audience. The more minimal and direct the *exordium* is, the more honorable Paul may think he and his case are to his audience. Insinuation uses an indirect approach to steal into the minds of the audience. It emphasizes the strong points of the case, avoids weak points and deflates the opponent's claims. Anywhere Paul uses insinuation, a difficulty between himself and his audience or his audience with his case is indicated. Certain techniques are used in such cases to remove prejudice which must be noted in constructing the rhetorical situation. These include techniques to diminish or weaken prejudice. For example, motives may be substituted, claims made to have intended something else, or claims made that something was an accident (Aristotle, *Rhet*. 3.15; Cicero, *De Part. Or.* 8.28).

To foster goodwill for the case the rhetor uses the *exordium* to present the actions of opponents as base, haughty, cruel and malicious; the opponents as misusers of power, wealth or family; or the opponents as lazy, careless, slothful or pursuers of wealth. The rhetor was instructed to make himself appear virtuous and the struggling underdog and to dishonor opponents by strengthening the prejudice against them to the rhetor's own advantage.[58] Rhetors throw contemptuous allusions at their opponent's cases in order to deride and trivialize them.[59] Emotional appeal is made in favor of the rhetor and his case and against the opponents and their case.[60] The *exordium* will require exaggeration and extenuation as expediency demands (Quintilian, 4.1.15). The *exordium* may produce the impression that the subject is of greater or lesser importance than it really is, and may be drawn from either irrelevant material or material akin to the subject (Quintilian, 3.8.7-9; 4.1.30-32).

---

57. Cicero, *Inv.* 1.15.20–16.21; 1.17; *Rhet. ad Her.* 1.3.5–4.6; 1.6.9–7.11; Quintilian, 4.1.40-50.

58. Cicero, *Inv.* 1.16.22; *De Or.* 2.79.321; *De Part. Or.* 8.28; *Rhet. ad Her.* 1.5.8; Quintilian, 4.1.6-29.

59. Cicero, *Inv.* 1.16.22; *De Or.* 2.79.322; Quintilian, 4.1.38-39.

60. Cicero, *De Or.* 2.77.310-11; *De Part. Or.* 8.27; Quintilian, 4.1.27-29.

To make matters even more tenuous, Quintilian advises that falsehood could be used in the *exordium* if necessary (4.1.33). The emotional appeal and exaggeration element of the *exordium* must be taken into consideration in constructing the rhetorical situation of a Pauline epistle.

The *exordium* introduces important *topoi* and propositions to be developed in the *probatio*.[61] The *exordium* anticipates the argumentation of the opposition (Quintilian, 4.1.49-50). The element considered the most effective is used first in the *exordium*, and especially can be borrowed from the speech of the opposition (Quintilian, 4.1.54). The *exordium* of a Pauline epistle is a key source for issues within the rhetorical situation. Some elements may be borrowed from the speech of the opposition and give us insight as to their nature as well.

The relationship of the *exordium* to the species of rhetoric is informative for constructing the rhetorical situation of a Pauline epistle. If an *exordium* is used in epideictic rhetoric, the rhetor has great freedom, but should include the main subject or propositions and refute any misrepresentation of his own. The *exordium* may derive from what is worthy of praise or blame, and exhortation and dissuasion (Aristotle, *Rhet*. 3.14.1414b.1–1415a.4; *Rhet. ad Alex*. 35.1440b.5-13).

Deliberative rhetoric does not have an *exordium* if the audience has sought the opinion of the rhetor and is naturally well disposed (Quintilian, 3.8.6; cf. Cicero, *De Part. Or*. 4.13). An *exordium* only belongs to deliberative rhetoric when there are differing opinions on a subject (Aristotle, *Rhet*. 3.13.1414b.3). An *exordium* is used if there is opposition, or the audience is not acquainted with the subject or attaches too much or too little importance to the issue in the estimation of the rhetor. In these cases the rhetor excites or removes prejudice, and magnifies or minimizes the importance of the subject (Aristotle, *Rhet*. 3.14.1415b.12). To secure the goodwill of the friendly audience, the rhetor pointed out his faithfulness and the value of his past advice. To secure the goodwill of the hostile audience, the rhetor stressed that his proposal is advantageous for the audience. When the audience is prejudiced against the rhetor, he anticipates its prejudice and raises arguments in his defense and shows that his advice is just and expedient. If the audience is friendly, the rhetor sets the proposal out immediately, and if hostile, he anticipates audience reaction and defends the proposal (*Rhet. ad Alex*. 29.1436b.5–1438a.41).

---

61. Cicero, *De Or*. 2.80.325; Quintilian, 4.1.23-27; cf. Cicero, *De Or*. 2.79.320.

In judicial rhetoric, the *exordium* should make the subject clear and can be skipped if the subject is clear or unimportant. The defendant tries to remove prejudice for his case in the *exordium* (and the accuser tries to create it for the defendant in the *peroratio*). To obtain audience attention, he makes the audience believe that what will be said about the case is important to it, concerns its interests, and is astonishing or agreeable. Just a simple statement of the subject is needed if the audience is ready to listen to the case and has good judgment (Aristotle, *Rhet.* 3.14.1415a.5–1415b.11). To obtain goodwill, he uses the same techniques for friendly and hostile audiences or, where prejudice exists, as outlined for deliberate *exordia* (outlined above). If the audience is neither favorable nor unfavorable to the case, the defendant praises it as possessing qualities it values, and abuses the opposition as not having these qualities. If there is prejudice against the rhetor or the case, he anticipates the objections of the opposition (*Rhet. ad Alex.* 36.1441b.30–1442b.28).

The *exordium* may not accurately portray the rhetorical situation. It is a biased presentation which favors the case of the rhetor and disparages the case of the opposition. It downplays the negative elements that the rhetor has to discuss and accentuates those of the opposition. It may contain exaggeration, falsehood or material which helps the rhetor but does not derive from the situation. Any assessment of the rhetorical situation based on the *exordium* will need to be balanced by the analysis of the entire work to see upon what the case is based and the types of argument used to confirm and refute. What is true of the initial *exordium* is also true for other portions of the discourse which are given the same function of introducing topics and emotional appeal and can be considered secondary *exordia* (Aristotle, *Rhet.* 3.14.1415b.9; Quintilian, 4.1.72-75; 4.3.9). These can provide further insight into the exigence as they help Paul develop and structure his arguments.

2. *The Narratio and Partitio.* The *narratio* is 'the persuasive exposition of that which either has been done, or is supposed to have been done... a speech instructing the audience as to the nature of the case in dispute'.[62] The *narratio* is usually discussed in relation to judicial

---

62. Quintilian, 4.2.31. See Aristotle, *Rhet.* 3.16; *Rhet. ad Alex.* 30–31; Cicero, *Inv.* 1.19-21; *De Part. Or.* 9.31-32; *Rhet. ad Her.* 1.8-9; Quintilian, 4.2.3; Lausberg, *Handbuch der literarischen Rhetorik*, I, pp. 163-90, §§289-347; Martin, *Antike Rhetorik*, pp. 75-89.

rhetoric, but can apply to deliberative and epideictic rhetoric as well (see below). The *narratio* has the virtues of brevity, clarity and plausibility. Thus only the essential details of a case are given; the details of the case should be carried only to the point needing consideration; digression should be rare; prejudicial details and those offering no advantage are to be omitted; and details should be presented in the order they occurred.[63] The *narratio* usually ends where the point of controversy begins (Quintilian, 4.2.132). The *narratio* is convincing if the facts narrated are in accordance with the persons, times, places, actions and evidence of the case (Cicero, *De Part. Or.* 9.31-32). It should introduce traits characteristic of the rhetor and his opponents (Aristotle, *Rhet.* 3.16.1417a.10).

When conforming to these conventions the *narratio* is perhaps the clearest statement of the details of the rhetorical situation (at least clearer than that offered by the *exordium*). Once identified, it is the *narratio* of the Pauline epistle that may give us the clearest insights into the rhetorical situation Paul is addressing, and its closing is the best indication of the main point of controversy. Elements of the narrative giving offense to the audience are distributed piecemeal throughout the speech and mitigated in argumentation and will not appear in the *narratio* (Cicero, *Inv.* 1.21.30). The entire content of a Pauline epistle must be examined closely to determine what elements of the narrative are distributed throughout the epistle because they are offensive to his audience. These are elements needed to assess more fully the rhetorical situation.

However, as was the case with the *exordium*, the *narratio* must be used with caution when constructing the rhetorical situation. Quintilian advises, 'For the purpose of the *statement of facts* is not merely to instruct, but rather to persuade the judge' (4.2.21). The *narratio* contains the case, but often digresses to attack somebody or to amplify (Cicero, *Inv.* 1.19.27). The *narratio* can be altered to suit the rhetor and his case (Quintilian, 4.2.67, 76) or even be entirely fictitious (*Rhet. ad Her.* 1.9.16; Quintilian, 4.2.19, 88-100). When constructing the rhetorical situation the interpreter must beware of amplification and vituperation in the *narratio* of a Pauline epistle.

---

63. Cicero, *Inv.* 1.20.28–21.29; *Rhet. ad Her.* 1.8-9; Quintilian, 4.2.31-60, 67. In difficult cases Quintilian allows for varying the actual order of events, but such cases are unusual (4.2.83-84, 87).

It must be kept in mind that the *narratio* does not have to be limited to the beginning of a discourse, but can be placed throughout, especially in complicated or damaging cases (Aristotle, *Rhet.* 3.16.1417b.11; Quintilian, 4.2.85). This function of the *narratio* should be noted in constructing the rhetorical situation of a longer Pauline epistle. Not all the elements of the exigence may be stated initially.

The *partitio* is the element of arrangement which enumerates the propositions of the orator to be developed in the *probatio* and, in judicial rhetoric, the propositions of the opposition to be refuted.[64] It usually follows the *narratio* and, as a listing of propositions, is perhaps the greatest indicator of the issues involved in the historical situation. The *partitio* is not needed if only one proposition is involved (Cicero, *Inv.* 1.23.33; Quintilian, 4.5.8). If a Pauline epistle contains no *partitio*, the main issue is probably found in the *narratio*.

3. *The Probatio.* The *probatio* develops the propositions of the *narratio* and *partitio*. It is composed of *confirmatio* which proves the propositions of the rhetor,[65] and *refutatio* which weakens or disproves the propositions of the opposition.[66] Arrangement of proofs within the *probatio* is enlightening for evaluating the most and least important elements in the rhetorical situation. Arrangement of argumentation should be guided by the needs of the individual case (Quintilian, 5.12.14).

It was advised that a strong or the strongest point be placed first, moderate points in the middle which may need to be grouped together to be effective, and a strong point at the end.[67] A strong argument could stand alone, but weak arguments should be grouped together (Quintilian, 5.12.4-5). Never descend from the strongest to the weakest

64. Cicero, *Inv.* 1.22-23; *Rhet. ad Her.* 1.3.4; 1.10.17; Quintilian, 3.9.1-5; 4.4-5; Lausberg, *Handbuch der literarischen Rhetorik*, I, p. 190, §347; Martin, *Antike Rhetorik*, pp. 91-95.

65. Aristotle, *Rhet.* 3.17; *Rhet. ad Alex.* 32–33; Cicero, *Inv.* 1.24.34–41.77; *De Part. Or.* 9.33–14.51; *Or.* 34.122; *Rhet. ad Her.* 1.3.4; 3.9-10; Quintilian, 5.1-12; Lausberg, *Handbuch der literarischen Rhetorik*, I, pp. 190-236, §§348-430; Martin, *Antike Rhetorik*, pp. 95-137.

66. Aristotle, *Rhet.* 2.25; 3.13.1414b.4; *Rhet. ad Alex.* 13; 34.1439b.37–1440a.25; Cicero, *Inv.* 1.42.78–51.96; *De Or.* 2.53.215-16; *De Part. Or.* 12.44; *Rhet. ad Her.* 1.3.4; Quintilian, 3.9.5; 5.13; Martin, *Antike Rhetorik*, pp. 124-33.

67. Cicero, *De Or.* 2.78.313-14; *Or.* 15.50; *Rhet. ad Her.* 3.10.18; Quintilian, 6.4.22. In Quintilian's time it was debated whether the strongest points should be first, last, or divided between the two (5.12.14; 7.1.10).

argument in proof, but ascend from weaker to stronger (Quintilian, 5.12.14; 7.1.16-22). Disregard weak arguments in argumentation (Cicero, *De Or.* 2.78.314). In the *probatio* of Paul's epistles, the arguments beginning and ending a unit of argumentation may be the strongest. These Paul can assume his audience will find compelling. Weaker arguments of which he is unsure will be sandwiched between. Such placement of strong and weak argument helps us delineate the contours of Paul's problem with his audience through what he considers strong and weak. Within the *probatio*, ἐπιμονή or *commoratio* is a figure of thought which 'occurs when one remains rather long upon, and often returns to, the strongest topic on which the whole cause rests'.[68] Repetition and continued development of topics are indicative of the main reason Paul addresses an audience.

In judicial rhetoric the prosecutor or accuser begins with a strong argument and ends with the strongest argument, with the weaker arguments between. The defense should dispose of the strongest argument first, then the minor ones. This procedure should alter if the minor arguments are obviously false and refutation is easy and the strong argument will take time to refute. In this case, one reverses the order of refutation to leave the impression that all the arguments are easily refuted (Quintilian, 7.1.10-11). Quintilian argues that in defense when advancing a number of points to support a single proposition the arguments should be presented from the weaker to the stronger (Quintilian, 7.1.16-19). In portions of judicial rhetoric Paul's arrangement of arguments indicates his assessment of the strength of his own arguments in accusation, and the opposition's in defense. When accusing, one should look for Paul's strongest arguments to be first and last in the unit of argumentation. When defending himself, one should look for the argument he deems strongest with his audience to be refuted first. If a series of smaller arguments is refuted prior to an extensive refutation, then Paul considers the former to be weak and the latter to be strong with the audience.

If the opponent's charges are weak, they can be repeated verbatim, but if strong, they should be toned down. The opponent's charges should never be repeated along with the proofs (unless to make light of them), for this only amplifies them. A rhetor has the option of summa-

68. *Rhet. ad Her.* 4.45.58. See also Cicero, *Or.* 40.137; *De Or.* 3.53.202 = Quintilian, 9.1.27; Quintilian, 9.2.4; Lausberg, *Handbuch der literarischen Rhetorik*, I, pp. 413-14, §830; p. 415, §835; Martin, *Antike Rhetorik*, p. 135 n. 3.

rizing the opponent's charges and refuting them together, especially if
the restatement emphasizes their implausibility, but a point-by-point
refutation is the safest approach (Quintilian, 5.13.25-28). Paul's arrangement in refutation may indicate his perception of the strength of the
position of his opposition. If he is repeating charges, he considers them
weak; if he summarizes them, he considers them implausible; and if he
refutes them one by one, he considers them strong.

Anticipation is a method used in all three species of rhetoric by
which the rhetor anticipates and forestalls the objections of the audience or opponents.[69] It was observed that if speaking ahead of the
opposition, 'arguments misrepresented in advance, even though quite
strong ones really, do not appear so important to an audience that has
heard them already' (*Rhet. ad Alex.* 18.1433a.38ff.). The rhetor was
advised to amplify his own arguments and make those of opponents
'weak and trifling' (*Rhet. ad Alex.* 33.1439b.10ff.). On the other hand,
the rhetor was advised to refute the anticipations of opponents which
misrepresent his position (*Rhet. ad Alex.* 18.1433b.1-14; 34.1440a.24-
25). The use of anticipation is instructive for what may or may not be
affirmed about Paul's opposition. On the one hand, arguments of the
opposition advanced by Paul may or may not be true representations.
On the other hand, when Paul is dealing with the accusations of opponents and against him, he may very well be representing these quite
accurately as he carefully defines which parts of the accusations are
accurate and which are misrepresentations.

In judicial and deliberative rhetoric, the first to speak begins with
proof and ends with refutation. If second to speak, one immediately
refutes the proofs of the opponents, especially when they are strong and
meeting with approval, and then gives one's own proofs (Aristotle,
Rhet. 3.1418b.17.14-15). Paul often finds himself responding to the
arguments of opponents and the placement of refutation may be an
indication of how much strength he attributes to the arguments of the
opposition and how much he believes the audience gives them credence. If they are placed first, more strength is indicated; if later, less.
In judicial rhetoric, the defense refutes only those proofs which the
audience perceives as probable (*Rhet. ad Alex.* 36.1443b.25ff.), and in
recapitulation the defense poses questions to its strongest points and its

---

69. *Rhet. ad Alex.* 18; 33; 36.1443a.7–1443b.14; Quintilian, 4.1.49-50; 9.2.16-
18; Lausberg, *Handbuch der literarischen Rhetorik*, I, pp. 424-25, §§854-55;
Martin, *Antike Rhetorik*, pp. 277-79.

opponent's weakest points (*Rhet. ad Alex.* 36.1444b.31ff.). When responding to opponents, proofs that Paul refutes are likely to be those he assumes the audience finds probable. When he summarizes within argumentation, questions posed to the opposition or to their proofs indicate which proofs he considers weak.

Proof in deliberative rhetoric uses supporting examples that are akin to the case and well known to the audience. No proof is needed if the statement alone carries conviction with the audience (*Rhet. ad Alex.* 32.1438b.29–1439a.10). In deliberative portions of his epistles, the more proof Paul uses the less likely the proposition he is supporting carries conviction with his audience.

In epideictic rhetoric, there is no need of proof because facts are taken on trust (Aristotle, *Rhet.* 3.17.1417b.3). This is because the rhetor praises or blames according to the views of the audience and generally received opinion in order for such to be effective (Quintilian, 3.7.23-25). Vituperation uses narrative that mirrors the character of the opposition and amplifies it (*Rhet. ad Alex.* 35.1441b.14-29). Thus values, both positive and negative, that are assumed in epideictic portions of Paul's epistles probably reflect those of the audience, but may be overly negative if describing his opposition. However, vituperation of opposition is likely to be exaggerated and amplified.

The *digressio* is 'the handling of some theme, which must however have some bearing on the case, in a passage that involves digression from the logical order of our speech' (Quintilian, 4.3.14). The *digressio* praises and blames people, amplifies topics and appeals to emotion.[70] The more important the case, the greater the role of the *digressio* (Cicero, *De Or.* 2.77.311-12). Thus the more Paul relies upon *digressio* the greater the importance of the situation from his perspective. Topics amplified in *digressio* will be central for constructing the rhetorical situation.

Jesting is especially employed in refutation to deny, rebut or make light of a charge. The rhetor pretends to agree, adds something more biting to a charge being denied, lies, feigns confession, distorts meaning, insinuates and uses misrepresentation based on irony and pretense (Quintilian, 6.3.72-92): 'There remains the prettiest of all forms of humour, namely the jest which depends for success on deceiving antic-

---

70. Cicero, *Inv.* 1.51.97; *De Or.* 2.19.80; 2.77.311-12; Quintilian, 4.3.12-17; Lausberg, *Handbuch der literarischen Rhetorik*, I, pp. 187-88, §§340-42; Martin, *Antike Rhetorik*, pp. 89-91.

ipations or taking another's words in a sense other than he intended'
(Quintilian, 6.3.84; cf. Cicero, *De Or.* 2.67.273). 'Indeed the essence of
all wit lies in the distortion of the true and natural meaning of words'
(Quintilian, 6.3.89). When Paul jests he cannot be expected to be presenting his opposition and their words in any exact manner.

4. *The Peroratio*. The *peroratio* is the conclusion of a rhetorical work
where the rhetor both recapitulates the case and, through amplification
and depreciation, arouses emotions for his case and against that of the
opposition.[71] The recapitulation demonstrates what facets of the case
the rhetor deems most important for the decision of the audience.
Recapitulation is prescribed to conclude divisions of a rhetorical piece
as well as the piece as a whole.[72] Methods of recapitulation include cal-
culations, proposal of policy or line of action, interrogation, and
enumerations of what has been proven (*Rhet. ad Alex.* 20.1433b.29ff.;
33.1439b.12ff.). The proposal of a policy is particularly indicative of
the rhetorical situation because it states explicitly what the rhetor wants
the audience to do to meet the exigence.

   In its capacity of recapitulation, the *peroratio* of a Pauline epistle
gives us insight into the rhetorical situation's most important facets as
understood by Paul. Proposals of policy, usually in the form of exhortation, make it clear what Paul is desiring most to change about the
rhetorical situation and what he assumes is within the capacity of the
audience to change.

   There is more emotional appeal in the *peroratio* than in the *exordium*
(Quintilian, 4.1.28; 6.1.9-10, 12, 51-52). The emotional appeal helps
the rhetor place his own case in unusually great light and impugn the
case of the opposition. This emotive role of the *peroratio* requires caution when using it for constructing the rhetorical situation of a Pauline
epistle. However, what is appreciated and what is depreciated in the
peroratio are indicative of Paul's understanding of the value system of
his audience.

---

   71. Aristotle, *Rhet.* 3.19; *Rhet. ad Alex.* 20–21; 36.1444b.21–1445a.29; Cicero,
Inv. 1.52-56; *De Part. Or.* 15–17; *Rhet. ad Her.* 2.30-31; Quintilian, 6.1; Lausberg,
Handbuch der literarischen Rhetorik, I, pp. 236-40, §§431-42; Martin, *Antike
Rhetorik*, pp. 147-66.
   72. *Rhet. ad Alex.* 20; 21.1434a.30ff.; 22.1434b.1-10; 32.1439a.19-24; Quintil-
ian, 6.1.8; cf. *Rhet. ad Her.* 2.30.47.

In the *peroratio* of judicial rhetoric, the prosecutor uses recapitulation and topics conducive to anger, while the defendant uses less recapitulation and topics conducive to compassion (Cicero, *De Part. Or.* 17.58). Both sides should keep their outstanding resources for the *peroratio* (Cicero, *De Or.* 2.78.314). Thus where Paul recapitulates in judicial portions of his epistles his use of topics conducive to compassion indicate that he is defending himself against opponents, and those resources he believes are the best to use in the situation (which should be carefully noted in constructing the rhetorical situation). Recapitulation only belongs to deliberative rhetoric when there are differing opinions (Aristotle, *Rhet.* 3.13.1414b.3; cf. Cicero, *De Part. Or.* 17.59). Thus, in a mainly deliberative epistle or portion of an epistle, recapitulation may indicate that Paul's audience is not in total agreement with him or with the course of action he is advocating.

e. *From Style*
The style of a work may indicate the social level of the rhetor and the audience, as well as other facets of the rhetorical situation.[73] Language was to be appropriate to the subject matter. The more important the subject, the more elevated the style.[74] 'Style is proportionate to the subject matter when neither weighty matters are treated offhand, nor trifling matters with dignity, and no embellishment is attached to an ordinary word' (Aristotle, *Rhet.* 3.7.1408a.2). Style was also to be appropriate to the occasion and the audience (*Rhet. ad Alex.* 22.1434b.27ff.; Cicero, *Or.* 21.71; 35.123-25). Compound words, epithets and foreign words are appropriate when the audience is enthusiastic (Aristotle, *Rhet.* 3.7.1408b.11) and arguments which the audience finds suspect can be disguised with charming style (Quintilian, 5.14.35).

Applied to the Pauline epistles, style may be indicative of the importance of the subject. Both the style of a Pauline epistle as a whole and of smaller portions may indicate the importance Paul places on the subject in regard to the rhetorical situation he is addressing. The more elevated the more important, and the less elevated the less important. Heavier use of compound words and epithets by Paul in a portion of his

73. For example, see A.H. Snyman, 'Style and the Rhetorical Situation of Romans 8.31-39', *NTS* 34 (1988), pp. 218-31.
74. Aristotle, *Rhet.* 3.7; Cicero, *Or.* 21.71–22.74; 28.100–29.101; Quintilian, 5.14.33-35.

epistle may indicate that he believes that the audience is enthusiastic for the topic discussed. Pauline arguments which are unusually ornate may be those Paul believes his audience would find suspect or the ones Paul considers the most important.

'Amplification…is a sort of weightier affirmation, designed to win credence in the course of speaking by arousing emotion' (Cicero, *De Part. Or.* 15.53). Amplification is effected by a number of means including strong words, augmentation, comparison, accumulation, vigorous attack on vices, and exaggeration.[75] The type of amplification used should be appropriate to the case (Cicero, *De Or.* 3.27.106). Amplification aims to persuade the audience and misrepresentation is expected. Note this definition of epideictic rhetoric: 'The eulogistic species of oratory consists…in the amplification of creditable purposes and actions and speeches and the attribution of qualities that do not exist, while the vituperative species is the opposite, the minimization of creditable qualities and the amplification of discreditable ones' (*Rhet. ad Alex.* 3.1425b.36ff.).

Degree and type of amplification are indicative of Paul's main concerns and where he thinks his audience is most likely to need instruction, dismiss his case, or be hostile to his case. Any surmise about the rhetorical situation must be careful that in portions in which amplification is heavily used, the portrayal of the overall rhetorical situation, characters and issues involved may be amplified, both positively and negatively.

3. *Conclusion*

Paul had freedom in reading the historical situation and creating the exigence and rhetorical situation of each epistle. He may not have interpreted the facts of the historical situation and created the exigence exactly as his audience would in every instance. He also operates with a somewhat different set of constraints (e.g. apostolic authority) which overlapped that of his audiences (e.g. shared tradition). However, his rhetorical exigence would certainly be tied to the facts of the historical

---

75. Aristotle, *Rhet.* 1.9.1368a.38-40; Cicero, *De Or.* 3.26.104–27.108; *De Part. Or.* 15.52–17.58; Longinus, *Subl.* 11.1–12.2; Quintilian, 8.4; Lausberg, *Handbuch der literarischen Rhetorik*, I, pp. 220-27, §§400-409; Martin, *Antike Rhetorik*, pp. 153-58, 208-10.

situation in order for him to communicate with an audience working with the same historial situation.

Once the rhetorical situation of a Pauline epistle is constructed the historical situation can also be constructed. At this step our knowledge of the historical, cultural and social dimensions of the Greco-Roman world contemporaneous with the Pauline epistles is needed to construct the broader historical situation which makes sense of all the facets of the rhetorical situation. This final step needs to be done in such a way that the rhetorical situation is not merely substituted for the historical situation. This step is rarely discussed in the literature and I suspect will initially find voice in interdisciplinary studies incorporating classical, social-scientific and rhetorical studies.

Part II

RHETORICAL INTERPRETATION OF LUKE'S GOSPEL AND ACTS

.

THE PREFACE TO THE LUKAN WRITINGS
AND RHETORICAL HISTORIOGRAPHY*

Kota Yamada

Inasmuch as many people took in hand to draw up a narrative concerning the things that have been confirmed among us, just as those who were the eyewitnesses and ministers of the Word from the beginning transmitted to us, it seemed good to me also that I write to you in order, investigating everything accurately from the very beginning, most excellent Theophilus, that you might know the certainty of the words that you were instructed (Lk. 1.1-4; my translation).

I

The beginning of the Lukan writings is written in the form of a preface, which was the literary convention of Hellenistic-Roman literary works. The preface to Luke's Gospel has been studied very well, since it is the only place in the Synoptic Gospels that depicts the author's intentions, as well as his literary consciousness. Thus, the preface to Luke's Gospel has been regarded as important, in spite of its brevity, in order to investigate not only the tradition history of earliest Christianity and the literary process and purpose of the author, but also the literary genre of the Lukan writings.

But the meaning of the preface has been disputed in many articles, books, commentaries and dictionaries, as many *hapax legomena* (ἐπειδήπερ [inasmuch as], ἀνατάσσεσθαι [draw up], αὐτόπτης [eyewitness], παρακολουθεῖν [investigate, participate]) and peculiar Lukan words (ἐπιχειρεῖν [take in hand], καθεξῆς [in order], κράτιστος [most

---

*   This is a revised version of my paper, 'Rukabunsyo no Jyobun to Syuji-gaku-teki Rekisi (The Preface to the Lukan Writings and Rhetorical Historiography)', which was read at the thirty-third annual meeting of the Japanese Society for New Testament Studies in Tokyo in September 1993, and now appears in *Keiwa Gakuen Daigaku Kenkyu Kiyo* (*The Bulletin of Keiwa College*) 4 (1995), pp. 1-23.

excellent]) are seen in it; and, further, each word has ambiguous meanings. What does the author of the Lukan writings intend to say in it? This essay is an attempt to add a new perspective to the past discussions.

Generally speaking, what is the function of prefaces in Hellenistic-Roman works? Aristotle mentions the *prooimion* of speeches as follows: 'The Introduction is the beginning of a speech, corresponding to the prologue in poetry and prelude in flute-music; they are all beginnings, paving the way, as it were, for what is to follow'.[1] Cicero, following Aristotle, also refers to the introduction in speeches in this way: 'An *exordium* is a passage which brings the mind of the auditor into a proper condition to receive the rest of the speech. This will be accomplished if he becomes well-disposed, attentive and receptive.'[2]

The preface in Hellenistic-Roman works seems to have had a similar function as the *prooimion* or *exordium* in speeches. For example, Lucian speaks about the preface in historiography in a similar way, but a little differently:

> Whenever he does use a preface, he will make two points only, not three like the orators. He will omit the appeal for a favorable hearing and give his audience what will interest and instruct them. For they will give him their attention if he shows that what he is going to say will be important, essential, personal or useful. He will make what is to come easy to understand and quite clear, if he sets forth the causes and outlines the main events.[3]

So far, it seems right to say that the preface in Hellenistic-Roman works has the same function—to make the reader 'well-disposed, attentive and receptive'.

Before embarking on our inquiries another question must be raised, as to whether the preface to Luke's Gospel was intended to be written to cover only the Third Gospel[4] or both the Third Gospel and the Acts

---

1. Aristotle, *Rhet.* 3.14.1 (1414b1.19-21) (ET J. Barnes, *The Complete Works of Aristotle* [Princeton, NJ: Princeton University Press, 1985]).

2. Cicero, *Inv.* 1.15.20 (LCL). Cf. Aristotle, *Rhet.* 3.14.7; Anaximenes, *Rhet.* 29; Ps.-Cicero, *Rhet. ad Her.* 1.4.6, 1.7.11; Quintilian, 4.1.5; R. Volkmann, *Die Rhetorik der Griechen und Römer* (Leipzig: Teubner, 1885), pp. 127-48; H. Lausberg, *Handbuch der literarischen Rhetorik: Eine Grundlegung der Literaturwissenschaft* (2 vols.; Munich: Heuber, 1960 [2nd edn. 1975]), §§263-88.

3. Lucian, *Hist. Conscr.* 53 (LCL).

4. E.g. E. Haenchen, 'Das "Wir" in der Apostelgeschichte und das Itinerar', *ZTK* 58 (1961), pp. 329-66 (362); *idem*, *Die Apostelgeschichte* (MeyerK, 3; Göttin-

of the Apostles—that is, the whole of the Lukan writings.[5] This problem is not likely to be solved by inquiring into the meaning of each
word. The Hellenistic-Roman authors used to write the preface to the
whole writing in the first volume of a multi-volumed work, and then
wrote prefaces to the second and following volumes, in which they
summarized the contents of the previous one or outlined those of the
present one. The Hellenistic-Roman historians often followed this

gen: Vandenhoeck & Ruprecht, 7th edn, 1977), p. 143 n. 3; H. Conzelmann, *Die
Mitte der Zeit: Studien zur Theologie des Lukas* (Tübingen: J.C.B. Mohr, 5th edn,
1964), p. 7 n. 1; *idem, Die Apostelgeschichte* (HNT, 7; Tübingen: J.C.B. Mohr, 2nd
edn, 1972), pp. 25-26; H. Schürmann, 'Evangelienschrift und Kirchliche Unter-
weisung: Die repräsentative Funktion der Schrift nach Lk 1,1-4', in *idem,
Traditionsgeschichtliche Untersuchungen zu den synoptischen Evangelien* (Düssel-
dorf: Patmos, 1968), pp. 251-71; *idem, Das Lukasevangelium* (2 vols.; HTKNT, 3;
Freiburg: Herder, 1969), I, pp. 1-17; G. Schneider, 'Der Zweck des lukanischen
Doppelwerks', *BZ* 21 (1977), pp. 45-66; *idem, Die Apostelgeschichte* (2 vols.;
HTKNT, 5; Freiburg: Herder, 1980–82), I, p. 81; S. Brown, 'The Role of the
Prologue in Determining the Purpose of Luke–Acts', in C.H. Talbert (ed.), *Per-
spectives on Luke–Acts* (Edinburgh: T. & T. Clark, 1978), pp. 99-111; R.J. Dillon,
'Previewing Luke's Project from his Prologue (Luke 1:1-4)', *CBQ* 43 (1981),
pp. 205-27, esp. p. 206 n. 3, p. 217 n. 37; E. Schweizer, *Das Evangelium nach
Lukas* (NTD, 3; Göttingen: Vandenhoeck & Ruprecht, 1986), p. 11; J. Nolland,
Luke 1–9:50 (Waco, TX: Word Books, 1989), pp. 11-12; L. Alexander, *The Pre-
face to Luke's Gospel: Literary Convention and Social Context in Luke 1.1-4 and
Acts 1.1* (Cambridge: Cambridge University Press, 1993).
    5.   E.g. H. Cadbury, 'Commentary on the Preface of Luke', in F.J. Foakes
Jackson and K. Lake (eds.), *The Beginnings of Christianity. I. The Acts of the
Apostles* (5 vols.; London: Macmillan, 1922), II, pp. 489-510, esp. pp. 421-22; J.M.
Creed, *The Gospel According to St Luke* (London: Macmillan, 1930), p. 1; G.
Klein, 'Lukas 1,1-4 als theologisches Programm', in E. Dinkler (ed.), *Zeit und
Geschichte: Dankesgabe an Rudolf Bultmann zum 80. Geburtstag* (Tübingen:
J.C.B. Mohr, 1964), pp. 170-203; A.J.B. Higgins, 'The Preface to Luke and the
Kerygma in Acts', in W.W. Gasque and R. Martin (eds.), *Apostolic History and the
Gospel: Biblical and Historical Essays Presented to F.F. Bruce* (Exeter: Paternos-
ter Press; Grand Rapids: Eerdmans, 1970), pp. 78-91, esp. pp. 78-79; E. Kloster-
mann, *Das Lukasevangelium* (HNT, 5; Tübingen: J.C.B. Mohr, 3rd edn, 1975),
p. 1; R. Maddox, *The Purpose of Luke–Acts* (Edinburgh: T. & T. Clark, 1981),
pp. 1-6; J.A. Fitzmyer, *The Gospel According to Luke I–IX* (AB, 28; New York:
Doubleday, 1981), p. 389; F. Bovon, *Das Evangelium nach Lukas (Lk. 1,1–9,50)*
(Neukirchen–Vluyn: Neukirchener Verlag, 1989), pp. 41-42; C.F. Evans, *Saint
Luke* (TPI New Testament Commentaries; London: SCM Press; Philadelphia:
Trinity Press International, 1990), pp. 120-21.

custom, taking after Ephorus and Diodorus.[6]

The author of the Lukan writings seems to have followed this custom, and wrote the preface to the whole of the Lukan writings in the first volume, Luke's Gospel, as is evident from the fact that he summarizes briefly the contents of the first volume in the preface to the second volume, the Acts of the Apostles. If this is right, it also leads to the following consequences: first, 'the things that have been confirmed among us' implies not only the contents of Luke's Gospel but also those of the Acts of the Apostles; secondly, 'those who were the eyewitnesses and ministers of the Word' handed down the traditions of earliest Christianity as well as those of Jesus; thirdly, the author compiled both Luke's Gospel and the Acts of the Apostles as 'a narrative', that is, as a single literary work; fourthly, the author investigated and narrated in an orderly way not only the material of Luke's Gospel, but also that of the Acts of the Apostles; and, fifthly, the words 'Theophilus, you were instructed' seem to have included the teachings both of Jesus and of the earliest church, and the author made an effort to show 'the certainty' of both teachings.[7]

II

H. Cadbury coined a hyphenated word, 'Luke–Acts', to reveal the unity of the Lukan writings, with the underlying thought that the preface to Luke's Gospel deals with the whole of the Lukan writings. However, he has compared the 'we' in the preface to Luke's Gospel (Lk. 1.2) and the 'we' in the so-called 'we passages' in the Acts of the Apostles (Acts 16.10-17; 20.5-15; 21.1-18; 27.1-28), and has concluded, following the traditional view, that the author of the Lukan writings was a traveling companion of Paul. He has also held the view that παρηκολουθηκότι in Lk. 1.3 does not mean 'investigate', as has been thought, but

---

6. E.g. Polybius; Josephus, *Ant.* 8, 13, 14. Cf. R. Laqueur, 'Ephoros 1: Die Proömien', *Hermes* 46 (1911), pp. 161-206; K.S. Sacks, 'The Lesser Prooemia of Diodorus Siculus', *Hermes* 110 (1982), pp. 434-43.

7. Cf. C.K. Barrett, 'The Third Gospel as a Preface to Acts? Some Reflections', in F. Van Segbroeck *et al.* (eds.), *The Four Gospels 1992: Festschrift Frans Neirynck* (3 vols.; Leuven: Leuven University Press, 1992), II, pp. 1451-66, esp. pp. 1463-64; I.H. Marshall, 'Acts and the "Former Treatise"', in B.W. Winter and A.D. Clarke (eds.), *The Book of Acts in its First Century Setting. I. The Book of Acts in its Ancient Literary Setting* (5 vols.; Grand Rapids: Eerdmans; Carlisle: Paternoster, 1993), pp. 163-82, esp. p. 177.

'participate', and has written a precise commentary on the preface to Luke's Gospel.[8] Since then his interpretation has had a significant influence, although Haenchen, Klein and others have maintained the meaning of παρηκολουθηκότι as 'investigate', distinguishing 'we' in the preface from 'we' in the 'we passages'.[9]

If the author of the Lukan writings was an eyewitness and directly participated in the sequence of events as a traveling companion of Paul, as Cadbury has described, then first, the three different generations of tradition history which are evidently distinguished in the preface—that is (1) 'those who were the eyewitnesses and ministers of the Word from the beginning', (2) 'many people' who 'took in hand to draw up a narrative', and (3) 'I' who try to 'write in order, investigating everything accurately from the very beginning—are blurred, particularly between (1) and (3), identifying 'I' with an eyewitness and a traveling companion. Secondly, Cadbury has to make a distinction between 'we' in 'the things that have been confirmed among us' (v. 1) and 'we' in 'those who were eyewitnesses and ministers of the Word from the beginning transmitted to us' (v. 2), taking the former as Christians in general and the latter as the generation of the author of the Lukan writings. Hence, he has to take different denotations of the same word 'we'. Such an interpretation seems to be unlikely.

Recently, in her rewritten and published doctoral thesis, L. Alexander has investigated the preface to Luke's Gospel more precisely than Cadbury.[10] In her detailed discussion, the following points are important. First, according to Alexander, the prefaces of the Greco-Roman historical works are longer than that of the Lukan writings and they are not so clearly separated from the narrative, as can be seen in Luke's Gospel. Secondly, the Greek historical prefaces are conventionally written in the third person; an address in the second person is not used. Using this theory, Alexander states her unique hypothesis that the preface to the Lukan writings is not a historical one but a scientific one;

---

8.   Cadbury, 'Commentary on the Preface of Luke'. Cf. for Cadbury, J.H. Ropes, 'St Luke's Preface: ἀσφάλεια and παρακολουθεῖν', *JTS* 25 (1923–24), pp. 67-71: against Cadbury, F.H. Colson, 'Notes on St Luke's Preface', *JTS* 24 (1922–23), pp. 300-309; A.T. Robertson, 'The Implications in Luke's Preface', *ExpTim* 35 (1923–24), pp. 319-21.

9.   Haenchen, 'Das "Wir"'; Klein, 'Lukas 1,1-4'.

10.   Alexander, *The Preface to Luke's Gospel*; cf. *idem*, 'Luke's Preface in the Context of Greek Preface-Writing', *NovT* 28 (1986), pp. 48-74.

scientific ones being distinctively separated from the narrative and usually written briefly in the first person with an address in the second person, that is, written in the form of 'label and address'. Consequently, Alexander tries to show numerous parallel passages in the scientific prefaces that are related to the preface to the Lukan writings in terms of structure, style and vocabulary in order to promote her hypothesis. Alexander selects the four most similar scientific prefaces to that of the Lukan writings in terms of structure, namely, the prefaces of Diocles of Carytus's *Letter to Antigosnus*, Demetrius's *Formae Epistolicae*, Hero of Alexandria's *Pneumatica I* and Galen of Pergamon's *De Typsis*. In this way, Alexander indicates a strong linkage between Lukan author-ship and the society of craftsmen for his social background, though she does not try to confirm the traditional view of the 'beloved physician' (Col. 4.14). But is her overall hypothesis true?

First, with regard to the brevity of Luke's preface (it consists of one sentence, containing 42 words): some scientific prefaces are longer than Luke's (e.g. Archimedes's *Methodus*) and some historical prefaces are shorter (e.g. Herodotus, 1 proem—one sentence containing 39 words). Thus, the length of the prefaces is not primarily related to their form. Further, it should be pointed out that there were criticisms of long his-torical prefaces and thus tendencies to avoid them.[11] Moreover, histori-cal prefaces can be classified into three groups (as mentioned below in detail); historical prefaces, with the causes or outlines of historical events (προέκθεσις), tend to be longer, whereas those without them (προγραφή), as in the case of the Lukan writings, tend to be shorter. Such prefaces are clearly separated from the narratives.

Secondly, with regard to the grammatical person of Luke's preface (written in the first person with a second-person address), the literary convention of using the third person in prefaces can be seen in the his-torical works of the classical period, such as Herodotus and Thucy-dides, whereas the Hellenistic-Roman historians customarily use the first person[12] in the prefaces and the third person in the narratives. In

---

11. Lucian, *Hist. Conscr.* 23; 2 Macc. 2.32: 'Here, then, without adding any-thing further, I begin my narrative. It would be absurd to make a lengthy introduc-tion to the history and cut short the history itself' (NEB).

12. In the first person singular, Polybius; 2 Maccabees; Livy; in the first person plural, Dionysius of Halicarnassus; Josephus, *Ant.*, *War*; Tacitus, *Historia*; Appian; Dio Cassius.

addition, the second-person address does not have anything to do with the form of prefaces or their literary genre, but may be more related to the familiar relationship between the author and the reader.

According to the study of R.J. Starr, literary texts in the Roman age circulated in three stages: (1) the inner circle of the author's friends, that is, by the author reading the text in front of his close friends, his dedication of the text as gift copies to his friends and the circulation of the text among its dedicatees; (2) the outer circle of strangers, that is, by the author reading or copying the text among friends of friends, who were not directly acquainted with the author; and (3) the circulation by professional bookdealers.[13]

If this hypothesis is right, and the Lukan writings circulated in a similar way, it seems likely that the Lukan writings were written, whether actually or fictitiously, conscious of the inner circle of friends, not the outer circle of strangers. For Luke's preface has only the name of the dedicatee, not the author's own name, which indicates that the author is well known to the inner circle and did not need to be mentioned in the preface. Hence, the second-person address in Luke's preface should not be ascribed to the form of prefaces, but rather to the intimate relationship between the author and the reader.

Thirdly, with regard to the premise that the words in Luke's preface are typically used in historical prefaces,[14] Alexander tries to show (with a number of examples) that these words are common to the scientific prefaces. But these typical words are rarely seen in the four most simi-

---

13. R.J. Starr, 'The Circulation of Literary Text in the Roman World', *ClQ* 37 (1987), pp. 213-23.

14. E.g. ἐπειδήπερ, Josephus, *War* 1.1.17: ἐπιχειρεῖν, Dionysius of Halicarnassus, 1.7.3: διήγησις, Dionysius of Halicarnassus, 1.8.2; Josephus, *Ant.* 1.67: πράγματα, Polybius, 1.1.3; Josephus, *Ant.* 1.26: there are a number of references to αὐτόπτης, καθεξῆς or ἀκριβῶς in the historical prefaces. The following articles are written in order to support Luke the historian: W.C. van Unnik, 'The "Book of Acts": The Confirmation of the Gospel', *NovT* 4 (1960), pp. 25-59; *idem*, 'Remarks on the Purpose of Luke's Historical Writings (Luke I 1-4)', in *idem, Sparsa Collecta* (3 vols.; Leiden: E.J. Brill, 1973), I, pp. 6-15; D.J. Sneen, 'An Exegesis of Luke 1:1-4 with Special Regard to Luke's Purpose as a Historian', *ExpTim* 83 (1971–72), pp. 40-43; I.I. du Plessis, 'Once More: The Purpose of Luke's Prologue (Lk I 1-4)', *NovT* 16 (1972), pp. 259-71; T. Callan, 'The Preface of Luke–Acts and Historiography', *NTS* 31 (1985), pp. 576-81; C.J. Hemer, *The Book of Acts in the Setting of Hellenistic History* (Tübingen: J.C.B. Mohr, 1989), pp. 321-28.

lar prefaces to Luke's that Alexander has selected in terms of structure. Thus it is not possible to decide whether Luke's preface is a scientific one or a historical one solely by vocabulary or by structure. Instead, we have to analyse the structure of the historical prefaces, which Alexander has failed to look at. Then the problem is whether the typical and common vocabulary can be seen in reference to the structure of the historical prefaces or not. For these reasons, it is not tenable to say, as does Alexander, that Luke's preface is a scientific one in the 'label and address' form.

III

Although the Hellenistic-Roman historical works do not always have prefaces,[15] if they are there, what kind of structure do they have? Lucian points out two elements of the historical prefaces: one theme is to tell the significance, necessity or utility of a historical subject, and the other is to show the causes or outlines of historical events. He mentions the prefaces by Herodotus and Thucydides as good examples.[16]

D. Earl states that the historical prefaces consist of three elements, adding the presentation of the historical subject to Lucian's indications, namely: (1) the presentation of a historical subject; (2) the importance of the subject; and (3) the outline of historical events. He also says that such a form of historical preface can be seen in works from Herodotus and Thucydides, passing through Livy, Josephus, Florus and Appian, to Bede in the seventh century.[17]

However, as we observe the prefaces of the Hellenistic-Roman historical works more carefully and precisely, it seems likely that they are composed of more detailed elements, that is: (1) the historical subject and its importance; (2) criticism against predecessors; (3) the sources or qualifications of the historian; (4) the causes or outlines of historical events; and (5) the purpose of historiography. These elements are the ideal types, so the order of the elements may be different in some cases, or certain elements may be missing in others.

15. Lucian, *Hist. Conscr.* 23, compares the history without a preface to 'the body without the head'.

16. Lucian, *Hist. Conscr.* 53.

17. D. Earl, 'Prologue-Form in Ancient Historiography', in *ANRW*, pp. 842-56.

1. The subject and its importance. A historical subject as an object of historiography tends to be told at the beginning of prefaces, sometimes briefly and sometimes in detail.[18] This is mentioned consistently from Herodotus onwards. The importance of the subject of historiography is often mentioned with it.[19]

2. Criticism against predecessors. The treatments of the same subject by preceding historians are said to be inadequate, so the necessity to write a history in a new way is described.[20] This is a tradition developed from Hecataeus and Thucydides onwards.

3. The sources or qualifications of the historian. The Hellenistic-Roman historians often refer to the sources of historiography or, in the case of describing what they have experienced, make reference to their qualifications to relate properly as historians, instead of the sources.[21]

4. The causes or outlines of historical events. The Hellenistic-Roman historians often mention why the historical events took place previously,[22] or summarize the historical events that are going to be told.[23] This is a custom seen since Thucydides.

5. The purpose of historiography. The Hellenistic-Roman historians make known the purpose of historiography, or why they write histories. Sometimes this is mentioned in the middle of the preface; at other times it comes at the end.[24] This is a tradition noted since Herodotus.

The historical prefaces can be mainly divided into two groups: the preface to the whole work in the first volume; and the preface to each

18. E.g. Polybius, 1.1.1-6; Dionysius of Halicarnassus, 1.1-3; Josephus, *War* 1.1, *Ant.* 1.5-9; 2 Macc. 2.19-32; Livy, 1.1-5.

19. E.g. Polybius, 1.2.1-8; Dionysius of Halicarnassus, 1.4; Josephus, *War* 1.13-16.

20. E.g. Polybius, 1.4.1-9: Dionysius of Halicarnassus, 1.6; Josephus, *War* 1.2, 7-8, *Ant.* 1.1-3; 2 Macc. 2.24.

21. E.g. Dionysius of Halicarnassus, 1.7; Josephus, *War* 1.3, 17-18, *Ant.* 1.10-26; Livy, 1.6-9; Dio Cassius, 1.2.

22. E.g. Josephus, *War* 1.4-5.

23. E.g. Polybius, 1.5.1-5; Dionysius of Halicarnassus, 1.8; Josephus, *War* 1.19-30.

24. E.g. Polybius, 1.4.10-11; Dionysius of Halicarnassus, 1.5; Josephus, *War* 1.9-12, *Ant.* 1.4; 2 Macc. 2.25-32; Livy, 1.10-13; Dio Cassius, 1.3.

volume in the series. Furthermore, the former can be divided into two: the type called προγραφή, which lacks the element of (4), following Herodotus;[25] and the type called προέκθεσις, which includes the element of (4), following Thucydides.[26] The latter is the type called ἀνακεφαλαίωσις, which summarizes the contents of the previous volume. Compared with this structure of the Hellenistic-Roman historical prefaces, the preface to Luke's Gospel can be analysed as follows.

1. The subject of the Lukan writings is briefly mentioned after περί: 'concerning the things that have been confirmed among us'. 'The things that have been confirmed' (v. 1) are the events of Jesus Christ—that is, the crucifixion and resurrection, the gospel, and its development.

2. The phrase 'inasmuch as many people took in hand to draw up a narrative' (v. 1) refers to the predecessors. The expression 'it seemed good to me also that I write to you in order, investigating everything accurately from the very beginning' (v. 3) implies criticism against these predecessors—that is, the historical treatments of the predecessors are not detailed enough, so the author intends to check them thoroughly and rewrite the account again.

3. 'Just as those who were the eyewitnesses and ministers of the Word from the beginning transmitted to us' (v. 2): the word 'transmitted' here implies the existence of oral traditions. Moreover, the phrase 'many people took in hand to draw up a narrative' (v. 1) presupposes the existence of certain written traditions. Further, the expression 'investigating everything accurately from the very beginning' refers to how to deal with these oral and written traditions.

4. The preface to Luke's Gospel is written very briefly so it lacks the causes or outlines of historical events.

5. The phrase 'in order that you might know the certainty of the words that you were instructed' (v. 4) explicitly mentions the literary purpose of the Lukan writings.

Hence, it is evident that the preface to Luke's Gospel tallies with the

25. E.g. Josephus, *Ant.*; 2 Macc.; Livy; Dio Cassius. Concerning προγραφή, προέκθεσις and ἀνακεφαλαίωσις, cf. Laqueur, 'Ephoros'; Cadbury, 'Commentary on the Preface of Luke', p. 491 n. 1: but I correct their contradicted concepts here.

26. E.g. Polybius; Dionysius of Halicarnassus; Josephus, *War*.

structure of the Hellenistic-Roman historical prefaces, particularly with the type called προγραφή. However, the preface to the Acts of the Apostles, the second volume of the Lukan writings, summarizes the contents of Luke's Gospel, the first volume, very concisely (Acts 1.1-2), which follows the pattern of ἀνακεφαλαίωσις.

IV

In this way, the author of the Lukan writings composes the preface in the manner of the Hellenistic-Roman historical works, not that of the scientific ones. In the preface to Luke's Gospel there are many conventional words which can be found in historical prefaces, including the *hapax legomena* and rare words which are typically seen in the Lukan writings;[27] some rhetorical elements are also found in it.

First, the author of the Lukan writings uses the word διήγησις (narrative), instead of Mark's εὐαγγέλιον (good news) (Mk 1.1), in order to refer to the contents of his description, which is often employed in the historical prefaces,[28] not in the scientific ones. Yet it also has a rhetorical sense which denotes a narrative, *narratio*, distinguished from a preface, *exordium*. Rhetoric is the way to persuade the audience or to make people believe by the statement (*narratio*) as Cicero and Quintilian mention: 'The statement is an explanation of the facts and as it were a base and foundation for the establishment of belief';[29] 'The statement of facts consists in the persuasive exposition of that which either has been done or is supposed to have been done'.[30] In historiography such persuasive perspective is also retained by telling stories in dramatic episodic style.[31] The word πράγματα is also utilized both in historiography and in rhetoric.

Secondly, the word πεπληροφορημένων is employed when referring to the subject of the Lukan writings. It is a perfect passive of a compound verb πληροῦν with φορεῖν, and has ambiguous meanings such as (1) 'to be accomplished';[32] (2) 'to be confirmed';[33] and (3) 'to be

27. One example of historical prefaces that is quite similar to Luke's preface is shown as follows, in which many typical words are compiled: Josephus, *War* 1.17.

28. Cf. n. 14.

29. Cicero, *De Part. Or.* 9.31 (LCL).

30. Quintilian, 4.2.31 (LCL).

31. Cf. E. Plümacher, *Lukas als hellenistischer Schriftsteller* (Göttingen: Vandenhoeck & Ruprecht, 1972).

32. E.g. A. Plummer, *The Gospel According to S. Luke* (ICC; Edinburgh: T. &

fulfilled'.[34] This word is particularly connected to the theological concept of the fulfilment of the Old Testament, which is also seen in the Lukan writings,[35] and the verb πληροφορεῖν is thought to be a synonym of πληροῦν so that most commentators take it to mean 'to be accomplished' or 'to be fulfilled'. However, as Rengstorf and Grundmann have pointed out in their commentaries, it has another possible meaning: 'to be confirmed'.[36] Therefore, if the literary purpose of the Lukan writings is to reveal the certainty (ἀσφάλεια) of the instructed teachings, it is better to interpret it as 'the things that have been confirmed among us' than to interpret it as 'the things that have been accomplished among us' or 'the things that have been fulfilled among us', in order to make it clear that the subject and the literary purpose of the Lukan writings correspond to each other consistently. That is, the literary purpose of the Lukan writings is to make the reader believe that 'the things that have been confirmed among us' have 'certainty'. If this is the correct sense, the verb πληροφορεῖν is closely related to the rhetorical term πληροφολία (assurance). In other words, rhetoric is a technique used to persuade the other party; it is an art to give assurance to the persuaded side.[37]

Thirdly, the word πολλοί (many [people]) is seen in the author's criticism against his predecessors. It has been pointed out that πολύς and its equivalents are rhetorically utilized in the introductory part of

T. Clark, 1901), p. 3; Cadbury, 'Commentary on the Preface of Luke', pp. 495-96; Klostermann, *Lukasevangelium*, p. 2; Brown, 'The Role of the Prologue', pp. 102-103; Dillon, 'Previewing Luke's Project', pp. 221-22.

33. E.g. K.H. Rengstorf, *Das Evangelium nach Lukas* (NTD, 3; Göttingen: Vandenhoeck & Ruprecht, 1974), pp. 43-44; W. Grundmann, *Das Evangelium nach Lukas* (THKNT, 3; Berlin: Evangelische Verlagsanstalt, 1978), pp. 43-44.

34. E.g. Creed, *St Luke*, p. 3; I.H. Marshall, *Gospel of Luke* (NIGTC; Exeter: Paternoster, 1978), p. 41; Fitzmyer, *Luke*, p. 283.

35. Cf. M.C. Parsons, *The Departure of Jesus in Luke–Acts: The Ascension Narratives in Conflict* (JSNTSup, 21; Sheffield: JSOT Press, 1987), pp. 83-91; D. Peterson, 'The Motif of Fulfilment and the Purpose of Luke–Acts', in Winter and Clarke (eds.), *The Book of Acts in its Ancient Literary Setting*, pp. 83-104.

36. LSJ and BAGD mention that 'to be assured or convinced' is applied to the person and in the passive, while 'to be fulfilled or accomplished' is of the thing and in the passive, and most commentaries follow these distinctions. But 'to be assured' is implied of the thing and in the passive, as in Ignatius, *Phld. prescr.*, in that case of the instituted church.

37. E.g. Plato, *Gorgias* 453a, πειθοῦς δημιουργός ἐστιν ἡ ῥητορική; Aristotle, *Rhet.* 1.2; Cicero, *Inv.* 2.2.6; Quintilian, 2.15.13.

the speeches and arguments.[38] The positive attitude to his predecessors, namely 'many people', is seen, on the one hand, in the expressions like 'just as' (καθώς) and 'it seemed good to me also' (ἔδοξε κἀμοί), showing his intention to follow his predecessors, using them as his models.[39] On the other hand, a negative attitude is also found in phrases such as 'I write to you in order...investigating everything accurately from the very beginning', implying he felt his predecessors to be inadequate.[40] In this way, the 'many people' that the author of the Lukan writings describes in positive and negative ways can be identified as mainly two predecessors, that is, Mark's Gospel and 'Q'—particularly the former, which gives the framework of Luke's Gospel and is revised by the author at the same time, rather than the latter, which seems to retain the original traditions more faithfully in Luke's Gospel. It is a rhetorical emphasis to refer to a very limited number of examples as 'many people'. Thus, the author tries to appeal to the antiquity of traditions with the phrase 'from the beginning' (ἀπ' ἀρχῆς), as well as to a number of traditions with the emphatic expression 'many people' in order to persuade the reader.

Fourthly, the word καθεξῆς is used in the historical treatment of the sources. Since this adverb has ambiguous meanings, it has been discussed in various ways. For example, some try to take it as equivalent to ἑξῆς ('one after another' or 'as it follows') which is often found in the historical works.[41] Certainly, in some instances καθεξῆς is interchangeable with ἑξῆς,[42] and in other cases it has another sense of 'in order',[43] therefore, it does not always have the same meaning. On the

---

38. J. Bauer, 'POLLOI LUKE I.1', *NovT* 4 (1960), pp. 263-66.

39. Cadbury, 'Commentary on the Preface of Luke', pp. 493-94; Brown, 'The Role of the Prologue', p. 103; Marshall, *Luke*, p. 41; Schneider, *Die Apostelgeschichte*, I, p. 38; Schweizer, *Lukas*, p. 11.

40. Klein, Conzelmann, Haenchen and others point out that ἐπιχειρεῖν has a negative nuance, based on the other two examples, critical to the predecessors. On the other hand, G.E. Sterling, *Historiography and Self-Definition: Josephos, Luke–Acts and Apologetic Historiography* (Leiden: E.J. Brill, 1992), pp. 341-45, mentions it as ambivalent to the predecessors, referring to Josephus, *Ant.* 1.10-13, as an example.

41. Cadbury, 'Commentary on the Preface of Luke', p. 505; J. Kurzingeer, 'Lk 1:3: ἀκριβῶς καθεξῆς σοι γράφαι', *BZ* 18 (1974), pp. 249-55; Brown, 'The Role of the Prologue'.

42. Lk. 8.1; Acts 3.24, 18.23.

43. Acts 11.4. Cf. ἑξῆς, Lk. 7.11, 9.37; Acts 21.1, 25.17, 27.18.

other hand, Klein interprets it in the sense of 'chronologically structured',[44] Völkel as 'materially structured'[45] and Moessner as 'getting
his story straight'.[46] If criticism against the predecessors is seen in
καθεξῆς as mentioned above, it is better to take the positive meanings
such as 'chronologically structured', 'materially structured' or 'getting
his story straight' than to take the negative ones such as 'one after
another' or 'as it follows'. However, it is evident that Mark's Gospel
(which gives the framework of Luke's Gospel) is not written in chronological order like a history or a biography, as form criticism has
revealed, and that Luke's Gospel, the revised edition of Mark, is not
restructured in chronological order (as can be seen from one example,
that Jesus' inaugural speech at Nazareth [Lk. 5] is placed at the beginning of the Galilean mission and understood as the theme speech). In
this respect it seems likely that καθεξῆς here means 'in order' with a
nuance of 'materially structured' or 'getting his story straight' in the
narratological sense. If such interpretation is right, καθεξῆς in this
sense is synonymous with the rhetorical expressions ἐν τάξει or κατὰ
τάξιν (orderly).

According to Lucian, a historian first collects the historical materials
(written documents and oral traditions), then makes them into 'a series
of notes' (ὑπομνήματα) without beauty and continuity, and finally
'arranges them into order' (ἐπιθεὶς τὴν τάξιν), giving beauty and continuity with charms of expression, figure and rhythm.[47] If this process
of historiography is applied to that used in the Lukan writings, it seems
likely that the author, who has a literary consciousness as evident from

44. Klein, 'Lukas I.1-4', p. 195, 'chronologisch strukturiert'; further, concerning the chronological and historical order, cf. Marshall, *Luke*, p. 43. Schneider
('Zur Bedeutung von καθεξῆς im lukanischen Doppelwerk', *ZNW* 68 [1977], pp.
128-31, and *Apostelgeschichte*, I, p. 39) adds a salvation-historical nuance to it.

45. M. Völkel, 'Exegetische Erwagungen zum Verstandnis des Begriffs
kathexes im lukanischen Prolog', *NTS* 20 (1973–74), pp. 289-99, esp. p. 299,
'sachlich structuriert'; F. Mussner ('Καθεξῆς im Lukasprolog', in E.E. Ellis and E.
Grässer [eds.], *Jesus und Paulus: Festschrift für W.G. Kümmel zum 70. Geburtstag*
[Göttingen: Vandenhoeck & Ruprecht, 1975], pp. 253-55) adds a nuance 'perfectly
without exceptions' (lückenlos ohne Ausnahme) to it.

46. D.P. Moessner, 'The Meaning of ΚΑΘΕΞΕΣ in the Lukan Prologue as a
Key to the Distinctive Contribution of Luke's Narrative among the "Many"', in
Van Segbroeck *et al.* (eds.), *The Four Gospels*, II, pp. 1513-28.

47. Lucian, *Hist. Conscr.* 48.

the preface to Luke's Gospel, recognizes Mark's Gospel as 'a series of notes' without rhetorical order and embellishments when it is handed over to him. Thus, the author uses the 'Q' source and other materials (1) to initiate the beautiful opening scenes, in order to correct the abrupt beginning of Mark's Gospel by introducing the birth narrative (Lk. 1–2); (2) to supplement the sudden and incomplete ending of Mark's Gospel by adding other traditions in the resurrection narrative (Lk. 24); (3) to insert the Samaritan Journey in the central section (Lk. 9.51–18.14) in order to complement the inadequate episodes and teachings of Jesus in Mark's Gospel and transform the two-part structure of Mark's Gospel (Galilee–Jerusalem) into three (Galilee–Samaria–Jerusalem); (4) to add the speeches in the middle of the Galilean section (Lk. 6.17-49) and at the beginning of the Samaritan section (Lk. 10.1-12) in order to supplement the speech part; (5) to make clear the theme of Jesus' mission in the inaugural speech at Nazareth; and, finally, (6) in the second volume of the Lukan writings, equivalent to the first volume, to fill up the gap in the period after Mark. In this way, the word καθεξῆς has a rhetorical sense of to 'arrange in order', 'a series of notes', namely, Mark's Gospel.

Fifthly, the author employs the word ἀσφάλεια to clarify the literary purpose of the Lukan writings. This is an ambiguous word which has several meanings, such as 'certainty' and 'safety'. Most historical works were written for the sake of 'truth' (ἀληθεία), 'usefulness' (ὠφελεία) or 'pleasure' (φυχαγωγία). However, the Lukan writings were written for 'certainty' or 'safety', not for the sake of 'truth'.[48] If so, this ἀσφάλεια is a rhetorical term like πληροφολία, as mentioned above. That is, it is a technical term to persuade the reader to make them believe in the certainty, to convince them. The Lukan writings are written in order to give the reader 'certainty', which is the goal of rhetoric. Moreover, such persuasive ways have two phases: one is by way of using testimonies of eyewitnesses and documents, but not in the proper persuasive technique (ἀτεχνή); the other is by way of rhetoric proper (ἐν τεχνή). The author of the Lukan writings does not try to prove his argument as a rhetorician, but rather attempts to utilize testimonies and documents as a historian. However, when he intends to narrate a history to 'arrange them in order', he writes not as a simple

48. BAGD, van Unnik ('The "Book of Acts"') and others almost identify 'truth' with 'certainty'.

historian, but as a historian in the literary sense, that is, as a rhetorical historian with a number of rhetorical techniques.

V

It is evident from the argument above that the preface to the Lukan writings is not a scientific one, as Alexander has discussed, but rather a historical one, and that the author's rhetorical intention can also be seen in it. In other words, the subject of the Lukan writings is 'the things that have been convinced' which can lead to 'belief' (πίστις) by way of 'persuasion' (πειθεῖν). 'The things' are rewritten following and criticizing 'many people' at the same time—but in fact the predecessor is mainly Mark's Gospel—adding other sources and traditions and 'arranging them in order'. Moreover, they are depicted in order to make the reader know that the transmitted teachings are 'certain'. There were chiefly two trends of historiography in the Hellenistic-Roman age, namely, political historiography and rhetorical historiography. The historiography of the Lukan writings belongs to the latter, which includes the literary elements in it and persuades the reader of its purpose.[49]

As a result, the author and the reader can be considered at several levels. First, what can we know of the real author in the preface? The author is traditionally ascribed to the co-worker of Paul, 'Luke the physician' (Col. 4.14; 2 Tim. 4.11; Phlm. 11). However, this tradition goes back to the so-called 'anti-Marcionite prologue', Irenaeus and the Muratorian Canon at the end of the second century, but not earlier than that.[50] Moreover, the original texts seem to have lacked titles '(The

---

49. On the difference between political historiography and rhetorical historiography, cf. K. Yamada, 'A Rhetorical History: The Literary Genre of the Acts of the Apostles', in S.E. Porter and T.H. Olbricht (eds.), *Rhetoric, Scripture and Theology: Essays from the 1994 Pretoria Conference* (JSNTSup, 131; Sheffield: Sheffield Academic Press, 1996), pp. 234-54. Related to this article, see other attempts to read rhetorical elements in Luke's preface in different perspectives, such as F.H. Colson, 'Τάξει in Papias', *JTS* 24 (1922–23), pp. 62-69; W.S. Kurz, 'Hellenistic Rhetoric in the Christological Proof of Luke–Acts', *CBQ* 42 (1980), pp. 171-95; E. Guttgemanns, 'In welchem Sinne ist Lukas "Historiker"? Die Beziehungen von Luk 1,1-4 und Papias zur antiken Rhetorik', *LB* 54 (1983), pp. 9-26; F. Siegert, 'Lukas—ein Historiker, d.h. ein Rhetor?', *LB* 55 (1984), pp. 57-60.

50. The so-called 'anti-Marcionite prologue' (the prologue to Luke); Irenaeus, *Ad. haer.* 3.1.1, 3.14.1; Canon Muratori, ll. 1-8, 34-39: cf. H.J. Cadbury, 'The Tradition', in Foakes Jackson and Lake (eds.), *The Beginnings of Christianity*, II,

Gospel) According to Luke' (κατὰ Λούκαν) and 'The Acts of the Apostles' (πράξεις 'Αποστόλων). Rather, these titles were added to the manuscripts in later days, which is evident from the fact that the first and second volumes of the Lukan writings have different titles. That means, when the titles were added to the manuscripts, they had already been separated and were considered to be different genres. Thus there is no trace of identification of authorship in the original texts. Further-more, it has often been pointed out that medical language can be found in the Lukan writings. However, such medical language is not only limited to the medical works, but can also be seen in the literary works by the Hellenistic-Roman *literati*.[51] Hence, we know nearly nothing about the real author, though we still use the traditional term 'Luke' or 'Lukan', which does not imply the historical man 'Luke the physician'. But it is evident from the preface to Luke's Gospel that the implied author of the text is a male[52] who seems to have got so acquainted with the implied reader that he did not need to mention his own name; moreover, he is a rhetorical historian who is going to persuade the implied reader. Further, the first person 'I' or 'we' in the preface does not seem to refer to the real author or the implied author, but rather the narrator who tells the narrative world of the Lukan writings in which Jesus (the protagonist), the religious authorities (the antagonists), the disciples and followers of Jesus, the people and Jews, and so on, appear as *dramatis personae*.[53]

pp. 209-64; A. Huck and H. Lietzmann, *Synopse der drei ersten Evangelien* (Tübingen: J.C.B. Mohr, 11th edn, 1970), pp. vii-ix; C.K. Barrett, *The Acts of the Apostles* (ICC; 2 vols.; Edinburgh: T. & T. Clark, 1994–98), I, pp. 30-48.

51. Against W.K. Hobart (*The Medical Language of St Luke* [Dublin: Hodges & Figgs; London: Longmans & Green, 1892]), see H. Cadbury, *The Style and Literary Method of Luke* (Cambridge, MA: Harvard University Press, 1920); *idem*, *The Making of Luke–Acts* (New York: Macmillan, 1927; repr. London: SPCK, 1958), pp. 219-20.

52. The word παρηκολουθηκότι is an active perfect participle masculine singular dative of παρακολουθεῖν.

53. T. Onuki, in *Hukuinsyo Kenkyu to Bungaku Syakaigaku* [*Studies for the Gospels and Sociology of Literature*] (Tokyo: Iwanami Syoten, 1992), pp. 52-54, takes 'I' as 'a fictitious narrator' and 'Theophilus' as 'a fictitious narratee'.

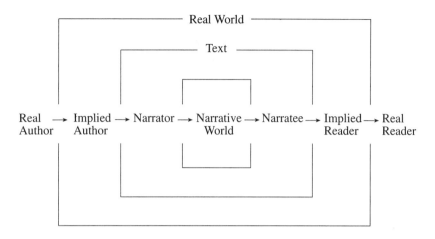

Then who is the real reader? The Lukan writings are dedicated to a person called 'Theophilus', as seen in the prefaces to Luke's Gospel and the Acts of the Apostles. Who was Theophilus and did he really exist or not? First, concerning the honorary form of address κράτιστος: it has sometimes been argued that Theophilus was a Roman officer of a high position, based on the fact that this form of address was used when referring to a higher social rank than the knight class, particularly to the Roman procurators (Acts 23.26; 24.3; 26.25). But the usage of this term was not limited to the Roman bureaucratic society—it was also used as a form of polite address to a respected person without any official connotation in outer circles of the bureaucratic society.[54] Thus it cannot be said whether Theophilus was a Roman officer of a high rank or not. Secondly, it is often said that Theophilus was a catechumen or a Christian, based on the sentence 'in order that you might know the certainty of the words that you were instructed'. The word 'catechumenos' (κατηχούμενος)—he who is instructed by catechism before baptism— derives from the word 'instructed' (κατηχήθης); however, it did not have such a limited connotation at this time. Moreover, although it is obvious that Theophilus received Christian teachings, it is not certain from this simple fact whether he was a Christian or not. Thirdly, it is affirmed that the dedicatee was a patron or a publisher.[55] Surely, Atticus, to whom Cicero had written a number of letters, was a

54. Cf. Josephus, *Life* 430; *Apion* 1.1: Epaphroditus is addressed by the honorary title, 'most excellent', but he seems to have been a libertine.

55. E.J. Goodspeed, 'Some Greek Notes I: Was Theophilus Luke's Publisher?', *JBL* 73 (1954), p. 84; Haenchen, *Die Apostelgeschichte*, p. 143 n. 4.

publisher of Cicero, and Epaphroditus, to whom Josephus had dedicated his literary works, was a publisher of Josephus.[56] But it cannot be said that since the dedicatees were *often* patrons or publishers, the dedicatees were *always* patrons or publishers. On this evidence, various aspects could be considered about the historical man Theophilus; however, there are no definite ones. Hence, we know nearly nothing about the real reader. The implied reader of the text in the preface was instructed in the Christian teachings and is the object of the rhetorical persuasion. 'Theophilus' in this sense is rather a narratee of the historical story-world of the Lukan writings. In that case the name 'Theophilus' (Θεοφίλος) has a symbolic nuance, 'a friend of God (θεοφίλος). In other words, it is expected in this story-world to be 'a friend of God' persuaded by the Word of God and warned not to be 'an enemy of God' (θεομάχος) opposing it (Acts 5.39).[57]

As mentioned above, the real author and the real reader are not known to us in the preface, although it can be seen that the implied author intends to persuade the implied reader. Thus the first person 'I' or 'we' who appears in the preface is a narrator of the story-world and 'Theophilus' is a narratee. The historical story-world is going to be developed by the *dramatis personae* of Jesus, the protagonist, the religious authorities (the antagonists), the disciples, the people and others between this narrator 'I' or 'we' and its narratee 'Theophilus'. In this way, the rhetorical program of the Lukan writings is described in the preface.

56. Josephus, *Life* 430, *Ant.* 1.1.2, *Apion* 1.1.

57. The Acts of the Apostles is very much related to the literary topos of θεομάχια; cf. W. Nestle, 'Legenden vom Tod der Gottesverächter', *ARW* 33 (1936), pp. 246-69; J. Kamerbeek, 'On the Conception of θεομάχος in Relation with Greek Tragedy', *Mnemosyne* 4th series, 1 (1948), pp. 271-83.

RHETORICAL ARGUMENTATION AND
THE CULTURE OF APOCALYPTIC:
A SOCIO-RHETORICAL ANALYSIS OF LUKE 21

L. Gregory Bloomquist

In his 1995 programmatic essay for the London rhetoric conference, Vernon Robbins pointed to the need to determine kinds of rhetorical argumentation more carefully. In his presentation, he astutely singled out apocalyptic, which, though long an object of scholarly interest,[1] has largely been absent from scholarly studies of rhetoric until recently.[2] One of the reasons for this absence is because 'apocalyptic rhetoric' has simply not been prominent as an object of study by those interested either in the rhetorical analysis of Scripture or in the study of apocalyp-

1.   See especially J.J. Collins (ed.), *Apocalypse: The Morphology of a Genre*, *Semeia* 14 (1979); and David Hellholm (ed.), *Apocalypticism in the Mediterranean World and the Near East: Proceedings of the International Colloquium on Apocalypticism, Uppsala, August 12–17, 1979* (Tübingen: J.C.B. Mohr, 1983).

2.   Among the first to treat it as such was Amos Niven Wilder ('The Rhetoric of Ancient and Modern Apocalyptic', *Int* 25 [1971], pp. 436-53). See now also, however, Ronald F. Reid, 'Apocalypticism and Typology: Rhetorical Dimensions of a Symbolic Reality', *Quarterly Journal of Speech* 69 (1983), pp. 229-48; Barry Brummett, *Contemporary Apocalyptic Rhetoric* (New York: Praeger, 1991); Stephen D. O'Leary, 'A Dramatistic Theory of Apocalyptic Rhetoric', *Quarterly Journal of Speech* 79 (1993), pp. 385-426; *idem, Arguing the Apocalypse: A Theory of Millennial Rhetoric* (Oxford: Oxford University Press, 1994); and Edith Humphrey, '"I Saw Satan Fall": The Rhetoric of Vision', *ARC: Journal of the Faculty of Religious Studies, McGill University* 21 (1993), pp. 75-88. See also representative directions in papers at the 1995 London Conference: Gary S. Selby, 'Paul the Seer: The Rhetorical Persona in 1 Corinthians 2.1-16'; and Verena Jegher-Bucher, '"The Thorn in the Flesh"/"Der Pfahl im Fleisch": Considerations about 2 Corinthians 12.7-10 in Connection with 12.1-13', both in S.E. Porter and T.H. Olbricht (eds.), *The Rhetorical Analysis of Scripture: Essays from the 1995 London Conference* (JSNTSup, 146; Sheffield: Sheffield Academic Press, 1997), pp. 351-73, 388-97 respectively.

tic.[3] Furthermore, a definition of 'apocalyptic rhetoric' is difficult.[4] Not only was apocalyptic not a subject matter of rhetorical handbooks in antiquity, but, according to Stephen O'Leary, modern interest in apocalyptic has been largely limited to 'trying to explain the appeal of apocalyptic discourse by discovering audience predispositions based in conditions of social and economic class, in experience of calamity, or in psychological anomie', in other words, everywhere but in discourse.[5]

In this essay I propose to use the insights gained from socio-rhetorical criticism to examine the so-called apocalyptic material found in Luke 21 in order to determine what kind of material in fact it is.[6] Following Vernon Robbins's lead, I shall first set forth the data for my study in terms of attention to innertexture, which, according to Robbins, yields 'initial insight into the argumentation in the text'.[7] I shall then proceed to analysis of the intertexture, a comparison of patterns in the subject text with other patterns, in an attempt to deal with the question 'with what texts does this text stand in dialogue?'[8] Thirdly, I shall

---

3.   There is no dedicated treatment of apocalyptic rhetoric in Hellholm (ed.), *Apocalypticism in the Mediterranean World and the Near East*.

4.   According to O'Leary, *Arguing the Apocalypse*, p. 15, the approach to apocalyptic rhetoric that seeks to determine genre reaches a dead-end; therefore, O'Leary argues for a 'dramatistic and argumentative analysis guided by the root metaphor of contextualism'. The larger methodological question here is the one that I pose in a paper entitled 'Methodological Criteria for the Determination of Apocalyptic Rhetoric', presented to the Rhetoric and the New Testament Group of the SBL in November 1996, New Orleans, LA.

5.   O'Leary, *Arguing the Apocalypse*, p. 11.

6.   Greg Carey has also sought to address this question. Carey's work first appeared in the form of a paper to the 1995 Sociology of Early Christianity Workshop (Montreal, Québec) to which I was the respondent. I am thankful to Mr Carey for the privilege to have been the respondent at the SEC Workshop to his paper.

7.   Vernon K. Robbins, 'Socio-Rhetorical Criticism: Mary, Elizabeth and the Magnificat as a Test Case', in E.S. Malbon and E.V. McKnight (eds.), *The New Literary Criticism and the New Testament* (JSNTSup, 109; Sheffield: JSOT Press, 1994), pp. 164-209, esp. p. 171, following C. Perelman and L. Olbrechts-Tyteca, *The New Rhetoric: A Treatise on Argumentation* (trans. J. Wilkinson and P. Weaver; Notre Dame: University of Notre Dame Press, 1969).

8.   Robbins, 'Socio-Rhetorical Criticism', p. 179. V.K. Robbins, 'Summary of Socio-Rhetorical Analysis and Interpretation', unpublished paper, 1995, p. 7, notes that these 'texts' are to be understood in the widest sense: 'In other words, the interaction of the text being interpreted with other material and physical "objects",

examine the socio-cultural texture to which the patterns and comparisons point, since, as socio-rhetorical analysis presupposes, richly textured texts have an existence in a complex web not just of literary relationships (intertexture) but also of social and cultural relationships. Finally, I shall analyze the ideological texture, which relates to the patterns of reading not in terms of 'how' but in terms of 'why'.[9] Here we begin to bring together the use of rhetoric to understand ancient texts and the insights of wider rhetorical analysis as taught in a variety of contexts, including implications for rhetorical argumentation in an ancient and in a contemporary mode.

Because analysis of ideological texture is the least developed and most debated aspect of socio-rhetorical analysis, the implications for this analysis of the work of people such as Thomas Olbricht is very significant at precisely this point. Olbricht's work in this field not only suggests the need to expand on rhetorical analysis as applied to biblical study, but also suggests ways of doing so. It is entirely appropriate then, in a volume of studies that honours the work of Tom Olbricht, that the influence of his work on this new method of analysis be more fully brought to light.

1. *Innertextural Analysis*

Attention to innertexture is a stage of attention that is prior to any analysis of meanings. According to Robbins, the critic at this stage attends to 'words, word patterns, voices, structures, devices, and modes in the text' as 'the context for meanings and meaning effects which are then analyzed with the other readings of the text'.[10]

Robbins identifies five groupings of elements in the study of the innertexture of a text:[11] 'repetitive texture and pattern' (repetition of

with historical events, with other texts, and with customs, values, roles, institutions, and systems'. I believe that Robbins involves interpretive steps here that should again be understood to have their proper place in the 'social-cultural texture' analysis.

9. According to Robbins ('Summary', p. 15), the analysis of the ideological texture of a text 'focuses on self-interests. What and whose self-interests are being negotiated in this text? If the dominant voices in the text persuade people to act according to their premises, who will gain and who will lose? What will be gained and what will be lost?'

10. Robbins, 'Summary', p. 4.

11. Robbins, 'Socio-Rhetorical Criticism', p. 165. The basic rhetorical elements

words, phrases, and topics throughout the unit); 'progressive texture and pattern' (sequences of words, phrases and topics that form patterns throughout the unit); 'narrational texture and pattern' (attention to the patterns formed by the voices of those in the text, including narrator and actors); 'opening-middle-closing texture and pattern'; and 'argumentative texture and pattern' (support via argumentation for statements made in the text).[12]

In determining the outlines of an initial sketch of the innertexture, we may first note some salient elements of repetition found in Luke (and, where relevant, in Acts).[13] At this stage of the study, we wish to attend to lexical patterns of repetition, such as connectives and particles (μή and οὐ, τις and τι), verbs, pronouns (αὐτός and its derivates), as well as to things, subjects, place names ('Ιεροσόλυμα, 'Ισραήλ) and persons (θεός, χριστός, 'Ιησοῦς, κύριος, πατήρ, 'Ιουδαῖος) as well as themes. We also wish to note major sequences or lines of progression through the narrative.[14] Finally, we will wish to observe patterns in the text created by settings, actors, their actions and resulting situations.[15]

of language according to Kenneth Burke are 'the repetitive, progressive, conventional and minor rhetorical forms of language' (Kenneth Burke, *Counter-Statement* [Berkeley: University of California Press, 1931], pp. 123-83).

12. Whereas Robbins assigns the analysis of the indebtedness to rhetorical theory of these argumentative patterns, I would suggest that such analysis belongs more properly to the realm of intertextual analysis, since it compares one form with another arising from a different context. Robbins, 'Summary', p. 5, also includes under 'innertextual' analysis 'aesthetic texture and pattern', but this seems more properly dealt with under the heading of socio-cultural analysis, since the points to which Robbins alludes, 'range of senses' (including body zones, motions, purposeful actions), are culturally conditioned and cannot simply be attended to outside of cultural considerations.

13. Source, form and redaction critics are no strangers to these elements. Yet, even such important works as Robert Morgenthaler's statistical analysis (*Statistik des neutestamentlichen Wortschatzes* [Zürich: Gotthelf, 1958]) and J.C. Hawkins's *Horae Synopticae* (Oxford: Clarendon Press, 1899) assume certain intertextural relationships (specifically, synoptic relationships) and are thus secondary to the more basic task of attending to normative patterns within discrete texts.

14. Again, redaction critics have blazed a trail for us here; however, here, too, the work of redaction critics must be disentangled from the form-critical presuppositions that suggest what are data on the basis of formal parallels with other literature (i.e. intertextural analysis).

15. The work of John Firth appears to parallel these foci of attention. See the

We first need to determine which patterns provide openings and closings to determine a focus for analysis. Bearing in mind that 19.47-48 corresponds lexically to 21.37-38, and what precedes 19.47 and what follows 21.38 is different in setting, characters and action, a first suggestion is that 19.47–21.38 forms a unit introduced by Jesus' violent entry into the Temple area (19.45-46).[16] Within this unit, we appear to have the following, relatively cohesive, sections, each formed by Jesus' interaction with his interlocutors: 20.1-19 with the high-priests, scribes and elders; 20.20-26 with the hypocritical spies (following on from 20.1-19); 20.27-38 with the Sadducees; 20.39-45 with the scribes (following on from 20.27-38); 20.45-47 with the people and his disciples; 21.1-4 (connected to 20.45-47 by the reference to χῆραι, whether there is a change of audience or not); 21.5-36 with 'some'.[17] Within the section 21.5-36, sub-units are created by Jesus' brief words in 21.5-6, which elicit the question (21.7) that leads to his more extensive teaching about what is coming (21.8-28).[18] The latter is followed by an explanatory parable (21.29-33) and a concluding paraenesis (21.34-36).

Accordingly, a first observation is that analysis of Luke 21 cannot be limited to Luke 21 alone; rather, we need to attend to the larger context of 19.45–21.38. In this respect, our attention to innertexture resonates with certain conclusions of literary analysis.[19] Secondly, it seems that 21.5-36 is intended for the same audience as 20.45-47 and (possibly) 21.1-4, that is, not primarily the disciples but rather the people who are in hearing range.[20]

discussion of Firth's contribution in the article by Gustavo Martín-Asensio in this volume (pp. 94-97).

16. So, too, Charles Talbert, *Reading Luke: A Literary and Theological Commentary on the Third Gospel* (New York: Crossroad, 1982), p. 185. Talbert actually sees 19.45–21.38 as the first part of a larger section 19.45–24.53, of which the second section is 'the Passion itself'.

17. Cf. Talbert, *Reading Luke*, pp. 199-200, for an alternative series.

18. *Pace* Talbert, *Reading Luke*, p. 200, the events as narrated do *not* run as an ordered series, except for those narrated near the end.

19. For example, cf. Robert L. Brawley, *Centering on God: Method and Message in Luke–Acts* (Literary Currents in Biblical Interpretation; Louisville, KY: Westminster/John Knox Press, 1990), p. 81.

20. So, too, Brawley, *Centering on God*, p. 81. Talbert's suggestion (*Reading Luke*, p. 188) that 19.45–21.38 'falls into two parts: (1) 19.45–21.5 and (2) 21.5-38' is unjustified and is probably indebted to a previous assumption that the so-called 'apocalyptic section' is a consistent whole independent of 19.45–21.38.

Within this larger section, we also discern lexical and thematic repetitions and progression of repetitions. A key word appears to be ἱερόν (19.45, 47; 20.1; 21.5, 37, 38), which was introduced in Luke 2 (2.27, 37, 46) but is used only five other times, including the final verse of the Gospel (4.9; 18.10; 22.52, 53; 24.53).[21] In contrast, the related word ναός is used only in 1.9, 21, 22 and 23.45, while in Acts it is used only in 17.24 and 19.24 and there to describe pagan temples.

Connected to this word are the *dramatis personae* of our section. Connected to but depicted, perhaps surprisingly, somewhat independent of ἱερόν is the chief grouping of personnel associated with the Temple, namely, ἀρχιερεῖς (ἀρχιερεύς is used independently of ἱερόν in 3.2; 9.22; 20.19; 22.2, 4, 66; 23.4, 10, 13; 24.20). We note that the word is used in conjunction with ἱερόν only in our section (19.47 and 20.1) and the trial of Jesus (22.50, 52, 54)—that is, at moments when Jesus is in or near the ἱερόν in a conflictual situation. The πρεσβύτεροι, named in our section in conjunction with the scribes and the high-priests, are named only rarely in the Gospel according to Luke, but always when the high-priests are named and mainly in the same conflictual, Jesus-in-the-Temple situations: 9.22; 20.1; 22.52 (cf. the one exception: 7.3). The γραμματεῖς are always named in the first half of the Gospel with the Pharisees (5.21, 30; 6.7; 11.53; 15.2; cf. the one exception 9.22) but in the second half are named almost exclusively with the ἀρχιερεῖς in the conflictual situations described earlier (19.47; 20.1, 19; 22.2, 66; 23.10; cf. the two exceptions found in our section, 20.39 and 46, where the γραμματεῖς are named alone, and the sole use of Σαδδουκαῖος in 20.27). Jesus' engagement up to this point in the text, then, is only with high-priests, scribes and elders, in a Temple context, and is highly conflictual.[22]

At this point, we note what at first glance is a striking exception to Jesus' interlocutors. The μαθηταί, mentioned frequently (38 times) throughout the Gospel, are mentioned only once in our section (20.45). On the other hand, λαός, mentioned almost as frequently (37 times), is found 10 times in our section. This, combined with the observation that λαός is used 8 times in Luke 1–2—in relation either to ναός or ἱερόν—

---

21. Cf. Talbert, *Reading Luke*, pp. 185, 188.

22. The extensive, public engagements with the Pharisees end at Lk. 19.39. The Pharisees reappear, and that in a not entirely unsympathetic light, in Acts, starting with Gamaliel's words (5.34).

and 8 times in Luke 22–24, means that only one-third of the uses of the word occur outside of the initial two chapters or in the conflictual ending. Similarly, χήρα, a term which, like ἱερόν, is introduced in ch. 2 (2.37), is also found relatively often in our section (20.47; 21.2, 3). Though used more extensively outside of the section, the term is found elsewhere in some relation to ἱερόν (namely, 4.25, 26—cf. ἱερόν 4.9– 7.12; 18.3, 5—cf. ἱερόν 18.10). For some reason, Luke appears to involve the λαός and a particular class of woman (χήρα) in the Temple conflicts and to exclude the μαθηταί.

In terms of actions, a common Lukan word group, διδασκ-, is present in the form of the verb διδάσκω in both opening and closing verses of our unit, as well as throughout Luke 20. Jesus' teaching appears directed to the λαός but to be triggered by questions from the particular interlocutors named above. The noun διδάσκαλος is also frequently used in our section, usually in the vocative form, but no single group can be said to have used it exclusively to refer to Jesus. Nevertheless, it should be noted that the word is never reported as having been used by Jesus' inner circle; however, it is used widely by those who might be considered to be opposed to Jesus but who in this section are generally reported simply to be asking questions of Jesus.

This again is surprising, at least at first: Jesus is pictured as the teacher of a much larger group than of select μαθηταί. Furthermore, those interlocutors are seen to speak to Jesus and ask him to speak to them (20.2), are seen to ask him questions (20.21, 27; 21.7: ἐπερωτάω—used frequently in Luke of all speakers, including Jesus), and answer him (20.39). In sum, all words used here to initiate a response from Jesus are used frequently throughout the Gospel and are used neutrally (i.e. they can be used in a positive way or a negative way, depending on further modifiers). There is no justification for speaking of consistent attempts by Jesus' interloctuors to 'discredit' Jesus.[23]

The subject of these interlocutors' questions is varied. In 21.7, however, the question concerns a σημεῖον. In 21.11, 25, Jesus goes on to respond. The word σημεῖον is used elsewhere in the Gospel, almost always in a form that clusters it with other uses of the word: 2.12 and

---

23. *Pace* Talbert, *Reading Luke*, p. 194. The only clearly negative approach is the phrase that introduces 20.21, namely, 20.19-20 (spoken of the scribes and chief priests).

34; 11.16, 29 and 30; and finally 23.8. In our section it also appears that it is used in conjunction with παραβολή (21.29). This connection between σημεῖον and παραβολή appears to focus on ἐξουσία (20.2, 8, 20)/ἔξεστιν (20.22). The connection raises the question of Jesus' ἐξουσία and his interlocutors' hypocrisy (namely, γραμματεῖς, who, though they appear to laud Jesus [20.39], are described by Jesus as hypocrites [20.45-47; cf. 20.20]) vis-à-vis the γυνή (20.27-38) and the χήρα (20.45—21.4). The hypocrisy is brought into full view through the contrast between the hypocrites (viewed in light of γυνή and χήρα) and Jesus, whose ἐξουσία becomes clear in the teaching that follows, namely, the warnings for the future, warnings that evidence his knowledge of the σημεῖα.

Accordingly, it appears that Jesus' exposition of signs functions primarily in terms of revelation, a revelation made clear through warning concerning future events.[24] Second-person plural imperatives (21.8-9, 14, 20-21, 28, 34, 36) are interwoven with future tense verbs (21.9-13, 15-19, 20, 22-27, 34-35; cf. vv. 29-33). Among the various imperatives, some verbs of warning are also clear from their lexical repetition.[25] The verb προσέχω is only ever used by the author of the Gospel in the second-person plural imperative and is used twice in this way in 19.45–21.38 (20.46; 21.34; cf. also 12.1; 17.3). The verb βλέπω is used in terms of warning only three times, two of which are in our section (second-person plural imperative: 8.18; 21.8; plural participle introducing another second-person plural imperative: 21.30). Underscoring that the future is not a distant one is the frequent use in Luke— and specifically within our section—of the words ἐγγίζω and ἐγγύς. Finally, we should note that, while not a prominent element in this section, the strongly Lukan theme of prayer (δέομαι) figures here as well (21.36) as a proper mode of response to Jesus' warnings. These exhortations make sense, however, only if the one delivering the warning can be completely believed.

Much remains to be done for a complete overview of the innertexture of the text with which we are concerned. First, one needs a complete overview of the innertexture of the Gospel, as well as an overview of

24. According to Talbert, persecution and warnings dominate (*Reading Luke*, pp. 201-202). It is true that the signs do include persecution, but they are not limited to that.

25. The single uses of some verbs, such as ἀγρυπνέω (21.36), is not significant because of lexical repetition but because of syntactical repetition.

Luke and Acts together. Secondly, one needs an overview of the innertexture of the specific section 19.45–21.38, possibly 19.45–24.53. Thirdly, as is clear from the previous points, one needs to be able to identify more accurately the range of objects of innertextual attention (e.g. letters, words, phrases, sounds, etc.).

Nevertheless, initial and tentative observations can be made. The Temple appears to be a principal piece of the fabric of the Lukan innertexture, as does Jesus' engagement ('teaching') with his interlocutors, primarily on the basis of questions of authority and power. This teaching does not appear to be first of all a demonstration of power but rather a means of demonstrating his authority through his knowledge of the signs. This teaching gives credence to the exhortations that follow.

2. *Intertextural Analysis*

Analysis of the intertexture involves texts that may be part of a related corpus (e.g. in the case of Luke, the New Testament would be a related *corpus*) or that may be interpreted in light of texts from other traditions (e.g. in the case of Luke, we may wish to compare the Gospel with rhetorical handbooks or exercises in earlier, later or contemporary Hellenistic traditions).[26] As such, analysis of intertexture is clearly a second stage of attention, a stage that may properly be the starting-point of analysis as such.

According to Robbins, analysis of intertexture involves analysis of (1) 'reference' ('with what texts and textual traditions are these phrases in dialogue?'), (2) 'recitation' (including the 'rehearsal of attributed speech in exact, modified or different words from other accounts of the attributed speech, and rehearsal of an episode or series of episodes, with or without using some words from another account of the story'), (3) 'recontextualization' ('the placing of attributed narration or speech in a new context without announcing its previous attribution'), and (4) 'reconfiguration' (modification of a word, phrase, topic or theme).[27] It

---

26. Robbins, 'Socio-Rhetorical Criticism', p. 181, citing T. Eagleton, *Literary Theory: An Introduction* (Minneapolis: University of Minnesota Press, 1983), pp. 1-53. For example, can we interpret Luke and Acts uniquely in the context of their canonical connection within the New Testament, or even with the Christian Scriptures, or does intertextuality demand that we transcend these boundaries that are the imposition of another age?

27. Robbins, 'Socio-Rhetorical Criticism', p. 179. Robbins also speaks of a fifth

will be appropriate in our section to examine, among other comparisons, patterns of the morphology of rhetorical argumentation in an apocalyptic mode via the examination of selected enthymemes and their elaborations.

There would appear to be at least four textual traditions to which Lk. 19.25–21.38 refers: (1) extant Christian texts that may have provided the author with direct source material (e.g. Mark); (2) non-extant and hypothetical Christian texts that may have provided the author with direct source material (e.g. Q, L and other unknown sources); (3) extant and non-extant Jewish textual traditions from which the author may have drawn (including, but not limited to, the Jewish Scriptures, the Greek translations of the Jewish Scriptures, targumic literature, other non-liturgical or independently sacred Second Temple literature, including the so-called 'apocalyptic literature', and commentary on any texts from the preceding traditions); and (4) extant and non-extant Greco-Roman textual traditions (including, but not limited to, rhetorical handbooks and exercises, novels, commentaries and histories). While we cannot possibly do justice to this complete range of textures, we can begin to show how intertextural analysis provides a significant interpretive moment.

a. *Extant Christian Texts*

The assumption made by most New Testament scholars today that the author of the Gospel has used the Gospel of Mark more or less as it presently exists is widely held and for good reasons. If we adopt this assumption, our Gospel would appear to have followed the general outline of Mk 11.15–13.37 in Lk. 19.45–21.38. Luke follows Mark through the main moments of the teaching of Jesus, including the parallels to Lk. 21.5-36. Lukan recitation of Mark is, then, extensive.

Nevertheless, Luke has not followed Mark strictly. Luke transposes Mark's disputation on the great commandment (12.28-34) to an earlier point (Lk. 10.25-28), thus preserving only the scribal commendation of Jesus in this section (Mk 12.32; Lk. 20.39). There are also significant differences between the two Gospels that suggest significant recontextualization and reconfiguration. Furthermore, many of these modifications underscore Lukan themes already discerned by attending to innertexture. For example, the briefer Lukan introduction to the entire

component, 'intertextual echo'; however, in my opinion, this is found in each of the already named four components (p. 181).

section (19.45-46; cf. Mk 11.18-19) leads the reader of the Gospel to attend directly to Jesus (19.47-48; cf. Mk 11.18) and to focus on Jesus' teaching by omitting Mk 11.20-26. Such a focus implies that Jesus' teaching in 21.5-36 takes place *within* the Temple precinct (rather than outside of it). The focus also yields an indistinct character of Jesus' audience (τινων; cf. Mk 13.1), rather than a more carefully defined one. This reconfiguration is intertwined with Luke's emphasis on the λαός in 19.47, an emphasis that suggests that the leaders fear the people (cf. 22.2), not Jesus (as in Mk 11.18).[28] The shift, then, from Jesus' teaching directed to disciples to Jesus' teaching directed to the people, may have, at least in part, been due to the author's understanding that the people are the object of the leaders' fears.

The subject matter of Jesus' teaching in Luke is also reconfigured from the Markan model in a way that is consistent with what we have seen in our attention to innertexture. For example, Luke appears either to echo or to reconfigure Mark so as to present (1) extensive use of future tenses (e.g. the Lukan introduction of ἐλεύσονται and ἀφεθήσεται, 21.6 and the admission of the Markan ἔσται Mk 13.4; Lk. 21.7), (2) the relative proximity (ἐγγ-) of that future (e.g. Markan source: Mk 13.28-29 and Lk. 21.30-31; and Lukan introduction: 21.8, 28; οὐκ εὐθέως Lk. 21.9), (3) references to Jesus as διδάσκαλος (e.g. Lk. 21.7; cf. Mk 13.1), (4) cautionary (e.g. 21.12) or hopeful (e.g. 21.28) exhortations directed to the audience concerning what has generally been called persecution (cf. especially Luke's echo of Mk 13.9 and his expansion of it in 21.12), especially in the form of second-person plural imperatives (e.g. Mk 13.5 and Lk. 21.8 βλέπετε, but also Lk. 21.8 μὴ πορευθῆτε), and (5) commands for how to deal with the warnings (cf. Lk. 21.14), including a role given to prayer (δέομαι 21.36), which is completely absent from Mark.

An element that did not surface in our initial attention to the innertexture, however, was Luke's evident development of certain aspects of the Markan signs. For example, Lk. 21.11 expands Mark considerably in order to point to the frightful nature of the future happenings. Thus, where Mk 13.8 mentions σεισμοί, λιμοί, Lk. 21.11 adds λοιμοί, φόβητρα and ἀπ' οὐρανοῦ σημεῖα μεγάλα. Luke 21.25-26 greatly expands on Mk 13.24-25 (σημεῖα ἐν ἡλίῳ καὶ σελήνη καὶ

---

28. This statement also provides a further inclusion, along with 21.37-38, for this entire section.

ἄστροις and αἱ δυνάμεις) by including the following greatly expanded list of signs: καὶ ἐπὶ τῆς γῆς συνοχὴ ἐθῶν ἐν ἀπορίᾳ ἤχους θαλάσσης καὶ σάλου, ἀποψυχόντων ἀνθρώπων ἀπὸ φόβου καὶ προσδοκίας τῶν ἐπερχομένων τῇ οἰκουμένῃ. Also, Lk. 21.20-24 is much more specific than Mk 13.14 regarding the nature of the attack on the holy place: the language used clearly depicts Jerusalem under siege by armies, a time for the inhabitants of Jerusalem to flee and the wholesale slaughter or captivity as the Gentiles take the city. Finally, another element that surfaces in the intertextual analysis but that did not surface in my initial attention to innertexture is the combination of somewhat rare themes such as ὑπομονή/ὑπομένω (Lk. 21.19), καιρός (21.8, 24, 36), the appearance of the Son of Man (21.27) and ἀπολύτρωσις (21.28). A fuller intertexutural analysis needs to consider the role these elements play in the Lukan reconfiguration of Mark.

We may already conclude tentatively that, while many of Mark's interests are underscored in Luke, he clearly takes his Markan source a significant step forward. He directs his teaching to the people and, while accepting the Markan vision of the future, apparently heightens the initial sense of impending doom that pervades Mark and, at the same time, introduces significant moments of hoped-for salvation. If we assume for the moment that these observations are accurate, we still need to ask whether Luke carried out these transformations on his own or utilized other sources in the reconfiguration.

b. *Non-Extant Christian Texts*
One possible answer to this question is that Luke may have recontextualized and reconfigured Mark on the basis of Q material. Lukan use of Q is respectful. Yet, as John Kloppenborg and Arland Jacobson note, it is not that Luke does not know of apocalyptic material in Q; rather, he appears to have taken the Q apocalyptic material and kept it separate from the Markan apocalyptic material by putting the former in 17.20-37 and keeping the latter here.[29] The material here is markedly different from both the cynic-based Q material[30] and the

29. John S. Kloppenborg, *The Formation of Q: Trajectories in Ancient Wisdom Collections* (Studies in Antiquity and Christianity; Philadelphia: Fortress Press, 1987), p. 154; Arland D. Jacobson, *The First Gospel: An Introduction to Q* (Sonoma, CA: Polebridge Press, 1992), pp. 230-31.

30. Kingdom language (which occurs in our section, 21.31) is often found in first-stratum Q materials, where it is often found in apothegmatic, non-apocalyptic

apocalyptic Q material. The appearance, however, of ὁ υἱὸς τοῦ ἀνθρώ-
που in both the Q-based Lk. 17.24 (also one of the four 'prophetic
correlatives' in Luke) and its use in our section in 21.27, especially in
light of the Qumran parallel, 4QpsDanA[a31] may be significant: this
reconfiguration of the Markan story-line may be due to Luke's reading
of Q.[32]

Consideration of Luke's indebtedness to non-extant materials has,
however, not been limited to Q alone. Reformulating Jan Lambrecht's
earlier suggestion that Mark composed his entire apocalyptic section on
the basis of Q material, I.H. Marshall suggests that the language of Lk.
21.5-36 is evidence of 'a non-Marcan source', one that is also the
source of Revelation 6.[33] Against this view, however, we note that the
references in Revelation 6 are to those elements already contained in
the Markan parallel, namely λιμός, σεισμός and ἀστέρες. If the source
is non-Markan, it is likely also pre-Markan (as Lambrecht suggested)
and used by Luke through the latter's use of Mark.

macarisms: 6.20 (J.S. Kloppenborg, 'Blessing and Marginality: The "Persecution
Beatitude" in Q, Thomas, and Early Christianity', *Forum* 2/3 [1986], pp. 36-37);
11.2, 17, 20; 12.31 and 32 (J.S. Kloppenborg, 'The Function of Apocalyptic
Language in Q', in *Society of Biblical Literature: Seminar Papers 1986* [SBLSP,
25; Atlanta: Scholars Press, 1986], pp. 226-27). The single kingdom reference in
our section appears to be very different from the cynic-inspired (non-apocalyptic)
kingdom language found in Luke's use elsewhere of Q: while markedly apocalyptic
in meaning, it does not convey the ethos of social reversal.

31. See the discussion in Kloppenborg, *The Formation of Q*, pp. 155-56.

32. Cf. Jirair S. Tashjian, 'The Social Setting of the Q Mission: Three
Dissertations', in *SBL Seminar Papers 1988* (SBLSP, 27; Atlanta: Scholars Press,
1988), p. 638. Luke is especially interested in using and nuancing the cynic foun-
dation of much of Q. See my 'Methodological Considerations in the Determination
of the Social Context of Cynic Rhetorical Practice: Implications for our Present
Studies of the Jesus Traditions', in Porter and Olbricht (eds.), *The Rhetorical
Analysis of Scripture*, pp. 200-231. The absence of Q materials in this section of
Luke, for example, leads to a complete absence of cynic-like materials in this
section. While certainly not a sole measure, it is telling that F.G. Downing's work,
*Christ and the Cynics: Jesus and Other Radical Preachers in First-Century
Tradition* (Manuals, 4; Sheffield: JSOT Press, 1988) contains no references to
Cynic parallels from our section 19.45–21.38.

33. I.H. Marshall, *The Gospel of Luke: A Commentary on the Greek Text*
(NIGTC; Grand Rapids: Eerdmans, 1979), p. 765. See Jan Lambrecht, *Die Redak-
tion der Markus-Apokalypse: Literarische Analyse und Strukturuntersuchung*
(Rome: Pontifical Biblical Institute, 1967).

So while it is not impossible that Luke has interwoven non-Markan, Christian sources into this section of his work, there is no scholarly consensus as to what such a source would have been, other than possibly Q material that is primarily woven into an earlier section that Luke has clearly kept separate from the one at hand.

c. *Jewish Textual Traditions*

At various points in the work, Luke recites an array of Jewish textual traditions that are not found in his Markan source. In the introduction to our section, Jesus quotes Isa. 56.7 (LXX) and alludes to Jer. 7.11 (19.46) in condemning those who have made the Temple—or as the Isaiah and Jeremiah passages have it, God's house (οἶκος)—an emporium. The parable in 20.9-19 is often viewed as being shaped by Isa. 5.1-9 (LXX) and includes a quotation from Ps. 117.22-23 (LXX). The discussion in 20.41-44 is over Ps. 109.1 (LXX). Finally, Lk. 21.5-36 expands the imagery of various Old Testament prophetic passages cited or not by Mark. For example, the added emphasis on nearness (ἐγγ-) of the right time (καιρός) may be an echo of Dan. 7.22 (cf. also Rev. 1.3). Or again, Lk. 21.11 considerably expands the number and range of references that Mk 13.8 draws from the Old Testament. Luke's expansion and explicitation of the destruction of Jerusalem (21.20-24) carries echoes of Old Testament passages such as Deut. 32.25, 35; Hos. 9.7; 13.16; and especially Jeremiah (e.g. 46.10). This is especially true in the imagery that underlies 21.23-24 (cf. Deut. 28.64; Ezek. 32.9; Est. 9.7; Zech. 12.3; Sir. 28.18; *Pss. Sol.* 17.25; Tob. 14.5; Dan. 12.7). Luke 21.25-28 (esp. vv. 25-26) also expands the cosmic signs found in Mk 13.24-27 on the basis of further Old Testament imagery (cf. Joel 3.3-4; Isa. 24.19; Ps. 65.8; 46.4; 89.10; Wis. 5.22; Jon. 1.15). The final Lukan warnings (21.34-36) are unique to Luke but draw on Old Testament imagery (e.g. Isa. 24.17 and Jer. 25.29). Such an abundance of Old Testament echoes throughout the section, but especially in 21.5-36, would suggest extensive interaction with Jewish textual traditions, well beyond the recitation and reconfiguration of Mark or his sources of the same traditions.

Such use of the Old Testament in Luke leads to the question of whether Luke has derived this imagery from or intended it to be understood in relation to its Old Testament referents or whether he derived it from other sources (e.g. other non-extant Christian sources or other non-biblical Jesus sources) and intended it to be understood accordingly. That the latter is possible is clear from the way other Jewish writers of Luke's day used some of the same imagery used by Luke to underscore dramatic events. According to Josephus (*War* 6.288-315) signs like those listed by Luke were said to have occurred before the fall of Jerusalem.[34] In fact, E. Meyer, M. Albertz and R. Pesch have discussed the possibility of a Jewish apocalyptic *Urtext* underlying Mark 13 and reflected in Luke.[35] Here again, as with Marshall's suggestion, it must be objected that if traces of such an *Urtext* can be found in Luke, it would be because of Mark's use of it, not Luke's independent use of it.[36]

In sum, however strong the case for Mark's (or Revelation's) indebtedness to an *Urtext*, it does not account for Luke's expansions of Mark. These are better accounted for by considering the possibility of further, independent reflection by Luke, not only on Mark's text, but on the Old Testament passages to which Mark's work points and on related passages to which those Old Testament passages point. No other consistent pattern than Luke's own creative interaction has yet been adduced that would give strong support to Luke's use of either a non-biblical Jewish or Christian *Urtext*.

Furthermore, Thomas Louis Brodie's comments on Luke's rhetorical style may explain how in fact Luke has used the Old Testament, namely, as a source for imitation.[37] Following Brodie's insight allows us to see Luke's work as mimesis and 'careful consistent adaptation' of

34. Cf. Marshall, *Gospel of Luke*, p. 765.

35. Eduard Meyer, *Ursprung und Anfänge des Christentums* (3 vols.; Berlin: Alfred Töpelmann, 4th edn, 1925), I, pp. 129-30; M. Albertz, *Die Botschaft des Neuen Testaments* (2 vols.; Zürich: Zollikon, 1952–54), I, pp. 180-81; Rudolf Pesch, *Naherwartungen: Tradition und Redaktion in Mk. 13* (Düsseldorf: Patmos, 1968), pp. 207-23. These texts are cited in David E. Aune, *Prophecy in Early Christianity and the Ancient Mediterranean World* (Grand Rapids: Eerdmans, 1983), p. 184. Aune, however, simply dismisses the hypothesis as 'unnecessary' without arguing against it.

36. Also, we should add here that the fact that the same material is found in both Mk 13 and Rev. 6 could simply indicate a borrowing of Mark from Revelation or vice versa, or even independent borrowings of Mark and Revelation from the Old Testament itself.

37. Thomas Louis Brodie, 'Greco-Roman Imitation of Texts as a Partial Guide to Luke's Use of Sources', in C.H. Talbert (ed.), *Luke–Acts: New Perspectives from the Society of Biblical Literature Seminar* (New York: Crossroad, 1984), pp. 17-46 (33). Brodie's use of 'imitation' is in the technical sense found in the Greco-Roman rhetorical tradition.

the Old Testament.[38] In other words, Jesus in Lk. 21.5-36 not only borrows heavily from a traditional series of Old Testament prophetic denunciations but also adapts them as his own. He thus not only recites earlier prophetic denunciations of Jerusalem (and Egypt) but also becomes the prophet who denounces Jerusalem.

d. *Greco-Roman Textual Traditions*
Because of Luke's expansion of Jewish material in our section, it should come as no surprise that this material has been viewed almost exclusively as dependent on Jewish textual traditions. Nevertheless, the suggestion that Luke has used *imitatio* in reconfiguring the Jewish traditions also suggests the presence of Greco-Roman elements in our section.

David Aune has argued that some of these Hellenistic features are shared with the Markan text.[39] First, the 'abbreviated peripatetic dialogue' is an 'essentially introductory setting for a [Greco-Roman] literary dialogue'.[40] Secondly, 'a seated dialogue in full view of the temple' had become in Greco-Roman literature a frequent companion to the first element, the *peripatos*. Mark, and more explicitly Luke in his modification, seems to have combined these two forms with the *Kirchen-* or *Tempeldialog*, so defined because a *peripatos* leads the dialogue partners into a Temple context or proximity to a Temple for the discussion on the Temple or feasts.[41] Thirdly, the setting of 'two questions which are intended to elicit the prophetic speech which follows' (Mk 13.1-4) 'is unique in the New Testament, since it is the only place an oracle is given in response to a question', a prophetic response that is 'entirely at home in the Greco-Roman world' but odd in a Jewish context.[42] Fourthly, as was already noted by L. Hartman, the emphases in Mark's so-called apocalyptic text, especially the parenetic details that are used to make application to the reader of the

38. Brodie, 'Greco-Roman Imitation', p. 33.

39. Aune, *Prophecy in Early Christianity*, p. 186.

40. See Aune, *Prophecy in Early Christianity*, p. 399 n. 93, for an overview of the origins and developments of the *peripatos*.

41. See Aune, *Prophecy in Early Christianity*, p. 400 n. 93, for a complete overview of these two facets of the continuation of the dialogue. Aune, *Prophecy in Early Christianity*, p. 187, notes especially two Temple dialogues by Plutarch, *De defectu oraculorum* and *De Pythiae oraculis*.

42. Aune, *Prophecy in Early Christianity*, p. 186.

apocalyptic prediction, are not characteristic of Jewish apocalyptic texts.[43]

In his reconfiguration of Mark, Luke develops and expands on these Greco-Roman elements even as he did on the Jewish traditions. For example, Jesus' entire discourse in our section falls within the realm of a rhetorically deliberative address: Jesus seeks to instill in his listeners a new way of acting in their world by a new way of considering him. In order to achieve this end, he follows Mark by combining prophetic utterance with parenetic warning, fleshed out by expanded 'imitation' of the Old Testament prophetic utterances.

Analysis from the vantage point of Greco-Roman rhetorical style confirms this observation. For we note in 21.7-36 that the argumentation of the entire section is carried forward by a series of 'hortatory enthymemes' from the mouth of Jesus (Lk. 21.29-33 is a special case that demands separate attention; see below). These 'hortatory enthymemes' are, like all enthymemes, deductive arguments, usually missing a major premise, but are hortatory in that they are intended to lead the hearer not only to a right conclusion, but more importantly to right action on the basis of authoritative pronouncement, in this case, the interpretation of the σημεῖον by Jesus.[44] Each of these enthymemes is further couched in the larger framework of prophetic utterances that function as rhetorical examples or paradigms.

The first 'hortatory enthymeme' comes in the shape of Jesus' response to the initial query of the mysterious τινων (21.8). It is made more explicit in Luke by the addition of γάρ.

43. L. Hartman, *Prophecy Interpreted: The Formation of Some Jewish Apocalyptic Texts and of the Eschatological Discourse Mark 13 par.* (Lund: C.W.K. Gleerup, 1966), p. 208. See also Aune, *Prophecy in Early Christianity*, p. 185.

44. The discussion of my paper at the Malibu conference suggested to me that the neologism 'hortatory enthymeme' is not only appropriate but also something that further underscores the value of examining Greco-Roman intertexture in this text. For, as colleagues reminded me, we have not only the strongly hortatory nature of maxims as support, but also the deliberative genus itself. Given the difficulty of successfully discussing paraenesis in rhetoric it would seem that this avenue of exploration of paraenetic statements in a rhetorical context might be fruitful.

Exhortation:	Beware that you are not led astray
Reason:	for many will come in my name saying 'I am He' and 'the time has come'.
Implicit (major) premise:	You are to be wary of the many who come saying 'I am He' and 'the time has come' for they will want to lead you astray.

This is immediately followed by another 'hortatory enthymeme', again made more explicit in Luke by the addition of γάρ (21.9):

Exhortation:	Do not be terrified (when you hear of these things)
Reason:	for these things must take place first.
Implicit (major) premise:	You do not need to be terrified of what takes place first.

The implicit premises that undergird both of these 'hortatory enthymemes' suggest an argumentation based on certain assumptions of future scenarios that will involve those who are reading Luke. I believe that 21.10-11, which follows this 'hortatory enthymeme', is not only an oracular pronouncement (as argued by Aune) but also a rhetorical 'example', giving further (inductive) evidence as to how the hearers are to know and live rightly, and implicitly how they alone know and judge Jesus to be correct in his assessment.

These examples also serve to give further shape to the assumptions of future scenarios that lie behind the hortatory enthymemes. For though this rhetorical example is found in Mark, it is significantly fleshed out by Luke's own inclusion of a wider array of texts from the Old Testament. Here, then, is where the hearer or reader would have learned more about the nature of the 'things' that must first take place, and would have been led to conclude concerning the rightness of Jesus' words about the future. They would have been drawn in their entirety from the Old Testament, which we may then have to see as having been not only normative for Jesus and his immediate audience in Luke's mind, but also for Luke and *his* immediate audience.

The 'hortatory enthymeme' in 21.14-15 (again made more visible by the Lukan inclusion of γάρ) is a Lukan configuration of Mk 13.11 and is bordered on each side by rhetorical examples, namely, 21.12, 16-17 (completed by two *chreiai*, vv. 18, 19), which, as in the first case, corroborate the rightness of Jesus' words.

Exhortation:	Make up your minds not to be anxious how to respond
Reason:	for I will give you utterance and wisdom that none or all of your opponents will be able to withstand or contradict.
Implicit (major) premise:	You do not need to be anxious (during this time) if you have God's unvanquishable utterance and wisdom.

This hortatory enthymeme points to the source of particular hearers'/ readers' peace of mind. It thus presupposes some understanding of what that source is and what the content of the peace involves. The rhetorical examples on either side underscore the source and the content by pointing to God's provision and to God's victory: the victorious nature of the witness comes to the fore in the time of persecution understood as primarily a time for bearing witness to Jesus (21.12); the persecution also reveals not only its harshness but God's provision in the midst of it (21.16-17). Two apparently independent *chreiai* (21.18 and 19) are bound to the example by polysyndeton (16-18).

Luke 21.20 is very similar in form to 21.9: a subordinate clause introduced by ὅταν δέ, an exhortation, and a follow up explanation introduced by τότε. Nevertheless, the crucial element that would make 21.20 a complete 'hortatory enthymeme' is missing, namely, the reason (cf. 21.9c introduced by γάρ). In fact, had Luke followed Mk 13.14 here, as Mt. 24.15 does, then he would have had the materials for an enthymeme. Instead, we are left with a truncated enthymeme, which compares only with the exhortation of 21.9:

Exhortation:	Know that the desolation of Jerusalem has come near (when armies surround Jerusalem).

In this case, the reader is left to fill in both premises:

Implicit (major) premise:	You are to be those who know the meaning of armies surrounding Jerusalem.

> *Implicit (minor) premise*:   The meaning of armies surrounding Jerusalem
>   is that the desolation of Jerusalem is near.

The import of this truncated form of argumentation appears to be to underscore the hearers'/readers' apparent insight into the events being described. So clear is it to the Lukan Jesus that those hearing him will understand his meaning, that he does not even need to state the premises, only the hortatory conclusion! In actual fact, the point of the subtle silence of this Lukan reconfiguration of the Markan narrative achieves the same purpose as the more overt (and possibly unoriginal) statement: ὁ ἀναγινώσκων νοείτω (Mk 13.14; Mt. 24.15), namely, the hearers/readers are by this time to have discerned the pattern of the Old Testament references and to see that the references there to the fall of Egypt and the fall of Jerusalem are being reconfigured here to describe a new fall of Jerusalem.

This truncated but highly significant enthymeme is followed immediately by another, complete enthymeme in 21.21-22.[45]

> *Exhortation*:   Flee to the mountains if you are in Judea; flee
>   the city if you are in it; do not enter the city if
>   you are not in it [i.e. if you are in the country]
>
> *Reason*:   for [ὅτι] these are the days of vengeance that
>   were predicted.
>
> *Implicit (major) premise*: You are to flee the city of Jerusalem and the
>   immediately surrounding regions when the
>   predicted days of vengeance dawn.

Not surprisingly, this uniquely Lukan hortatory enthymeme follows up directly on the previous one and expands on the prophetic elements missing from the truncated enthymeme in 21.21. The reference to predictions is here made explicit (21.22).

The enthymeme found in 21.23 follows immediately on the previous one and is a reconfigured mirror of the Markan enthymeme (13.19).

> *Exhortation*:   Woe to the pregnant and the nursing in those
>   days

---

45. Note that in 21.9-10, the pattern that concludes with τοτε is followed here, but 21.10 does not introduce a new enthymeme, as 21.21 does.

Reason:	for there will be great distress on earth and wrath upon the people.
Implicit (major) premise:	When there is great distress and wrath, the most distressed and the most clear recipients of wrath are the pregnant and the nursing.

In this case the expansion is (1) of the stated premise of the enthymeme itself, here in terms of additional Old Testament imagery and the Lukan theme of λαός as the immediate recipients of God's wrath, and (2) by a specifically Lukan oracular prediction or rhetorical example (21.23-24) that corroborates the deductive conclusion of the enthymeme, and which again contains additional Old Testament imagery and specific, favorite Lukan themes (e.g. ἄχρι οὗ πληρωθῶσιν καιροὶ ἐθνῶν, 21.24; cf. 3.5; 4.21; etc.).

This enthymeme is followed by two oracular predictions that function as rhetorical examples underscoring the coming terrors for the λαός. The first (21.25-26) is found in more general form in Mk 13.24-25 but is greatly expanded by Luke from Old Testament imagery; the second (21.27) is shortened by Luke in such a way that it mentions only the Son of Man, while the Markan imagery of angels at the service of God and the gathering of the elect (Mk 13.27) are omitted.

How this second example is to be viewed by Jesus' hearers/readers is clear from the uniquely Lukan (cf. also the use of ἐγγίζω here) hortatory enthymeme in 21.28.

Exhortation:	Look up and raise your heads (when these things happen; cf. 21.9)
Reason:	for your redemption is near.
Implicit (major) premise:	You know that when these things happen, your redemption is near and you are to be expectant.

Contrasting starkly with the terror of the mass of people, those who understand and accept the rightness of Jesus' interpretation of the signs are hopeful. The reduction by Luke of all focus of attention in 21.27 to the Son of Man serves further to marry the hopefulness of this group for its redemption to the appearance of the Son of Man alone. It also serves to show that the terrifying elements that Luke has added to the Markan apocalypse are functional: they serve to heighten the drama through an imitation of Old Testament prophetic pronouncements and thus to show what a great salvation the group that receives Jesus' word experiences.

Luke borrows almost in its entirety from Mk 13.28-32 a combination rhetorical parable (21.29) plus another truncated, hortatory enthymeme (21.30, after the example of 21.20). In this way, the Lukan and Markan Jesus is seen to drive home the point of the argumentation in this section. The inductive logic of the parable seems to be:

> When a tree brings forth leaf, you know that summer is near.
> Therefore, when the things described take place, you know that the
>   kingdom of God is near.

The logic of the parable is then underscored in a truncated enthymeme:

Exhortation:	Know that the kingdom of God is near (when you see these things).[46]
Implicit (minor) premise:	You are to be those who know the meaning of these things.
Implicit (major) premise:	The meaning of these things is that the kingdom of God is near.

Again, as in 21.20, the import of this truncated form of argumentation is to point to the hearers'/readers' apparent insight into the events being described, but this time not with a view to the terror that accompanies the events of armies laying siege to the city, but with a view to the meaning of the fall of the city as the inauguration of the kingdom and salvation of God.

The result of this parable–enthymeme combination in its placement here, a placement that is held over by Luke from the original Markan sequence, is to make 21.29-33 function as a kind of larger commentary on the previous hortatory enthymemes, even as the other examples do on their related hortatory enthymemes. In this way, 21.29-33 can be judged to be a kind of concluding inductive and deductive proof of the rightness of Jesus' approach to the σημεῖα and to the judgment due to their lack of knowing that will ultimately separate some members of the

---

46. Joseph A. Fitzmyer, *The Gospel According to Luke* (2 vols.; AB, 28, 28A; Garden City, NY: Doubleday, 1981–85), II, p. 1351, takes γινώσκετε as an imperative.

λαός from those who do heed and follow Jesus.

The section is brought to a close by a uniquely Lukan hortatory enthymeme that in fact contains two hortatory conclusions.

Exhortation (1):	Take heed that your hearts not be weighed down by dissipation, drunkenness and the cares of life, such that the day catch you in a snare.
Exhortation (2):	Be alert at all times, praying that you may have strength to escape all things and to stand before the Son of Man
Reason:	for (it) will come upon all who dwell on the face of the earth.
Implicit (major) premise:	In order to escape (it), you must be different from all the rest who dwell on the face of the earth (1) by taking heed, etc. and (2) by being alert, etc.

In this Lukan hortatory enthymeme the stress appears now to be fully on the uniqueness of those from among the people who will not be caught by surprise when the Son of Man appears but who rather will greet the coming Son of Man as their Savior. Their only assurance of being part of this different group, the company of the redeemed, however, is not doctrine but rather their alertness and awareness, pictured by Luke as a posture of prayer.

In concluding this section, I would suggest that the above analysis of Greco-Roman intertexture ought to lead us to conclude not only that Luke is 'imitating' the prophetic utterances of Jewish literature, but that he is doing so for a particular, well-recognized rhetorical purpose, namely, to summon out from among the people those who will hear and follow. As noted, it is the people that the Jewish leaders in Luke are said to fear; they, not Jesus, are the ones who will testify to the ἐξουσία of Jesus by giving him credence. The leaders and others who focus on what the people think are characterized by fear and helplessness in the face of Jesus' wisdom and in the face of the future wrath of God, while those who focus on Jesus and on the Son of Man are those who have hope. This so-called apocalyptic text, then, is both a call for separation—and, in that sense, a call for judgment—and also a call to those who understand to live in hope.

3. *Socio-Cultural Texture*

According to Robbins, analysis of socio-cultural texture involves an analysis of the common social and cultural topics 'that everyone living in an area knows either consciously or instinctively'.[47] Analysis of this web of relationships 'raises questions about the response to the world, the social and cultural systems and institutions, and the cultural alliances and conflicts evoked by the text'.[48] In this stage of the analysis, we should be able to delineate the discursive culture to which this argumentation may be considered to point.[49]

Robbins includes among the topics of interest here: (1) overarching cultural and anthropological questions, such as honour, guilt, purity, rights and legal arrangements;[50] (2) forms of social interaction (such as challenge-response and dialectic interaction); (3) economic wealth exchanges common to the means of production (agriculture, industry, information technology); (4) social relations arising from these exchanges; and (5) self-understanding, including understandings of the body.

One way of looking at these topics in religious texts will be in terms of religious responses to social situations. Here Robbins has been guided by Bryan Wilson's typology of religious sects into (1) the conversionist, (2) the revolutionist, (3) the introversionist, (4) the manipulationist or gnostic, (5) the thaumaturgic, (6) the reformist and (7) the utopian.[51] Also, we need to consider looking at topics that are more

47. Robbins, 'Summary', p. 12.

48. Even classical rhetorical theory was aware that such phenomena were 'primary topics' (Robbins, 'Socio-Rhetorical Criticism', p. 185, citing Roger Fowler, *Linguistic Criticism* [Oxford: Oxford University Press, 1986], pp. 85-101; and Aristotle, *Rhet.* 1.2.21-22; 2.22.1–23.30; 3.15.1-4).

49. Seeking to use modern forms of rhetorical analysis to uncover the meaning of the text, Carey attempts to probe the social context of Lk. 21. Unfortunately, I do not feel that Carey's work is sufficiently refined, either methodologically or in terms of content, to provide a clear direction for this study (see n. 6).

50. This might involve, for example, an examination of individualist and dyadic personalities. 'A dyadic personality is one who needs another person continually in order to know who he or she really is… The dyadic personality is an individual who perceives himself/herself and forms his/her self-image in terms of what others perceive and feed back to him/her' (Robbins, 'Summary', p. 13).

51. Brian R. Wilson, 'A Typology of Sects', in R. Robertson (ed.), *Sociology of Religion* (Harmondsworth: Penguin Books, 1969), pp. 361-83.

crucial, what Aristotle called 'final topics'. These are the topics 'that most decisively identify one's cultural location' and concern 'the manner in which people present their propositions, reasons and arguments both to themselves and to other people'.[52] Robbins identifies four 'final topics' of cultural rhetoric: (1) dominant culture rhetoric, (2) subculture rhetoric, (3) counterculture rhetoric, and (4) contraculture rhetoric.[53]

Certain elements of the socio-cultural texture of our text have already been touched on. The Temple appears to be the context for and focus of Jesus' teaching. The centrality of the Temple, clear both from attention to innertexture and from the appearance in various layers of the inter-texture, is crucial for our understanding of the passage 19.45–21.38,[54] for it appears in this section that the fates of Jerusalem and the Temple are inextricably bound together.[55] The fate of Jerusalem is bound to that of the Temple, and vice versa, precisely because from the Holy of Holies in the Temple—the place where, in some sense, God dwelt—radiated 'gradated zones of holiness'.[56] These zones were more zealously guarded the closer they were to the holiest zone itself, so the Holy of Holies was obviously the most zealously guarded space in Jerusalem. But these zones did not cease with the actual Temple complex.[57] The actual, protected 'space' was much greater than either the immediate physical Temple precinct or even the walled city of Jerusalem.

Nor were the zones limited to physical space. As John Elliott notes, 'temple' does not just mean 'holy place of prayer and sacrifice' but also the network of 'priests, rulers, law and lawyers, purity observance'. As such, notes Elliott, we need to consider not just the lexical referents to the physical Temple when talking about the reality of the Temple, but

52. Robbins, 'Summary', p. 19.

53. Robbins, 'Summary', p. 20, citing K.A. Roberts, 'Toward a Generic Concept of Counter-Culture', *Sociological Focus* 11 (1978), pp. 111-26.

54. For a description of the Temple and the cult associated with it in the day of Jesus, see Philip Francis Esler, *Community and Gospel in Luke–Acts* (SNTSMS, 57; New York: Cambridge University Press, 1987), pp. 148-57.

55. Cf. Esler, *Community and Gospel*, p. 131.

56. Esler, *Community and Gospel*, p. 154.

57. Shmuel Safrai notes that the public administrative institutions of Jerusalem were located in the Temple courtyards. See his 'The Temple', in S. Safrai and M. Stern (eds.), *The Jewish People in the First Century: Historical Geography, Political History, Social, Cultural and Religious Life and Institutions* (CRINT, 2; Philadelphia: Fortress Press, 1976), p. 865.

also the larger semantic field invoked by the terms (e.g. 'connected groups, roles, structures, patterns of behaviour, norms, values, cultural symbols, economic, political, and ideological features').[58] Via this network, the 'Temple' created boundaries, for the network of connections that centered on the Temple 'symbolized a holy people's union with the Holy One of Israel...and their demarcation from all that was unholy'.[59] In practical terms, such boundaries touched on the meaning of purity (or its absence) not only in terms of the land and places, but also in terms of classes of persons and their interrelationships, times and bodily functions.[60]

Eventually, it is this 'dominating public center of Jewish society and a web of social relations' that represents the final conflict for Jesus.[61] For throughout Luke knowledge of and action on such matters as forgiveness of sins and purity are seen by the author to reside with Jesus (not in the Temple or with the Temple authorities), and to be offered to all people, including Gentiles who were excluded from the Temple. Accordingly, the author appears to assume that Jesus stood in direct opposition not to the Temple building,[62] but via Jesus' teaching to the entire Temple structure, both physical and cultural. Luke does not see the Temple as inherently opposed to Jesus (as demonstrated by Lk. 1–2 and what the Temple could be) but as derivatively opposed, that is, opposed through what others had made of the Temple. The future of *this* Temple understood as a culture is its destruction.

If this is correct, it would suggest that the Lukan Jesus' position is characteristically 'revolutionist'. Only through the destruction of the Temple culture, which will happen at the hand of God, could those who hear Jesus' message and bear testimony be able to return to the Temple to worship. This happens proleptically in Lk. 24.53. It is also revolutionist for the destruction of the Temple is the destruction of the Jewish 'world', since the Temple *was* the Jewish world, the 'cosmos' or cultural world in which the λαός lived and had its being. The Temple

58. John H. Elliott, 'Temple versus Household in Luke–Acts: A Contrast in Social Institutions', in J. Neyrey (ed.), *The Social World of Luke–Acts: Models for Interpretation* (Peabody, MA: Hendrickson, 1991), pp. 211-40, esp. p. 212.

59. Elliott, 'Temple versus Household', pp. 218-19.

60. Elliott, 'Temple versus Household', p. 221.

61. Elliott, 'Temple versus Household', p. 220.

62. *Pace* Esler, *Community and Gospel*, p. 159.

was the tangible microcosm of the much larger cultural world Luke inhabited.

Already there were signs that this world was being destroyed. Luke's world was characterized by disease and scarcity. The eastern Mediterranean land-based agrarian economies of the early Roman period (in which the self-sufficient 'household' was the main economic unit of a kinship-based economy) had yielded to a growing *new* urbanism brought with it by imperial Rome.[63] One of the key problems faced in the Palestine of Jesus' day was the breakdown in the patronage system caused by this urbanism.[64] In fact, it may be that the Hellenistic East, including Herodian Palestine, 'excelled at this aspect of the imperial system'.[65]

In the 'new' model the two key players were patrons, who controlled 'access to key social resources', and their clients, who were acquired;

63. Douglas E. Oakman, *Jesus and the Economic Questions of his Day* (Studies in the Bible and Early Christianity, 8; Lewiston, NY: Edwin Mellen Press, 1986), pp. 17-18.

64. See, for example, S.N. Eisenstadt and Luis Roniger, 'Patron–Client Relations as a Model of Structuring Social Exchange', *Comparative Studies in Society and History* 22 (1980), pp. 42-78; *idem, Patrons, Clients and Friends: Interpersonal Relations and the Structure of Trust in Society* (Cambridge: Cambridge University Press, 1984); *idem*, 'The Study of Patron–Client Relations and Recent Developments in Sociological Theory', in S.N. Eisenstadt and R. Lemarchand (eds.), *Political Clientelism, Patronage and Development* (London: Sage, 1981), pp. 271-96. In his MA thesis for the Department of Religious Studies at the University of Ottawa, entitled 'Patron–Client Dynamics in Flavius Josephus' *Vita*: A Cross-Disciplinary Analysis' (available by anonymous htp from aix1.uottawa.ca), Michael Strangelove helpfully overviews the history of patron–client studies. See now also Halvor Moxnes, 'Patron–Client Relations and the New Community in Luke–Acts', in Neyrey (ed.), *The Social World of Luke–Acts*, pp. 241-68.

65. Specifically, 'Judea and Galilee were deeply insinuated into the imperial political system' as evidenced by 'the prominent building projects in this region during the first and early second centuries'. These projects announced 'Judean and Galilean participation in a pattern involving the expectation of public building, royal benefaction, and civic appreciation at all political levels' (J. Andrew Overman, 'Matthew's Parables and Roman Politics: The Imperial Setting of Matthew's Narrative with Special Reference to his Parables', in Eugene H. Lovering [ed.], *Society of Biblical Literature 1995: Seminar Papers* [SBLSP, 34; Atlanta: Scholars Press, 1995], pp. 428-29). See also J.A. Overman, 'Recent Advances in the Archaeology of the Galilee in the Roman Period', *Currents in Research: Biblical Studies* 1 (1993), pp. 35-58.

this relationship was 'inherently unstable':[66] while the patron was over-whelmingly superior to the client, monopolizing access to production, its means, major markets and the elite of the society,[67] the peasant saw his world disintegrating through 'exploitative urbanism' and overly powerful landholding central institutions.[68] Wealth of the land moved out of the sphere of reciprocal distribution characteristic of village life based on kinship into 'urban areas, temple complexes, or state coffers'. As it did so, the cultivator became necessarily impoverished, and village life degenerated into a 'survivalist mentality'.[69] Urbanism encouraged the very kind of 'acquisitive attitudes, insensitive exploitation of the agricultural produces, and the worship of Mammon' condemned throughout the pages of Luke's works.[70] This was a world that was in the process of destroying itself, and the people, with it.

The Lukan Jesus calls for an essentially subversive approach to the Temple culture of his day as the immediate expression and vehicle of this impoverishment and destruction. But though we may best describe the Lukan Jesus' approach as 'revolutionist', the discursive culture to which this Jesus' teaching points is best described as 'subcultural'.[71]

66. Oakman, *Jesus*, p. 208.

67. Eisenstadt and Roniger, *Patrons, Clients and Friends*, pp. 48-49. See my work 'Rhetorical Analysis and Sociological Analysis in Historical Jesus Research', from the Sociology of Early Christianity Workshop, Toronto, 1994, published in *Method and Theory in the Study of Religion* 2 (1997), pp. 139-54. See also the work by Steven Grosby, 'Kinship, Territory, and the Nation in the Historiography of Ancient Israel', *ZAW* 105 (1993), pp. 3-18.

68. Oakman, *Jesus*, p. 211.

69. Oakman, *Jesus*, pp. 79-80. In order not to go into 'a hopeless spiral of debt that would lead to the loss of the family plot, the peasant would have to curtail consumption. The option of extending the production base was not available since more arable land was not available.'

70. Oakman, *Jesus*, p. 211.

71. As a subculture, Luke's audience is, as Carey notes, an intracommunal, Christian one; however, I fail to see how Carey can conclude that Luke's 'implied' audience is 'a relatively comfortable one' and that Luke 'may have been challenging it to more rigorous standards of discipleship' (Carey, 'Social and Rhetorical Functions'). Carey's position does not find support even among those who hold to the traditional, critical approaches to our text, which hold the text to be an example of apocalyptic. For example, Elisabeth Schüssler Fiorenza argues that apocalyptic in general is intended to encourage one to hold fast (*The Book of Revelation: Justice and Judgment* [Philadelphia: Fortress Press, 1985], p. 168) and

That is, via the teaching of Jesus to the Temple cult of Israel and to the λαός defined by that culture and via the invocation of extensive Old Testament passages, the Lukan Jesus speaks to a subculture. That is, he enacts 'the attitudes, values and disposition and norms' of the dominant culture better than the members of the dominant status.[72] In this, the Lukan Jesus also fulfills the picture of the Old Testament prophets whose role and function was remarkably similar.[73] After Jesus' death, his immediate followers, the apostles, will take on this role.

Yet, even without appeal to the possible, apocalyptic genre present in Lk. 19.45–21.38, it seems more likely that Luke is imitating a prophetic rebuke of the dominant culture while, at the same time, imitating the words of comfort issued to the responsive group from among the λαός who would heed Jesus' words and who would, as such, bear testimony to Jesus as the one who best fulfills the very essence of Israel's historical mission. As such, this message would seem to have been preached to—or at least memorized by—*responsive* 'brokers' of the traditional, patronage model,[74] the rising class of householders that were following and providing a physical meeting and welcome space for what Luke will later refer to as 'the Way'.[75] These individuals, who

John Gager suggests that apocalyptic has a kind of 'therapeutic function' via which the audience comes to experience the future as present (*Kingdom and Community: The Social World of Early Christianity* [Englewood Cliffs, NJ: Prentice–Hall, 1975]). Following Schüssler Fiorenza, we would expect encouragement of the listener, not rebuke, to be found here. This would accord with Carey's indication of the Lukan word ὑπομονή, but not with Carey's understanding of the use of this word to signify reprimand, more than encouragement. Following Gager, we observe not a chastising of the community as Carey would have it but a Lukan stress on the 'imminent' aspects of Lukan language and the place of prayer. Earlier, Norman B. Johnson had pointed to the same proleptic significance of prayer noted by Gager, namely, that an important facet of prayer in the Second Temple period was precisely to beseech God to bring the future to reality in the present (*Prayer in the Apocrypha and Pseudepigrapha: A Study of the Jewish Concept of God* [JBLMS, 2; Philadelphia: Society of Biblical Literature and Exegesis, 1948], pp. 29-34).

72. Cf. Robbins, 'Socio-Rhetorical Criticism', p. 189, following Roberts.

73. Cf. O. Plöger, *Theocracy and Eschatology* (trans. S. Rudman; Richmond, VA: John Knox Press, 1968), p. 45. See also David L. Petersen, *Late Israelite Prophecy: Studies in Deutero-Prophetic Literature and in Chronicles* (Missoula, MT: Scholars Press, 1977), pp. 2-5.

74. Oakman, *Jesus*, pp. 213-15.

75. See Anthony J. Blasi, 'Role Structures in the Early Hellenistic Church',

appear to be portrayed positively throughout Luke over against the
members of the Jewish elite as the power-brokers in Jesus' day—if not
in Luke's[76]—would form the foundations of the new apostolic community. The apostles as the bureaucracy of the new empire, the subculture called 'the kingdom of God', would govern a responsive, if not
always harmonious, community that was capable of living in freedom
under the rule of law.[77] In this way, the community would be a living
example of the subversion of the present, dying order created by the
Temple authorities and generally made possible by Caesar Augustus
until such time as the divine order to which the Old Testament points
would be fully restored.

4. *Ideological Texture*

In his 1995 presentation to the London Conference on the Rhetorical
Analysis of Scriptures, entitled 'The Flowering of Rhetorical Criticism
in America',[78] Tom Olbricht noted the significant influence in his own
work and in the work of American rhetoric scholars of the book by
Lester Thonssen and A. Craig Baird, *Speech Criticism: The Development of Standards for Rhetorical Appraisal*.[79] This work, which
Olbricht describes as the 'Bible' of American rhetorical criticism, described rhetorical criticism as 'a comparative study in which standards
of judgment deriving from the social interaction of a speech situation
are applied to public addresses to determine the immediate or delayed
effect of the speeches upon specific audiences, and ultimately, upon
society'.[80] Rhetorical criticism thus understood would not simply look

Sociological Analysis 47 (1986), pp. 226-48.

76. Lloyd Gaston, *No Stone on Another: Studies in the Significance of the Fall
of Jerusalem in the Synoptic Gospels* (NovTSup, 23; Leiden: E.J. Brill, 1970), pp.
331-33. *Pace* Robert J. Maddox, *The Purpose of Luke–Acts* (FRLANT, 126;
Göttingen: Vandenhoeck & Ruprecht, 1982), p. 45; Carey, 'Social and Rhetorical
Functions'.

77. The freedom is visibly expressed by the new apostolic life-style (Acts 2.42-
46) and the rule of law is shown vividly in the treatment of offenders, such as
Ananias and Sapphira (Acts 5.1-11).

78. In Porter and Olbricht (eds.), *The Rhetorical Analysis of Scripture*, pp. 79-
102.

79. New York: Ronald Press, 1948.

80. Thonssen and Baird, *Speech Criticism*, p. 16, quoted in Olbricht, 'Flowering', p. 7.

to style, arrangement and delivery as the keys to understanding a rhetorical address but rather to the standards of judgment used to assess the effect of the address both on a specific audience and on the larger society.[81]

By focusing on this packed definition in the work of Thonssen and Baird, Olbricht helps us to see how the larger practice of rhetorical analysis can assist those of us who wish to apply it concretely to scriptural texts. For, given our historical-critical prejudices, we are often content simply to examine the effect of the ancient address on the specific ancient audience. Thonssen and Baird would probably say that such an approach is inadequate. We will certainly want to examine the text in its day but ultimately we may also have to consider how the text has been understood subsequent to that day, even down to our own.[82] In this, then, we should probably talk less about rhetorical (or even socio-rhetorical) *criticism*—as if it were limited to the same objectives as historical-critical studies—and speak more broadly about rhetorical (or socio-rhetorical) *analysis*.

We can already see the importance of this dynamic view in the ancient context itself when we look at Luke. For already by Luke's time it appears that an earlier, Christian, contracultural language of cynicism, a language that appears to have represented a very early appropriation of Jesus' teaching, was proving inadequate. The popular pronouncements that form the earliest strata of Jesus traditions had been designed to influence in a broad way all of those who had power to institute change in the distribution of wealth (the 'haves') as opposed to those who had no power (the 'have nots'); however, by Luke's time the strictures were beginning to be limited to Luke's own growing community. In this way, Luke's works reflect a shift in the earliest Christian 'response to the problems of social formation' from a broadly issued 'alternative community ethos and ethic among those willing to consider an alternative social vision'[83] to a more complex social

---

81. Carey, who has also been influenced by this wider approach to rhetoric, notes that 'rhetorical investigations study texts for their motivations and effects in particular social and political contexts' (Carey, 'Social and Rhetorical Functions').

82. Here we enter the realm of the 'responsible' use of ancient texts, as spoken of by Bernard Lonergan, *Method in Theology* (New York: Herder & Herder, 1973), pp. 9, 27-55.

83. Burton L. Mack, *The Lost Gospel: The Book of Q and Christian Origins* (San Francisco: HarperSanFrancisco, 1993), p. 127.

formation, characterized by membership, meetings, property holdings, and so on.[84] For example, in Luke the contracultural, anti-family ethos of early Q sayings begins to yield to the positive role to be played by those households willing to be involved in the expansion of the Word.

Strikingly, the motor or dynamic of this expansion and growth was, in Luke's understanding, the waves created by the violence waged against the kingdom of God by the violence of empire and Temple. Though it is beyond the scope of this essay to determine whether the role of violence and persecution contributed to the Jesus movement becoming subcultural,[85] it seems clear that Luke understands violence and persecution as the prominent factor not only in the creation of the Jesus movement (Luke 21) but also in its ongoing growth (Acts).

In a brilliant adaptation of the rhetorical elements bequeathed to him, Luke inverts the dynamic of the Augustan imperial rhetoric that sees the empire moving out from the centre—Rome—to the limits of empire through the expansion of military and business power and through the resultant restoration of all land to full productive powers by showing how the 'kingdom of God' rides the ebb or reflux of the imperial wave. This reflux, which moves from the periphery back toward the centre, from the client Temple-state of Jerusalem toward the mainstay of that state, Rome, moves from home to home. In doing so, it in effect reverses the wave of history and turns what *had* been central into what is becoming *peripheral*. And yet this wave is not peaceful or violent, for the motor of that reflux is the very violence that carries the Roman

84. So Willi Braun, ACTS-L discussion list, 6 March 1995, commenting on Mack, *The Lost Gospel*, p. 121. In my paper to the London Conference in 1995 I suggested that something similar could be seen to be occurring in the literature of other cynic movements. If so, then we need to note that the religious response of cynicism was not, as is often supposed, monolithically utopian (that is, a response that 'presupposes that people must take an active and constructive role in replacing the entire present social system with a new social organization in which evil is absent'; so Robbins, 'Socio-Rhetorical Criticism', p. 186, citing Brian Wilson, *Magic and the Millennium: A Sociological Study of Religious Movements of Protest among Tribal and Third-World Peoples* (New York: Harper & Row, 1973), pp. 22-26) but at times in the stage of development of 'reformist' or even 'revolutionary' cynicism and that it, too, led to the creation of a sub-culture, both within classical Greece and within imperial Rome.

85. Cf. Brian Wilson's discussion of persecution related to various native American movements and the resulting impact on social organization (*Magic and the Millennium*, pp. 436-40).

imperial order and its rhetoric out from its centre but will now carry the Word of the gospel back to the centre-now-become-periphery.[86]

Our section plays an important role in this whole by foreshadowing the role of the Temple culture as first the context for hearing and affirming that Jesus is the authorized source of prophetic utterance regarding its future, and subsequently in the Lukan passion account and in the Acts as the source of the persecution described in this section. Yet, it is the Temple, understood broadly within the imperial context, that is the very source of the tidal wave of change that Luke sees the Christians riding toward Rome. Therefore, as noted above, the emphasis in this section is not so much on the destruction of the Temple and its subsequent culture as on the accompanying signs of the message moving out (in the language of Acts 1.8) or back (in the language of the inversion of imperial rhetoric). In the end, it is the same wave, coming back and washing over the Temple cult of Jerusalem, that will wash away everything corrupt in its wake.

The above is not only crucial for the progress of the gospel as envisioned by Luke but is also characteristic of apocalyptic as it is defined by O'Leary.[87] The characteristics of what O'Leary identifies as apocalyptic matches well the characteristics that our wider socio-rhetorical analysis of this section has revealed. For example, O'Leary describes apocalyptic as a revolutionary '*epochal discourse*: a systematic symbolic division of historical time that accords weight to actions and events in history by mediating the relationship of past, present, and future'.[88] As we have seen, via an 'imitation' of the past—both the Old Testament and Greco-Roman modes of rhetorical address—Luke portrays Jesus as mediating past prophetic utterances through a present suffering that will necessarily lead to a future fulfilment of the Kingdom as God brings it about.

Such an epochal picture is made possible for Luke because of the

---

86. See my description of this process in 'Whose Rhetoric? Whose Empire? The Subversion of Augustan Rhetoric in the Gospel of Luke', a paper presented at the conference 'Augustus: Le visage d'un empire/The face of Empire' (Carleton University/University of Ottawa, 15–16 March 1996).

87. O'Leary, 'Dramatistic Theory', p. 385.

88. In his definition, O'Leary follows John Angus Campbell, according to whom a 'rhetorical epoch' is 'an era so marked by a strategic, stylized symbolism that it divides history into a "before" and "after"' (John Angus Campbell, 'A Rhetorical Interpretation of History', *Rhetorica* 2 [1984], pp. 227-66 [229]).

authoritative person of Jesus and the complete acceptance of his followers. As O'Leary notes, the revolutionary discourse that is apocalyptic is possible because of an authority based on an '"extra-ordinary and personal gift of grace"', one that depends on '"the abso-lutely personal devotion and personal confidence in revelation, heroism, or other qualities of individual leadership"'.[89] According to O'Leary, 'since legitimation can be viewed as a primary function of rhetoric, little imagination is required to consider Weber's typology of legitima-tion as a catalogue of argumentative strategies employed by those who seek to achieve or maintain spiritual, as well as political, authority'.[90]

Jesus is clearly the focus of this authority in our section. Other rival authorities and claims to power stand clearly opposed to Jesus and to his authority, and are shown finally to be judged as such. This is true even of possible parallel authorities within the Christian community, such as the apostles, who simply do not figure in this section because it is not their 'epoch'. The emphasis is strictly on those who have received Jesus' authoritative word and who follow him in witness. The picture in this section of the Gospel of Luke is, then, a very different picture to the one found in Acts where the legitimation of the apostles (including Paul) is clearly the central issue.

Yet Luke's presentation of Jesus and of his followers here does resemble Acts in another way, namely, that both are 'comedic' presen-tations. Because the 'eschatological *topoi* of Authority, Time,[91] and Evil are elaborated differently in the tragic and comic interpretations of apocalypse',[92] the elements of suffering in Luke and Acts do not overwhelm. For, if it is true that Luke has borrowed elements from so-called apocalyptic sections of the Old Testament or even from so-called postbiblical apocalyptic texts, he has not done so through simple borrowing or through simple repetition of inspired oracular discourse, but through the reception and mediation through reinscription, inter-

89. O'Leary cites Weber's essay, 'Politics as a Vocation' (1946), in *From Max Weber: Essays in Sociology* (ed. and trans. H.H. Gerth and C. Wright Mills; New York: Oxford University Press, 1958).

90. O'Leary, 'Dramatistic Theory', p. 401.

91. According to O'Leary, the 'historical influence of this discourse is achieved precisely through its symbolic constructions of time: apocalyptic succeeds or fails with its audiences to the degree that it persuades them of their situation within the particular historical pattern of temporal fulfillment represented in its mythic imagery' (*Arguing the Apocalypse*, p. 13).

92. O'Leary, 'Dramatistic Theory', p. 386.

pretation and rationalization to which those texts and those utterances have been subjected.[93] With regard to Luke, this means that earlier tragic portrayals have been redefined to present a comedic interpretation of the original message or variants of it.[94]

Strikingly, though, and sadly, Luke's own interpretation of Jesus' words *became* a tragic portrayal when, in the work of subsequent Western authors, Luke's own rhetorical reversal was reinverted and the reflux and violence of the Augustan imperial model once again reappeared. For by the fourth century, Rome had once again become the seat of imperial power, a power that was by then Christianized, and the emperors were pictured more as Augustus had once been in his own rhetorical instruments.[95] Rather than suffering violence, Christian emperors and their apologists now saw it as their means of exercising ἐξουσία. Ironically, and truly tragically, the picture that results is the very inverse of Luke's and thus a reversion to the Augustan one! And yet, it was Luke's own agenda that allowed for that later reversal since his original, rhetorical reversal had blazed the way for later Christians to appropriate and transform apparently opposing rhetorical elements,[96] be they classical (as in Luke's case) or early Christian (as in the case of fourth- and fifth-century Christian writers).

5. *Conclusions*

The outlines and initial overview for a socio-rhetorical analysis of the material in Luke 21 suggest that there is much value in the multi-disciplinary approach called socio-rhetorical analysis. Not only does this approach help us to overcome the severe fragmentation to which

93. In this, O'Leary depends heavily on the work of Hans Blumenberg, *Work on Myth* (trans. Robert M. Wallace; Studies in Contemporary German Social Thought; Cambridge, MA: MIT Press, 1985). O'Leary here engages in a similar mode of analysis to that of Vernon Robbins in his intertextual analysis.

94. It is of course possible that we should not view the Old Testament or Second Temple so-called apocalyptic passages as 'tragic'. In this case, there is less Lukan reconfiguration.

95. In the early Christian apologies, the earthly king begins to be spoken of as the embodiment of the Logos, much as Philo had done with Augustus (cf. W.H.C. Frend, *The Rise of Christianity* [Philadelphia: Fortress Press, 1984], p. 36).

96. So Robert D. Sider, *Ancient Rhetoric and the Art of Tertullian* (London: Oxford University Press, 1971).

the discipline of New Testament studies is subject these days, but it also assists us to avoid the hasty determination of materials on the basis of supposed parallels. We have been able to assess various features of Lk. 19.45–21.38 without forcing elements of this text into the form-critical mold prepared for it.

Socio-rhetorical analysis also underscores the value of understanding rhetoric more widely than the historical-critical canons would suggest. From this vantage point, what we see to be at stake in the Lukan portrayal of Jesus in the section we have examined is a conflicting rhetorical presentation of how rhetorical and social boundaries affect the λαός and of the way in which those who possess ἐξουσία can change the boundaries. The focus of the debate leading up to 21.5-38 suggests that what is really at stake is a debate over what is permitted (namely, that over which one has power). According to Jesus' opponents, the boundaries need to be fortified around the Temple, and they will do it; according to Jesus, the boundaries need to be eliminated, and he and his followers will do it. In the end, Jesus argues, he and his followers know which approach God will favor and Jesus' interpretation of the σημεῖα prove him right.

Elements of this scenario fit the classical scenarios of so-called apocalyptic texts. But where Luke clearly differs is that, as Acts shows, the enlargement of the boundaries and the transformation takes place in the household (οἶκος), which is the countervailing force to the Temple.[97] In this, Luke not only inverts normal Jewish apocalyptic expectations but also forces the Augustan imperial rhetoric of abundance and transformation to serve his purposes of the advance of the kingdom of God in the common everyday life of Christians.

Luke's approach to this question had significant influence on subsequent Christian discourse. Subsequent Christian discourse, through its contact with the surrounding world, also significantly transformed the original Lukan model. As Averil Cameron has noted, the study of Christian discourse in the Roman world is a study not merely of 'how Christian discourse made its impact on society at large, but [of how] it was itself transformed and shaped in the endeavor'.[98] In the end, Luke

97. On the implications of the transformation of households, see the study by Willi Braun, *Feasting and Social Rhetoric in Luke 14* (SNTSMS, 85; Cambridge: Cambridge University Press, 1995).

98. Averil Cameron, *Christianity and the Rhetoric of Empire: The Development of Christian Discourse* (Berkeley: University of California Press, 1991), p. 4.

memorialized for us a critique of Temple culture that, in its constant ebb and flow, has been a rhetorical platform used by Christians against others, by others against Christians, and finally by Christians against alternative Christian understandings of Temples now become Christian.

The Lukan Account of Paul's Conversion
and Hermagorean Stasis Theory

Ira J. Jolivet, Jr

Biblical scholars have long grappled with the presence of a number of discrepancies between Luke's depiction of Paul's conversion in Acts 9 and the retelling of that event in Paul's defense speeches in chs. 22 and 26. The nature of the scholarly discussion generated by these discrepancies has naturally evolved coincidentally with the methodological development of biblical studies in general. Few, if any, modern analysts, for instance, share in the interests of those earlier historical critics who sought to prove the accuracy of the accounts or to harmonize all the disparate details which they contained. Nor are they interested, as source critics once were, in attributing the discrepancies to divergent sources underlying the written text.

But building on the work of form, redaction and secular literary critics, modern scholars are much more likely to be interested in deducing the theological intentions of the author by analyzing the literary aspects of the discrepancies as they function in the framework of the entire narrative. This methodological shift may be clearly seen in the following statements of Dennis Hamm:

> It is widely accepted among Lucan scholars that the variations of event, detail and expression in the three accounts of Paul's experience on the road to Damascus (Acts 9; 22 and 26) are best accounted for as the work of Luke rather than as deriving from a diversity of sources. Whatever his sources, Luke the historian, theologian and narrator is in control and his fifty-two chapter, two-volume work is a unified whole. Where Luke creates a 'theme with variations', e.g. speeches with similar content or in repeated narratives of the same event (esp. the Cornelius material [Acts 10–11 and 15] and the conversion/call accounts), these are privileged *loci* for exploring Luke's method and meaning.[1]

---

1.   D. Hamm, 'Paul's Blindness and its Healing: Clues to Symbolic Intent

Hamm subsequently concludes that by subtly varying the details of the blindness motif in the three accounts,

> Luke moves from a story in which Paul experiences blindness as a punitive act of God and recovery of sight as a divine healing (Acts 9) to a story in which the same loss and recovery of sight is told in muted and ambiguous language (Acts 22) and, finally (in Acts 26), to a story in which Paul's own experience of loss and recovery of physical vision is transmuted to a metaphor describing the end-time mission of Israel, Jesus and Paul.[2]

The significance of Hamm's approach and conclusions and those of other modern scholars[3] who have attempted to address the problem of the discrepancies in the conversion accounts should neither be overlooked nor minimized. As a student of ancient Greco-Roman rhetorical theory and practice, however, I am convinced that the newly resurrected methodology of rhetorical criticism can also contribute to the understanding of the nature of the discrepancies.

I therefore offer this analysis as a rhetorical solution to the problem of the discrepancies between the initial Lukan account of Paul's conversion in Acts 9 and the later retelling of that event in the account of Paul's defense. Since William R. Long deals with the disparities between chs. 9 and 22, albeit in a cursory manner, in his rhetorical analysis 'The *Paulusbild* in the Trial of Paul',[4] and for the sake of brevity, I shall focus solely on the discrepancies between chs. 9 and 26.

The analysis consists of three major sections. In the first section I shall briefly describe stasis theory—the system of classifying rhetorical topics developed by Hermagoras of Temnos in the second century BCE. In the second section I shall suggest that Paul's defense speech in Acts 26 is best understood in light of insights from the Hermagorean stasis *antestasis*, the 'issue of comparison'. In the final section I shall examine

(Acts 9; 22 and 26)', *Bib* 71 (1990), pp. 63-72.

2.   Hamm, 'Paul's Blindness', p. 71.

3.   See also for content and bibliography, C.W. Hedrick, 'Paul's Conversion/ Call: A Comparative Analysis of Three Reports in Acts', *JBL* 100 (1981), pp. 415-32; and R.C. Tannehill's narrative-critical approach to the problem in *The Narrative Unity of Luke–Acts: A Literary Interpretation*. II. *The Acts of the Apostles* (Minneapolis: Fortress Press, 1990), pp. 321-22.

4.   W.R. Long, 'The *Paulusbild* in the Trial of Paul', in *Society of Biblical Literature: Seminar Papers 1983* (Atlanta: Scholars Press, 1983), pp. 87-105.

the discrepancies between chs. 9 and 26 from the perspective gained from specific topics under this issue.

1. *Hermagorean Stasis Theory*

With regard to the specific contributions of the ancient Greek theorists to the universal field of rhetoric George A. Kennedy writes:

> What is unique about Greek rhetoric, and what makes it useful for criticism, is the degree to which it was conceptualized. The Greeks gave names to rhetorical techniques, many of which are found all over the world. They organized these techniques into a system which could be taught and learned. What we mean by classical rhetorical theory is this structured system which describes the universal phenomenon of rhetoric in Greek terms.[5]

In yet another work Kennedy attributes the fullest development of ancient Greek rhetorical theory to Hermagoras.[6] Ray Nadeau agrees with Kennedy's assessment and goes on to describe Hermagoras's system of classification of rhetorical topics according to 'stasis' or issue:

> In his fourfold system, *stochasmos* means stasis of conjecture on—for instance, whether an act took place; *horos* means stasis of definition, having to do with what a thing is through its essential qualities; *poiotes* means quality of nonessential kinds as distinguished from essential qualities noted in a definition; *metalēpsis* means objection to a charge on technical grounds.[7]

In other words, when the question in a forensic case is the fundamental one of whether the accused committed an act such as murder, the stasis is *stochasmos*, the issue of conjecture or fact. In such a case the defense relies on irrefutable proofs and probable arguments to deny that the accused committed the alleged act. If, however, the accused does not deny that an act was committed but claims that the act should be called something else—for example, manslaughter rather than murder— then the stasis is *horos*, the issue of definition. Or, should the accused

---

5.   G.A. Kennedy, *New Testament Interpretation through Rhetorical Criticism* (Chapel Hill, NC: University of North Carolina Press, 1984), p. 11.

6.   G.A Kennedy, *The Art of Persuasion in Greece* (Princeton, NJ: Princeton University Press, 1963), p. 318.

7.   R. Nadeau, 'Hermagoras' *On Stasis*: A Translation with an Introduction', *Speech Monographs* 31 (1964), pp. 362-424.

admit to performing an act but claim justification due to some extenuating circumstance such as self-defense or temporary insanity, the issue is qualitative stasis, *poiotes*. This issue is divided into further subdivisions which will be introduced as they become pertinent. Finally, if the defendant seeks dismissal of the case due to some technicality, the stasis is *metalēpsis*, the issue of objection.

2. *Stasis in Acts 26*

Three factors external to the text of Acts point to the probability of the use of Hermagorean stasis theory in Luke's narration of Paul's speech before Agrippa in ch. 26. First, the teaching and practice of rhetoric pervaded the educational, literary and social environs of the period in which Luke wrote.[8] The rhetoric which both Hellenists and Romans taught and practiced during this period was based on Hermagorean stasis theory. Secondly, as a 'Hellenistic historian'[9] Luke was probably inclined to use whatever training he had acquired to fabricate or embellish the speeches in his history.[10] Finally, by using stases in the defense speeches Luke would have appeared as a more reliable historian to his first-century readers who would have expected Paul to use appropriate and plausible arguments in his own defense.

Internal evidence also suggests that stasis theory is at work in Acts 26. Kennedy points in the direction of this evidence when he writes:

> When compared to Paul's address to the Jews in Jerusalem and his defense before Felix...this speech shows an attempt to adapt the same basic materials to a different audience, in this case the hellenized Jewish king Agrippa. Paul has clearly had an opportunity to prepare his address in advance, something which was not possible when he spoke in Jerusalem. Stasis remains metastasis, transference of responsibility to God.[11]

Kennedy's rhetorically trained eye has perceived two characteristics of Paul's speech before Agrippa which are relevant to this study. First, he has noted that Paul is actively trying to defend himself against the charges leveled at him. This point is not insignificant because a number

8. Kennedy, *New Testament Interpretation*, pp. 8-10.
9. D.E. Aune, *The New Testament in its Literary Environment* (Philadelphia: Westminster Press, 1987), p. 138.
10. Aune, *The New Testament*, p. 83.
11. Kennedy, *New Testament Interpretation*, p. 137.

of biblical literary scholars (Martin Dibelius[12] and Ernst Haenchen[13] to name two of the most notable) tend to see Paul's defense as non-existent or at least as secondary to the literary and theological intentions of the author.

Now I am not suggesting that Luke does not have a literary or theological agenda. I am merely saying that an analyst who begins with the presupposition that these agendas are the only factors worth investigating runs the double risk of overlooking the artistic subtlety of the author, and, more importantly, of misunderstanding the theological implications of the discrepancies. Such an analyst would perhaps do well to take note of the following observation by Henry J. Cadbury:

> Even though devoid of historical basis in genuine tradition the speeches in Acts have considerable historical value. There is reason to suppose that the talented author of Acts expended upon them not only his artistic skill, but also a considerable amount of historic imagination.[14]

Thus Kennedy's rhetorical training allows him to read Paul's speech before Agrippa as a first-century reader might have, and to notice the subtle nuances of the arguments. Which brings us to Kennedy's second point, that Paul's legal strategy is built on stasis *metastasis*, shifting the responsibility to God.

In the Hermagorean system *metastasis* is one of the four final subdivisions of the 'assumptive branch' of the issue of quality which, we recall, had to do with extenuating circumstances. *Metastasis* or 'shifting of the charge', occurs, according to Cicero, 'when the accusation for the offense which is alleged by the prosecutor is shifted to another person or thing. It is done in two ways: sometimes the responsibility is shifted and sometimes the act itself.'[15]

Kennedy does not offer a great deal of evidence in support of his conclusion that Paul is seeking to transfer the responsibility for his actions to God. In reference to the speech in Acts he merely states: 'Since Paul does not deny that his actions have been inconsistent with

12. M. Dibelius, *Studies in the Acts of the Apostles* (ed. H. Greeven; London: SCM Press, 1956), p. 180.

13. E. Haenchen, *The Acts of the Apostles: A Commentary* (Philadelphia: Westminster Press, 1971), pp. 104, 327.

14. H.J. Cadbury, 'The Speeches in Acts', in K. Lake and H.J. Cadbury (eds.), *The Beginnings of Christianity*. I. *The Acts of the Apostles* (5 vols.; repr.; Grand Rapids: Baker Book House, 1966), V, pp. 402-27 (426).

15. Cicero, *Inv.* 2.29.86 (LCL).

the law, the stasis is best regarded as metastasis, transferring responsibility to God'.[16] Supporting evidence for his similar conclusion about the speech in ch. 26 is equally meager. 'The proof (19-23)', Kennedy writes, 'argues that Paul (like Peter) had no choice and adds scriptural evidence'.[17]

I would like to suggest that textual evidence with regard to Paul's legal strategy in ch. 26 is actually more in line with topics under the heading of another of the four assumptive subdivisions of the issue of quality, stasis *antestasis*, the issue of 'comparison'.

Comparison, as defined by Cicero, 'is the case where some act which cannot be approved by itself, is defended by reference to the end for which it was done'.[18] Taken alone this description of the stasis of comparison is far too vague to shed any light on the speech in Acts 26. Fortunately, Cicero proceeds to describe the appropriate arguments or topics under the heading of this issue. He describes the first of the three 'common topics', those arguments which are suitable for both prosecutor and defendant, as follows:

> The common topics will be: of the prosecutor, to inveigh against a man who when he confesses to a deed that is base or disadvantageous or both, yet seeks some defence, and to bring out the inexpediency or baseness of the deed with great indignation; of the counsel for the defence, that no deed should be judged inexpedient or base, or for that matter advantageous or honourable unless it is known with what intent, at what time and for what reason it was done.[19]

A contemporary practical illustration of this type of argument appears in a newspaper account of the first day of testimony in Lieutenant Colonel Oliver North's 1989 trial on a number of charges including making false statements to and obstructing Congress. The prosecutor, John Keker, opened the trial by telling jurors that

> they would hear that North 'considers himself a very patriotic person who knows what's best for our country, what's best for us'.
>
> 'But there is no higher patriotism than protecting our system of government. To lie to Congress, even if you mistrust them, is a crime, not a defense.'[20]

16. Kennedy, *New Testament Interpretation*, p. 134.
17. Kennedy, *New Testament Interpretation*, p. 137.
18. Cicero, *Inv.* 2.24.72 (LCL).
19. Cicero, *Inv.* 2.25.77 (LCL).
20. A. Epstein, 'North Called a Liar, Patriot as Long-Awaited Trial Opens',

Here the prosecutor is clearly trying to refute the anticipated argument of the defense that North's actions were expedient and honorable rather than criminal.

Attorney for the defense Brendan Sullivan paints an entirely different picture of North and his actions, however, claiming that his client

> was motivated by a 'strong sense of duty and patriotism' and a desire to obey Reagan's policy of helping the Contras to dislodge communism from Nicaragua and to prevent Nicaraguans from fleeing to 'take places in schools and jobs' in the United States.
>
> 'He was always faithful to this country, to his commander-in-chief, to his family and to those whose lives depended on him', Sullivan said of the former White House national security aide.[21]

The implication here is that Colonel North stood at a historical cross-roads where the red tide of communism lapped at the shores of North America and where potential unchecked hordes of political refugees threatened the USA's economic and educational well-being. North's actions were intended to check both of these evils and were therefore, according to Sullivan, to be viewed as honorable and expedient rather than as criminal.

The same general type of legal strategy may be observed in Paul's trials in Acts in which he was initially charged with being 'a pestilent fellow, an agitator among all the Jews throughout the world, and a ringleader of the sect of the Nazarenes' (24.5). He was also accused of trying to profane the Temple in Jerusalem (24.6). The charges seem to have become less specific with the passage of time due to court delays and the disappearance from the scene of the Asian Jews who had been witnesses to the alleged defilement of the Temple (21.27; 24.18-19). By the time of the trial before Agrippa in Acts 26 it seems that Paul has become more concerned with defending himself against the more serious charge, at least as far as the Roman authorities were concerned, of threatening the tranquillity and security of the empire through riots which resulted from his preaching.

Paul's legal strategy has also undergone various changes according to the juridical situation. In 24.10-21, for example, Paul seems to be arguing both from conjecture (24.12-18) and on procedural grounds (24.18-19). The abbreviated exchange between Festus and Paul in 25.8-

---

Austin American Statesman, 22 February 1989, p. 8(A).
   21. Epstein, 'North Called a Liar', p. 8(A).

11 also contains hints that Paul is still seeking dismissal of the charges on procedural grounds as well.

In 26.2-23, however, he apparently shifts his strategy to the issue of comparison. At this point Paul, like Oliver North according to his defense attorney, stood at a historical crossroads, the time of fulfillment of the 'promises made by God to our fathers' through the resurrection of Jesus (26.6-7). And not unlike Oliver North's defense attorney, Paul also claims that both his intentions and his actions were always honorable and expedient. With regard to his intentions, Paul implies that his desire to preach Christ, to share in proclaiming 'light both to the people and to the Gentiles', was consistent with his former manner of life (26.4-5) and with the well-intended but misguided convictions which led him to persecute the Christians (26.9-11). Paul also shows clearly that in comparison with his former activities of imprisoning, coercing and participating in the executions of innocent people, his post-conversion action of preaching hope and salvation was much more honorable and expedient.

And there are other indications in Acts 26 that Paul is using a strategy of comparison in his defense. These indications involve the second and third topics under the heading of the issue of comparison and may now be discussed in conjuction with the discrepancies between ch. 26 and ch. 9.

3. *Honor, Advantage and Necessity in Paul's Legal Strategy*

Cicero states that the second common topic from comparison 'is that in which the magnitude of the service performed is demonstrated and enlarged upon by reference to the advantage or honour or necessity of the deed'.[22] Since the terms advantage, honor and necessity are also topics under the heading of 'deliberative' oratory, another slight digression is in order.

Deliberative rhetoric was generally the discourse of the political assembly where orators debated the honor, advantage or necessity of undertaking some future course of action. Arguments of this type, however, were also used in the forensic arena. The first topics, honor and advantage, are categories under which certain things are classified according to whether they are to be sought or to be avoided. The category of honor consists of anything which 'draws us to it by its intrinsic

22. Cicero, *Inv.* 2.26.77 (LCL).

merit, not winning us by any prospect of gain, but attracting us by its own worth'.[23] To this category belong such abstract but inherently valuable things as virtue, knowledge and truth. 'But there is something else', Cicero continues, 'that is to be sought not because of its own merit and natural goodness, but because of some profit or advantage to be derived from it. Money is in this class.'[24] Finally, there is 'something which unites qualities from both these classes; by its own merit and worth it entices us and leads us on, and also holds out to us a prospect of some advantage to induce us to seek it more eagerly. Examples are friendship and a good reputation.'[25]

The above categories pertain to Paul's legal strategy in Acts 26 in that here he is demonstrating and enlarging upon the magnitude of the service he has rendered to people of all nations with reference to the honor and advantage which results from his preaching. The honor and advantage to which Paul refers is implicitly embedded in Jesus' address on the road to Damascus. In 26.18 Jesus says that he is sending Paul to the people and to the Gentiles 'to open their eyes, that they may turn from darkness to light and from the power of Satan to God, that they may receive forgiveness of sins and a place among those who are sanctified by faith in me'. This concise statement offers the promise of such honorable things as glory and friendship with God and such advantageous things as immortality and everlasting security.

The other element mentioned in topic two, necessity, also figures into Paul's legal strategy in Acts 26 and therefore merits some discussion. Once again, Cicero: 'I regard necessity as something that no force can resist and thereby one is prevented from accomplishing some possible task; and this necessity cannot be altered or alleviated'.[26] To use one of Cicero's examples which also seems relevant to Acts 26, it is necessary that every human being die at some time or other.

Some necessities inherently possess qualifications. We might say, for example, that it is necessary for all human beings to eat food. But a person may choose not to eat food and to starve to death instead. The qualification in this instance, then, is that one must eat food *if one does not wish to die*.

This topic is relevant to Paul's defense in Acts 26 because both the

23. Cicero, *Inv.* 2.52.157 (LCL).
24. Cicero, *Inv.* 2.52.157 (LCL).
25. Cicero, *Inv.* 2.52.157 (LCL).
26. Cicero, *Inv.* 2.57.170 (LCL).

content and tone of the speech convey the idea that the course of action prescribed by Paul's preaching—that is, faith in Jesus—is necessary if one wishes to attain the honors and advantages that accrue to salvation.

At this point it is fair to ask what all this has to do with the discrepancies between Acts 9 and 26. Clearly we should now be able to say that it is quite probable that Paul in Acts 26 is actively trying to defend himself against the charges leveled at him by means of topics 1 and 2 from the issue of comparison. He has shown, for example, that the action of which he is accused, preaching the resurrection of Jesus, is not a crime but rather is more honorable, advantageous and necessary than the well-intended but misguided actions which he performed as a Pharisee.

Paul, then, has a legal strategy; a legal strategy which calls for him to use an embellished and heightened form of language—much, as we have seen, as the language Brendan Sullivan used in Oliver North's defense. Consequently, we can understand that whereas in Acts 9.3 Luke narrates in a relatively subdued way that as Paul journeyed 'a light from heaven flashed about him'; in 26.13 the light is said by Paul to be brighter than the midday sun. We can also see why only Paul fell to the ground in response to the flash of light in 9.4, but in 26.14 Paul and the entire traveling party reacted to the overpowering light.

While some of the discrepancies between Acts 9 and 26 may be attributed to embellishments in accordance with topics 1 and 2 from comparison, the two major differences—the addition of the statement by Jesus in 26.14, that 'It hurts you to kick against the goads', and the absence of any mention of the role of Ananias in Paul's conversion—must be attributed to topic 3. According to Cicero this topic is one

> in which by a vivid verbal picture the event is brought before the eyes of the audience, so they will think that they too would have done the same if they had been confronted with the situation and the same cause for action at the same time.[27]

This topic is essential for understanding what Luke is doing when in Acts 26.12-18 he reshapes Paul's encounter with the Lord in the framework of a legal defense.

Here Luke has Paul paint for Agrippa a very vivid picture of the cause of his action, the event which compelled him to begin declaring the resurrection of Jesus. Ananias must be omitted so that Paul can

---

27. Cicero, *Inv.* 2.26.78 (LCL).

receive his orders directly from the powerful risen Lord. An added element of compulsion is imparted by the phrase, 'It hurts you to kick against the goads'. Who would be brave or foolish enough to be disobedient to the heavenly vision? Certainly not Paul. And hopefully Agrippa would put himself in Paul's place and agree by his decision that he also would have done the same thing. In a sense Paul's strategy was successful because Agrippa assented with Festus to Paul's innocence (26.31-32). Alas, however, Paul's fate had already been sealed by his appeal to Caesar.

4. *Conclusion*

In this essay I have attempted to analyze Paul's defense speech in Acts 26 in light of ancient Greco-Roman theory and to account rhetorically for the discrepancies between the accounts of Paul's conversion in Acts 9 and 26. More specifically, I have sought to attribute the discrepancies to a legal strategy which used topics from stasis *antestasis*, the issue of comparison. I believe that rhetorically literate ancient readers would have recognized the artistic value of the strategic embellishments. Such readers would certainly have had more understanding of and appreciation for Luke's rhetorical and literary skills than modern readers who are more concerned with the pursuit of 'objective scientific truth'.

Part III

RHETORICAL INTERPRETATION OF PAUL'S WRITINGS

PAUL AS EPISTOLOGRAPHER *AND* RHETORICIAN?[*]

Stanley E. Porter

1. *Introduction*

Our knowledge of Paul comes from two principal sources, his letters and the book of Acts, but these are not the same kinds of sources. One is a set of letters and the other a narrative; one is a primary source and the other a secondary source, so far as Paul is concerned. What we learn about Paul and his background from his letters is not nearly as great as we would like. In fact, much of what is tacitly assumed to be reliable knowledge of Paul is dependent upon the book of Acts. For example, a clear statement of Paul's conversion experience on the Damascus road (Acts 9, 22, 26; but cf. Gal. 1.11-24; 1 Cor. 15.8), the itinerary of his several missionary journeys, the Hellenistic side of his background and experience, including his coming from Tarsus and his Roman citizenship—all of these are found primarily in Acts and not in the Pauline letters. Consequently, critical scholarship has often raised questions about whether these are accurate depictions of Paul. There are a number of other items related to Paul's life and experience that are only known from Acts and that critical scholarship doubts even more seriously, such as his numerous public speeches, for example at Athens (Acts 17.22-31). This raises several important questions regarding the relationship between the Paul of Acts and the Paul of his letters, that is, between Paul the speechmaker and Paul the letterwriter. How do these relate to each other—are they compatible or exclusive? What can we make of the evidence that we get from each, especially in terms of rhetorical analysis of Paul and his compositions? In order to examine these questions adequately, general questions about the relationship

---

[*]   An expanded and developed form of this chapter may be found as Chapter 5 in S.E. Porter, *The Paul of Acts: Essays in Literary Criticism, Rhetoric, and Theology* (WUNT, 115; Tübingen: Mohr Siebeck, 1999), pp. 98-125.

between the Paul of Acts and the letters must be asked, before discussing each of these corpora in more detail.

2. *The Relationship between the Paul of the Letters and the Paul of Acts*

The traditional view of authorship of Acts is that the volume is the second of two composed by a traveling companion of Paul, Luke the physician.[1] Although this tradition is reasonably early (second century), it must be recognized that the Gospel and Acts are formally anonymous, and so certainty regarding authorship cannot be established. Scholars have debated the evidence regarding how certain the traditional view is, giving various amounts of credibility to references in Paul's letters to Luke (Col. 4.14; 2 Tim. 4.11; Phlm. 24). Further support for Lukan authorship is often found in the 'we' passages of Acts (16.10-17; 20.5-15; 21.1-18; 27.1-29; 28.1-16) and the fact that Luke was among the faithful companions of Paul (Col. 4.14; 2 Tim. 4.11; Phlm. 24). Critical scholarship of the last hundred years, however, has called this attribution into question. The thought that the author of Luke–Acts was a physician can no longer be definitively supported from the text itself, since the medical language is typical of writers of Luke's level and style,[2] and the majority of references to Luke are found in the disputed Pauline letters.[3] Furthermore, there are a number of possibilities for explaining the use of the 'we' passages, and the first-hand account is only one of them. The 'we' passages have been viewed as a fictional device to tell of a sea voyage, they have been seen as an indication of the redactional activity of the author, they have been thought to indicate the incorporation of a source document, and they have been thought to indicate that the author is citing his own first-hand

1.   On authorship of Acts, see W.G. Kümmel, *Introduction to the New Testament* (trans. H.C. Kee; Nashville: Abingdon Press, 1975), pp. 147-50.

2.   On the use of medical language in Luke–Acts as reflecting a higher register of usage, see H.J. Cadbury, *Style and Literary Method of Luke* (Cambridge, MA: Harvard University Press, 1920), arguing against W.K. Hobart, *The Medical Language of St Luke* (London: Longmans, Green, 1882) and A. Harnack, *Luke the Physician: The Author of the Third Gospel and the Acts of the Apostles* (trans. J.R. Wilkinson; London: Williams & Norgate, 2nd edn, 1909).

3.   On authorship of these letters, see L.M. McDonald and S.E. Porter, *Early Christianity and its Sacred Literature* (Peabody, MA: Hendrickson, forthcoming), Chapter 10.

account.[4] Even if the 'we' passages are thought to represent a first-hand account (the language does not necessarily mean an eyewitness), in the light of the author's leaving this indicator in the text, the most that can probably be argued is that another source is being used.[5] It does not resolve the issue of authorship, and certainly not the issue of the relationship between the Paul of Acts and the Paul of the letters.

Important still for the discussion are a number of questions that have been raised regarding the accuracy and reliability of Acts in relationship to what is known about Paul through his letters.[6] A number of these factors seem to some scholars to be so at odds with the picture of

4.   See, among others, V.K. Robbins, 'By Land and by Sea: The We-Passages and Ancient Voyages', in C.H. Talbert (ed.), *Perspectives on Luke–Acts* (Edinburgh: T. & T. Clark, 1980), pp. 215-42; V.K. Robbins, 'The We-Passages in Acts and Ancient Sea-Voyages', *BibRes* 20 (1975), pp. 5-18, for the sea-voyage view; M. Dibelius, *Studies in the Acts of the Apostles* (ed. H. Greeven; trans. M. Ling; London: SCM Press, 1956), pp. 204-206 and *passim*; H. Conzelmann and A. Lindemann, *Interpreting the New Testament: An Introduction to the Principles and Methods of New Testament Exegesis* (trans. S.S. Schatzmann; Peabody, MA: Hendrickson, 1988), p. 241; G. Lüdemann, *Early Christianity According to the Traditions in Acts: A Commentary* (trans. J. Bowden; Philadelphia: Fortress Press, 1987), *passim*, for the redactional view; J. Dupont, *The Sources of Acts: The Present Position* (trans. K. Pond; London: Darton, Longman & Todd, 1964), esp. pp. 76-165, on various source theories; and C.J. Hemer, *The Book of Acts in the Setting of Hellenistic History* (ed. C.H. Gempf; WUNT, 49; Tübingen: Mohr Siebeck, 1989), pp. 308-34; *idem*, 'First Person Narrative in Acts 27–28', *TynBul* 36 (1986), pp. 79-109, esp. pp. 79-86, on first-hand accounts.

5.   See S.E. Porter, 'The "We" Passages', in D.W.J. Gill and C. Gempf (eds.), *The Book of Acts in its First Century Setting. II. The Book of Acts in its Graeco-Roman Setting* (5 vols.; Grand Rapids: Eerdmans, 1994), pp. 546-74, where the independent source document is endorsed, as well as a critique of previous positions being offered. This essay is now revised and expanded in Porter, *The Paul of Acts*, Chapter 2.

6.   The standard treatments of these issues are P. Vielhauer, 'On the "Paulinism" of Acts', in L.E. Keck and J.L. Martyn (eds.), *Studies in Luke–Acts* (Philadelphia: Fortress Press, 1966), pp. 33-50; and E. Haenchen, *The Acts of the Apostles: A Commentary* (trans. B. Noble *et al.*; Philadelphia: Westminster Press, 1971 [1965]), pp. 112-16. For recent discussions of these issues, see L.T. Johnson, *The Writings of the New Testament: An Interpretation* (Minneapolis: Fortress Press, 1986), pp. 231-38; B. Witherington III, *The Acts of the Apostles: A Socio-Rhetorical Commentary* (Grand Rapids: Eerdmans, 1998), pp. 430-38; and Porter, *The Paul of Acts*, Chapter 9.

Paul that is gained through his letters as to raise the question of whether the person who wrote Acts could possibly have been a first-hand witness or close acquaintance. In the light of the concerns of this chapter, the following points are worth enumerating, before turning to the issues of rhetoric and epistolography.

1. Whereas Paul is only known as a letterwriter in the writings attributed to him in the New Testament, the author of Acts never depicts Paul as a letterwriter, but as a speechmaker. Nowhere in Acts is Paul seen carrying on the kind of ministry that is depicted in his letters, that is, maintaining and guarding his relationships with his churches through his epistolary correspondence. Furthermore, the author of Acts, regardless of his knowledge of Paul's writing activities, does not overtly refer to or use the letters in his composition, although there may be allusions.[7] Instead, in Acts Paul carries out his missionary strategy through speaking in various ways.

2. Whereas Paul apparently was not able personally to convince his audiences on several occasions, at least according to his own words in his letters (e.g. 2 Cor. 10.10, although one must be careful in interpreting this passage), in Acts Paul is, for the most part, a highly convincing rhetorician (Acts 13.9-11, 16-41; 14.15-17; 17.22-31; 22.1-21; 24.10-21; 26.2-26). These speeches have been analyzed in some detail recently, and it is to this that I wish to return.[8]

3. One would not be able to gather from Acts that Paul jealously guarded his relationship as apostle with, for example, the Corinthian church, warranting the kind of epistolary exchange that we find in the letters themselves. Instead he delivers speeches and then moves on, very much reminiscent of the itinerant evangelists ridiculed so severely in Lucian's *Peregrinus* and warned about in the *Didache* (11–13), as

---

7. For discussion of the question of whether Paul knew or used Paul's letters, see W.O. Walker, 'Acts and the Pauline Corpus Reconsidered', *JSNT* 24 (1985), pp. 3-23, repr. in S.E. Porter and C.A. Evans (eds.), *The Pauline Writings: A Sheffield Reader* (The Biblical Seminar, 34; Sheffield: Sheffield Academic Press, 1995), pp. 55-74.

8. For a recent analyses of the speeches in Acts, see M.L. Soards, *The Speeches in Acts: Their Content, Context, and Concerns* (Louisville, KY: Westminster/John Knox Press, 1994); cf. Porter, *The Paul of Acts*, Chapters 6 and 7. Still valuable is H.J. Cadbury, 'The Speeches in Acts', in F.J. Foakes Jackson and K. Lake (eds.), *The Beginnings of Christianity*. I. *The Acts of the Apostles* (5 vols.; London: Macmillan, 1933), V, pp. 402-27.

well as being similar to various other kinds of itinerant philosophers of the times, such as the Cynics.[9]

These kinds of contrasts can clearly be overdrawn,[10] but they do illustrate that there are issues to be raised regarding the relationship between Paul the rhetorician and Paul the epistolographer, so much so that some would say that all we can know is Paul the epistolographer, since there is not an accurate depiction of Paul to be found in Acts. Is it possible to entertain his being both, or must we say that he is only one?

3. *The Rhetoric of Paul and his Letters*

That Paul was a letter writer is beyond dispute, and will not be argued here.[11] Although the use of the amanuensis adds a heretofore unquantifiable factor to authorial composition,[12] and although composition in the ancient world may well have been conceived of in terms other than those used today,[13] despite these caveats it cannot be seriously denied that Paul was the author of a number of letters in the New Testament. I would argue that these number 13, but even if others argue for another number the point is that the authentic writings of Paul are all letters, regardless of the number.

9.   See A.J. Malherbe, *The Cynic Epistles: A Study Edition* (SBLSBS, 12; Missoula, MT: Scholars Press, 1977); *idem, Paul and the Popular Philosophers* (Minneapolis: Fortress Press, 1989).

10.   The issues above, with response, are discussed in more detail in McDonald and Porter, *Early Christianity and its Sacred Literature*, Chapter 10.

11.   On Paul's letters, see W.G. Doty, *Letters in Primitive Christianity* (Philadelphia: Fortress Press, 1973); S.K. Stowers, *Letter Writing in Greco-Roman Antiquity* (LEC; Philadelphia: Westminster Press, 1986); J.L. White, 'New Testament Epistolary Literature in the Framework of Ancient Epistolography', *ANRW* 2.25.2 (1984), pp. 1730-56; *idem,* 'Ancient Greek Letters', in D.E. Aune (ed.), *Greco-Roman Literature and the New Testament: Selected Forms and Genres* (SBLSBS, 21; Atlanta: Scholars Press, 1988), pp. 85-105; L. Alexander, 'Hellenistic Letter-Forms and the Structure of Philippians', *JSNT* 37 (1989), pp. 87-101; repr. in Porter and Evans (eds.), *The Pauline Writings*, pp. 232-46; H. Probst, *Paulus und der Brief: Die Rhetorik des antiken Briefes als Form der paulinischen Korintherkorrespondenz (1 Kor 8–10)* (WUNT, 2.45; Tübingen: Mohr Siebeck, 1991), pp. 29-105.

12.   See E.R. Richards, *The Secretary in the Letters of Paul* (WUNT, 2.42; Tübingen: Mohr Siebeck, 1991).

13.   See S.E. Porter, 'Pauline Authorship and the Pastoral Epistles: Implications for Canon', *BBR* 5 (1995), pp. 105-23.

A major question in Pauline rhetorical study is whether, in fact, Paul the letterwriter is also a rhetorician. Part of the problem with this is what is meant by the terms rhetorician and rhetoric. A number of questions can be raised that will help to penetrate this issue.

Was Paul writing letters or was he in fact writing speeches, as did Demosthenes, Isocrates and Lysias?[14] That Paul was indeed writing speeches appears to have been advocated by George Kennedy.[15] Kennedy and his followers approach the letters of Paul as essentially speeches that must be interpreted along these lines, with the epistolary opening and closing treated as almost incidental features. This is not confined to Kennedy, however, since those following the work of H.D. Betz strongly advocate the existence of a hybrid literary form that combines epistolary and rhetorical features.[16] As a result, rather than a single agreed-upon rhetorial outline, there are several types of analyses of Paul's letters that are to be found. For example, in some, the opening and closing are retained, but are not seen to be integral to the rhetorical structure of the bulk of the letter. Kennedy's analysis of Galatians treats the salutation (1.1-5) as separate from the *proem/exordium* (1.6-10), with the epistolary closing labeled an epilogue (6.11-14).[17] In others, the opening and closing are jettisoned altogether. Thus Smit does not even treat the epistolary prescript (1.1-5) in his rhetorical analysis, seeing it as having a solely epistolary and hence non-rhetorical func-

14. On ancient rhetoric and epistolography, see J.T. Reed, 'The Epistle', in S.E. Porter (ed.), *Handbook of Classical Rhetoric in the Hellenistic Period 330 B.C.– A.D. 400* (Leiden: E.J. Brill, 1997), pp. 171-93.

15. See G.A. Kennedy, *New Testament Interpretation through Rhetorical Criticism* (Chapel Hill, NC: University of North Carolina Press, 1984), pp. 86-87. See also K. Berger, 'Hellenistische Gattungen im Neuen Testament', *ANRW* 2.25.2 (1984), pp. 1326-63.

16. See H.D. Betz, *Galatians: A Commentary on Paul's Letter to the Churches in Galatia* (Hermeneia; Philadelphia: Fortress Press, 1979); *idem*, 'The Literary Composition and Function of Paul's Letter to the Galatians', *NTS* 21 (1974–75), pp. 353-79; *idem, 2 Corinthians 8 and 9: A Commentary on Two Administrative Letters of the Apostle Paul* (Hermeneia; Philadelphia: Fortress Press, 1985); and M.M. Mitchell, *Paul and the Rhetoric of Reconciliation: An Exegetical Investigation of the Language and Composition of 1 Corinthians* (HUT, 28; Tübingen: Mohr Siebeck, 1991), esp. p. 22.

17. Kennedy, *New Testament Interpretation*, p. 145. But see also Betz, *Galatians*, pp. 14-25, and M. Bachmann, *Sünder oder Übertreter: Studien zur Argumentation in Gal 2,15ff.* (WUNT, 59; Tübingen: Mohr Siebeck, 1992), pp. 156-60, who do similarly.

tion. He labels the epistolary closing as *amplificatio* (6.11-18). He also excises from analysis 5.12–6.10, since (he contends) parenesis has no place within classical rhetoric.[18] Still others simply overlook the epistolary elements altogether. For example, Jewett analyses 1 and 2 Thessalonians in entirely rhetorical terms. He begins with an *exordium* (1 Thess. 1.1-5; 2 Thess. 1.1-12) and closes with a *peroratio* (1 Thess. 5.23-28; 2 Thess. 3.16-18).[19]

Even though many rhetorical analysts of the Pauline letters have approached them as essentially speeches or speeches in the disguise of letters, this approach is unsatisfactory, since it either minimizes or altogether neglects the clear epistolary features of the Pauline letters. Regardless of whether one argues for a three-, four- or five-part Pauline epistolary structure, the failure to take into account the clear elements of the opening or the closing, whether this means bracketing them out of discussion or considering them appendages, starts the entire discussion off in the wrong direction, since it demands that we analyze the clear in terms of the unclear, that is, the epistolary as secondary to the rhetorical. The epistolary features of the Pauline letters are the clear generic features that allow identification of the literary form, and regardless of whatever else is done with the letters, these elements must be satisfactorily explained before moving to further explanation. The opening and closing clearly reflect the conventions of the ancient world abundantly attested in the documentary papyri. The rhetorical features are less clearly perceived, as can be seen in the simple fact that some rhetorical analysts include the epistolary opening, others exclude it and others still relabel it. There is no consistency at this point, because the rhetorical features are not clear features in the same way that the epistolary opening and closing are. There is further lack of agreement when the other parts of the letter/speech are analyzed.[20]

Was Paul formally trained as a rhetorician or were rhetorical categories in use in the ancient world no matter what the form of communication? Rhetorical analysts have argued both ways on this question. Some have wanted to maintain that Paul reflects formal training as a

18. J. Smit, 'The Letter of Paul to the Galatians: A Deliberative Speech', *NTS* 35 (1989), pp. 1-26.

19. R. Jewett, *The Thessalonian Correspondence: Pauline Rhetoric and Millenarian Piety* (FFNT; Philadelphia: Fortress Press, 1986), pp. 221, 225.

20. Further examples and discussion are provided in S.E. Porter, 'Paul of Tarsus and his Letters', in Porter (ed.), *Handbook of Classical Rhetoric*, pp. 533-85.

rhetorician. Although it is firmly established that Paul was born in Tarsus of Cilicia, a city known as a centre of learning especially in the areas of philosophy and rhetoric (Strabo, 14.5.3), and one with a fully developed Greco-Roman educational system, it is doubtful that Paul proceeded very far in this educational system.[21] This is seen in two ways. The first is the lack of evidence from his letters of classical knowledge. At various times it has been argued that Paul reflects classical writers or uses classical or rhetorical language and terminology, but most remain firmly unconvinced.[22] His few quotations of classical writers can be attributed to basic knowledge, and his use of such terms as ἀλληγορέω (Gal. 4.24) is conventional and not technical.[23] The second evidence is what he himself is recorded as saying in Acts 22.3. The statement there is grammatically ambiguous, but most interpreters believe that Paul is saying that although he was born in Tarsus and may have lived there for a portion of his life, he was reared in Jerusalem.[24] Thus, he may have been able to receive primary education in Tarsus, but he does not seem to have been able to receive secondary or tertiary education, and therefore would not have been able to receive formal rhetorical training in Tarsus. Although there is significant influence of Hellenism on rabbinical thought,[25] it is not sufficient to posit that this would constitute formal training in Greco-Roman rhetoric.

The supposition of a universal form of rhetoric does not go far to

21. On Greco-Roman education, see H.I. Marrou, *A History of Education in Antiquity* (trans. G. Lamb; London: Sheed & Ward, 1956), esp. pp. 229-329; D.L. Clark, *Rhetoric in Greco-Roman Education* (New York: Columbia University Press, 1957), esp. pp. 59-66; and S.F. Bonner, *Education in Ancient Rome: From the Elder Cato to the Younger Pliny* (London: Methuen, 1977), *passim*.

22. For recent discussion, see J. Fairweather, 'The Epistle to the Galatians and Classical Rhetoric: Parts 1 & 2', *TynBul* 45.1 (1994), pp. 1-38, esp. pp. 23-30; D. Litfin, *St Paul's Theology of Proclamation: 1 Corinthians 1–4 and Greco-Roman Rhetoric* (SNTSMS, 79; Cambridge: Cambridge University Press, 1994), pp. 137-40. Cf. the still important finds of E.B. Howell, 'St Paul and the Greek World', *Greece and Rome* 11 (1964), pp. 7-29, although few biblical scholars would endorse his conclusions now (the same may not be true for classicists, however).

23. For a list of such terms, as well as discussion, see C.J. Classen, 'Philologische Bemerkungen zur Sprache des Apostels Paulus', *Wiener Studien* 107–108 (1994–95), pp. 321-35.

24. See M. Hengel with R. Deines, *The Pre-Christian Paul* (London: SCM Press, 1991), pp. 18-39.

25. See D. Daube, 'Rabbinic Methods of Interpretation and Hellenistic Rhetoric', *HUCA* 22 (1949), pp. 239-64.

answering the question either, however, since what is being discussed is not whether individuals have always had the ability to marshall persuasive arguments, but whether these arguments are clearly couched in the terminology of ancient Greco-Roman rhetoric. The claim that Paul, even though he may not have received formal training in rhetoric exemplifies a number of features of rhetoric simply because either he was intelligent and widely travelled enough to have availed himself of informal training in rhetoric or there was sufficient rhetorical influence in the Greco-Roman world of the time to make it plausible that he inadvertently picked up the rudiments of rhetoric, overlooks the nature of rhetorical training and practice in the ancient world. Even though the times were litigious, we distort the social composition of the world to think that so many had clear access to the legal system; far fewer still were formally trained in rhetoric, especially when at most 20 to 30 per cent of the *men* were even literate.[26] This training was intense and rigorous, as the handbooks attest, not the kind of thing that the vast majority had the luxury of time or of sufficient money to engage in.

Are ancient rhetorical and epistolary categories to be equated? Although some have found it easy to equate epistolary and rhetorical categories,[27] there are two major problems with such equations. The first is found in the analyses of arrangement of the Pauline letters themselves. Even by those who wish to 'find' rhetorical categories appropriate to the Pauline letters there is widespread divergence regarding what these categories are and the extent of their presence in a given letter.[28] A survey of the rhetorical outlines of Paul's letters reveals virtually no two analyses the same, even by those who have worked together in the common task of doing such analyses. Although this failure to arrive at common results does not necessarily mitigate the task, it does raise questions about the usefulness of the categories. This

26. See W.A. Meeks, *The First Urban Christians: The Social World of the Apostle Paul* (New Haven: Yale University Press, 1983), *passim*, on the social composition of Corinth; and W.V. Harris, *Ancient Literacy* (Cambridge, MA: Harvard University Press, 1989), pp. 116-46, on literacy in the Hellenistic period, with p. 141 for statistics. For a sociologist's view of the rise of the early Church, see R. Stark, *The Rise of Christianity: A Sociologist Reconsiders History* (Princeton, NJ: Princeton University Press, 1996).

27. See, for example, F.W. Hughes, *Early Christian Rhetoric and 2 Thessalonians* (JSNTSup, 30; Sheffield: JSOT Press, 1989), esp. pp. 34-43, among many others.

28. See Porter, 'Paul of Tarsus and his Letters', *passim*, for examples.

kind of confusion is certainly not to be found in discussion of the epistolary structure of the letters, where most if not virtually all commentators agree on the extent of the epistolary openings and closings, as well as the limits of the thanksgivings, bodies and parenesis, even if they do not believe that they constitute discrete sections in epistolary structure. The second major problem is how the rhetorical categories are determined. When examining the rhetorical categories used in epistolary analysis, there is rarely a consistent utilization of categories from one of the handbooks or authors on rhetoric. Sometimes Roman and sometimes Greek categories are used, in most instances there being a mix of the two.[29] Since no clear set of categories appears to have been found, it is difficult to know how they can in any way be equated with the rather more straightforward categories of epistolary analysis. The only set of categories that seems to be consistently applied is that of Aristotle. Although it is plausible that Paul could have known and used the categories of Aristotelian rhetoric, there is little if any evidence that he did, and very few Aristotelian readings of Pauline letters have been advanced.[30] The relative simplicity of the categories has not resulted in the analyses proving to be the most penetrating.

If the terms of rhetorical and epistolary analysis are not to be equated, did the ancients recognize a cross-over between these two sets of categories and use rhetorical theory to discuss the composition and analysis of letters?[31] Such evidence is clearly lacking. This is seen in

---

29. See H. Lausberg, *Handbuch der literarischen Rhetorik: Eine Grundlegung der Literaturwissenschaft* (2 vols.; Munich: Heuber, 1960), I, pp. 148-49, for a synoptic chart of the categories of arrangement in the various authors and handbooks; and Porter, 'Paul of Tarsus and his Letters', pp. 539-61, for examples applied to the New Testament.

30. Two Aristotelian rhetorical analyses of Pauline letters worth noting are R.G. Hall, 'The Rhetorical Outline for Galatians: A Reconsideration', *JBL* 106 (1987), pp. 277-87; T.H. Olbricht, 'An Aristotelian Rhetorical Analysis of 1 Thessalonians', in D.L. Balch, E. Ferguson and W.A. Meeks (eds.), *Greeks, Romans, and Christians: Essays in Honor of Abraham J. Malherbe* (Philadelphia: Fortress Press, 1990), pp. 224-36.

31. Those familiar with my writing will readily recognize the arguments here having been first proposed in S.E. Porter, 'The Theoretical Justification for Application of Rhetorical Categories to Pauline Epistolary Literature', in S.E. Porter and T.H. Olbricht (eds.), *Rhetoric and the New Testament: Essays from the 1992 Heidelberg Conference* (JSNTSup, 90; Sheffield: JSOT Press, 1993), pp. 100-122. Cf. also R.D. Anderson, Jr, *Ancient Rhetorical Theory and Paul* (Kampen: Kok Pharos, 1996), esp. pp. 93-109, who concludes similarly.

two major ways. The first is that epistolary theory only becomes a part of rhetorical theory much later than the composition of the New Testament. It is not until Julius Victor in the fourth century in an appendix to his *Art of Rhetoric* (§27) that there is a section devoted to letterwriting in a rhetorical handbook.[32] The second is that where letters are mentioned in discussion of rhetoric, in virtually all instances a distinction between the two is made. For example, Pseudo-Demetrius's *On Style*, perhaps written in the first century BCE, has comments in an excursus on letters, but primarily to distinguish letterwriting from oratory. There certainly is no theoretical basis assumed or established for analyzing letters according to the categories of rhetoric. The same can be said for the others who mention letters in their writings. In none of the handbooks or other writers is the practice of epistolary composition evoked as a way of instructing in rhetorical composition. There is no evidence regarding the use of rhetorical categories to analyze letters until much later than the time of the composition of the New Testament. In the fourth and fifth centuries such fathers of the church as John Chrysostom and Augustine make rhetorical comments about the Pauline letters,[33] but this coincides with epistolary theory being later integrated with rhetorical theory. The evidence clearly indicates that this was a later development in Christian hermeneutics, perhaps when the Church was concerned to establish itself as intellectually and literarily respectable in the ancient world even though it was a religion based upon letters.

Is it, then, illegitimate to use the categories of ancient rhetoric to study Paul's letters? It is evident that there are clear functional relations between some of the categories of ancient rhetoric and the categories of ancient letters.[34] This can be accounted for, however, by virtue of the need to communicate and the finite linguistic means by which this is made possible. Therefore, no matter what form of discourse is concerned, there are bound to be a number of functional similarities with, for example, the opening gambit in most such discourses. Likewise, when such communication comes to an end, there is bound to be

32. See A.J. Malherbe, *Ancient Epistolary Theorists* (SBLSBS, 19; Atlanta: Scholars Press, 1988) for collection of the epistolary theorists.

33. See Fairweather, 'Galatians and Classical Rhetoric', pp. 2-22 and Kennedy, *New Testament Interpretation*, p. 11.

34. See J.T. Reed, 'Using Ancient Rhetorical Categories to Interpret Paul's Letters: A Question of Genre', in Porter and Olbricht (eds.), *Rhetoric and the New Testament*, pp. 294-314.

significant functional correspondence in the light of the finite closing functions of these discourses. Similarly, the way that an argument unfolds is bound to have certain (although perhaps fewer) functional similarities. These functional similarities allow the interpreter to draw upon a much wider range of resources for analysis than simply those of the ancient rhetoricians. In fact, this is bound to have a certain liberating effect as categories of thought and analysis from a variety of disciplines are utilized. These could well include not only the new rhetoric (as important as that is) but recent work in discourse analysis and other forms of what is sometimes called text-linguistics, as well as various other linguistic models that have a concern for the ways in which discourses are created and interpreted.[35] Now, however, we have crossed a major boundary, one which liberates us from the categories of ancient rhetoric altogether. There is no necessary need to retain the categories of ancient rhetoric, and certainly not with reference to how they are defined and used in the ancient handbooks or even utilized in the speeches themselves. We can recognize that the categories and conventions of ancient rhetoric were developed by practitioners of the time to aid them in their communicative tasks, in the same way that in our day and age we ought to develop and utilize useful sets of categories for our own analysis.[36]

At best, whereas there is a sense in which rhetoric is universal, and as much with us today as it was in ancient times, this does not necessarily mean that the categories of ancient rhetoric are the most useful for analysis of ancient discourse. Whereas there is merit in utilizing the categories of ancient rhetoric in discussion of ancient speeches, it cannot be shown that Paul's letters constitute examples of ancient speeches. The only firm evidence is that they are ancient letters and must be analyzed at least in the first instance as examples of epistolography. Whereas there may be functional value in discussing these letters in terms of some of the categories of ancient rhetoric, when such

---

35. Cf. S.E. Porter, 'Rhetorical Analysis and Discourse Analysis of the Pauline Corpus', in S.E. Porter and T.H. Olbricht (eds.), *The Rhetorical Analysis of Scripture: Essays from the 1995 London Conference* (JSNTSup, 146; Sheffield: Sheffield Academic Press, 1997), pp. 249-74.

36. See, for example, D.L. Stamps, 'Rhetorical Criticism of the New Testament: Ancient and Modern Evaluations of Argumentation', in S.E. Porter and D. Tombs (eds.), *Approaches to New Testament Study* (JSNTSup, 120; Sheffield: Sheffield Academic Press, 1995), pp. 129-69, esp. pp. 151-57.

an enterprise is undertaken, we must remember that this is not how these categories were utilized by the ancients. There is no clear evidence for epistolary theory and rhetorical theory being equated, especially since epistolary theory did not become a part of rhetorical theory until much later than the time of the composition of the New Testament. Therefore, the Paul of the letters is Paul the epistolographer.

4. *The Rhetoric of Paul and the Speeches in Acts*

Having concluded that, on the basis of his letters, Paul is an epistolographer, I turn now to Acts, in order to see if there is a sense in which he is a rhetorician. In dealing with the speeches in Acts, there are two major questions that must be addressed. The first is with regard to how speeches were recorded in the ancient world, including the book of Acts.[37] There have been two major positions regarding the speeches in Acts. The first holds that since each speech suits the speaker, audience and circumstances of delivery there is good reason to believe that the speeches were not invented by the author but condensed accounts of speeches actually delivered and retained by the early Church.[38] The

37. For a fuller exposition of the issues involved, including an analysis of Thucydides 1.22.1, see S.E. Porter, 'Thucydides 1.22.1 and Speeches in Acts: Is There a Thucydidean View?', *NovT* 32 (1990), pp. 121-42; repr. with modifications in S.E. Porter, *Studies in the Greek of the New Testament: Theory and Practice* (SBG, 5; New York: Peter Lang, 1996), pp. 173-93, from which the following is summarized and occasionally quoted. Endorsements of this article's concern for the difficulties of this passage are in C. Gempf, 'Public Speaking and Published Accounts', and P.E. Satterthwaite, 'Acts against the Background of Classical Rhetoric', both in B.W. Winter and A.D. Clarke (eds.), *TheBook of Acts in its First Century Setting*. I. *The Book of Acts in its Ancient Literary Setting* (5 vols.; Grand Rapids: Eerdmans, 1993), pp. 259-303 (266) and pp. 337-79 (355-56) respectively; J.B. Polhill, *Acts* (New American Commentary, 26; Nashville: Broadman, 1992), p. 45. See also W.J. McCoy, 'In the Shadow of Thucydides', in B. Witherington III (ed.), *History, Literature and Society in the Book of Acts* (Cambridge: Cambridge University Press, 1996), pp. 3-23, esp. pp. 15-16.

38. See, for example, F.F. Bruce, *The Speeches in the Acts of the Apostles* (London: Tyndale Press, 1942), esp. p. 27; cf. also *idem*, 'The Speeches in Acts: Thirty Years After', in R. Banks (ed.), *Reconciliation and Hope: New Testament Essays on Atonement and Eschatology* (Festschrift L.L. Morris; Grand Rapids: Eerdmans, 1974), pp. 530-68; F.F. Bruce, 'The Acts of the Apostles: Historical Record or Theological Reflection?', *ANRW* 2.25.2 (1985), pp. 2582-88. See also W.W. Gasque, 'The Speeches of Acts: Dibelius Reconsidered', in R.N. Longe-

second position holds the contrary position, arguing that the speeches are creations by the author of Acts, since they can be paralleled in other historical practices of the time and purportedly reflect a later viewpoint than the one of the chronology of the book.[39] Each of these positions establishes itself in large part by appeal to the well-known statement in Thucydides 1.22.1 regarding speeches. The first position usually assumes that there is such thing as a 'Thucydidean view' that endorses faithful retention and reproduction of the speeches, while the second maintains that Thucydides is speaking of reconstructing the intention of the speechmakers. But is there such a thing as a Thucydidean view of speeches?

An examination of Thucydides 1.22.1 reveals that there are at least seven problematic words or phrases. The statement in Jowett's translation, with the contentious wording included for reference (note that, due to the nature of the translation, the Greek wording does not necssarily appear in this order), is thus:

> As to the speeches which were made either before or during the war, it was hard [χαλεπόν] for me, and for others who reported them to me, to recollect the exact words [τὴν ἀκρίβειαν αὐτὴν τῶν λεχθέντων]. I have therefore put into the mouth of each speaker the sentiments proper to the occasion [τὰ δέοντα], expressed as I thought he would be likely [μάλιστα] to express them [ὡς… ἄν… ἐμοὶ… εἰπεῖν], while at the same

necker and M.C. Tenney (eds.), *New Directions in New Testament Study* (Grand Rapids: Zondervan, 1974), pp. 232-50; Hemer, *Book of Acts*, pp. 63-100; Gempf, 'Public Speaking and Public Accounts', pp. 265-85; and B. Witherington III, 'Editor's Addendum', in *idem* (ed.), *History, Literature and Society*, esp. pp. 24-26. Advocates of this position, even when they recognize the speeches as condensed summaries, tend to treat the words of the speeches as if they were the 'words of Paul', and they become part of the corpus of 'Pauline' material. Even Soards tends to analyze the speeches as if they were a body of hard data regarding Paul.

39. See, for example, Dibelius, *Studies in the Acts of the Apostles*, esp. pp. 138-85; H.J. Cadbury *et al.*, 'The Greek and Jewish Traditions of Writing History', in F.J. Foakes Jackson and K. Lake (eds.), *Beginnings of Christianity*. I. *The Acts of the Apostles* (5 vols.; London: Macmillan, 1922), II, pp. 7-29; B. Gärtner, *The Areopagus Speech and Natural Revelation* (ASNU, 21; Uppsala: C.W.K. Gleerup, 1955), esp. pp. 7-36; E. Schweizer, 'Concerning the Speeches in Acts', and H. Conzelmann, 'The Address of Paul on the Areopagus', both in Keck and Martyn (eds.), *Studies in Luke–Acts*, pp. 208-16 and 217-30 respectively; Haenchen, *Acts*, pp. 90-112; and G. Schneider, *Die Apostelgeschichte* (2 vols.; HTKNT, 5; Freiburg: Herder, 1980–82), I, pp. 95-103, esp. p. 97.

time I endeavoured, as nearly as I could [ὅτι ἐγγύτατα], to give the general purport [τῆς ξυμπάσης γνώμης] of what was actually said [τῶν ἀληθῶς λεχθέντων].⁴⁰

The following items merit discussion. The first is the meaning of the word often translated 'difficult' (χαλεπόν), whether this should be rendered 'difficult, but within the realm of possibility', 'difficult, and in fact not readily accomplishable, perhaps under any circumstance', or the intermediary position 'difficult, even impossible, unless some intervening action or circumstance occurs'. It is not altogether clear which is the best understanding. The last has probably the most to commend it, with Thucydides saying that, whereas reconstructing the speeches was virtually impossible, he was able to render a close approximation, if he applied his particular method. The second is the meaning of the phrase often rendered 'the exact words' (τὴν ἀκρίβειαν αὐτὴν τῶν λεχθέντων). The question is whether this refers to the specific individual utterances themselves or to the accuracy of the statements taken as a whole. The word 'exact' itself is not an absolute but a relative term, depending upon the nature of the action spoken about.

Third is the phrase that should probably be glossed 'as they [the speakers] seemed to me as they would have spoken (if they could have been heard)' (ὡς ... ἂν ... ἐμοὶ ... εἰπεῖν), in which there is an apparent contrast with the similar phrase in the next section, 1.22.2 (οὐδ' ὡς ἐμοὶ ἐδόκει). The adverb 'likely' or, better, 'especially' (μάλιστα) can be taken with 'the things that are necessary' as in 'what was roughly or precisely required', with 'to speak' as in 'to speak roughly or precisely', or with the entire clause as in 'to speak the things that are required, as certainly as possible'.

Fourthly, the phrase rendered by Jowett 'proper to the occasion', or more precisely 'the necessary things' (τὰ δέοντα), raises the question of necessary for whom or for what purpose. Is it that these things are necessary for Thucydides, the occasion, his audience or the individual speakers involved? A case can be, and has been, made for each of them. The fifth is the phrase 'that is nearest' (ὅτι ἐγγύτατα), meaning either 'keeping as close as possible to the general sense of what Thucydides himself saw as necessary', or 'keeping as close as possible to the general sense of what was said in the light of what was necessary for whatever reason'. The sixth is the phrase given by Jowett as 'general

40. B. Jowett, *Thucydides* (2 vols.; Oxford: Clarendon Press, 2nd edn, 1900), I, p. 16.

purport' and often rendered 'general sense' (τῆς ξυμπάσης γνώμης). This interpretation is often objected to, however. Two suggestions are that it means 'the gist of the message' or 'the line taken by the speaker'. The seventh is the phrase 'spoken truly' (τῶν ἀληθῶς λεχθέντων), often rendered 'spoken truthfully' or 'truly spoken'.

In the light of the varied interpretations suggested above, the degree of precision that one can attribute to this statement by Thucydides is open to serious question. Certainly more weight has been placed on it by both sides in the debate than the statement itself can hold. As a result of various interpretive configurations, Thucydides's statement in 1.22.1 can be interpreted as saying something from the fairly conservative 'it has been difficult (but I have done it) to remember with accuracy the things which were stated, but the speeches are given as they were required on the basis of the events, possessing an accuracy of the specific words which were spoken truthfully' to the more skeptical 'it has been impossible to remember with any accuracy the things which were stated, so the speeches are given as seemed required for my purposes, possessing an accuracy equivalent to a consensual view of the things said by those who would have really spoken'. Thus, it is difficult to appeal to any sort of notion of a programmatic statement in Thucydides to justify a particular kind of recording of the speeches in Acts. Neither side in the discussion has clear support for its supposition regarding accuracy of recording.

With the theoretical issue inconclusive, the second issue in Acts, the actual speeches themselves, must be raised. Failing a systematic statement in Thucydides to appeal to either way regarding the accuracy of the speeches, one must turn to the speeches to determine the possibility of establishing Paul as a rhetorician.

Before proceeding with discussion of any actual speeches, however, two preliminary points must be made, which threaten the entire enterprise. First, if what was said above regarding the lack of formal knowledge of rhetoric by the Paul of the letters is true, then it is only logical to think that, if it is the same Paul found in Acts, he has the same lack of formal training in rhetoric. (Of course, if the Paul of Acts has no actual relation with the Paul of the letters, rhetoric alone cannot establish such a link.) Secondly, perhaps the single most limiting factor for analysis of the speeches of Acts is that we do not know whether we have any example of a complete speech, as both views on the statement in Thucydides recognize. This may well be true of even the one or two sentence 'speeches' that are recorded in Acts (e.g. 1.4b-5, 7-8, 11; 18.6; 21.11; 21.13, 28; 23.9), but is almost certainly true of the so-called 'major speeches', none of which is more than a couple of minutes in reading length. This says nothing of what to do with those that are interrupted. One must appreciate the importance of these factors for analysis of the speeches in Acts. Rhetorical analysis is designed to examine the process by which a rhetorician formulated his argument, whether it was designed to be epideictic, deliberative or forensic, or a combination of them.[41] In order to do this, there were various conventions that were maintained, regarding invention, arrangement, style, memory and delivery.[42] It is difficult to know how much the integrity of a given speech in Acts was maintained, even if it were an actual oration that followed these conventions at all. If the speeches are not preserved in their entirety, even if one takes the view that the speeches in Acts reflect the content of what was actually said on the occasion (one of the several possible interpretations of Thucydides 1.22.1), and a possibility in the light of apparent ancient practice of recording summaries of forensic speeches (see Diodorus Siculus, 1.76),[43] one must wonder whether the categories of rhetoric can be systematically or comprehensively applied. If the speeches are analyzed as they appear in Acts, all that may result is rhetorical analysis of either a summary or the final form constructed by Luke, not the actual speech of Paul (or anyone else).

Analysis of two of the most important speeches by Paul in Acts confirms what has been said above.

a. *Paul's Speech to the Ephesian Elders at Miletus (Acts 20.18-35)*
The first speech to consider is Paul's speech to the Ephesian elders at Miletus (Acts 20.18-35). This speech must take priority in examining

41. On the 'species' of rhetoric, see G.A. Kennedy, 'The Genres of Rhetoric', in Porter (ed.), *Handbook of Classical Rhetoric*, pp. 43-50.

42. On invention, see M. Heath, 'Invention'; on arrangement, see W. Wuellner, 'Arrangement'; on style, see G.O. Rowe, 'Style'; and on delivery and memory, see T.H. Olbricht, 'Delivery and Memory'; all in Porter (ed.), *Handbook of Classical Rhetoric*, pp. 89-119, 51-87, 121-57, 159-67 respectively.

43. See B.W. Winter, 'Official Proceedings and the Forensic Speeches in Acts 24–26', in Winter and Clarke (eds.), *Acts in its Ancient Literary Setting*, p. 307. Winter admits that this process results in a summary made by a scribe, which makes the basis for his subsequent detailed analysis difficult to understand. See also Witherington, *Acts*, p. 518, who does the same.

the speeches of Acts in relation to the letters of Paul, since, as Colin Hemer has pointed out following others, it is

> the only one of the larger speeches addressed to a Christian audience, actually of leaders of a church previously founded by Paul, and so likely to be nearer to the pastoral function of Paul's writing in the epistles than any other. It therefore offers the best prospect of direct comparison between the Paul of Acts and the Paul of the letters.[44]

Several scholars accept this relationship of the speech to the writings of Paul, but this is where the agreements apparently end. The disputes over the speech include at least the following.

The first is the type of speech that it is. Dibelius calls it an encomium biography. Hemer and Soards, among others, say that it is a speech of farewell. Watson agrees that it is a speech of farewell, which (he notes) is a type of epideictic speech, although he provides no rationale for introducing the categories of classical rhetoric apart from citing Menander Rhetor, 2.15 (also noting, however, that the *topoi* he discusses are not found in this speech). Kennedy says it is a speech of farewell as well, although he states categorically that Paul's speech here does not conform to the rhetorical conventions of Menander Rhetor. Conzelmann notes that it has elements of popular rhetoric.[45] Thus, whereas we may well be able to agree that it is a farewell speech, it is difficult to equate it easily with an epideictic speech.

The second dispute is concerning the structure of the speech. Opinions here too vary considerably. Dibelius posits four sections: vv. 18-21 retrospect and self-defense; vv. 22-27 anticipation of death; vv. 28-31 the apostle's statement; and vv. 32-34 the closing (blessing, concluding). Soards proposes: vv. 18b-21 Paul's recalling of his Asian ministry; vv. 22-27 words about the future; vv. 28-31 advice for the elders;

---

44. C. Hemer, 'The Speeches of Acts I. The Ephesian Elders at Miletus', *TynBul* 40 (1989), pp. 77-85 (77). See also Cadbury, 'Speeches in Acts', p. 412. Witherington (*Acts*, pp. 610-11) provides a synoptic chart of Acts and Paul's letters, illustrating points of conceptual correlation.

45. See Dibelius, *Studies in the Acts of the Apostles*, p. 155; Hemer, 'Speeches of Acts', p. 81; Soards, *Speeches in Acts*, p. 105; D.F. Watson, 'Paul's Speech to the Ephesian Elders (Acts 20.17-38): Epideictic Rhetoric of Farewell', in D.F. Watson (ed.), *Persuasive Artistry: Studies in New Testament Rhetoric in Honor of George A. Kennedy* (JSNTSup, 50; Sheffield: JSOT Press, 1991), pp. 184-208 (190-91); Kennedy, *New Testament Criticism*, pp. 132-33; H. Conzelmann, *Die Apostelgeschichte* (HNT, 7; Tübingen: Mohr Siebeck, 1963), p. 117.

and vv. 32-35 concluding blessing and admonition. Whereas the first
two analyses have much in common, Kennedy's is quite different.
Kennedy posits that vv. 18-27 constitutes an extended *proem*, v. 28
a proposition, v. 29 a metaphor, v. 31 an example and vv. 32-35 an
epilogue (he does not treat v. 30). Different still is that of Lambrecht,
who posits six sections within two larger sections: self-defense and
announcement (Acts 20.18b-27), consisting of vv. 18b-21, previous
conduct; vv. 22-25, announcement of departure and future suffering;
and vv. 26-27, previous conduct (apology); and exhortations and farewell (18.28-35), consisting of vv. 28-31, warning: vigilance in face of
imminent dangers; v. 32, farewell; and vv. 33-35, warning: help for the
weak. Whereas the first four analyses at least stayed within the boundaries of the speech itself, a fifth, by Watson, does not. His includes five
sections: vv. 17-18a historical preface; vv. 18b-24 *exordium*; vv. 25-31
probatio; vv. 32-35 *peroratio*; vv. 36-38 narrative summary.[46]
Watson's analysis is instructive, since it is not merely an analysis of the
Pauline speech, but an analysis of Acts 20.17-38. There seems to be
some ambiguity in Watson's analysis regarding what constitutes the
speech and what constitutes the rhetorical unit, and what this may
imply regarding the contribution of Paul and that of the author of Acts.

The third dispute is over the relationship of the speech to Pauline
style in the letters. It is routinely denied that Luke knew or represents
authentic Pauline material in Acts, including in the speeches, since the
style of Acts is often said to be thoroughly consistent. However, there
are a number of parallels between this speech and the Pauline letters
worth considering. The first are verbal parallels, including 'being a ser-
vant of the lord' (Acts 20.19; Rom. 12.11), 'with all humility' (Acts
20.19; Eph. 4.2), 'Jews and Greeks' (Acts 20.21; and especially
Romans), 'complete the course' (Acts 20.24; 2 Tim. 4.7), 'complete
service' (Acts 20.24; 2 Tim. 4.5; Col. 4.17), 'the service which we
received from our Lord Jesus' (Acts 20.24; Col. 4.17), 'grace of God'
(Acts 20.24, 32; elsewhere in Paul), 'the church of God' (Acts 20.28),

46. Dibelius, *Studies in the Acts of the Apostles*, p. 157; Soards, *Speeches in Acts*, p. 105; Kennedy, *New Testament Interpretation*, p. 133; J. Lambrecht, 'Paul's Farewell-Address at Miletus (Acts 20, 17-38)', in J. Kremer (ed.), *Les Actes des Apôtres: Traditions, rédaction, théologie* (BETL, 48; Gembloux: Duculot; Leuven: Leuven University Press, 1979), pp. 307-37, esp. p. 318; Watson, 'Paul's Speech', p. 208.

'watch out for yourselves' (Acts 20.28; 1 Tim. 4.16), 'consider' (Acts 20.31; 1 Cor. 16.13; Col. 4.2; 1 Thess. 5.6, 10), 'build up' (Acts 20.32; Rom. 15.20; 1 Cor. 8.1, 10; 10.23; 14.4, 17; Gal. 2.18; 1 Thess. 5.11), 'inheritance among the saints' (Acts 20.32; Col. 1.12), 'hands...working' (Acts 20.34-35; 1 Cor. 4.12; Eph. 4.28), and repeated language of earnestness (Acts 20.31; 1 Thess. 2.7-8). The second are biographical details, including Paul's not wishing to be a burden to his churches (Acts 20.33-34; 1 Cor. 9; 2 Cor. 11.7-11; 1 Thess. 2.9-12) and the length of his stay with the Ephesians. The third are theological similarities, including reference in Acts 20.28 to 'the blood of his own'. This redemptive language is untypical of Luke, both in the Gospel and in Acts.[47]

How to assess this material has been highly debated. Some have contended that all of these individual elements can be found in various ways in simply the language and thinking of the larger Christian community.[48] The confluence of such factors prompts most scholars to recognize that Luke's inclusion of them was to render his work with an authentic Pauline stamp. This raises the question, however, of how Luke knew what was or was not an authentic Pauline stamp. There seem to be only two real options. The first is that he knew the Pauline letters. If this is the case, then he in fact did know and use the Pauline letters, something denied by many if not most scholars. The second is that if he did not know the letters he must have known Paul or someone very like him. In either case, it is difficult to show that this speech is a reflection of Paul as rhetorician. It is more likely that this speech shows Paul delivering a farewell testimony to close friends, reflecting a similar pastoral and theological approach to that found in his letters (which have already been shown not to be formally rhetorical according to ancient standards). The other alternative, which Watson's analysis seems to point to, is that any rhetorical analysis is not of Paul's speech but of what Luke has done with it.

47. See Hemer, *Book of Acts*, pp. 425-26; Cadbury, 'Speeches in Acts', pp. 412-13; R. Pesch, *Die Apostelgeschichte* (2 vols.; EKKNT, 5; Solothurn: Benziger; Neukirchen–Vluyn: Neukirchener Verlag, 1995 [2nd edn], 1986), II, pp. 201-206; among others. Contra Lambrecht, 'Paul's Farewell-Address', esp. pp. 325-26, who emphasizes Lukanisms, disputing Pauline parallels (pp. 319-20).
48. See Cadbury, 'Speeches in Acts', pp. 416-17.

b. *Paul's Speech on the Areopagus in Athens (Acts 17.22-31)*
The second speech for analysis is Paul's speech on the Areopagus (Acts 17.22-31). This is certainly the best known of Paul's speeches in Acts, and one that has generated a number of analyses and interpretations.[49] Schneider categorizes it as a missionary speech before Gentiles,[50] but not all scholars agree that this is what is occurring in this incident. Several interpreters have noticed that Paul begins his discussions in Athens by reasoning in the synagogue with the Jews and godfearers, and in the market place with whoever happened to be there. This would have included the Stoics and Epicureans. On one occasion, he is taken to the Areopagus, in response to the question that they desire to know about his new teaching, which sounds strange to their ears. It is in this setting that Paul makes his speech (not that of the synagogue).[51] But what exactly is the context? There is a distinct missionary feel about the situation, in that the philosophers are responding to the discussions that Paul has previously had in the market place, where Paul first spent some time noticing their various religious monuments, which provoked him to discussion. This would not have required that Paul be taken to the Areopagus to be examined, however. On the other hand, therefore, some have claimed that Paul is actually undergoing a form of trial, or at least preliminary hearing before the leading people of the city, in order to determine if he is perhaps disseminating some form of subversive doctrine. In this case, the question that is asked of Paul may be more of

49. A sample of the most important secondary literature (excluding commentaries) includes Dibelius, *Studies in the Acts of the Apostles*, pp. 26-83; E. Norden, *Agnostos Theos: Untersuchungen zur formengeschichte Religiöser Rede* (repr.; Darmstadt: Wissenschaftliche, 1956), pp. 1-124; Gärtner, *Areopagus Speech*, *passim*; P. Schubert, 'The Place of the Areopagus Speech in the Composition of Acts', in J.C. Rylaarsdam (ed.), *Transitions in Biblical Scholarship* (Chicago: University of Chicago Press, 1968), pp. 235-61; Conzelmann, 'Address of Paul on the Areopagus', pp. 217-30; N.B. Stonehouse, *Paul before the Areopagus and Other New Testament Studies* (London: Tyndale Press, 1957), pp. 1-40; C.J. Hemer, 'The Speeches of Acts: II. The Areopagus Address', *TynBul* 40.2 (1989), pp. 239-59; D.L. Balch, 'The Areopagus Speech: An Appeal to the Stoic Historian Posidonius against Later Stoics and the Epicureans', and J.H. Neyrey, 'Acts 17, Epicureans, and Theodicy: A Study in Stereotypes', both in Balch, Ferguson and Meeks (eds.), *Greeks, Romans, and Christians*, pp. 52-79, 118-34 respectively.

50. Schneider, *Die Apostelgeschichte*, I, pp. 95-103, esp. p. 96. See G. Schille, *Die Apostelgeschichte des Lukas* (THNT; Berlin: Evangelische, 1983), pp. 360-61, for a survey of opinion on the origins of this speech.

51. See Schille, *Die Apostelgeschichte*, p. 354.

an informal charge,[52] a charge that in some ways resembles that brought against Socrates in the same city almost 450 years before.[53] It is difficult to know the full extent of the context, since so little information is given. Although it is worth noting that Dionysius, one of the converts on the occasion of Paul's speech, is called an Areopagite, perhaps conveying that he had a position of responsibility in the proceedings, in most other trial scenes Luke leaves no ambiguity regarding the nature of the enquiry.[54]

There are three features of this speech worth noting. First, Paul, standing in their midst, a posture used elsewhere by Paul and by others in Acts, addresses his audience as 'Athenian men' (17.22). This is consonant with his speeches elsewhere, in which he often specifies his audience. Nevertheless, Kennedy has drawn attention to the fact that this may well have been an improper word of address in the light of the circumstances. Instead of 'Athenian men', Paul perhaps should have addressed them as 'gentlemen'.[55] It is unclear what bearing this has on the account in terms of its authorship, since the author of Acts may have recorded what he knew to be true just as much as he may have conformed the word of address to many of Paul's other speeches. Nevertheless, Paul does address his audience with a specific title, perhaps warranted on the basis of his having discussed with them previously and established a certain amount of familiarity.

Secondly, Paul appeals to his audience's 'religiousness' (not 'superstition') as a way of invoking a form of natural theology (vv. 22-29). This introduction is a form of *captatio benevolentiae*, designed to curry their favour and find a common ground for discussion,[56] even if it may have alienated some of the Epicurean elements of his audience.[57] He

---

52. See, for example, Kennedy, *New Testament Interpretation*, pp. 129-30; T.D. Barnes, 'An Apostle on Trial', *JTS* 20 (1969), pp. 407-19; contra B.W. Winter, 'On Introducing Gods to Athens: An Alternative Reading of Acts 17:18-20', *TynBul* 47.1 (1996), pp. 71-90, esp. pp. 79-80, 90.

53. See Haenchen, *Acts*, p. 518; cf. K.O. Sandnes, 'Paul and Socrates: The Aim of Paul's Areopagus Speech', *JSNT* 50 (1993), pp. 13-26 (20-24).

54. See Haenchen, *Acts*, pp. 518-19.

55. Kennedy, *New Testament Interpretation*, p. 130.

56. Conzelmann, *Die Apostelgeschichte*, p. 97; L.T. Johnson, *The Acts of the Apostles* (SP, 5; Collegeville, MN: Liturgical Press, 1992), p. 314; cf. D. Zweck, 'The *Exordium* of the Areopagus Speech, Acts 17.22-23', *NTS* 35 (1989), pp. 94-103; contra Witherington, *Acts*, p. 520.

57. On the appropriateness of Paul's words especially to a Stoic audience, but

selects their altar dedicated 'to an unknown god', and bluntly states that
he can proclaim that unknown god to them. Despite not having found
an altar with this very inscription on it, the fact that a number of ancient
authors speak of altars to unknown gods in and around Athens shows
that the speech, if not historically accurate, is at least placed in the right
context.[58]

As many scholars have noted, the body of this speech discusses three
main, intertwined themes: God's self-sufficiency, humans created to
need God, and worship of God excluding images.[59] Paul moves directly
from the assertion of knowledge of this god to the God who made the
world and everything in it. The transition is rough, whether that was
because Paul himself was pushing to get to the point, or whether the
editor has excised several important steps in the logical process. That
the speech is probably a summary is made apparent by the quick transition from creation of the world and being Lord of heaven and earth
back to the dwelling place of this God. Paul states that it is not in man-
made temples, which indicates that he is not beholden to humans in any
way. God is in fact the creator of humanity, with the purpose of their
seeking after him. Although Stoics and Paul would perhaps understand

---

less so to an Epicurean one, see Balch, 'Areopagus Speech', esp. pp. 54-79;
Neyrey, 'Acts 17, Epicureans, and Theodicy', pp. 122-29. The points of similarity
include providence in nature and history and opposition to images of deity.

58. See Pausanias, 1.4.1; Diogenes Laertius, 1.110; Philostratus, *Apol. Tyana*
6.3.5, as well as one and possibly two recently published inscriptions. See P.W. van
der Horst, 'The Altar of the "Unknown God" in Athens (Acts 17:23) and the Cults
of "Unknown Gods" in the Graeco-Roman World', repr. from *ANRW* 2.18.2
(1989), pp. 4226-56 in *idem, Hellenism–Judaism–Christianity: Essays on their
Interaction* (Kampen: Kok Pharos, 1994), pp. 165-202, who makes a very plausible
case for the accuracy of Luke's language, as well as suggesting that the reference
may be to the God of the Jews (contra Haenchen, *Acts*, p. 521 n. 2; Schille, *Die
Apostelgeschichte*, p. 356, who takes the reference as merely literary). Winter
('Introducing Gods', p. 84) notes that singular and plural are often interchangeable
in Greek discussion of god/s. See also his 'In Public and in Private: Early Christian
Interactions with Religious Pluralism', in A.D. Clarke and B.W. Winter (eds.), *One
God, One Lord: Christianity in a World of Religious Pluralism* (Cambridge: Tyn-
dale House, 1991), pp. 112-34 (118-19), for examples, such as Cleanthes' *Hymn to
Zeus* 1-7; Diogenes Laertius, 7.119.

59. See, for example, Dibelius, *Studies in the Acts of the Apostles*, p. 27;
Balch, 'Areopagus Speech', p. 54. But cf. Kennedy, *New Testament Interpretation*,
pp. 130-31; Soards, *Speeches in Acts*, p. 96.

this creator-God differently, Kennedy thinks that the argumentation in Acts 17.24-25 that God's not living in temples is proved by his not needing humans would have been mutually intelligible.[60] For example, Paul and the Stoics have at least parallel thinking regarding God as creator. In support of the notion that humanity exists only because of this God, Paul may cite two lines from pagan poets in v. 28. There is disagreement whether 'in him we live and move and are' is from the poet Epimenides (also cited by Paul in Titus 1.12).[61] More certain is that there is citation in the second part of the verse of a line from the poet Aratus, *Phainomena* 5: 'for we also are his offspring' (cf. Cleanthes, *Hymn to Zeus* 4). Aristobulus the Hellenistic Jewish philosopher also cites this poem (fragment 4 in Eusebius, *Prep. Evang.* 13.12.3). As Johnson says, 'Luke has Paul citing pagan *auctoritates* in virtually the same way that he cites Torah for his Jewish listeners'.[62] The link between God and humanity through this concept of generation allows Paul to dismiss idolatry as foreign to the divine nature. The worship of things made out of gold, silver or stone reveals ignorance, which God has been willing to overlook until the designated time of his divine judgment (cf. Rom. 3.25-26). Although the concept of the judgment of the world is not found frequently in Acts, it is found abundantly in Paul, and was a familiar concept to the Stoics, who believed that the world would end in destruction (Diogenes Laertius, 7.156).[63] This judgment, according to Paul, is going to be carried out by a man designated for such a purpose, and shown to be worthy of this task because of God having raised him from the dead. Kee notes that

60. Kennedy, *New Testament Interpretation*, p. 130.

61. See F.F. Bruce, *The Acts of the Apostles* (Grand Rapids: Eerdmans, 2nd edn, 1952), p. 338 (the text is reconstructed from a later Syriac text by Isho'dad; and references in Clement of Alexandria, *Strom.* 1.14.59.1-2; Diogenes Laertius, 1.111, 112); although most do not agree: e.g. Johnson, *Acts*, p. 316. For a discussion of possible quotations of pagan writers in Acts, see H.J. Cadbury, *The Book of Acts in History* (London: A. & C. Black, 1955), pp. 44-52.

62. Johnson, *Acts*, p. 316. This of course does not mean that Paul believed that the pagan authors had the same status or authority as the Old Testament for him.

63. See Balch, 'Areopagus Speech', pp. 58-67, on the Stoic view of judgment. On belief in cosmic conflagration, see P.W. van der Horst, ' "The Elements Will Be Dissolved with Fire": The Idea of Cosmic Conflagration in Hellenism, Ancient Judaism, and Early Christianity', in *idem, Hellenism–Judaism–Christianity*, pp. 227-51.

The strategy of this address is remarkable. The choice of Stoic principles as a point of entry and the quotation of familiar Greek writers virtually guarantees attention and a sympathetic hearing—at least initially. The degree of overlap between the concepts in this popular philosophy and what the author regards as the basic Christian worldview is striking, and serves the reader as a demonstration of what can be done in approaching with the gospel those who have no familiarity with the teachings of the Jewish scriptures.[64]

Thirdly, the proof for Paul of the appointment of this man as the worthy judge of humanity is his having been raised from the dead (Acts 17.30-31). At the mention of the resurrection, Paul's audience reacts strongly. Some are entirely dismissive, others say that they will hear Paul on this topic at another time (possibly indicating a more polite dismissal, or even the need for time to contemplate fully what it is that they have just heard), and still others seem to believe what Paul has said. For Paul, it appears to be a natural step to progress from natural revelation in the created order to a further day of reckoning. The fact that he appeals to an act that is not part of the natural order, however, seems to have disrupted the flow of thought on the part of the audience. Nevertheless, his audience reacts to this. It is not that Paul's logic has been grossly inconsistent. It appears more that he has introduced something into the argument that his audience would not have fully accepted. The problem for Greek thinking was not the idea of spiritual existence or even continual existence after death. The point of contention would have been the apparent resuscitation to physical life of a dead body. Both the Epicureans and Stoics were materialists.[65] The Epicureans believed that the world as we know it was made up of very small particles, an early form of atomic theory. At death, one simply

64. H.C. Kee, *The Good News to the Ends of the Earth: The Theology of Acts* (London: SCM Press, 1990), p. 65.

65. On Stoic and Epicurean thought, besides Balch and Neyrey, see T.R. Glover, *The Conflict of Religions in the Early Roman Empire* (London: Methuen, 1909), pp. 33-74; W. Tarn and G.T. Griffith, *Hellenistic Civilisation* (London: Edward Arnold, 3rd edn, 1952), pp. 325-60; W.T. Jones, *The Classical Mind* (New York: Harcourt Brace Jovanovich, 2nd edn, 1970), pp. 317-33; A.A. Long (ed.), *Problems in Stoicism* (London: Athlone Press, 1971); F.H. Sandbach, *The Stoics* (London: Chatto & Windus, 1975), esp. pp. 149-78; A.A. Long, *Hellenistic Philosophy: Stoics, Epicureans, Sceptics* (London: Gerald Duckworth, 2nd edn, 1986), pp. 14-74, 107-209; E. Ferguson, *Backgrounds of Early Christianity* (Grand Rapids: Eerdmans, 1987), pp. 281-301; and Winter, 'In Public and in Private', pp. 118-22.

returned to the condition of one's particular state. The Stoics believed that the material substance of the universe was the principle of rationality, the logos, etc., and that the goal of life was to align oneself with this divine principle of rationality. Both were agreed that death was an escape from physical existence. Therefore, the idea of continued existence was not a problem, since both believed that material did in fact persist. The problem was that one would return to a human physical state. This was a condition that one ought to be glad to be relieved of.[66] This apparent conflict is what leads Paul's audience to interrupt him and not allow him to continue. Some scholars believe that this is not a genuine interruption, the argument being that the speech is complete,[67] but this cannot be correct. The balance of the speech is completely wrong, with the only distinctly Christian part, mention of the resurrection, coming at the very end of v. 31.

Concerning Acts, it is difficult to posit on the basis of what has been said above that we have sufficient evidence to provide an analysis of the rhetoric of Paul. We might well posit that we have sufficient confidence in the speeches of Acts to have a firm idea of what Paul said on the occasion, even in terms of his approach (*stasis*) to various topics (*topoi*),[68] but we do not have a sufficient quantity of those words in the proper form to allow us to perform rhetorical analysis of the speeches as *speeches* of Paul. As conservative a commentator as Colin Hemer says that 'The crucial question of historicity here concerns only the essential content of the speeches. We need not be concerned with any supposition that they are verbatim reports; there is a clear argument against such an extreme position.' As Hemer states further, Paul must have spoken at great length (see Acts 20.7; cf. Acts 2.40; 9.22; 14.1, 3): 'The brief summary paragraphs we possess do not purport to reproduce more than perhaps a *précis* of the distinctive highlights. They do not read as transcripts of oral delivery and the responses of the audience to

66. Bruce (*Acts*, p. 340) cites Aeschylus, *Eum.* 647–48 against the idea of Greeks believing in a bodily resurrection. But cf. Euripides, *Alcestis*, where Heracles brings Alcestis back from the dead. See S.E. Porter, 'Resurrection, the Greeks, and the New Testament', in S.E. Porter, M.A. Hayes and D. Tombs (eds.), *Resurrection* (Roehampton Institute London Papers, 5; JSNTSup, 186; Sheffield: Sheffield Academic Press, 1999).

67. E.g. Dibelius, *Studies in the Acts of the Apostles*, p. 57; followed by Haenchen, *Acts*, p. 526; Soards, *Speeches in Acts*, p. 100.

68. See Porter, 'Paul of Tarsus and his Letters', pp. 570-76.

them do not relate realistically to the bald words reported.'[69] The same conclusion is arrived at by Cadbury: 'the probability is against any extensive verbal agreement of the ultimate record with the original. Memory must have considerably condensed the actual utterance, and, indeed, the speeches that we have are all relatively brief and succinct and capable of explanation as summaries of longer addresses.'[70] Thus, there is little firm ground for positing Paul the rhetorician even in the book of Acts, at least in any way that provides firm data for close analysis of his speeches as clearly Pauline rhetoric.

5. *Conclusion*

Others would obviously conclude differently regarding the rhetoric of Paul, wishing to assert that Paul the rhetorician can be found in both his letters and his speeches in Acts. Instead, I am compelled to conclude that we cannot find Paul the ancient rhetorician in the letters, primarily because Paul was a letterwriter. To be a letterwriter was to be doing something different than being a speechmaker in the Greco-Roman world. On the basis of the letters, we cannot examine Paul as a rhetorician in terms of the categories of construction of speeches in the ancient world. But can we find Paul the rhetorician in Acts? The answer here must be yes and no. On the one hand, it is highly debatable whether we have direct access to the historical Paul as speechmaker, and this for two reasons. The first is that there is a highly debatable relationship in ancient historiography between the delivery of speeches and their record in later literary works. The second is that what is found in Acts is for various reasons not complete Pauline speeches but at best later summaries or even prematurely curtailed speeches possibly designed to give the gist of the original speech. These cannot provide an adequate basis for rhetorical analysis of the speeches of the historical Paul. Nevertheless, if these strictures are taken into account, there are still grounds for examining the speeches in Acts, including those of Paul, in terms of how they are presented by the author of the book. In that case, although the speeches may have had their origins in the historical Paul and reflect the context of what was said by him, the rhetorical analysis is of the speeches in Acts as they were shaped and presented by its author.

69. Hemer, *Book of Acts*, p. 418.
70. Cadbury, 'Speeches in Acts', pp. 406-407.

Dennis L. Stamps

1. *Introduction*

As rhetorical criticism has exploded as a method of analysing the biblical text, there have been a number of suggestions that the persuasive
discourse of the Bible is somehow distinct. Critics have begun to discuss with regard to the New Testament writings a concept of Christian
rhetoric. In this essay, I want to explore this notion particularly as it
pertains to Pauline rhetoric and argumentation. In this exploration, several issues need examination. First, what is being said about the nature
or characteristics of Christian rhetoric? Secondly, what is meant by
argumentation and how does a critic analyse this dimension of Pauline
discourse? Thirdly, after examining notions of Christian rhetoric and
Pauline argumentation, what implications are there for using these concepts to further an understanding of Pauline theological rhetoric?

2. *What Is Christian Rhetoric?*

G.A. Kennedy, as an eminent classical scholar, has posited a definition
of Christian rhetoric over against classical rhetoric. In his book, *Classical Rhetoric and its Christian and Secular Tradition from Ancient to
Modern Times*, Kennedy concludes that the rhetoric of the Gospels is
proclamation.[1] As such it is distinctive from classical persuasion:
'Christian preaching is thus not persuasion, but proclamation, and is
based on authority and grace, not on proof'.[2] Further, in response to the
idea of 'the Word' in John 1, he states, 'The concept of the Word carries within it the three factors of Christian rhetoric we have identified—

---

1.   G.A. Kennedy, *Classical Rhetoric and its Christian and Secular Tradition
from Ancient to Modern Times* (Chapel Hill, NC: University of North Carolina
Press, 1980), p. 127.
2.   Kennedy, *Classical Rhetoric*, p. 127.

grace, authority, and the message "proclaimed" to mankind'.[3] With regard to the rhetoric of the New Testament epistles, after surveying 1 Corinthians 1–2, Kennedy concludes:

> This passage may be said to reject the whole of classical philosophy and rhetoric. For rhetoric the Christian can rely on God, both to supply words and to accomplish persuasion if it is God's will. In place of worldly philosophy there exists a higher philosophy, only dimly apprehended by man. Much of the work of Christian exegesis in the following centuries is built on the assumption that there is a wisdom in the Scriptures, deliberately obscure, which man can, in part, come to understand with God's help.[4]

In his later book, *New Testament Interpretation through Rhetorical Criticism*, Kennedy refined this wholesale distinction of Christian rhetoric from classical rhetoric to a notion that within the scriptural writings there is Christian rhetoric that uses classical rhetorical persuasion and there is *radical* Christian rhetoric.[5] Still using the idea of Christian rhetoric as proclamation, Kennedy notes that some parts of the Bible 'give a reason why the proclamation should be received and thus [appeal], at least in part, to human rationality'.[6] Radical Christian rhetoric is different in that it does not appeal to rational argument: 'When a doctrine is purely proclaimed and not couched in enthymemes I call the technique *radical Christian rhetoric*'.[7] He develops his idea of radical Christian rhetoric based on a summary of E. Grassi's five characteristics of the rhetoric of sacred language:

> (1) It has a purely revealing or evangelical character, not a demonstrative or proving function; it does not arise out of a process of inference, but authoritatively proclaims the truth. (2) Its statements are immediate, formulated without mediation or contemplation. (3) They are imagistic and metaphorical, lending the reality of sensory appearances to a new meaning. (4) Its assertions are absolute and urgent; whatever does not fit with them is treated as outrageous. (5) Its pronouncements are outside time.[8]

3. Kennedy, *Classical Rhetoric*, pp. 128-29.

4. Kennedy, *Classical Rhetoric*, pp. 131-32.

5. G.A. Kennedy, *New Testament Interpretation through Rhetorical Criticism* (Chapel Hill, NC: University of North Carolina Press, 1984), pp. 6-8.

6. Kennedy, *New Testament Interpretation*, p. 7.

7. Kennedy, *New Testament Interpretation*, p. 7.

8. E. Grassi, *Rhetoric as Philosophy: The Humanist Tradition* (University Park: Pennsylvania State University Press, 1980), pp. 103-104, as quoted in

Kennedy further defines the nature of radical Christian rhetoric as including the perspective (he says doctrine) that 'the speaker is a vehicle of God's will'.[9] He adds to this the idea that radical Christian persuasion depends not on the capacity of a human mind to understand the message, but on whether God's love allows a person's heart to be moved or withholds that grace.[10]

J.R. Levison has offered a critique of Kennedy's notion of Christian rhetoric.[11] Levison first explores the Jewish concept of the Spirit as giving inspired, authoritative speech, a concept that undergirds Kennedy's assertions about early Christian rhetoric. Then Levison examines whether there is any appeal to the Jewish concept of Spirit-inspired speech in Paul's renowned discussion of wisdom and the Spirit in 1 Corinthians 1–2. Levison concludes that what Paul says corresponds to this notion of authoritative, Spirit-inspired speech, but how Paul presents his thesis is 'with all the resources of classical rhetoric'.[12] In view of this, Levison rejects the concept of radical Christian rhetoric as defined by Kennedy, yet he does not abandon the idea that there is something distinctive about Christian rhetoric.[13]

In general, many rhetoricians or linguists recognize that there is something distinctive about religious or sacred discourse, particularly biblical utterances.[14] D. Leith and G. Myerson make a typical comment: 'What we can loosely term religious utterances, then, occupy part of the

Kennedy, *New Testament Interpretation*, p. 6.

9. Kennedy, *New Testament Interpretation*, p. 7.

10. Kennedy, *New Testament Interpretation*, p. 8.

11. J.R. Levison, 'Did the Spirit Inspire Rhetoric? An Exploration of George Kennedy's Definition of Early Christian Rhetoric', in D.F. Watson (ed.), *Persuasive Artistry: Studies in New Testament Rhetoric in Honor of George A. Kennedy* (JSNTSup, 50; Sheffield: JSOT Press, 1991), pp. 25-40.

12. Levison, 'Did the Spirit Inspire Rhetoric?', p. 39.

13. Levison, 'Did the Spirit Inspire Rhetoric?', p. 40: 'The true rhetoric to which Paul adheres is the studied rhetoric of the sage who pores over ancient wisdom and turns of phrase, and who is renowned for instructive and persuasive speech'.

14. For example, Y. Gitay, 'Rhetorical Criticism', in S.R. Haynes and S.L. McKenzie (eds.), *To Each its Own Meaning: An Introduction to Biblical Criticisms and their Applications* (Louisville, KY: Westminster/John Knox Press, 1993), pp. 135-49, says on p. 135: 'The argument contained in this prophetic "proof" is quasi-logical rather than scientific. It occupies a middle ground between rational, mathematical proof and emotional appeal. This kind of argumentation is typical of religious rhetoric.'

same cultural space as literature: both make use of the idea that things can be known or understood which are beyond the power of language to verbalize in the form of referential propositions'.[15] Leith and Myerson, in essence, are recognizing that religious discourse appeals to transcendentals which cannot be verified by a closed system of linguistic reference.

It appears when one begins to try to define the nature of religious discourse, or more specifically for this study, Christian rhetoric; the heart of the matter is the manner of appeal, the nature of the argument. No one seems to dispute that there is argumentation that seeks to persuade in the biblical writings. But as one begins to analyse the ways and means of that argumentation or its rhetoric—that is, what makes it persuasive—does Christian rhetoric distinguish itself from its Hellenistic environment by not utilizing Graeco-Roman rationality associated with the classical rhetorical tradition?

3. *Pauline Argumentation and Pauline Rhetoric*

It was Wilhelm Wuellner who broke new ground in the discussion of the rhetoric and argumentation in Paul's letters in his article, 'Paul's Rhetoric of Argumentation in Romans: An Alternative to the Donfried–Karris Debate over Romans'. It is worth quoting in full his opening remarks which reset the methodological agenda:

> I propose to replace the traditional priority on propositional theology and the more recent priority on letters as literature with the new priority on letters as argumentation. Traditional theology, even biblical or Pauline theology, was based on the traditional model of logic and dialectic. The approach to Paul's letters as literature was based on traditional or modern theories of literature or poetics. Instead I am proposing that we consider Paul's letters primarily as argumentative. We understand argumentation as the use of discourse 'to influence the intensity of an audience's adherence to certain theses', the study of which belongs to traditional or 'new' rhetoric. I propose that in the rediscovery of the nature and purpose of argumentation as a basically rhetorical process we will find a more satisfactory way of accounting not only for the dialectical and logical dimensions, and for the literary dimensions in Paul's discourses, but also for the situational and social dimensions presupposed in Paul's letters.[16]

15. D. Leith and G. Myerson, *The Power of Address: Explorations in Rhetoric* (London: Routledge, 1989), p. 136.

16. W. Wuellner, 'Paul's Rhetoric of Argumentation in Romans: An Alter-

Wuellner's agenda suggests several important issues. First, what do we mean by argumentation? Secondly, what is the rhetorical nature of this argumentation, particularly in Paul's letters? Thirdly, what does this new agenda suggest for how we do biblical theology?

a. *Argumentation versus Rhetoric*
Wuellner's appeal to Perelman and Olbrechts-Tyteca's *The New Rhetoric* in order to define argumentation provides an interesting start-ing-point: 'We understand argumentation as the use of discourse "to influence the intensity of an audience's adherence to certain theses", the study of which belongs to traditional or "new" rhetoric'.[17] In *The New Rhetoric*, Perelman and Olbrechts-Tyteca distinguish between demon-stration and argumentation.[18] Demonstration is equated with formal logic 'which is limited to the examination of demonstrative methods of proof'.[19] Argumentation, on the other hand, is the use of discourse in the deliberation between two parties in order 'to influence the intensity of one party's adherence to certain theses'.[20] More simply put, argu-mentation is any means of persuasion in order to convince the other party. This makes argumentation a broad category of discourse that is always rhetorical with demonstration as one means of argumentation.

This general and rhetorical understanding of argumentation is differ-ent from that suggested by J. Kopperschmidt.[21] He defines an 'argu-ment' as 'the use of a statement in a logical process of argumentation to support or weaken another statement whose validity is questionable or contentious'.[22] His is a narrow understanding of argumentation com-pared to Perelman and Olbrechts-Tyteca, corresponding more closely with their understanding of demonstration.

To relate back to the above discussion regarding Christian rhetoric

native to the Donfried–Karris Debate over Romans', *CBQ* 38 (1976), pp. 330-51 (330-31).

   17. Wuellner, 'Paul's Rhetoric', p. 330.

   18. C. Perelman and L. Olbrechts-Tyteca, *The New Rhetoric: A Treatise on Argumentation* (trans. J. Wilkinson and P. Weaver; Notre Dame: University of Notre Dame Press, 1969), pp. 13-62, esp. pp. 13-14.

   19. Perelman and Olbrechts-Tyteca, *The New Rhetoric*, p. 13.

   20. Perelman and Olbrechts-Tyteca, *The New Rhetoric*, p. 14.

   21. J. Kopperschmidt, 'An Analysis of Argumentation', in T.A. van Dijk (ed.), *Handbook of Discourse Analysis*. II. *Dimensions of Discourse* (London: Academic Press, 1985), pp. 159-68.

   22. Kopperschmidt, 'An Analysis of Argumentation', p. 159.

and its relation to classical rhetoric, Wuellner's understanding of argumentation confronts Kennedy's distinction between classical rhetoric as appeal to rationality and radical Christian rhetoric as authoritative assertion without rational appeal. Whereas Kopperschmidt preserves the distinction, Wuellner's understanding does distinguish between social and cultural forms of argumentation so that one can speak of Christian rhetoric, Jewish rhetoric, classical Greek rhetoric, and so forth. In so doing, he is not prioritizing one particular mode of argumentation, but noting the commonalty of certain kinds of argumentation. Wuellner in effect collapses rhetoric into argumentation and argumentation into rhetoric.[23]

Kopperschmidt represents a different philosophical stream which prioritizes *logos*. In this understanding, argumentation is one thing; rhetoric is another. Discourse is analysed to evaluate the mode of argumentation, not its rhetoric. If argumentation, as defined above, is absent from the discourse, then some other means of persuasion is operative.

These two different perspectives on argumentation correspond with the well-known debate, philosophy versus rhetoric.[24] Moreover, it has important consequences for how rhetorical criticism conceives its methodology. The application of ancient Graeco-Roman categories of oratorical rhetoric to analyse the Pauline letters is in one sense an analysis of the argumentation of that letter. But by limiting the analysis of the Pauline letter to ancient conventions of Graeco-Roman rhetoric, is there an implicit assumption on the critic's part about the nature or mode of argumentation that the critic expects to find in Paul's letters? It is interesting that Wuellner's broad interpretation of argumentation and rhetoric has resulted in him using a wide range of critical perspectives and methods and not only conventions of Graeco-Roman rhetoric to expose the persuasive power of the biblical text.

b. *Rhetorical Analyses of Pauline Argumentation*
Wuellner's remarks quoted above suggest that New Testament studies has tended in the past to analyse Pauline discourse in theological terms and in literary terms. In sum, exegesis was interested in positing what Paul said (content criticism) and how the text corresponded to its liter-

23. W. Wuellner, 'Hermeneutics and Rhetorics: From "Truth and Method" to "Truth and Power"', *Scriptura* Sup3 (1989), pp. 1-54 (33-34).
24. See the survey of the debate in B. Vickers, *In Defence of Rhetoric* (Oxford: Clarendon Press, 1988), pp. 148-213.

ary environment in terms of genre and literary forms (literary form criticism). But there has always been a concern in Pauline studies to discern the manner of argumentation.[25] Yet, as Wuellner recognizes, this concern was basically interested in the manner of argumentation in order to determine Paul's theological method. The two main perspectives for analysing Pauline argumentation were logic (the rational or propositional nature of his theology) and Jewish theological discourse (the use of midrash, halakah, haggadah and pesher to reinterpret Paul's tradition, the Old Testament and Judaism). In recent years a third method of analysing Pauline argumentation has emerged: rhetorical criticism (the ways and means and the effect of Pauline argumentation), which has emphasized the Hellenistic context of Paul.

Rhetorical analyses of Pauline argumentation abound.[26] One strand primarily uses aspects of modern rhetorical theory to illumine Pauline argumentation. Another strand primarily utilizes the categories of ancient Graeco-Roman rhetorical theory. If one confines one's interest to the second strand, one notes that such analyses seem to adopt different perspectives regarding the nature of Paul's argumentation. Some analyses seem to adopt a 'scientific' stance in which all the parts of a Pauline text are identified and labelled as a particular rhetorical convention and then correlated with the relevant discussion of rhetorical theory in the ancient rhetorical handbooks or treatises.[27] These same studies adopt a perspective which assumes that by so labelling and identifying the parts of the text the critic is reconstructing in accurate historical terms the intent of Paul at the time of writing.[28] From this perspective,

25. Examples include A.M. Gale, *Use of Analogy in the Letters of Paul* (Philadelphia: Westminster Press, 1964); R. Longenecker, *Biblical Exegesis in the Apostolic Period* (Grand Rapids: Eerdmans, 1975); and J.A. Fischer, 'Pauline Literary Forms and Thought Patterns', *CBQ* 39 (1977), pp. 209-23.

26. See the bibliography in D.F. Watson and A.J. Hauser, *Rhetorical Criticism of the Bible: A Comprehensive Bibliography with Notes on History and Method* (Biblical Interpretation Series, 4; Leiden: E.J. Brill, 1994).

27. See, for example, D.F. Watson, '1 Corinthians 10.23–11.1 in the Light of Greco-Roman Rhetoric', *JBL* 108 (1989), pp. 301-18; or J. Smit, 'Argument and Genre of 1 Corinthians 12–14', in S.E. Porter and T.H. Olbricht (eds.), *Rhetoric and the New Testament: Essays from the 1992 Heidelberg Conference* (JSNTSup, 90; Sheffield: JSOT Press, 1993), pp. 211-30.

28. Kennedy, *New Testament Interpretation*, p. 12, set the agenda for those who follow his model or method of rhetorical criticism: 'The ultimate goal of rhetorical

rhetorical criticism actually uncovers the argumentative design which was inscribed by the author at the time of writing.

Other rhetorical-critical studies are less 'scientific' in perspective. Wishing to avoid an a-historical perspective and to preserve some sense of historicity with regard to the text, they use dimensions of Graeco-Roman rhetoric to suggest the nature and tenor of the argument.[29] It is not so much establishing what the author intended as suggesting a way to make sense of the texture and progression of the argument found in the text.[30] From this perspective, rhetorical criticism highlights one possible way to understand the argument of the discourse.

To step back for a moment, the issue that emerges is quite crucial. Is there one correct method for analysing Pauline argumentation? Is all Pauline argumentation based on its Hellenistic milieu and formulated according to the practice of Graeco-Roman rhetoric? If so, is this what makes Pauline argumentation rhetorical? Or is Pauline argumentation constructed according to Jewish modes of argumentation? Or is the argumentation of *some* Pauline texts constructed according to Jewish argumentation and the argumentation of *other* texts according to Graeco-Roman rhetoric? Common sense suggests that a critic cannot determine this beforehand, but must let the features of the text dictate which theoretical perspective to adopt after a preliminary examination of the argument—but common sense is not always theoretically or methodologically appropriate. It does seem, however, that at times some rhetorical-critical studies assume any and all Pauline arguments can and should be analysed according to Graeco-Roman rhetoric.

Wuellner seems to suggest that all Pauline arguments are rhetorical, but not necessarily because they conform to Graeco-Roman rhetoric. Kennedy seems to suggest that while all Pauline arguments are rhetori-

analysis, briefly put, is the discovery of the author's intent and of how that is transmitted through a text to an audience'.

29. For example, T.H. Olbricht, 'An Aristotelian Rhetorical Analysis of 1 Thessalonians', in D.L. Balch, E. Ferguson and W.A. Meeks (eds.), *Greeks, Romans, and Christians: Essays in Honor of Abraham J. Malherbe* (Philadelphia: Fortress Press, 1990), pp. 216-36; or G.W. Hansen, *Abraham in Galatians: Epistolary and Thetorical Contexts* (JSNTSup, 29; Sheffield: JSOT Press, 1989).

30. See V.K. Robbins, 'The Present and Future of Rhetorical Analysis', in S.E. Porter and T.H. Olbricht, *The Rhetorical Analysis of Scripture: Essays from the 1995 London Conference* (JSNTSup, 146; Sheffield: Sheffield Academic Press, 1997), pp. 24-52, esp. pp. 30-32, for the use of the term 'texture' as a way to refer to rhetorical argumentation.

cal, some conform to modes of classical rhetorical argument and others to the features of radical Christian rhetoric. Rhetorical criticism may be in a bit of a muddle because it is not always clear what it means by rhetoric and because it is not always clear about what constitutes an 'argument'. The questions remain—does Christian rhetoric employ a different mode of argumentation than Graeco-Roman rhetoric? If so, what does that mean for how critics apply rhetorical criticism to Paul's arguments?

4. *The Theological Rhetoric of Paul's Argumentation*

To say that Paul is a theologian *par excellence* seems indisputable. Paul was perhaps the Church's first great theologian, and his theological contribution to Christianity has remained a bedrock for Christian theology ever since. In order to come to terms with Paul's theology, one needs to understand both how he argues and how he persuades, though it is not always easy to distinguish between the two and it may be methodologically improper to try to do so (much like distinguishing between form and content). In which case, a theological analysis of Paul's writings is interested in the argumentation and the rhetorical nature of that argumentation. For the sake of discussion, it seems reasonable to state that in his writings Paul attempts to present a theological idea/thesis and to argue for its truthfulness or at least its correctness. Part of that argument includes persuading the other party to assent or adhere to the thesis or theses presented. One way to conceive rhetorical criticism, then, is both as an analysis of the argument of the discourse and as an analysis of the persuasive techniques employed in the argument.

The importance of conceiving rhetorical criticism in this way is that one does not have to exclude an investigation into what is said (content criticism) from the investigation of how it is said. In this way, rhetorical criticism becomes an important methodology for understanding the theological rhetoric of Paul because it investigates content, form and persuasion. It recognizes that Paul as a theologian attempted in his letters to say something meaningful, to present or argue this in a form of argumentation, and to employ persuasive techniques to gain the assent of his readers/hearers. In many ways this is saying something similar to what Wuellner said at the end of his remarks on the new agenda for studying the rhetorical nature of Paul's argumentation:

> I propose that in the rediscovery of the nature and purpose of argumenta-
> tion as a basically rhetorical process we will find a more satisfactory way
> of accounting not only for the dialectical and logical dimensions, and for
> the literary dimensions in Paul's discourses, but also for the situational
> and social dimensions presupposed in Paul's letters.[31]

To endorse this agenda for rhetorical criticism implies that Kennedy's model or method for doing rhetorical criticism is inadequate. It is inadequate because those who use it generally limit their analysis of a biblical text to the conventions of Graeco-Roman rhetoric, and it seems that with regard to Paul both his mode of argumentation and his rhetorical means are not limited to such conventions. It is also inadequate because its end product can generally be labelled a kind of rhetorical form criticism, where identification of rhetorical features determines function. Further, it is inadequate because the end product of the method tends to be an evaluation of the effectiveness of the rhetorical features upon the original rhetorical situation. If one considers 1 Corinthians as an example, no matter how you identify the rhetorical features of the text, most rhetorical critics would agree that the letter is an effective rhetorical response to a complex rhetorical situation.[32] But it appears from what historical knowledge we have of the relationship between Paul and the Corinthians that 1 Corinthians was a failure rhetorically. It was a failure because it did not persuade enough people and thus did not solve the problems and disputes which existed between the two parties. The importance of 1 Corinthians is not limited to its use of Graeco-Roman conventions nor to its effectiveness as rhetoric in a historical moment between two parties. The importance of 1 Corinthians is that, as theological rhetoric, what it says and how it says it has informed the theological thinking of the Christian Church since it was written.

To return to the matter of the nature of Christian rhetoric. What distinguishes Christian rhetoric is not its rationality or its lack of rationality nor its authoritative assertion which lacks logical demonstration, but its appeal to the significance of Jesus Christ—his life, teaching and

---

31. Wuellner, 'Paul's Rhetoric', p. 331.

32. As in B. Witherington III, *Conflict and Community in Corinth: A Socio-Rhetorical Commentary on 1 and 2 Corinthians* (Carlisle: Paternoster Press, 1995); and M.M. Mitchell, *Paul and the Rhetoric of Reconciliation: An Exegetical Investigation of the Language and Composition of 1 Corinthians* (HUT, 28; Tübingen: J.C.B. Mohr, 1991).

ministry—for understanding the meaning of life, the truth about God and the ways of God. Appeal to the significance of Jesus Christ is done rationally, authoritatively, imaginatively, dramatically, and in many other modes of argumentation, but always rhetorically. It is always rhetorical because when appeal is made to the significance of Jesus Christ the argument attempts to say something meaningful, to argue for its correctness, and to persuade the readers/hearers to assent to its meaningfulness. It is rhetorical because the appeal to the significance of Jesus Christ becomes a theological foundation and argument for constructing a world of meaning and becomes a theological basis and argument for persuading others to faith. There may be other rhetorical elements which are common to Christian rhetoric, but the essence of Christian rhetoric is its christology. It would not be surprising to find that the theological rhetoric of the Pauline letters is, at least in essence, Christian rhetoric.

THE SELF AGAINST THE SELF IN ROMANS 7.7-25

Glenn S. Holland

Romans 7 is a perennial focus of exegetical attention. Several fundamental principles of Paul's theology seem to depend on its proper
interpretation. The apostle's beliefs about the human situation and the
means of salvation, his vision of the life lived 'in Christ' and his attitude towards the Jewish law—the resolution of all of these issues is
dependent in large part on how Romans 7 is read and understood.

But Rom. 7.7-25 also presents its own problems by virtue of Paul's
use of the first-person singular to describe the plight of the person
enslaved by sin. It is 'I' who was once alive apart from the law, it is 'I'
who knows what is right but does what is wrong, it is 'I' who is made
wretched by the power of sin. It is entirely reasonable to wonder why
Paul has chosen to use this particular rhetorical approach in these particular verses, as well as to ask what rhetorical function Rom. 7.7-25
serves within the larger strategy of the letter. But two other important
questions arise as well: How is Paul's use of the 'I' related to the *topos*
of self-example in the arguments of the Hellenistic moral philosophers?
And what does Paul's use of the 'I' in Romans 7 reveal about his
rhetorical intentions?

1. *Romans 7 in the Context of the Letter*

At least some of the problems associated with Romans 7 arise—like
many other problems in the letter—from the modern tendency to divide
the letter into discrete sections and to look at each section in isolation
from the others.[1] Romans 7.7-25 is only one part of an extended argument, an argument that begins in Rom. 1.16-17. What Paul says in
Romans 7 is anticipated and foreshadowed throughout the first part of

---

1.　Stanley K. Stowers gives a good account of this practice and the problems it
causes in *A Rereading of Romans: Justice, Jews, and Gentiles* (New Haven: Yale
University Press, 1994), pp. 6-11.

the letter, but most especially in what are now the two preceding chapters.

In his recent 'rereading' of Romans, Stanley Stowers has emphasized the close association between Rom. 1.18-32 and Rom. 7.7-25.[2] But it is in Romans 5 that Paul first addresses at length the contrast between the (present) life lived in Christ and the (past) life lived in bondage to sin and death. The new life was made possible by Christ's death 'while we were still weak' and 'ungodly' (Rom. 5.6), 'while we were still sinners' (Rom. 5.8b) and 'while we were still enemies' (Rom. 5.10a). Paul uses these increasingly severe terms to describe those (apparently including himself) who were under the sovereign power of death as a result of sin's presence in the world from the beginning of human history (Rom. 5.12-14). Paul in this chapter repeatedly contrasts the power of sin and death which once held sway over all humanity with the much greater power of divine grace and Christ's work of obedience which has now brought reconciliation (Rom. 5.9, 10, 15, 16, 17, 18, 19, 20b, 21). Romans 5 resonates both with what was once and what is now. Significantly, Romans 5 also takes up the place of the law in human history and its relationship to sin: sin was in the world before the law (Rom. 5.13a), and the law served to increase transgressions (Rom. 5.20a).

In Romans 6 the contrast between the life in Christ and the life lived in bondage to sin and death continues. Paul rejects the suggestion that continuing to sin might initiate greater grace from God by arguing that baptism into union with Christ is baptism into his death (Rom. 6.3). This death is death to sin, a death embraced 'so also we might set out on a new life' (Rom. 6.4). It is specifically the old humanity, the body of sin, that is crucified 'so that we may no longer be slaves to sin; for whoever dies is set free from sin' (Rom. 6.6b-7). Paul makes an obvious point—dead people cannot sin—but passes over another equally obvious point: death is one of the few means by which one can escape enslavement.

In Romans 6, sin, slavery and death as a sovereign power are associated closely enough that a reference to one implies a connection to the other two. Jesus, once dead, is no longer under death's dominion (Rom. 6.9) and so has died also to sin (Rom. 6.10). The baptized must regard themselves as dead to sin as well, and no longer allow it to hold sovereign power over their mortal bodies (Rom. 6.12). The exhortatory

2. Stowers, *A Rereading of Romans*, pp. 42-43.

implications of death to sin are brought out in Rom. 6.12-14: the new status must be lived out. Here also Paul speaks of 'the members of the body' as 'implements' (ὅπλα) at sin's disposal, as well as yielding the entire body to God as a 'member' to serve God, as an implement to do right (Rom. 6.13). In Rom. 6.14, sin's mastery is related to submission to ('being under') the law.

The association between sin and death becomes explicit in Rom. 6.15-23, while 'slavery' becomes a neutral term whose status depends on the master to whom one is enslaved.[3] Paul draws the contrast between slavery to sin and death and slavery to God and righteousness in Rom. 6.16b, making it clear that while the former was previously the readers' lot, they are now emancipated from sin and are slaves of righteousness (Rom. 6.17-18). Romans 6.19b reiterates the contrast between the readers' past and present situations, while raising again the idea of (then) yielding the members to serve impurity, and (now) to serve righteousness. In Rom. 6.20-23 Paul hammers home the contrast between the past and the present, while playing with the language of slavery and freedom: the readers, once slaves of sin, were then 'free' from righteousness; now they are slaves to God and 'free' from sin.

Romans 7.1-6 echoes Rom. 6.1-11 in crediting this change to a death, in this case the atoning death of Christ which the believer appropriates through baptism. Now, however, what one escapes through death is not sin or slavery, but the power and authority of the law. This idea is worked out in terms of the legal bonds that put a wife under the authority of her husband (Rom. 7.2-3). The consequence of being under authority is 'bearing fruit' (καρποφόρειν) for the one in authority. Christ 'has been raised from the dead in order that we may bear fruit for God' (Rom. 7.4b).

So it is that 'you will know them by their fruits'. Previously, 'while we were living in the flesh, our sinful passions, aroused by the law, were at work in our members to bear fruit for death' (Rom. 7.5). As in Rom. 6.13, it is only a part of the body or the self that is subjected to sin and death, the 'members' or the 'flesh'. As in Rom. 6.14, the authority of the law is associated with the authority of sin and death; here in fact the law arouses the passions, an idea already presented in

---

3.   This appears to represent accurately the situation of slaves in the Roman empire of the first century. See Dale B. Martin, *Slavery as Salvation: The Metaphor of Slavery in Pauline Christianity* (New Haven: Yale University Press, 1990), pp. 1-49.

Rom. 5.20. But that is in the past. 'Now we are discharged from the law, dead to that which held us captive' (Rom. 7.6a). The law is again associated with subjection to sin and death and with the readers' past. Their previous life was associated with 'the old way of the word' (παλαιότητι γράμματος), but their present life is 'the new way of the spirit' (καινόητι πνεύματος).

In Romans 5, 6 and 7.1-6, then, we find the major thematic and metaphorical constituents of Rom. 7.7-25. There is in both the striking contrast between the past and present situation of the readers, the description of the former situation as enslavement to sin and death, the idea of the members of the body serving as implements at the disposal of the one in authority, God's abounding grace to free those enslaved to sin, death (by baptism into Christ and his death) as the means by which freedom is gained from enslavement, and, strikingly, the law as the means by which transgressions increase.

Romans 7.7-25 is not the first time that Paul has employed the first person while discussing these ideas. Romans 5.1–7.6 sees the frequent and apparently careful use of the first-person plural. Paul appears to differentiate what can truly be said about his gentile readers, either in the past or the present, and what can truly be said about his own past or present situation.[4] In part, this use of the first-person plural contributes to the sense of solidarity with his readers that Paul establishes rather clumsily in Rom. 1.11-12. But it also fosters the intimacy which characterizes Rom. 6.1–7.6 as a direct address from Paul as author to his implied audience,[5] an intimacy which reaches its highest pitch when he calls his readers 'brothers' (Rom. 7.1, 4).[6] Significantly, this direct address appears just before Paul's identification with his readers in their past and present situation as described in Rom. 7.5-6. Within this context, Rom. 7.7-25 may be seen as a reiteration and expansion of ideas introduced and explored in the previous chapters, using the first-person singular in place of the first-person plural.

2. *Romans 7.7-25 as 'Speech-in-Character'*

Stowers argues in *A Rereading of Romans* that Paul's use of the first-

---

4.   Stowers builds on this distinction (cf. *A Rereading of Romans*, pp. 255-56), although he curiously overlooks its significance in Rom. 5.6-11 and 7.5-6.

5.   Stowers, *A Rereading of Romans*, pp. 269, 270, 292.

6.   Stowers, *A Rereading of Romans*, pp. 259, 277.

person singular in Rom. 7.7-25 is an example of 'speech-in-character' (προσωποποιία). 'Speech-in-character' was a familiar rhetorical device in the first century and its use was part of a basic rhetorical education.[7] Stowers argues that there are clear indications that Paul employs 'speech-in-character' in Rom. 7.7-25. First, 'The section begins in v. 7 with an abrupt change in voice following a rhetorical question that serves as a transition from Paul's authorial voice'.[8] Secondly,

> the passage seems to present a distinctive, coherent ethos with a particular life situation. As the handbooks recommend, the person speaks of his happy past before he learned about the law (7.7b-8 and especially 9), his present misery, and his future plight (7.24). Since this tragic characterization also centers on self-reflection and takes the form primarily of a monologue, the passage fits the classic models of speech-in-character.[9]

Stowers identifies the character speaking as a gentile 'God-fearer'. But he understands that designation in a particular way. The 'God-fearer' is a gentile who has accepted selected stipulations of the Torah as a means of gaining self-mastery (σωφροσύνη).[10] Citing the example of Philo and Josephus, Stowers maintains that some first-century Jewish teachers presented the stipulations of Torah as a superior moral code that could provide gentiles with the self-mastery promised by Hellenistic philosophy.[11] But the gentile 'God-fearer' Paul portrays by speech-in-character has found himself unable to conform to the demands of the law. As a gentile, he is still laboring under the condemnation pronounced by God against those 'who by their wickedness suppress the truth' (Rom. 1.18b). Like other gentiles, the gentile 'God-fearer' in Rom. 7.7-25 is still subjected to moral futility. Although he knows the law, he is unable to conform to it, and the self-mastery he seeks continues to elude him.[12]

Although Stowers's argument that Rom. 7.7-25 provides an example of προσωποποιία generally commends itself, there are some problems with the more specific question of just what character is portrayed in which speech. As Stowers notes, Rom. 7.7-12 depicts a past situation, while Rom. 7.14-25 depicts a present situation. The 'speaker' in Rom.

7.   Stowers, *A Rereading of Romans*, pp. 16-21.
8.   Stowers, *A Rereading of Romans*, p. 269.
9.   Stowers, *A Rereading of Romans*, p. 270.
10. Stowers, *A Rereading of Romans*, pp. 71-72.
11. Stowers, *A Rereading of Romans*, pp. 58-65.
12. Stowers, *A Rereading of Romans*, pp. 107-109, 277-78.

7.7-12 (actually, Rom. 7.7b-12) is someone who has come to know the law and, as a result, to know sin (Rom. 7.7b). In fact the speaker is able to say, 'I was alive once without the law' (Rom. 7.9a). Stowers, following Origen, considers such a statement impossible for Paul as a Jew,[13] but it is in fact just as impossible for a gentile, 'God-fearer' or not. As Paul demonstrates in Rom. 1.18-32, a passage with close affinities to Rom. 7.7-25,[14] gentiles are condemned to moral futility and a downward spiral of sin. In fact, since 'death held sway from Adam to Moses' (Rom. 6.14a), the only person who could say 'I was alive once without the law' would be Adam or Eve. The overtones of Genesis 3 in Rom. 7.7-12 have been discussed before, most notably by Lyonnet.[15] Although there are potential objections to such an identification,[16] it may still provide some insight into the character of the 'speaker' in Rom. 7.7-12.

But if Paul has Adam or Eve in mind here, it is not as the ancestor of all humanity. It is instead Adam or Eve as the prototypal gentile, who receives divine stipulations but is unable to fulfill them. It is Adam or Eve as the first person misled by sin and through sin subjected to death (Rom. 7.11). Paul does something similar in Romans 4 when he presents Abraham as the prototypal man of faith/faithfulness who is commended and accepted by God.

According to the account in Rom. 1.18-32, the Gentiles from the beginning turned away from God. God punished them by giving them free rein, so that they became enslaved to their passions and a downward spiral of corruption. Romans 7.7-12 describes this situation in images borrowed from the Genesis story.

Romans 7.14-25 then presents the gentile God-fearer who is aware, like Adam, of the true state of his soul and therefore wretched. Stowers has characterized the gentile 'God-fearer' speaking in Rom. 7.7-25 largely in terms of the second portion of the passage, Rom. 7.14-25.

---

13. Stowers, *A Rereading of Romans*, p. 266.

14. Stowers, *A Rereading of Romans*, pp. 42-43.

15. S. Lyonnet, 'L'histoire du salut selon le chapitre vii de l'épître aux Romains', *Bib* 43 (1962), pp. 117-51.

16. The most compelling has been that Adam is never explicitly evoked, but Stowers's explanation of προσωποποιία indicates that such an explicit identification is unnecessary (*A Rereading of Romans*, pp. 18-21). Stowers himself is wary of any conclusions drawn from the citation of Adam in Rom. 5 (*A Rereading of Romans*, pp. 253-55).

Here the 'I' speaks in the present tense of his 'wretchedness', a wretch-edness brought about by ἀκρασία, 'lack of self-mastery'.[17] Stowers has demonstrated that the speaker describes his inner conflict in terms evocative of the tragic heroine Medea and argues that Medea was the primary example of ἀκρασία for the Greco-Roman world.[18]

But she is more than that; she also represents the exact opposite of what the gentile 'God-fearer' has hoped to achieve through his attempts to obey the stipulations of Torah. He seeks the self-mastery which is essentially Roman and masculine;[19] she is a foreigner who epitomizes feminine ἀκρασία. He tries to rise above his pagan origins by acknow-ledging and obeying the one true God; she is an arch-pagan and a sorceress. He seeks the peace of mind and happiness which arise from doing what one knows to be good; she represents the wretchedness of one who can say *video meliora proboque, deteriora sequor*, 'I see and approve what is better, but I do the worse' (Ovid, *Met.* 7.20-21).

It is difficult for us, conditioned as we are by what Krister Stendahl has called the 'introspective conscience of the West',[20] to appreciate the radical debility described in Rom. 7.13-25. Paul describes a moral situ-

---

17. A. Van den Beld discusses the philosophical and ethical ramifications of the term in 'Romans 7.14-25 and the Problem of *Akrasia*', *RelS* 21 (1985), pp. 495-515.

18. 'The text remembered as the starting point for this tradition is Euripides' *Medea* 1077–80: "I am being overcome by evils. I know that what I am about to do is evil but passion is stronger than my reasoned reflection and this is the cause of the worst evils for humans." These words of Euripides' *Medea* became the classic text for the long and varied ancient discussion of *akrasia*, lack of self-mastery' (Stowers, *A Rereading of Romans*, p. 260).

In contrast to Euripides and Seneca, Ovid deals only briefly with Medea's murder of her sons by Jason as one in a series of crimes. He instead emphasizes Medea's ἀκρασία specifically in reference to her passion for Jason (*Met.* 7.7-99). She is aware that her love for him is in opposition to all demands of family and national loyalty; she blames it on the gods; she is unhappy; she is not herself; she nearly masters herself but sees Jason and is overwhelmed by passion; she admits, 'I see clearly what I am doing: it is not ignorance of the truth that will lead me astray, but love' (*Met.* 7.92-93). It would seem, then, that Medea's association with ἀκρασία was such that it was believed to epitomize her entire character, and any one of several different aspects of her story might be chosen to highlight that trait.

19. Stowers, *A Rereading of Romans*, pp. 46-56.

20. Krister Stendahl, 'The Apostle Paul and the Introspective Conscience of the West', in *idem*, *Paul among Jews and Gentiles and Other Essays* (Philadelphia: Fortress Press, 1976), pp. 78-96.

ation utterly beyond the ability of human reason to correct or control.

Paul here runs against the common opinion of first-century Hellenistic moral philosophy, which taught that true knowledge of the good inevitably led to correct moral behavior. As Albrecht Dihle has demonstrated, the Hellenistic philosophers maintained almost unanimously that the rational mind, the intellect, was the sole determinant of a person's behavior, and directed that behavior according to its own recognition of the good.[21] There could be a defective idea of the good, as in the case of Aristotle's morally weak man (*Eth. Nic.* 1150b30–1151a4), but the moral defect in such people was believed to be the result of impaired moral knowledge (*Eth. Nic.* 1152a8-24).[22]

A division within the self of the sort described in Romans 7 might be theorized, as in Plato's figure of the charioteer guiding the tractable horse and the resistant horse in the *Phaedrus* (246a3–257a2).[23] But even so, Plato asserted that knowledge enables the charioteer—the reason—to maintain control and conform the actions of the chariot—the self—to what the reason recognizes as good. Knowledge gives the reason undisputed power over the contrary elements in the human mind. The Hellenistic philosophers asserted that if what is good is truly known, morally correct behavior will be the inevitable result.[24]

Such is not the case in Rom. 7.13-25. There Paul, like Philo and Josephus, treats Torah as a means by which gentiles might gain self-mastery, and in that respect as something comparable to pagan philosophy. Knowledge of the good, presented specifically as knowledge of Torah, itself neither grants the reason power over the other elements in

21. Albrecht Dihle, *The Theory of Will in Classical Antiquity* (Berkeley: University of California Press, 1982), pp. 20-67.

22. Stowers, following Anthony Kenny (*Aristotle's Theory of the Will* [New Haven: Yale University Press, 1979], pp. 62-63), maintains that Aristotle rejected the idea that correct knowledge determines moral behavior (*A Rereading of Romans*, p. 261), but Van den Beld correctly observes that 'although he [Aristotle] originally recognizes that *akrasia* is a real phenomenon, his explanation ultimately entails a denial that it actually occurs' ('Romans 7.14-25', p. 501).

23. An instructive analysis of the palinode may be found in Charles L. Griswold, Jr, *Self-Knowledge in Plato's Phaedrus* (New Haven: Yale University Press, 1986), pp. 92-99.

24. Disagreement was more likely to arise over the difficulty of achieving real virtue, as, for example, in the position of Chrysippus, third leader of the Stoa: 'Man walks in wickedness all his life, or, at any rate, for the greater part of it. If he ever attains to virtue, it is late and at the very sunset of his days' (*SVF*, I, pp. 59-60).

the human mind nor leads to morally correct behavior. The enslaving power of sin leads instead to ἀκρασία and renders knowledge of the law ineffectual. Instead of leading to the σωφροσύνη extolled by the philosophers, the gentile attempt to obey Torah leads only to 'wretchedness' (ταλαιπωρία), the very state from which the popular philosophers offered salvation.[25]

'God-fearers' might assume that they can correct their situation by access to the wisdom of the law and the acknowledgment that the Lord is God, but they remain in bondage to sin. The knowledge of their moral futility leads to despair and 'wretchedness'. According to Stowers, this moral futility is a particularly gentile problem.[26] Yet Paul is able to identify with this plight and claim it as his own former situation as well.

As we have seen, Paul uses the first-person plural throughout Rom. 5.1–7.6, especially Rom. 6.1–7.6, to indicate his solidarity with his gentile readers while at the same time maintaining some distinctions between himself and them. Paul and his readers share the benefits of baptism and have been made right with God through Jesus Christ (Rom. 5.1-2, 8-10; 6.3-4, 5-9; 7.6). Paul reverts to the second-person plural when exhorting his readers (Rom. 6.11-14) or describing their former slavery to sin and contrasting it with their new situation as people of Christ (Rom. 6.16-23; 7.4).

But surprisingly, at the climax of his direct, intimate address to his 'brothers' in Rom. 7.1-6, Paul returns to the first-person plural to describe their common former condition of enslavement to sin (Rom. 7.5). He then again contrasts the past with the present (Rom. 7.6), but in so doing he further identifies himself with a past enslavement to sin and bondage to the law that he has otherwise ascribed to the gentiles alone. Moreover, Rom. 7.5-6 anticipates and summarizes the points to be made in Rom. 7.7-25 (Rom. 7.5) and Rom. 8.1-39 (Rom. 7.6). But since Rom. 6.15-23 also anticipates the soliloquy of Rom. 7.7-25, Rom. 7.5-6 not only foreshadows Rom. 7.7-25 and Rom. 8.1-39 but also reiterates a point already made. In other words, Paul presents very much the same situation in three distinctive 'voices': the second-person plural of Rom. 6.15-23, the first-person plural of Rom. 7.5-6 and the first-person singular of Rom. 7.7-25.

Although it may be true, then, that Rom. 7.7-25 represents not the

25. Cf. Arrian, *Epict. Diss.* 1.3.5; 1.12.28; 3.23.28.
26. Stowers, *A Rereading of Romans*, pp. 278-84.

voice of Paul himself but an example of 'speech-in-character', as Stowers believes, the cumulative effect of Paul's rhetorical self-presentation in the preceding two chapters would seem to require some sort of identification between Paul as author and the wretched 'I'. Although the details may derive from a specifically gentile context, as described in both Rom. 6.15-23 and Rom. 7.7-25, Paul is still able to identify with the plight of the wretched 'I' sufficiently to include himself among those who were once at the mercy of the sinful desires evoked by the law in Rom. 7.5.

3. *The Wretched 'I' and Pauline Self-Example*

By including himself in the 'wretchedness' of moral frustration, Paul subverts the philosophical *topos* of the teacher as a moral example and guide for his followers. He presents himself as one who shared in the former slavery to sin endured by his readers, so he cannot offer himself as an example for them to follow. But even if he could, it would do no good. It was not knowledge of the good or the examples of wise men that freed his readers from moral futility; it was the work of God through Jesus Christ.

The idea that the philosophical teacher taught not only through his words but also by his own moral example was widespread in the Greco-Roman world. Kathleen O'Brien Wicker notes, 'The general belief of antiquity, which Plutarch also shares, is that *paradeigmata…* examples of virtuous behavior, are more effective than logic or physical force in encouraging persons to perform the kinds of actions through which habits of virtue are acquired'.[27] Paul proves himself familiar with the practice. He often draws upon his own behavior as a guide for his readers: 'Be imitators of me, as I am of Christ' (1 Cor. 11.1; cf. Phil. 3.17; 4.9; 1 Cor. 4.16; 1 Thess. 1.6).[28] Paul is able to cite his own

27. Kathleen O'Brien Wicker, 'Mulierum Virtutes (Moralia 242E–263C)', in H.D. Betz (ed.), *Plutarch's Ethical Writings and Early Christian Literature* (SCHNT, 4; Leiden: E.J. Brill, 1978), p. 112.

28. For Paul's use of self-example, see D.M. Stanley, ' "Become Imitators of Me": The Pauline Conception of Apostolic Tradition', *Bib* 40 (1959), pp. 859-77; H.D. Betz, *Nachfolge und Nachahmung Jesu Christi im Neuen Testament* (BHT, 37; Tübingen: Mohr Siebeck, 1967), pp. 136-89; Benjamin Fiore, *The Function of Personal Example in the Socratic and Pastoral Epistles* (AnBib, 105; Rome: Biblical Institute Press, 1986), pp. 164-90.

example because his congregations have personal knowledge of both his character and his work as an apostle.

But Paul in Romans identifies with the plight of the wretched 'I' described in Rom. 7.7-25 as someone who was once at the mercy of the passions at work in his members. So in Romans 7 the *topos* of the teacher as a moral example and guide becomes for Paul's readers—if anything—a 'bad example', an example of moral futility and impotence that no one would wish to imitate. And yet, ironically, this is precisely the example all unredeemed humanity follows because of its bondage to sin.

The wretched 'I' is offered as an example of human moral failure precisely to encourage Paul's gentile readers to shun any hope of salvation that is based in the accumulation of knowledge or the practice of correct moral action. The one is useless and the other impossible. Rejection of these paths to salvation means rejection both of the teachings of philosophy and, as Paul presents the case, teachings based in the Jewish law. But Paul also shuns self-example as a form of moral pedagogy by claiming a share in the past 'wretchedness' his readers once experienced. No human example can save; that is the work of God alone.

Why does Paul adopt this sort of solidarity with his readers as a dominant rhetorical strategy in Romans? Because it addresses the needs of the situation. When Paul wrote to the Christians in Rome he could not assume that his readers would have a favorable impression of him, or that they would respect his authority as an apostle. If, as Stowers argues,[29] the letter is directed exclusively to believing gentiles, their attitudes towards Paul, the self-styled 'apostle to the gentiles', might reasonably be expected to run the gamut from outright hostility to strong support. Under these circumstances Paul could not simply assert his authority as an apostle from afar. He likewise could not depend upon his readers' trust or obedience based on previous experience. Nor could he base a claim to authority on his history as an apostle, which was not known directly by his Roman readers, and, to the extent that it was known at second or third hand, might be subject to partisan interpretation.[30] In such circumstances Paul chose to promote solidarity with his readers by styling them as fellow members of the community of

29. Stowers, *A Rereading of Romans*, pp. 21-22, 29-33.

30. One need only consider the wide variety in the interpretation of Paul's teaching and behavior in Corinth, in spite of his long personal relationship with the congregation there.

saints, as people saved, as Paul himself was, by nothing else than faith in Christ.

Paul's identification with the situation of the 'wretched I' in Rom. 7.7-25 is fully in keeping with his rhetorical strategy in writing to the Romans. He jettisons the privilege of apostolic status in favor of that of a brother in Christ who offers a 'spiritual gift' to the Romans, but who also expects to be 'mutually encouraged by each other's faith, both yours and mine' (Rom. 1.12). He does not offer his own example in his paraenesis, but instead evokes a fellowship with a common wretched past and a common blessed present, a fellowship strengthened by mutual forbearance and mutual support. Regardless of background, both Paul and his readers are people who were once enslaved by sin but are now set free, because 'there is...now no condemnation for those who are in Christ Jesus' (Rom. 8.1).

SPECIAL TOPICS IN 1 CORINTHIANS 8–10

Anders Eriksson

There is something different about early Christian rhetoric when it is compared to the classical rhetoric of the Greco-Roman world. The setting is neither the law court, the political assembly nor the festive occasion where an encomium would be delivered. The proofs that characterize early Christian rhetoric are not quite the same as those in the handbooks. Thomas Olbricht, in the Festschrift for Abraham Malherbe, has noted these differences and advanced the idea that the rhetoric of the New Testament is so different from the ordinary rhetoric of the Greco-Roman world that it is neither to be classified as juridical, deliberative or epideictic but instead as a separate genre. Olbricht has chosen to designate this new genre, 'church rhetoric'.[1]

A second point developed by Olbricht is that rhetorical criticism has entered a new phase which supersedes epistolary analysis. In his overview of rhetorical studies on 1 Thessalonians in the 1980s, Olbricht notes a shift from a focus upon structure to a focus upon rhetorical proofs: 'These studies have not been strong on relating rhetorical observations to Paul's theology so as to ascertain why he proceeded as he did. Only to a modest extent have these studies helped us to comprehend better the text's power.'[2] This interest in the text's power to

---

1. T.H. Olbricht, 'An Aristotelian Rhetorical Analysis of 1 Thessalonians', in D.L. Balch, E. Ferguson and W.A. Meeks (eds.), *Greeks, Romans, and Christians: Essays in Honor of Abraham J. Malherbe* (Minneapolis: Fortress Press, 1990), pp. 216-36 (225-26). He thereby engages in the old dispute 'as to whether there are three kinds [of genres] or more' (Quintilian, 3.4.1). Translations throughout are from the editions in the LCL.

2. Olbricht, 'An Aristotelian Rhetorical Analysis', p. 219. Olbricht's reference to the text's power is taken from an unpublished paper by Wilhelm Wuellner, presented at the 1988 Colloquium Biblicum Lovaniense, 'The Rhetorical Structure of 1 Thessalonians', p. 17. A similar reference is found in G.A. Kennedy, *New*

persuade is distinctive for the present-day phase of rhetorical criticism. Interest in the *dispositio* of the text has given way to an interest in the *inventio*: that is, the rhetorical situation, the rhetorical strategy and the argumentation in the text.

In this essay I would first like to describe an alternative understanding of the distinctive feature of early Christian rhetoric based on Aristotelian rhetoric and then attempt to show the power of the text by a study of the traditions in 1 Corinthians 8–10 as rhetorical proof. In conclusion I shall make some observations about Paul's argumentation as theology.

1. *Tradition as Special Topics in Early Christian Rhetoric*

The distinctive features of early Christian rhetoric were noted by Amos Wilder, already in 1964: 'The whole compendium of Israel's literature is built upon peculiar rhetorics that find no place in the textbooks of Aristotle and Quintilian'.[3] George Kennedy is ambivalent about the relationship between early Christian rhetoric and classical rhetoric. He claims that the three rhetorical genres are universally applicable, but at the same time he draws a disjuncture between early Christian and classical rhetoric by distinguishing a special class of rhetoric: the radical Christian rhetoric.[4] He concludes: 'Christian preaching is thus not persuasion, but proclamation, and is based on authority and grace, not on proof'.[5] John Levison finds this disjuncture too sharp. He asserts that Kennedy's evidence for the radical Christian rhetoric is scant and does not fully take into account the irony used by Paul in 1 Corinthians 1–2. In this passage, Paul, while he rejects the Corinthian's boastful rhetoric, simultaneously demonstrates his rhetorical skill by an impressive show of rhetorical figures. Levison finds the clue to the tension between proclamation and persuasion in early Christian rhetoric in the view of the Spirit as both overcomer and artificer in the Jewish tradition.[6]

Testament Interpretation through Rhetorical Criticism (Chapel Hill, NC: University of North Carolina Press, 1984), p. 158.

3. A.N. Wilder, *The Language of the Gospel: Early Christian Rhetoric* (New York: Harper & Row, 1964), p. 15.

4. Kennedy, *New Testament Interpretation*, p. 7.

5. G.A. Kennedy, *Classical Rhetoric and its Christian and Secular Tradition from Ancient to Modern Times* (Chapel Hill, NC: University of North Carolina Press, 1980), p. 127.

6. J.R. Levison, 'Did the Spirit Inspire Rhetoric? An Exploration of George

Burton Mack agrees with Kennedy that one of the distinguishing features of early Christian rhetoric is 'the issue of authority that over-whelms the readers of this discourse'.[7] Whereas persuasion in ordinary Greek rhetoric is grounded in cultural conventions, the Christian rhetoric appeals to external authorities (Jesus, the Holy Spirit, or God) as guarantors for given propositions. The appearance of this rhetoric is understandable in a new movement which is forming its own social structures and finds itself in tension with both the Jewish and Greco-Roman structures. Mack proposes that this early Christian rhetoric is based on two core convictions: Jesus as the founder teacher and the Christ as the founder martyr. Whereas Paul's authority as an apostle is contested, the authority of the kerygma is not.

According to Olbricht, the distinctive feature of 'church rhetoric', in contrast to Aristotelian rhetoric, is the Christian world-view: 'In the Christian view, the world is the arena in which God (through God's Son and the Spirit) carries out divine purposes among humans'.[8] Accordingly, this difference significantly affects Paul's rhetorical proofs, arrangement and style. Olbricht also demonstrates that the proof from *ethos* in 1 Thessalonians is based on Christian virtues rather than Hellenistic morals. Furthermore the proof from *pathos* is more dependent on close family and community metaphors than Aristotelian rhetoric would have anticipated.[9] Olbricht's idea of 'church rhetoric' has not yet been widely discussed. One exception is James Thompson's study of 1 Peter, where he finds a pattern of persuasion refined in a subculture shaped by 'church rhetoric'. He identifies the distinguishing feature of the argumentation in 1 Peter as the author's consistent appeal to authority. The author grounds his exhortations in Scripture citations and in the community's knowledge of its own tradition.[10]

Kennedy's Definition of Early Christian Rhetoric', in D.F. Watson (ed.), *Persuasive Artistry: Studies in New Testament Rhetoric in Honor of George A. Kennedy* (JSNTSup, 50; Sheffield: JSOT Press, 1991), pp. 25-40.

7.   B.L. Mack, *Rhetoric and the New Testament* (Minneapolis: Fortress Press, 1990), pp. 96, 98.

8.   Olbricht, 'An Aristotelian Rhetorical Analysis', p. 226. In the Aristotelian world-view 'humanity is the measure of all things' (*Eth. Nic.* 10.8).

9.   Olbricht, 'An Aristotelian Rhetorical Analysis', pp. 229-30.

10.   J.W. Thompson, 'The Rhetoric of 1 Peter', *Restoration Quarterly* 36 (1994), pp. 237-50 (245-47). He refers to a form of the sermon with example, conclusion and exhortation. This pattern is similar to the amplification of a theme in *Rhet. ad. Her.* 4.44.56-58 and the elaboration of the chreia in the *progymnasmata*.

I would like to take issue with Olbricht's suggestion that 'church rhetoric' is a fourth rhetorical genre, by presenting the Aristotelian concepts ἔνδοξα and ἴδιοι τόποι as keys to understanding the difference between ordinary rhetoric and early Christian rhetoric.[11] Note that Aristotle defines rhetoric as 'the faculty of discovering the possible means of persuasion in reference to any subject whatever'.[12] Therefore the primary object of rhetoric is to find a persuasive argument, that is, an argument which is believable (τὸ πιθανόν). This is admittedly difficult as the believable argument is dependent on the views held by the audience: 'That which is persuasive is persuasive in reference to some one'.[13] The truth argued in rhetoric can only be persuasive if it is acknowledged by the interlocutors and the truth value is limited to what is accepted by both partners. The speaker trying to persuade his audience is therefore dependent on the opinions shared by himself and his audience. Aristotle calls these opinions ἔνδοξα and understands them as those opinions 'that commend themselves to all or to the majority or to the wise—this is, to all of the wise or the majority or to the most famous and distinguished of them'.[14] The same insight is developed in the 'New Rhetoric' of Perelman and Olbrechts-Tyteca. They stress that the premises held by the audience are the necessary starting-point for argumentation.[15] The distinguishing feature of early Christian rhetoric is therefore dependent upon the audience to which it was addressed and is to be found in the ἔνδοξα shared by the Christian rhetor and his audience. I suggest that when Paul searches for a persuasive argument to use in argumentation with his congregations, his search for τὸ πιθανόν leads to a search for the ἔνδοξα, the reputable opinions shared by both. These would have been found in the shared Christian tradition.

In specifying the content of the distinctive early Christian rhetoric, the special topics in Aristotle's rhetoric are helpful. In contrast to the

11. I accept Olbricht's point that we should not be limited to the classical rhetoric for our rhetorical analysis, but note that no other accepted terminology has yet been developed to analyze his invention 'church rhetoric'.

12. *Rhet.* 1.2.1.

13. τὸ πιθανὸν τινὶ πιθανόν ἐστι (*Rhet.* 1.2.11).

14. *Top.* 1.1.100b. On the importance of ἔνδοξα in Aristotle's rhetoric, see L. Arnhart, *Aristotle on Political Reasoning: A Commentary on the 'Rhetoric'* (DeKalb, IL: Northern Illinois University Press, 1981), pp. 17-19, 28-32.

15. C. Perelman and L. Olbrechts-Tyteca, *The New Rhetoric: A Treatise on Argumentation* (trans. J. Wilkinson and P. Weaver; Notre Dame: University of Notre Dame Press, 1969), pp. 65-66.

common topics, which are the same for all subjects, the special topics, ἴδιοι τόποι, belong to the subject under study.[16] They are

> derived from propositions which are peculiar to each species or genus of things; there are...propositions about Physics which can furnish neither enthymemes nor syllogisms about Ethics, and there are propositions concerned with Ethics which will be useless for furnishing conclusions about Physics; and the same holds good in all cases... The happier a man is in his choice of propositions, the more he will unconsciously produce a science quite different from Dialectic and Rhetoric... Most enthymemes are constructed from these specific topics.[17]

Aristotle identifies the special topics for the political orator as 'ways and means, war and peace, the defence of the country, imports and exports, and legislation'.[18] These are the areas of knowledge in which the political orator needs expertise. When we apply the Aristotelian special topics to early Christian rhetoric, we need to seek the topics in which the Christian orator needs expertise. Which propositions are peculiar to early Christian rhetoric? Which special topics distinguish it from the ordinary topics of ancient rhetoric? I suggest that the special topics in use among early Christians were directly derived from the proclaimed kerygma. As the Christian gospel was proclaimed by Paul and then received by the converts, a common ground developed between the apostle and the congregations. This common ground contained the core convictions about Jesus as the founder teacher and the Christ as the founder martyr, as well as other beliefs which were widely shared by early Christians. The form-critical studies that have dealt with the faith of the early Christians can thus be of help now that the scholarly interest has turned to synchronic aspects of the text. The key role of tradition in the establishment of congregations can explain the significance of authority in early Christian rhetoric. The appeal to tradition as rhetorical proof is therefore central in Paul's argumentation.

2. Traditions as Rhetorical Proof in 1 Corinthians 8–10

During the era of form-critical investigation of the pre-Pauline traditions in the Pauline text, attention was focused on the pre-history of the

16. *Rhet.* 1.2.21.
17. *Rhet.* 1.2.21-22.
18. *Rhet.* 1.4.7. Each of these topics is discussed by Aristotle, but he concludes, 'All these things, however, belong to Politics and not to Rhetoric' (1.4.13).

text. The traditions found in the text were studied for what they could explain about the development of the early Church and the different christologies held by various groups. The interest was focused, not upon the phenomena in the text, but upon the history behind the text. In the new *inventio* phase of rhetorical criticism, attention is focused upon how these traditions function as rhetorical proofs in Paul's argumentation.

In the study of Paul's argumentation, we are helped by the patterns of persuasion presented in the rhetorical handbooks. These argumentative patterns are found in the parts of the handbooks dealing with invention. Corresponding to the Aristotelian division of reasoning into deductive and inductive modes, the handbooks present both inductive and deductive argumentative patterns.[19] The deductive patterns are a development of Aristotle's treatment of the enthymeme, the rhetorical syllogism.[20] The complete fivefold argument (with proposition, reason, proof of the reason, embellishment and résumé), developed in *Rhet. ad Her.* 2.18.27–19.30, is a mixture of inductive and deductive modes of reasoning.[21] A clearly inductive argument is spelled out in the amplification of a theme in seven parts, *Rhet. ad Her.* 4.44.57-58:

> But when we descant upon the same theme, we shall use a great many variations. Indeed, after having expressed the theme simply, we can subjoin the Reason, and then express the theme in another form, with or without the Reasons; next we can present the Contrary…then a Comparison and an Example…and finally the Conclusion.

The importance of this inductive pattern is seen when it is compared to the elaboration of the chreia in the elementary rhetorical exercises called the *progymnasmata*.[22] Hermogenes in his treatment περὶ χρείας

---

19. *Rhet.* 1.2.8: 'I call an enthymeme a rhetorical syllogism, and an example rhetorical induction. Now all orators produce belief by employing as proofs either examples or enthymemes and nothing else.'

20. So Cicero, *Inv.* 1.67-69 presents a syllogistic argument in five parts where the second and fourth are supports for the major and minor premises respectively. Similarly Quintilian's chapter on arguments starts with the syllogistic enthymemes and epicheiremes before treating the inductive arguments (5.10).

21. The parallels to inductive argumentation become clearer when the author explains the component part of embellishment as (1) analogy, *similes*; (2) examples, *exemplum*; (3) amplification, *amplificatio*; and (4) judgment, *res iudicata*, so *Rhet. ad Her.* 2.29.46.

22. The treatment of the χρεία in ancient rhetoric has been made available through the volume edited by R.F. Hock and E.N. O'Neil, *The Chreia in Ancient*

(7.10–8.14) includes the following points: (1) praise; (2) chreia; (3) rationale; (4) contrary; (5) analogy; (6) example; (7) judgment; (8) exhortation. This pattern is quite close to the elaboration of a theme in *Rhet. ad Her.*, with the chreia being the theme, the rationale the reason, and the presence of the arguments from contrary, analogy and example being identical.[23] One noteworthy difference is that Hermogenes includes a moral application of the chreia, an exhortation.[24] In the following I shall show how the argumentative pattern in each argument can elucidate that argument and explain the 'power of the text'.

a. *The Problem of Food Sacrificed to Idols*
In the rhetorical unit comprising 1 Cor. 8.1–11.1, Paul addresses the problem of food sacrificed to idols.[25] The Corinthians have written him a letter where the problem of εἰδωλόθυτα was brought up.[26] This problem had also been discussed previously by Paul and the Corinthians.

Rhetoric. I. *The Progymnasmata* (Atlanta: Scholars Press, 1986). The volume treats the principal texts on the chreia by Aelius Theon of Alexandria, Quintilian, Hermogenes of Tarsus, Priscian, Aphthonius of Antioch, Nicolaus of Myra and the Vatican Grammar with introductions, translations and comment. The importance of the chreia for the interpretation of the Synoptic Gospels, especially the pronouncement stories, is shown by B. Mack and V.K. Robbins, *Patterns of Persuasion in the Gospels* (Sonoma, CA: Polebridge Press, 1989). To this date the chreia has only sparingly been used in studies of Pauline argumentation. One exception is J. Hester, 'Placing the Blame: The Presence of Epideictic in Galatians 1 and 2', in Watson (ed.), *Persuasive Artistry*, pp. 299-307.

23. In the chreia the restatement of the theme is missing. Hermogenes's term 'judgment' is similar to the μαρτύρια τῶν παλαιῶν in *Rhet. ad Her.*

24. Ordinarily the exhortation would be a function of the *peroratio* in the rhetorical speech. This parallel to the chreia indicates that it was possible for each argumentative unit to conclude with an exhortation.

25. Due to her emphasis on the unity of the whole letter, Margaret Mitchell disregards smaller rhetorical units (M.M. Mitchell, *Paul and the Rhetoric of Reconciliation: An Exegetical Investigaion of the Language and Composition of 1 Corinthians* [HUT, 28; Tübingen: J.C.B. Mohr, 1991], pp. 15-19). Kennedy, *New Testament Interpretation*, pp. 33-34, on the contrary suggests that a text can be divided into successively smaller rhetorical units, with the smallest units consisting only five or six verses.

26. M.M. Mitchell, 'Concerning περὶ δέ in 1 Corinthians', *NovT* 31 (1989), pp. 229-56, argues that the περὶ δέ formula does not necessarily indicate anything more than that a new subject has been introduced. Most interpreters understand the formula here to be a reference to items in the Corinthian letter to Paul in analogy with the formula's first occurrence in 7.1, περὶ δὲ ὧν ἐγράψατε.

That discussion (or those discussions) seems to have involved some deliberate misunderstandings on the part of the Corinthians. These misunderstandings were similar to their interpretation of Paul's advice in 1 Cor. 5.9-11 'not to associate with immoral men' to mean that they should 'leave the world'. They also questioned Paul's vacillating praxis, sometimes eating idol sacrifices and sometimes refraining from eating.[27]

Paul chooses to deal with the problem of idol sacrifices as a complex issue (*quaestio coniuncta*),[28] by first treating the aspect he disallows then the one he allows. In Paul's text the actual problem is mentioned four times. The eating of market-place meat (10.25) and the eating of 'whatever is placed before you when invited by an unbeliever' (10.27) are allowed by Paul. These more innocent aspects of the problem of idol sacrifices could very well have been the issues brought forward by the Corinthians. For Paul, however, the real issue seems to be eating in an idol's temple (8.10) and any eating which would give κοινωνία with demons (10.19-21).

The stasis of the first controversial question is not fact (*coniectura*), but rather definition.[29] The first question expounded by Paul fits the description of the stasis of definition by Cicero:

> The controversy about a definition arises when there is agreement as to the fact and the question is by what word that which has been done is to be described. In this case there must be a dispute about the definition, because there is no agreement about the essential point, not because the fact is not certain, but because the deed appears differently to different people, and for that reason different people describe it in different terms.[30]

Paul chooses to regard εἰδωλόθυτα eaten in the temple as εἰδωλολατρία, a definition many of the Corinthians surely would have contested. The second controversial question in Paul's perspective is that of idol sacrifices eaten outside the temple setting. This question is dealt with

---

27. About the Corinthian's letter to Paul concerning immoral men, see J.C. Hurd, *The Origin of 1 Corinthians* (Macon, GA: Mercer University Press, 1983), pp. 149-54.

28. Quintilian, 3.10.1; Cicero, *Inv.* 1.12.17.

29. Quintilian, 3.6.80, agrees with the view of the authorities followed by Cicero, to the effect that 'there are three things on which enquiry is made in every case: we ask whether a thing is, what it is, and of what kind it is', i.e. *coniectura*, *definitionis* and *qualitatis*.

30. Cicero, *Inv.* 1.8.11.

under the stasis of quality, specifying the circumstances for the eating of idol sacrifices in direct reference to the cases brought forward by the Corinthians.

The handbooks also provide a case classification theory for the analysis of the rhetorical situation.[31] According to Cicero there are five kinds of cases: honorable, difficult, mean, ambiguous and obscure. Most pertinent here is the ambiguous case 'in which the point for decision is doubtful, or the case is partly honourable and partly discreditable so that it engenders both good-will and ill-will'.[32] In the case faced by Paul concerning idol sacrifices the point for decision is doubtful and his point about idolatry causes both good-will and ill-will.

In difficult rhetorical situations, the rhetorical strategy called *insinuatio* is recommended. This strategy 'by dissimulation and indirection unobtrusively steals into the mind of the auditor'.[33] *Rhetorica ad Herennium* describes several such situations, 'when our case is discreditable, that is when the subject itself alienates the hearer from us; and when the hearer has apparently been won over by the previous speakers of the opposition'.[34] In Paul's treatment of the problem of idol sacrifices in 1 Corinthians 8–10, his exhortation to flee idolatry (10.14) is discreditable to many of the hearers. As the majority of the church has already been won over to the side of the Corinthian wise, Paul uses the *insinuatio* as his rhetorical strategy. The *insinuatio* is first seen in the vagueness of Paul's language as he describes the problem. He uses circumlocutions and omits the object to ἐσθίω.[35] Secondly, the handbooks recommended that if the audience had been won by the opponents, the speaker should promise to begin with 'the point which our

31. For the various names employed by different writers in antiquity, see H. Lausberg, *Handbuch der literarischen Rhetorik: Eine Grundlegung der Literaturwissenschaft* (2 vols.; Munich: Hueber, 1960), I, §64.

32. Cicero, *Inv.* 1.15.20. Cf. *Rhet. ad Her.* 1.3.5. This view is shared by Quintilian, 4.1.40, who identifies it as the majority view.

33. Cicero, *Inv.* 1.15.20; cf. *Rhet. ad Her.* 1.4.6; Quintilian, 4.1.42.

34. *Rhet. ad Her.* 1.6.9.

35. It is clear that the problem concerns eating, but after the introductory περὶ δὲ τῶν εἰδωλοθύτων in 8.1 it is not at all clear what they actually eat. The object to ἐσθίω is conspicuously missing in a number of places, cf. 8.7, 8b, 8c; 10.28 and 31. The same vagueness is found in the various circumlocutions used by Paul, e.g. βρῶμα and κρέα in his dialogue with the 'wise' in ch. 8 and the curious antecedent to ἃ θύουσιν in 10.20. Is Paul implicitly saying that Corinthian Christians are involved in a sacrifice to demons consisting of idol food?

adversaries have regarded as their strongest support' and preferably 'with a statement made by the opponent'.[36] Paul's citations of Corinthian slogans in 1 Corinthians 8 should be seen as examples of this. A third indication of the *insinuatio* is that the real issue in Paul's eyes, the prohibition of idolatry, is not brought up until 10.14, after two and a half chapters of dissimulation and indirection.

Having described the rhetorical situation as involving a definitional and a qualitative issue, and as an ambiguous case with the chosen rhetorical strategy of an *insinuatio,* we are ready to look at the actual disposition of the rhetorical unit.

b. *The Rhetorical Disposition*
The *exordium* in 8.1-6 introduces the issue of idol sacrifices, cites the opinions of the opponents and suggests modifications of them. The *exordium* also contains a *partitio,* in which three points introduce the ensuing discussion. First in 8.1-3, the issue of love versus knowledge anticipates the argumentation in 8.7-13. The section in 8.4-5, introduced by περὶ τῆς βρώσεως οὖν τῶν εἰδωλοθύτων, concerns the actual eating of idol sacrifices, which is the topic of the argumentation in 10.1-22. The third part of the *partitio* is the tradition, the double εἷς-acclamation which is the common ground shared by Paul and the two groups in the Corinthian church, the wise and the weak. The tradition thereby anticipates the statement of Paul's own case (10.23-30).[37]

The *argumentatio* section in Paul's argumentation covers 8.7–10.30. The first *refutatio* (8.7-13) takes up the γνῶσις of the Corinthian wise, refutes it and in its stead places love, specified as concern for the weaker brother. The refutation ends in 8.13 with Paul as a positive

36. *Rhet. ad Her.* 1.6.10. Cf. Cicero, *Inv.* 1.17.25: 'promise to discuss first the argument which the opponents thought was their strongest and which the audience have especially approved'.

37. The first two parts of the *partitio* have been pointed out by J.F.M. Smit, '1 Cor 8,1-6: A Rhetorical Partitio. A Contribution to the Coherence of 1 Cor. 8,1-11,1', in R. Bieringer (ed.), *The Corinthian Correspondence* (Leuven: Leuven University Press, 1996), pp. 577-91 (588-89). He notes the importance of the confession, but does not see its function as the third part of the *partitio*: 'Form and position of this confession of faith give rise to the expectation that it forms the cornerstone of Paul's discussion, but the sequel does not appear to fulfill this' (p. 579). This oversight leads Smit to conclude that 'in 1 Cor. 10.23-11 Paul shifts attention away from idol offerings to an adjacent field. So strictly speaking, in adding this conclusion he transgresses an important rhetorical rule' (p. 591).

example, a theme which will be developed in the *digressio* (9.1-27). The theme of the second *refutatio* (10.1-22) is the actual eating of idol sacrifices in a temple setting. Paul refutes this practice in the direct imperative: 'flee from the worship of idols' (10.14). The statement of Paul's own view of the second controversial question follows in the *confirmatio* (10.23-30). Paul concedes the eating of idol sacrifices defined as food bought at the *macellum* and the food served by a pagan host, but tempers the concession with the repeated qualitative concern for the weaker brother. The brief *peroratio* (10.31–11.1) sums up the discussion by directly applying it to the Corinthians in three imperatives: 'Do everything to the glory of God'; 'give no offense to the Jews, the Greeks or the church of God'; and 'become imitators of me'.[38] This is an appropriate conclusion to a deliberative argumentation, whose goal it is to urge the audience to action in the future.

c. *The Double* εἰς-*acclamation in the Exordium, 1 Corinthians 8.1-6*
The tradition cited by Paul in 1 Cor. 8.6 has been claimed to be pre-Pauline in a number of form-critical studies.[39] The amount of redaction in the tradition is difficult to determine. The tradition is possibly a Pauline composition of already existing material,[40] since the confessions to the εἰς θεός and the εἰς κύριος were widespread in the early Church.[41] The background is the יהוה אחד of the *Shema'* (Deut. 6.4),

38. The first imperative is a maxim. The second alludes to the baptismal reunification formula that is the basis for their unity in Christ and contains also an appeal to the final category of deliberative rhetoric, τὸ σύμφορον. The third is a reference to Paul as positive example, behind whom the positive example of Christ himself can be discerned.

39. J. Murphy-O'Connor, '1 Cor. VIII, 6: Cosmology or Soteriology?', *RB* 85 (1978), pp. 253-67 (254-55) (with an overview of opinions); W. Kramer, *Christ, Lord, Son of God* (London: SCM Press, 1966), pp. 94-99; K. Wengst, *Christologische Formeln und Lieder des Urchristentums* (Gütersloh: Gütersloher Verlagshaus, 1972), p. 136. See also the shorter articles by R. Kerst, '1 Kor 8,6—ein vorpaulinisches Taufbekenntnis?', *ZNW* 66 (1975), pp. 130-39; and R.A. Horsley, 'The Background of the Confessional Formula in 1 Kor 8.6', *ZNW* 69 (1978), pp. 130-35.

40. V.H. Neufeld, *The Earliest Christian Confessions* (Leiden: E.J. Brill, 1963), pp. 65-66; J.D.G. Dunn, *Christology in the Making: A New Testament Inquiry into the Origins of the Doctrine of the Incarnation* (Philadelphia: Westminster Press, 1980), p. 181; G. Fee, *The First Epistle to the Corinthians* (NICNT; Grand Rapids: Eerdmans, 1987), p. 374.

41. The εἰς θεός is used as a set formula by Paul in Gal. 3.20 and Rom. 3.30

which became reformulated as εἷς θεός in Jewish missionary preaching,[42] and consequently taken over by the first Christian missionaries in the pagan world. Hence the formula could have contained the central tenets of the missionary preaching that the Corinthian Christians had previously listened to and which had led to their conversion. The form is an acclamation, 'die Rufe einer grossen Menge' ('shouts by a big crowd'),[43] and the *Sitz im Leben* would have been the public worship services of the church, possibly in connection with baptism.[44]

The double εἷς-acclamation, part of the tradition Paul knew and once had transmitted to the Corinthians, became the common ground between Paul and the Corinthians. It was therefore part of the audience's premises to which Paul could appeal, and which were a proper starting-point for argumentation.[45] Furthermore, both the weak and the wise could appeal to this tradition to strengthen their side in the quarrel concerning idol sacrifices.[46] The wise Corinthians' radical monotheism, which allowed them to eat idol sacrifices even in a temple setting, could be seen as a logical development of the formula's monotheism. The

(cf. Eph. 4.6, Jas 2.19), combined with εἷς μεσίτης in 1 Tim. 2.5. The confession to the one Lord is a variation of the basic confession in the early Church, κύριος Ἰησοῦς, found in 1 Cor. 12.3, Rom. 10.9, Phil. 2.11.

42. E. Peterson, *ΕΙΣ ΘΕΟΣ: Epigraphische, formgeschichtliche und religionsgeschichtliche Untersuchungen* (Göttingen: Vandenhoeck & Ruprecht, 1926), p. 216; followed by Kramer, *Christ*, p. 95. For Jewish proselytism, see L.H. Feldman, *Jew and Gentile in the Ancient World* (Princeton, NJ: Princeton University Press, 1993), pp. 288-382.

43. Peterson, *ΕΙΣ ΘΕΟΣ*, p. 141.

44. Murphy-O'Connor, '1 Cor. VIII, 6', pp. 257-58; Kerst, '1 Kor 8,6', p. 138.

45. Perelman and Olbrechts-Tyteca, *The New Rhetoric*, pp. 65-66.

46. For the historical reconstruction of the Corinthian church as divided into two groups called the 'weak' and the 'wise' (not the older 'weak' and 'strong'), I am dependent on the article by S.K. Stowers, 'Paul on the Use and Abuse of Reason', in Balch, Ferguson and Meeks (eds.), *Greeks, Romans, and Christians*, pp. 276-84. Stowers maintains that the wise Corinthians regarded the Christians who refused to eat idol sacrifices as suffering from an ἀσθένεια, interpreted as a moral deficiency or illness, in analogy with the sickness of the soul ascribed to the person who joined a philosophical school. The Corinthian wise consequently entered into a campaign to rid the weak of their false beliefs by making them participate in pagan cultic meals to achieve γνῶσις by praxis. Stowers's student Clarence Glad develops this *psychagogy* in his monograph, *Paul and Philodemus: Adaptability in Epicurean and Early Christian Psychagogy* (Leiden: E.J. Brill, 1995); on 1 Cor. 8, see pp. 277-90.

Corinthian slogans of 8.4 actually apply such a radical monotheism to the issue of idol sacrifices. The weak Corinthians, who refused to eat idol sacrifices, could find support for their stance in the fact that the tradition reflected Jewish and Christian missionary preaching with its turning away from idols to 'serve a living and true God' (1 Thess. 1.9). When Paul appeals to this tradition, he can use it as a unifying common ground since both sides in the discussion would accept the truth of the tradition. Both sides would be strongly affected by a reminder of how they had responded to the missionary preaching in connection with their conversion, and how they had used the acclamation in their worship services, possibly even in their own baptisms.

The tradition functions as the foundation for Paul's argumentation throughout the rhetorical unit. Paul finds support for his concern for the weaker brother in the tradition. The 'we to him' and the 'we through him' define the worshipping congregation as the eschatological people of God, who experience salvation through Christ. The unity of the new eschatological people of God is the reason why there should be no division between wise and weak (8.7-13). The salvation experienced by this people is the *causa infinita*[47] elaborated in the digression 9.1-27,[48] where Paul refrains from his rights so that he might win all.[49] The κοινωνία with the Lord Jesus Christ manifested by this people in the Lord's Supper celebrations makes partnership with other gods impossible. This is the argument of the second *refutatio*. Finally the theme of the eschatological people of God introduces a new perspective in the *confirmatio*, a *causa infinita*, which allows for concessions to the wise in two particular instances.[50]

---

47. The distinction between these two *causa* in rhetoric goes back to Hermagoras's distinction of deliberative rhetoric into *theses* and *hypotheses*, so G.A. Kennedy, *The Art of Persuasion in Greece* (Princeton, NJ: Princeton University Press, 1963), p. 305.

48. W.H. Wuellner, 'Greek Rhetoric and Pauline Argumentation', in W. Schoedel and R.L. Wilken (eds.), *Early Christian Literature and the Classical Intellectual Tradition: In Honorem Robert M. Grant* (Paris: Editions Beauchesne, 1979), pp. 182-88.

49. The theme is elaborated in seven ἵνα-clauses with the main verb κερδάνω in 9.19-23.

50. The *causa infinita* is expressed in the concern for the weaker brother and with the goal of deliberative rhetoric in 10.23, the final category advantage. These concessions are to be seen from the qualitative *stasis*. The other aspects of the problem Paul has previously given his own verdict in the stasis of definition.

So far in the discussion the function of the tradition has been studied as a proof from *logos*. According to Aristotle, the proofs from *ethos* and *pathos* are just as important,[51] but these aspects of the power of the text are unfortunately almost never explored by commentators.[52] According to Aristotle, *ethos* 'constitutes the most effective means of proof'.[53] The importance of the proof increases with the lack of certainty in the situation:

> We feel confidence in a greater degree and more readily in persons of worth in regard to everything in general, but where there is no certainty and there is room for doubt, our confidence is absolute.[54]

The problem faced by Paul is one where there is no certainty. Paul's rhetorical challenge is that his standing with the Corinthians is questioned and characterized by a certain hostility. The answer he is about to give concerning idol sacrifices is contrary to what they want to hear. Hence Paul has a great need for a good proof from *ethos* to strengthen the credibility of his argumentation.

The proof has three components, the *ethos* of the speaker, the matter and the audience.[55] Since Paul's own *ethos* is questioned, he avoids overt attempts to establish his authority. Instead he brings forward the *ethos* of the matter, the received tradition with a salvific message concerning the eschatological people of God. Paul hides the issue of his

---

51. 'Now the proofs furnished by the speech are of three kinds. The first depends upon the moral character of the speaker, the second upon putting the hearer into a certain frame of mind, the third upon the speech itself as it proves or seems to prove' (*Rhet.* 1.2.3).

52. Due to our Enlightenment heritage, biblical scholars have studied the text with a view for the rational argumentation. It is just quite recently that attention has been turned to the pragmatic function of texts and a psychological analysis of texts. One exception to the neglect of ethos and pathos appeal in New Testament research is the dissertation by S.J. Kraftchick, 'Ethos and Pathos Appeals in Galatians Five and Six: A Rhetorical Analysis' (PhD Dissertation, Emory University, 1985).

53. κυριωτάτην ἔχει πίστιν τὸ ἦθος (*Rhet.* 1.2.4).

54. *Rhet.* 1.2.4.

55. Kennedy, *The Art of Persuasion*, pp. 91-93. The *ethos* of the speaker, based on his moral character, is his trustworthiness in the eyes of the audience. The *ethos* of the matter concerns the reputability of the case defended. If a logographer was hired to write a speech for a defendent that speech was designed to fit his character through *ethopopoiia*. The *ethos* of the audience is derived from the character of the audience to which the rhetor must adapt his argumentation. This is the psychological approach to rhetoric.

own *ethos* behind the *ethos* of the tradition. The acclamation as uttered by the Corinthians themselves in their worship would have had a high *ethos*, and the Corinthians most probably could accept a teaching derived from the acclamation as trustworthy. A second aspect of this proof is that the tradition expresses the *ethos* of the Corinthians themselves. The acclamation expresses the Corinthians' own experience of conversion, baptism and joint worship. A third aspect is that the acclamation covertly strengthens Paul's own *ethos* by establishing a bond between himself and the audience.[56] Paul identifies with his audience, they all share the common experience, they are united in the second-person plural pronoun, ἡμεῖς.

The proof from *pathos* persuades the audience 'when they are roused to emotion by his speech'.[57] By reminding the Corinthians of their conversion, baptism and their joint worship Paul awakes their emotions. They would have been reminded of their response to the missionary preaching and turning away from false gods. They would have been reminded of their baptism, their initiation into the new fellowship. They would have been reminded of their worship together with other Christians in the church, of joint acclamations to the one God and the one Lord. The emotions thus aroused would have served to remind them of their unity.[58] The acclamation would have functioned as a proof from *pathos*.

d. *The Vicarious Death Formula in the First Refutatio, 1 Corinthians 8.7-13*
The second tradition Paul appeals to is the reference to the brother δι' ὃν Χριστὸς ἀπέθανεν, 1 Cor. 8.11b. This vicarious death formula is a

56. J.W. Marshall, 'Paul's Ethical Appeal in Philippians', in S.E. Porter and T.H. Olbricht (eds.), *Rhetoric and the New Testament: Essays from the 1992 Heidelberg Conference* (JSNTSup, 90; Sheffield: JSOT Press, 1993) pp. 357-71, shows how *ethos* is dependent on the identification of the rhetor with his audience and the relationship between the two.
57. *Rhet.* 1.2.5. It is characteristic of Aristotle's rhetoric that the passions are regarded as rational, responding to arguments, so Arnhart, *Aristotle on Political Reasoning*, pp. 114-18.
58. Already noted by J. Murphy-O'Connor, 'Freedom or the Ghetto', *RB* 85 (1978), pp. 542-74 (563): 'Paul intended the citation of the baptismal acclamation to function as an emotional trigger which would alert the Strong to the fact that they belonged to a community of brothers'.

variation of the first ὅτι-clause in the *pistis* formula of 1 Cor. 15.3-5.[59] Variations of this formula, describing the death of Christ as ὑπὲρ ἡμῶν, occur in Rom. 5.6, 8 and 14.15.[60] In this formula, the death of Christ, originally a stumbling block to the followers of Jesus, is interpreted as having salvific significance. The crucifixion was a sacrificial death for the benefit of others, which is evidenced by the ὑπὲρ ἡμῶν interpreting the death in sacrificial terms for the benefit of the believers.[61] The death of the Messiah thus has a corporate significance; it was through this death that the community of believers was established.

Since this understanding of the death of Christ is part of the *pistis* formula which Paul has transmitted to the Corinthians, he can presuppose that they share this belief.[62] By his death Christ had established a new community, which now saw themselves as brothers (the ἡμῶν in the formula). When Paul applies the vicarious death formula to the Corinthian situation, he sharpens the wording to διὰ ὅν by placing the traditional statement in apposition to ὁ ἀδελφός. Hence the weak person is not just a brother and a member of the new eschatological community, but he is a *special* brother because it was for his sake Christ died. There is a gradual shift in the designation of the weaker brother in these verses, but before an explication of that shift, we will have to examine Paul's argumentation in this first *refutatio*.

In this argumentative unit, Paul is engaged in a refutation of the position held by the Corinthian wise. Their position is expressed in the

59. That is, ὅτι Χριστὸς ἀπέθανεν ὑπὲρ τῶν ἁμαρτιῶν ἡμῶν. For form-critical studies of 1 Cor. 15.3-5, see the literature referred to by K. Lehmann, *Auferweckt am dritten Tag nach der Schrift: Früheste Christologie, Bekenntnisbildung und Schriftauslegung im Lichte von 1 Kor. 15, 3-5* (Freiburg: Herder, 1968). The designation *pistis* formula is from Kramer, *Christ*, p. 21, who has been followed by P. Vielhauer, *Geschichte der urchristlichen Literatur: Einleitung in das Neue Testament, die Apokryphen und die Apostolischen Väter* (Berlin: W. de Gruyter, 1975), pp. 13-14, 18.

60. Kramer, *Christ*, pp. 26-28.

61. The theology of atonement in this tradition is explored by H.N. Ridderbos, 'The Earliest Confession of the Atonement in Paul', in R. Banks (ed.), *Reconciliation and Hope: New Testament Essays on Atonement and Eschatology Presented to L.L. Morris on his 60th Birthday* (Exeter: Paternoster Press, 1974), pp. 76-89.

62. Paul emphasizes that he has delivered the gospel to them as is seen in the elaborate introduction to the tradition, with terminology from the transmission of tradition, παρέδωκα ὑμῖν ὃ καὶ παρέλαβον. He is, however, not sure that they still hold firmly to the message, 1 Cor. 15.2.

slogan 'all of us possess knowledge' (8.1) and the content of that knowledge is further specified in the radical, rationalistic monotheism of the slogans 'no idol in the world really exists' and 'there is no God but one' (8.4). Paul's refutation consists not in an outright attack on their theology, but in an argument concerning the effects of their behavior. This corresponds to the first point in the *partitio*: love instead of knowledge (8.1-3). The theme of Paul's argumentation is a contradiction of the assumption by the Corinthian wise that everyone has this knowledge and therefore ought to act upon the knowledge. Paul bluntly states, 'not everyone has this knowledge', thereby siding with the weak and becoming their spokesman.

Paul's argumentation is inductive and the sequence is similar to the amplification of a theme in *Rhet. ad Her.* 4.44.57-58:

1.   Theme: Not all have this knowledge (v. 7a).
2.   Reasons: (a) For τινές, accustomed to idols, eat ὡς εἰδωλό-θυτον (v. 7b); (b) The conflict caused by your slogans testify that not all have this knowledge (v. 8).
3.   Restatement of the theme: Take care so that this liberty of yours does not somehow become a stumbling block to the weak (v. 9).
4.   Argument from contrary: Your behavior when at table in an idol's temple contradicts the concern for the weaker brother (v. 10).
5.   Argument from example: The tradition in v. 11b is applied to the Corinthians in a double enthymeme (v. 12).
6.   Conclusion: Paul refraining to eat κρέα out of concern for the weaker brother is a personal example for them to follow (v. 13).

The argumentation starts with the thesis 'not all have this knowledge'. This theme is a refutation of the reasoning the Corinthians exemplified in their slogans. This first statement of the theme is general and the concern for the weaker brother is simply introduced in the unobtrusive 'not all'. To support his thesis Paul brings in two reasons. First, the fact that certain people (τινές used as a circumlocution for the weaker brother) eat something 'as idol sacrifice' shows that those people do not share the knowledge of the wise Corinthians. Hence the slogan of these wise Corinthians is false. Secondly, the strife brought about by the slogans in 8.8 further underlines the falsehood of their statement and exposes how presumptuous the wise are when pushing their understanding on the weak. By removing the negations from the verse, we arrive at what would presumably have been the Corinthian position: 'Food will bring us close to God.[63] We are worse off if we do not eat, and better off if we do.'[64] The way Paul corrects the slogans through negation,[65] instead of adding an extra clause,[66] has baffled the textual tradition[67] and the commentators.[68]

The restatement of the theme in 8.9 applies the more general rendering directly to the Corinthians. The point is not just the lack of knowledge by some, but the effects the wise Corinthians' knowledge have on the weaker brothers.[69] The weaker brothers are gradually brought in as

63. παριστάνω is a positive term 'bring before God = bring close to God', so BAGD, *s.v.* The common attempts to give it a forensic meaning 'bring before his judgment seat' are questionable and caused by the desire of interpreters to make the issue an *adiaphora* in an ethical discussion. For the positive meaning 'bring close to God' as reflecting court procedure, cf. B. Reicke, 'παρίστημι', *TDNT*, V, pp. 837-41 (840).

64. This statement would agree with the Corinthian position as reconstructed by Stowers and Glad but neither one of them takes the step to remove the negations.

65. W.L. Willis, *Idol Meat in Corinth: The Pauline Argument in 1 Corinthians 8 and 10* (Chico, CA: Scholars Press, 1985), pp. 96-98, is the first to note Paul's method of negating the Corinthian slogan.

66. The extra clause modifying the slogan is Paul's method of correction in 6.12, 13; 7.1; 8.1; 10.23.

67. The *lectio difficilior* adopted in modern critical editions is confined to Egypt (𝔓[46] B 81 630 and 1739). The alternative reading in ℵ A[c], the majority text and several church fathers moves μή to the last clause in accordance with the later church interpretation as an *adiaphora*: 'We are no better off if we eat, and no worse off if we do not'.

68. H. Lietzmann, *An die Korinther I & II* (Tübingen: J.C.B. Mohr, 1949), p. 38, notes that for 8.8 to be a Corinthian slogan, the negation should be shifted from the first clause to the second. Hurd, *The Origin of 1 Corinthians*, has constructed a table of scholarly opinions on the existence of slogans in 1 Corinthians, and notes that 'as 8.8 stands…it is probably preferable to take it as one item in a series of criticisms of the liberal position and thus as originating from Paul' (p. 123).

69. The restatement of the theme varies it slightly. Often the variation is an application of a more general theme as in *Rhet. ad Her.* 4.44.57 where the general theme, 'The wise man will, on the republic's behalf, shun no peril', is narrowed to an application of the case at hand in the reformulation: 'I say, then, that they who flee from the peril to be undergone on behalf of the republic act foolishly' upon which follows the reason, 'for they cannot avoid the disadvantages, and are found guilty of ingratitude towards the state'.

the real theme. Note the gradual shift in these verses. First the weak are vaguely described as a negation to the slogan (v. 7a). Then they are certain unnamed individuals (v. 7b), who have weak συνείδησις (v. 7c). In v. 8 they are the voices who together with Paul contradict the slogans of the Corinthian wise. In v. 9 they themselves are designated 'the weak', whereas they are more specifically called 'weaker brothers' in v. 11. Finally they are included in Christ in v. 12. By this gradual shift Paul 'steals into the mind of the auditor'.[70]

The presented arguments from contrary and example in 8.10-12 should be seen as reasons for the restated theme. The argument from the contrary uses the behavior of the wise Corinthians as a contradiction of the restated theme. When they eat in an idol's temple and encourage their weaker brothers to eat idol sacrifices, they contradict the concern for the weaker brother that is Paul's concern in the argumentation.

The argument from example in v. 11 uses the vicarious death formula to redefine the weak from being a morally deficient person needing the enlightening cure of γνῶσις, to a Christian brother deserving regard. By identifying the weaker brother with Christ, Paul reproaches the Corinthian wise for their behavior. This takes place in two steps, each in the form of an enthymeme. The first enthymeme redefines the weak as a Christian brother:

Major premise (unstated)	The one Christ dies for is a brother
Support for major premise (the tradition)	Christ died for us The weak is one for whom Christ died
Minor premise	Therefore, the weak is a Christian brother
Conclusion	

The major premise is unstated and relies on the acceptance of the audience. Since this acceptance is so vital for Paul's argument, he supports the major premise with the tradition. The vicarious death formula proves that the one Christ died for is a brother.[71] The vicarious death formula was foundational in early Christian theology, both in its capacity to interpret the vicarious suffering and death of Christ, and in its capacity to define the Christian community.[72] It is almost certain that

70. Cicero, *Inv.* 1.15.20. Quintilian, 4.1.42.

71. This sub-argument in the enthymeme is thus itself construed as an enthymeme where the tradition is the major premise: Christ died for us, we are brothers, therefore the one Christ died for is a brother.

72. The social function of theological statements as community shaping is noted

Paul could rely on the acceptance of the audience in this case. Given the importance of the vicarious death formula for the Corinthians' own self-definition, the enthymeme functions as a meeting of minds and is thus the σῶμα τῆς πίστεως.[73] The Corinthians could not reject the logical conclusion of their own premises. Thus the unstated major premise stands. It would also be difficult for the Corinthian wise to reject the minor premise. The weak are members of the Corinthian church and therefore included in the group of people for whom Christ died. To question this would be to question the salvation of the weaker brother. It would not be a step lightly taken, since both weak and wise probably shared the experience of conversion, baptism and initiation in the Church. Thus the logical conclusion is that the weak are Christian brothers, and should be treated as such.

The second enthymeme (1 Cor. 8.12) builds on the first. From the identification of the weaker brother with Christ, Paul builds an argument that entails a heavy accusation against the Corinthian wise:

Major premise (unstated)	Christ and the Christian are united
Minor premise (the conclusion above)	The weak is a Christian brother united with Christ
Conclusion	Therefore, sinning against the weak is sinning against Christ

The unstated major premise expresses a view widely held among Christians.[74] It is a *topos* that would have been included among the ἔνδοξα held by the Corinthian wise.[75] The minor premise is the conclusion of the previous enthymeme.[76] The resultant conclusion, derived from the Corinthians' own premises, constitutes a powerful rhetorical proof: sinning against the weak is sinning against Christ. The strength of the accusation is the reason why Paul chooses to relieve the tension

by W.A. Meeks, *The First Urban Christians: The Social World of the Apostle Paul* (New Haven: Yale University Press, 1983), pp. 164-92.

73. *Rhet.* 1.1.3.

74. This is seen in the prevalence of the expression ἐν Χριστῷ in the Pauline letters, which builds on a christology where Christ is the new Adam and Christians participate in a new humankind.

75. The union with Christ might even have been the presupposition of a theology of present resurrection in 1 Cor. 15.

76. Such a chain of interlocking enthymemes is called a *sorites*. It is an effective deductive rhetorical proof.

by means of the digression that follows in ch. 9.[77] Paul prepares for this digression in the conclusion of the argument in 8.13. The verse functions as a *transitus* to the digression. Paul's own personal example of not eating meat, if the eating would cause the fall of the weaker brother, is the conclusion to the argumentation. The wise are urged not to become a stumbling block to the weak and Paul himself vows to refrain from causing his brother to fall.[78] By the personal example they are urged to imitate him.[79]

Besides this proof from *logos*, the vicarious death formula functions as a proof from *ethos*. In this first *refutatio*, Paul is engaged in a refutation of the viewpoint of the Corinthian wise. The one who refutes and rebukes must have a strong *ethos* to be heeded. Paul enhances his own *ethos* by the appeal to the tradition. It is not just Paul who is saying this, it is the Christian tradition into which they themselves are embedded. Hardly anything could have a higher *ethos* for a Christian than the salvific work of Christ. It is Christ's saving work that achieved salvation. It is through his work that each and every Christian himself is saved and comes together with other believers. Paul skilfully hides his own disputed *ethos* behind the *ethos* of the tradition.

The persuasive power of the vicarious death formula as proof from *pathos* resides in the fact that it could arouse the Corinthians' emotions. In subsequent Christian history, few items have been able to evoke such an emotional response as the undeserved suffering of Christ on our behalf.[80] Even if it might be hazardous to ascribe the same feelings to them as to us when we are filled with compassion towards the innocent sufferer and rage against the evil-doers, it is probably safe to

77. Quintilian, 4.3.10 states: 'We shall employ such utterances [digressions] as emolients to soften the harder elements of our statement, in order that the ears of the jury may be more ready to take in what we have to say in the sequel... For it is hard to persuade a man to do anything against the grain.'

78. Notice the inclusio formed by πρόσκομμα and σκανδαλίζει whose noun form σκάνδαλον is almost synonymous with πρόσκομμα.

79. The use of personal examples in rhetorical theory, the kingship literature and epistolary exhortation is treated by B. Fiore, *The Function of Personal Example in the Socratic and Pastoral Epistles* (AnBib, 105; Rome: Biblical Institute Press, 1986); for Paul's use of example in 1 Corinthians, see pp. 168-83.

80. In Gal. 3.1 Paul uses the public portrayal of Christ as crucified as a rhetorical argument. This is a *descriptio* or vivid description, *Rhet. ad Her.* 4.39.51, which is useful for exciting the emotions, 2.30.49.

assume some similar emotions among the Corinthians. If the Corinthians were aroused to compassion, it would have served Paul's argumentative purpose admirably well.

e. *The Lord's Supper Allusion in the Second Refutatio, 1 Corinthians 10.1-22*

The Lord's Supper allusion (1 Cor. 10.16) is the third tradition in this rhetorical unit. This tradition is a rhetorically shaped reformulation of the words of institution of 1 Cor. 11.23-25, Lk. 22.19-20, Mk 14.22-24 and Mt. 26.26-28. The cup and the bread in the words of institution under Paul's pen become the main statements in two parallel rhetorical questions. Each includes a relative clause in the first-person plural, whereby the entire worshipping community partakes in the ritual of blessing the cup and breaking the bread. The tradition is a liturgical tradition, having its *Sitz im Leben* in the Lord's Supper celebrations. Paul can presuppose that the Corinthians accepted this tradition and that they understood the implication that whenever they broke the bread and blessed the cup, they individually became fellow sharers in Christ and manifested their unity in Christ as the body of Christ.

Paul applies the tradition to the Corinthian situation by reshaping the wording and by adding the deductive argument in 10.17. To form the rhetorical questions and to bring out the aspect of cultic fellowship established by the ritual, Paul adds οὐχὶ κοινωνία to the tradition. Note that all the other words are found in the words of institution. By adding κοινωνία, Paul develops the concept of the new covenant: the participants in the Lord's Supper constitute a new fellowship since they are members of a new covenant. Shaping the statement as a rhetorical question forces the Corinthians to think for themselves, and come to the only possible conclusion: assent to Paul's statement.[81] Before explicating the deductive argument, we need to look at the wider context, which is an inductive chain of reasoning.

The second *refutatio* contains Paul's direct confrontation with the

---

81. With οὐχί an affirmative is expected (BDF, §427.2). The function of the rhetorical questions in 1 Corinthians has been studied by D.F. Watson, '1 Corinthians 10.23–11.1 in the light of Greco-Roman Rhetoric: The Role of Rhetorical Questions', *JBL* 108 (1989), pp. 301-18. The subject was previously studied by W. Wuellner, 'Paul as Pastor: The Function of Rhetorical Questions in First Corinthians', in A. Vanhoye (ed.), *L'Apôtre Paul: Personnalité, style et conception du ministère* (Leuven: Leuven University Press, 1986), pp. 49-77.

most serious aspect of the problem of idol sacrifices: the idolatry that can result from eating in a temple setting. The warning examples of the Israelites in the desert establish an analogy between the Israelites and the Corinthians. Both have received spiritual blessings and both face the same temptation to fall away from God through idolatry. After the analogy has been established, Paul states his emphatic warning: 'flee from the worship of idols' (10.14). This warning is the main point of the refutation and forms the theme of the ensuing argumentation.

The argumentation in 10.14-22 is an inductive chain of reasoning elaborating a theme. The argumentative pattern is similar to the first *refutatio* and close to the elaborated argument in *Rhet. ad Her.* 4.44.57-58:

1. Theme: flee from the worship of idols (v. 14).
2. Reason: for you are sensible people; judge for yourselves what I say (v. 15).
3. The argument from example: κοινωνία with Christ in the Lord's Supper (v. 16) applied to the Corinthians with an enthymeme (v. 17).
4. The argument from analogy: the priests in the temple have κοινωνία with the altar (v. 18).
5. The argument from contrary: eating εἰδωλόθυτα (in a temple) means κοινωνία with demons (v. 19-20).
6. Conclusion: the Lord and the demons are two mutually exclusive spiritual realities (v. 21)
7. The conclusion is applied to the Corinthians in a double exhortation: do not provoke the Lord to jealousy; you are not stronger than he (v. 22).

The theme elaborated in this argumentation is the imperative 'flee from the worship of idols'. This theme is the governing idea in the whole argument and the various sub-arguments serve to establish the truth of this imperative and to persuade the Corinthians to flee from idolatry.

In the *reason*, Paul appeals to the good sense of the Corinthians, by asking them to judge for themselves.[82] If they only would exercise

82. The same kind of argument is used in 1 Cor. 11.13, 'Judge for yourself'. Paul seems to imply that they should have reached the same verdict as himself, if they had just used their sound judgment. Appealing to the good sense of the audience is a good rhetorical practice. The rhetorical figure is called *communicatio*, 'the figure…when we actually take our opponents into consultation' (Quintilian, 9.2.20).

sound judgment, they would themselves realize that their behavior is dangerous and would avoid eating idol sacrifices in the temple. Considering the ironical φρόνιμοι in 1 Cor. 4.10, Paul could here be appealing to the wisdom the Corinthians claimed to have, urging them to apply that 'wisdom' to the really important case: idolatry.

There is no restatement of the theme, but the three cases of κοινωνία in the next five verses all serve to support the theme of avoiding idolatry. The three cases follow the standard pattern of argument from contrary, argument from analogy and argument from example, but Paul varies the order of these arguments. The Lord's Supper allusion in 10.16 constitutes an argument from example and will be dealt with below. The reference to the priests and the people in the temple eating the sacrifices and having κοινωνία with the altar, is an argument from analogy.[83] The analogy between the Israelites and the Corinthians (10.1-11) is here developed as concerns the eating of sacrifice. The point of the analogy is that the eating establishes κοινωνία with the altar. Understanding κοινωνία to be a covenantal term, the word depicts an allegiance to the God of the covenant and the resulting fellowship in the cult.[84] The reference to eating sacrifices is especially appropriate since Paul's real concern is their eating of sacrifices in the temple setting. The analogy thus anticipates the argument from contrary in 10.19-20. In this argument Paul refers to the contrary of his thesis concerning the avoidance of idolatry: the Corinthians' own behavior. The argument also explains why this behavior is wrong. It implies a κοινωνία not with Christ or the God of the covenant, but on the contrary, a κοινωνία with demons.[85] The conclusion in a deliberative argument usually urges to action. In this case the Corinthians are enjoined to refrain from idolatry. The conclusion is phrased in a prohibition consisting of two repeated, and mutually excluding, allegiances. The cup of demons and the table of demons is a reference to the drinking

83. The special function of the argument from analogy is to ground the theme in common social and cultural phenomena. V.K. Robbins, *The Tapestry of Early Christian Discourse: Rhetoric, Society and Ideology* (London: Routledge, 1996), p. 82.

84. Willis, *Idol Meat in Corinth*, p. 209: 'κοινωνία means the relationship established among members of the covenant and the obligations ensuing from it'.

85. Note the renewed reference to εἰδωλόθυτα in 10.19. This time Paul clearly explains it as a dangerous food. Cf. P. Gooch, *Dangerous Food: 1 Corinthians 8–10 in its Context* (Waterloo: W. Laurier University Press, 1993), pp. 53-59.

and eating of idol sacrifices in a temple setting, Paul's concern ever since the *exordium*, which he now prohibits. The conclusion is accompanied by a reproach in 10.22.[86] Since the Corinthians' previous track record shows they have not heeded the prohibition, Paul shames them.[87]

After this overview of the rhetorical argumentation, we can return to the rhetorical function of the tradition in the argumentation. A first observation is that the allusion to the Lord's Supper is the first and decisive example of κοινωνία which lays the basis for the following two examples. The analogy established here between cultic behavior and spiritual allegiance is the force of the next two arguments. The significance of Paul's reformulation of the Lord's Supper tradition lies especially in the term κοινωνία, chosen deliberately as the basis for the extended analogy. Paul's point is that the celebration of the Lord's Supper establishes a partnership with the Lord Jesus Christ and with his body, the Church, which excludes all other loyalties.[88] The emphasis is on the eating and the drinking.

If the identification between the Church and the body of Christ is not clear in the traditional statement, this point is forcefully driven home by Paul in the enthymeme in 10.17.[89] The enthymeme applies the point derived from the tradition to the actual problem in Corinth. Even if both a vertical and a horizontal aspect are discernible in the tradition, the point developed by Paul is communal.[90] That the unity between

---

86. The reproach is not included in the amplification of a theme in *Rhet. ad Her.*, but as noted above, the exhortation is sometimes the last point in the elaboration of the chreia.

87. Paul's use of shame as a harsh psychagogue is noted by Glad, *Paul and Philodemus*, pp. 304-10.

88. As pointed out by Mitchell, *Paul and the Rhetoric of Reconciliation*, p. 254 n. 383, the common dichotomy in the interpretation of κοινωνία, sacramental or social, is overcome when one notes the function in Paul's argumentation: 'Cultic ties are commonly appealed to in attempts to get divided groups back together again'.

89. For various interpretations of the relationship between the tradition and the enthymeme, see the discussion in H. Probst, *Paulus und der Brief: Die Rhetorik des antiken Briefes als Form der paulinischen Korintherkorrespondenz (1 Kor 8–10)* (Tübingen: J.C.B. Mohr, 1991), pp. 245-58. He advocates the communal understanding of κοινωνία in Paul's argumentation.

90. Hence Paul can not be making a statement about the sacraments here, even though this has repeatedly been asserted in the history of exegesis.

Christians is Paul's major concern is underlined by the thrice-repeated εἷς in the enthymeme:

Major premise	There is one bread
Minor premise	We all partake of the one bread
Conclusion	Therefore, we who are many are one body

The major premise is taken from the tradition. The bread which is broken is rephrased as the one bread. At a basic level this is a reference to the common fact that the cake of bread is whole before it is broken. Hence the major premise is a common fact taken from their own experience. The minor premise introduces the individual Corinthian Christians. Whether weak or wise they all participate in the same Lord's Supper celebration. Hence the minor premise is also taken from their own experience. Paul's conclusion from these two premises is the unity of Christians in the body of Christ, a unity which is derived from the fact that all Christians partake of the same bread. Here the argument leaves the strict logic required of a syllogism. Even if the fellowship-forming character of a meal in the ancient Mediterranean culture is acknowledged, the mere eating of bread pieces that have originally been united does not ordinarily make the different partakers in the meal one body. However, the ritual setting makes Paul's argument work. It is not just any eating. The Lord's Supper is a meal in a covenantal setting and therefore it establishes unity between the participants in the meal.

The Lord's Supper allusion in 1 Cor. 10.16 also functions as a proof from *ethos*. The Lord's Supper as a ritual would have had a high *ethos* for the Corinthians. By bringing in the tradition, Paul shifts the focus from his own views to the authority of the Christian tradition and their own Lord's Supper celebrations. To question Paul in this matter would be to question their own experience of unity in Christ and their shared allegiance to Christ in the Lord's Supper celebrations.

The strength of the Lord's Supper allusion as a proof from *pathos* is increased by the fact that Paul is here referring to their own experiences of celebrating the Lord's Supper. By reminding them of their experiences, Paul rouses their emotions. If those emotions would have been related to exclusive devotion to Christ, they would have served Paul's persuasive purpose. Their devotion to Christ would have acted as proof from *pathos*, underlining their allegiance to Christ and none other. Hence the imperative to flee idolatry would have been strengthened by the positive emotions of their devotion to Christ.

298   *The Rhetorical Interpretation of Scripture*

3. *Theology in Context*

Throughout this rhetorical unit we have seen how Paul uses the traditions he himself had delivered to the Corinthians as the starting-point for argumentation. As a commissioned messenger with an authoritative message, Christian tradition is the apostle Paul's field of expertise. His relationship with the Corinthians is determined by the fact that he is their founding apostle, the messenger who brought the gospel to them. They have received the tradition and their acceptance of the gospel is the basis for the church in Corinth. The accepted tradition is therefore basic to the self-understanding of the Corinthians as Christians.

Considering this it is surprising that the role of tradition in Paul's argumentation has not previously been given detailed study.[91] Although many of the rhetorical analyses undertaken to date point out the parallels in Paul's letters to the rhetoric of the Greco-Roman world, the distinctive features of early Christian rhetoric have not been taken into account. In retrospect, historical-critical scholars have been more interested in the history behind the text than the argumentation in the text.[92] This diachronic use of rhetoric is in tension with the synchronic use by literary scholars, some of whom never leave the world of the text to enter into the historical reality behind the text. I am convinced that a study of the role played by tradition in Paul's argumentation breaks this

91. During the form-critical investigation of the pre-Pauline material in the 1960s, some attempts were made to see the function of the traditions in the texts, but these studies were mainly concerned with the redaction of the tradition and Paul's role as interpreter in relationship to his predecessors: K. Wegenast, *Das Verständnis der Tradition bei Paulus und in den Deuteropaulinen* (Neukirchen–Vluyn: Neukirchener Verlag, 1962); K. Wengst, 'Der Apostel und die Tradition: Zur theologischen Bedeutung urchristlicher Formeln bei Paulus', *ZTK* 69 (1972), pp. 145-62; H. von Lips, 'Paulus und die Tradition: Zitierung von Schriftworten, Herrenworten und urchristlichen Traditionen', *VF* 36 (1991), pp. 27-49 (31), states that: 'wie Paulus urchristliche Tradition aufgenommen hat, ist als umgreifendes Thema kaum monografisch behandelt worden'. He concludes, 'eine Genauere Untersuchung solcher literarischer Sachverhalte in der Verwendung von Zitaten insgesamt könnte auch neue Aspekte bringen, die für den Umgang des Paulus mit den unterschiedlichen Traditionsbereichen von Bedeutung sind' (p. 49).

92. One such example is Margaret Mitchell's learned monograph, *Paul and the Rhetoric of Reconciliation*, which is replete with parallels to contemporary rhetorical conventions, but which does not aim to study the argumentative power in the text.

impasse, by actively searching the argument in the text while at the same time keeping in mind the historical situation behind the text.

The inner Christian argumentation which has been studied in this essay is only one of the realms of argumentation employed by Paul. A study of the rhetorical functions of maxims shows how Paul relates to the cultural conventions of the Hellenistic world.[93] A study of the rhetorical function of Old Testament citations shows how Paul relates to his Jewish heritage.[94] My contention is that the inner Christian argumentation is the most important to gain an understanding of the communication between Paul and the churches to which he writes. The tradition seems to be the most important aspect of the special topics that are the basic premises for inner Christian argumentation in the developing field of early Christian knowledge. Aristotle called the realm of the special topics a 'science'.[95] After 2000 years of Church history we may call that science 'theology'.

The interesting aspect of Paul's theological argumentation is that it is to such a great degree based on tradition. Besides the fact that tradition is the accepted premise shared by the audience, it forms the basis for Paul's own theology. When Paul makes more substantial theological statements in 1 Corinthians 8–10, these statements are an elaboration of some theme found in the tradition. Sometimes the tradition contains several themes and the theme developed by Paul in his argumentation can be just one out of several themes. The Lord's Supper tradition, for example, contains a rich complex of themes out of which Paul picks the κοινωνία aspect in 1 Cor. 10.16-17, but develops a theme of judgment in 1 Cor. 11.26-31.

The application of a particular theme from the tradition to the issue of idol sacrifices in the Corinthian church is accomplished through an interplay between inductive and deductive modes of reasoning. Aristotle pointed out the two modes of argument in rhetoric as 'induction and

93. R.A. Ramsaran, *Liberating Words: Paul's Use of Rhetorical Maxims in 1 Corinthians 1–10* (Valley Forge, PA: Trinity Press International, 1996).

94. F. Siegert, *Argumentation bei Paulus: Gezeigt an Röm 9–11* (Tübingen: J.C.B. Mohr, 1985), pp. 157-64, has undertaken such a study from the perspective of the New Rhetoric.

95. Comparing theological argumentation to a 'science' (in the Aristotelian sense with special topics) implies that theological arguments are only acceptable to the particular audience which shares the same premises. Cf. the disussion on particular and universal audience in Perelman and Olbrechts-Tyteca, *The New Rhetoric*, pp. 31-35.

the syllogism...for the example is induction and the enthymeme a syllogism'.[96] The tradition taken by itself is an inductive example or παράδειγμα. In a rhetorical argumentation, it is seldom possible to list all the instances that would make the inductive conclusion valid; instead, the speaker would list the most relevant example which would lead to the desired conclusion.[97] Quintilian notes that examples are especially suited for deliberative discourse.[98] In the subsequent rhetorical tradition the argument from example was often connected with the testimony of antiquity. Combined, they form the sixth point in the amplification of a theme in *Rhetorica ad Herennium*.[99]

When the tradition is applied to the particular situation in Corinth, Paul employs a deductive mode of reasoning. A theme from the tradition is made the premise for an enthymeme whereby Paul deductively brings home his point. In 1 Cor. 8.11, the tradition 'Christ died for us' is a support for the major premise in the first enthymeme (the one Christ dies for is a brother), as well as a support for the major premise in the second enthymeme (Christ and the Christian are united). The conclusions to these enthymemes, where Paul applies the tradition to the Corinthians, were shown to be: 'therefore the weak is a Christian brother' and 'therefore sinning against the weak is sinning against

96. *Rhet.* 1.2.8. This distinction is basic to Aristotle's understanding of rhetoric.

97. 'One [example] alone is sufficient if [it is] put last; for even a single trustworthy witness is of use' (*Rhet.* 2.20.20).

98. Quintilian, 3.8.36, 66.

99. *Rhet. ad Her.* 4.44.57. This combination of example and testimony is also found in the rhetorical discussion of the κρίσεις and *auctoritas*. Hermogenes περὶ χρείας (8.4-12) lists the statement by an authority (ἐκ κρίσεως), right after the statement from example (ἐκ παραδείγματος). This is similar to the discussion of the *exornatio* in the complete argument in *Rhet. ad Her.* 2.29.46, where *exemplum* and *res iudicata* are two of the component parts. Quintilian, in a discussion whether examples and *auctoritas* are intrinsic or extrinsic proof, finally deciding for the former, states, 'Authority [*auctoritas*] also may be drawn from external sources to support a case. Those who follow the Greeks, who call such arguments κρίσεις, style them *judgments* or *adjudications* [*iudicia* aut *iudicationes*] thereby referring not to matters on which judicial sentence has been pronounced (for such decisions form examples or precedents), but to whatever may be regarded as expressing the opinion of nations, peoples, philosophers, distinguished citizens, or illustrious poets... They form a sort of testimony, which is rendered all the more impressive by the fact that it was not given to suit special cases, but was the utterance or action of minds swayed neither by prejudice or influence, simply because it seemed the most honourable or honest thing to say or do' (5.11.36-37).

Christ'. In 1 Cor. 10.17 the tradition is the basis for the major premise in the enthymeme ('there is one bread'), which gives the conclusion appropriate to the Corinthian situation: 'therefore we who are many are one body'. In 1 Cor. 8.11 the application of the tradition in the enthymemes leads to an implicit accusation so severe that Paul digresses in one whole chapter before returning to the case in point. In 1 Cor. 10.17 the unity of Christians in the Lord's Supper is made explicit through the enthymematic argumentation. In both cases one of the meanings of the tradition, in itself an inductive proof, is brought out by a deductive mode of reasoning.[100] This interplay between inductive and deductive rhetorical proof seems to be an important aspect of Paul's way of applying his theology in specific church situations.[101]

100. This perspective on Paul's theological method has certain similarities to the interplay between the coherent core and the contingent situation noted by J.C. Beker, *Paul the Apostle: The Triumph of God in Life and Thought* (Philadelphia: Fortress Press, 1980), pp. 23-36. Cf. his observations on Paul as interpreter of tradition, pp. 109-31.

101. My fuller account of Paul's argumentation in this passage is found in *Traditions as Rhetorical Proof: Pauline Argumentation in 1 Corinthians* (ConBNT, 29; Stockholm: Almqvist & Wiksell, 1998), pp. 135-73.

WAS PAUL ANGRY?
DERHETORIZING GALATIANS

Lauri Thurén

1. *Introduction*

James D.G. Dunn recently confessed that he is 'less enthused about the value' of literary and rhetorical criticism for the study of Pauline theology. He continued: 'In particular it seems to me fairly pointless to argue about whether Paul's letters are "epideictic" or "deliberative", or whatever'.[1]

I can understand Dunn's frustration. Much good basic work has been done in rhetorical criticism, but an ordinary scholar still fails to see its relevance to standard exegetical questions. Despite the continuing boom, rhetorical criticism has in fact already arrived at a crossroads. The big question is how to integrate the analyses into theological and historical problems. In this essay I shall put forward a tentative answer.

One of the principal tasks of a biblical scholar is to translate the text so that modern people can understand it. In so doing we are not working only with dictionaries and grammars: Rudolf Bultmann's idea of *demythologizing* the text was also an attempt to interpret the Bible's foreign approach to communication. Although he may not have succeeded, the quest still stands. In order to comprehend and examine the thinking behind any text, or even to use it as a historical source, we need to recognize and interpret its communicative techniques. In the Bible, the main obstacle may not be the mythical language, but the art of persuasion. Therefore, the text needs to be *derhetorized*.

Paul did not produce textbooks on dogmatics. His writing was guided not only by an effort to present his religious ideas but also—and perhaps primarily—to use them in order to affect his audience. This

---

1.   J.D.G. Dunn, 'Prolegomena to a Theology of Paul', *NTS* 40 (1994), pp. 407-32 (414).

indicates that in practice it is questionable whether a student of Paul's theology can take his expressions at their face value. I am not referring only to simple misconceptions of certain stylistic devices, for example, *hyperbole*, but the whole text.

The goal of Paul's letters was hardly to convey to the addressees what he thought or how he felt. From what Paul says we do not directly know what he thinks, nor can we easily draw a psychological portrait of him. Actually, the goal of Paul's texts was not even to make his addressees believe what he wanted them to believe. The aim was far more practical: to persuade, to modify the addressees' behavior. And in persuasion, almost everything is allowed.[2]

There are many signs of persuasive flexibility in Paul's texts.[3] This means that the strategic goals and tactical moves[4] complicate and embellish the thoughts presented, as compared with neutral description. Just like any other author, he utilizes devices on different levels—such as *insinuatio*—to affect the addressees in the way designed. The expressions often depend on the part of the speech in which they occur. For instance, at the beginning of the letter he has to be more careful and positive, in the end more outspoken. In front of another audience or in another situation he would express himself differently. Since different letters, such as Romans and Galatians, had very different goals, even the theology presented seems to be different. Only when this is fully recognized can we seek to discern what Paul really means.

Therefore, when analyzing Paul's *theological* universe—namely, the ideological religious system behind his letters—we must be able to look behind his rhetoric. No sound comparison between religious ideas presented in his texts or even different parts of a single letter can be made without a proper study of their function in the total persuasive strategy. But derhetorization is needed even before we can arrive at reliable *historical* conclusions from different clues in the text.[5]

Such a dynamic approach to the theology of Paul will not necessarily

---

2. Paul was often criticized for unduly flexible rhetoric (cf., e.g., 2 Cor. 1.13-18). Thus he has to emphasize that at least on some occasions the contents override his art of persuasion (Gal. 1.10, 20; Rom. 9.1-3). Or, are even these expressions mere rhetoric?

3. See, e.g., his own confession in 1 Cor. 9.22.

4. It is typical of modern rhetorical studies to use military terminology.

5. For an example, see L. Thurén, 'Hey Jude! Asking for the Original Situation and Message of a Catholic Epistle', *NTS* 43 (1997), pp. 451-65.

solve the problems inherent in his texts; it is possible that the opposite result will ensue. But even then the study can be focused on the real issues by eliminating misunderstandings, which are due to the interpreters' unduly static comprehension of the nature of the texts. This provides us with a more sensible basis.

When searching for a theology, we must be aware that we are asking the 'wrong question' of the text. We are reading it for another purpose than that for which it was originally written. We need a more realistic Pauline theology, but it is difficult indeed to ask a static question of a dynamic text. Although this is what theology is all about, the difficulties inherent in the wrong questions should be recognized and considered.[6]

Therefore the study of the theology behind a text, and the scrutiny of the tensions therein, need more than a contextual correction. We have to understand for what purpose the author writes as he does, and how this purpose modifies his explicit 'thoughts'. Only then can we hope to discern the ideological pattern behind what is said.

By translating the rhetoric of a text into historical or theological language, we can make full use of the results of the current basic rhetorical, epistolary and narratological studies, but simultaneously also integrate them with ordinary historical and theological questions. Derhetorization will thereby not only provide scholars with a new perspective on the Bible, but possibly also with new answers to old questions.

To substantiate this thesis I return to Galatians and offer some general observations on the nature of communication therein. I shall discuss some general persuasive features which may have affected the way in which Pauline theology is expressed in the letter. Thereby I hope to take the first step in derhetorizing the theologically essential statements in Galatians so that they may be compared with corresponding utterances in other Pauline texts.

2. *Was Paul Angry?*

It is commonly claimed that the apostle was so enraged when he wrote Galatians that he was too angry to present proper theology—or that he

6.	For example, the parable of the rich man and Lazarus (Lk. 16.19-31) does not directly provide us with material for deducing what was Jesus' or the evangelist's view on heaven or the life after death (cf. E. Schweizer, *Das Evangelium nach Lukas* [NTD, 3; Göttingen: Vandenhoeck & Ruprecht, 1982], p. 173: 'weil sie nicht dogmatisch über das Jenseits belehren').

happened to reveal his actual, inconsistent ideas.[7] This explanation often leads to depreciation of, for example, his sharp 'antinomistic' expressions in Galatians.

Paul is said to dictate 'under considerable emotion'[8], 'in a singularly passionate way' so that we learn to know 'his fiery temperament'.[9] The apostle is distressed by a painful situation and does not know what to do.[10] He writes 'mit glühendem Eifer',[11] 'im ersten Affekt',[12] in 'deep personal anguish'[13] clearly unable to formulate his utterances.

All this is claimed to have a defective impact on his explicit theology. According to one alternative, this indicates that the apostle paid little attention to serious theology, but let his feelings guide his speech.[14] Another explanation is that the usually thoughtful apostle was so upset by the new situation in Galatia, that he cannot be held responsible for what he said.[15] In his anger he even seems to have forgotten basic rhetorical skills.

Certainly this is the impression which occurs to the reader of the epistle. But how do we really know? What if this is only what the apostle wants his addressees to think, and we modern readers are similarly affected?

Let us visualize how a listener is expected to react when facing a respected speaker who now, surprisingly, is furious. I can imagine two things: first, he/she must take the speaker seriously. There is no room to suspect any rhetorical gimmicks or calculation when the speaker's

---

7. H. Räisänen, *Paul and the Law* (WUNT, 29; Tübingen: J.C.B. Mohr, 2nd edn, 1986), p. 133.

8. R.Y.K. Fung, *The Epistle to the Galatians* (NICNT; Grand Rapids: Eerdmans, 1988), p. 93.

9. H.N. Ridderbos, *The Epistle of Paul to the Churches of Galatia* (NICNT; Grand Rapids: Eerdmans, 1953), p. 18.

10. Ridderbos, *The Epistle of Paul*, pp. 170-71.

11. J. Rohde, *Der Brief des Paulus an die Galater* (THKNT, 9; Berlin: Evangelischer Verlagsanstalt, 1989), p. 13.

12. Rohde, *Der Brief des Paulus*, p. 11.

13. F. Thielman, *Paul and the Law: A Contextual Approach* (Downers Grove, IL: InterVarsity Press, 1994), p. 120.

14. E.g. Räisänen, *Paul and the Law*, p. 200, claims that Gal. 3.19 is written 'in heated debate'. The statement is 'steeped in emotion'; Paul dictates in anger and overreacts (pp. 132-33). This indicates, according to Räisänen, that 'Paul's mind was divided with regard to the law'.

15. C.E.B. Cranfield, 'St Paul and the Law', *SJT* 17 (1964), pp. 43-68 (62).

emotions seem strong and genuine. Another point is that the listener cannot remain calm, but is emotionally affected. This, however, is precisely the goal of the well-educated speaker; this is what he/she is trained to produce.[16]

If Galatians is as carefully planned as the modern rhetorical analyses—especially the commentaries of Betz[17] and Longenecker[18]—demonstrate, it would be no surprise if Paul's emotional statements served the *pathos* appeal of the text rather than represented his actual state of mind.[19] Of course, it was good for the cause if the speaker worked himself up into the same emotion.[20] If Paul, like a good modern salesman 'sold' the product to himself before meeting the customer, he was not really deceiving his addressees.

Notwithstanding, we must add that the use of rhetorical devices and strategies in a text does not prove that the author *could not* have been overwhelmed by the feelings this technical artifice is aimed to display. However, recognition of such clichés makes us wonder whether the opposite is to be believed. Thomas Olbricht once suggested that Paul's use of *pathos* is closely related to family metaphors.[21] Maybe Paul was just a good father, sounding angry in order to protect his children?

Let us take a closer look at the statements that convey an emotionally heated picture of Paul in Galatians.

In 1.6 Paul begins the letter with an expression of astonishment (θαυμάζω), instead of his standard εὐχαριστῶ. The normal thanks-

16. J. Martin, *Antike Rhetorik: Technik und Methode* (HbAltW, 2.3; Munich: Beck, 1974), pp. 158-66; S.J. Kraftchick, 'Ethos and Pathos Appeals in Galatians Five and Six: A Rhetorical Analysis' (PhD Dissertation, Emory University, 1985), pp. 137-43.

17. H.D. Betz, *Galatians: A Commentary on Paul's Letter to the Churches in Galatia* (Hermeneia; Philadelphia: Fortress Press, 1979). In March 1996, in Copenhagen I asked Professor Betz if his notions on the rhetoric in Galatians can be used for pondering whether the apostle really was angry. Betz emphatically dismissed such a question as mere psychology.

18. R. Longenecker, *Galatians* (WBC, 41; Waco, TX: Word Books, 1990).

19. Longenecker, *Galatians*, pp. cxviii-cxix, rightly counts some expressions in Galatians as aimed at the *pathos* appeal and thereby at persuading the addressees. He, however, does not draw any further conclusions from these observations.

20. Cf. Martin, *Antike Rhetorik*, p. 161.

21. T.H. Olbricht, 'An Aristotelian Rhetorical Analysis of 1 Thessalonians', in D.L. Balch, E. Ferguson and W.A. Meeks (eds.), *Greeks, Romans, and Christians: Essays in Honor of Abraham J. Malherbe* (Minneapolis: Fortress Press, 1990), pp. 216-36 (230).

giving section is replaced by a rebuke. Longenecker's explanation is typical: 'Paul evidently could not think of anything to commend them for, and so enters directly into the issues at hand. He had just received, it seems, news...and reacts to that news on the spot.'[22] Rohde argues that Paul here breaks the common epistolary pattern.[23] Ridderbos informs us that Paul's heart is full of pain.[24]

It is evident that the θαυμάζω-expression is intended to signal the importance of the issue. But what does it actually tell us about Paul's feelings? The addressees hardly knew how Paul was wont to begin his letters. Although unique in the *corpus Paulinum*, the expression is but a conventional letter-opening cliché, a standard rhetorical device designed to signal the author's unhappiness vis-à-vis the addressee's behavior and attitudes.[25] We do not know whether Paul really was astonished or, for example, irritated[26]—the only fact we have is that he uses a persuasive device for a certain purpose.

Galatians 1.8-9 is a curse, which can be seen as exceptional and emotionally based. Although certainly a strong, extreme expression, such a threat is by no means unknown to, for example, Quintilian.[27]

Galatians 1.10 is seen as an 'emotional outburst'; Paul 'speaks in fervor'.[28] However, even here we have technical terminology. The verse serves as a transitional formula between the *exordium* and the *narratio*.[29] In a classical oratory style, Paul is rejecting 'empty' persuasion, claiming to be free of unduly calculated rhetoric, in order to demon-

---

22. Longenecker, *Galatians*, p. 13.

23. Rohde, *Der Brief des Paulus*, p. 38.

24. Ridderbos, *The Epistle of Paul*, p. 46.

25. See H. Koskenniemi, *Studien zur Idee und Phraseologie des griechischen Briefes bis 400 n.Chr.* (Annales Academiae Scientiarum Fennicae, Series B, 102.2; Helsinki: Suomalainen tiedeakatemia, 1956), pp. 65-67; H. Lausberg, *Handbuch der literarischen Rhetorik: Eine Grundlegung der Literaturwissenschaft* (2 vols.; Munich: Hueber, 1960), I, p. 153, §270; Betz, *Galatians*, pp. 46-47; Longenecker, *Galatians*, pp. cv-cvii, 14 (who however does not draw any conclusions from this). Whether the expression contains some irony (Betz, *Galatians*, pp. 46-47), or not (F. Mussner, *Der Galaterbrief* [HTK, 9; Freiburg: Herder, 1974], p. 53), is not of importance.

26. T.Y. Mullins, 'Formulas in New Testament Epistles', *JBL* 91 (1972), pp. 380-95 (385).

27. See Betz, *Galatians*, pp. 45-46.

28. So, according to Longenecker, *Galatians*, pp. 18-19, and most modern commentators.

29. Betz, *Galatians*, p. 46.

strate his candor.[30] Although the reactions of the first readers are unknown to us, at least many modern commentators have been affected as planned by this device.

In 3.1-5 Paul wonders who has 'bewitched the foolish Galatians'. Once more he is said to speak 'with obvious emotion'[31] and 'strong feeling'.[32] But again—is Paul really angry? This section, being one of the most emotionally colored and apparently straightforward in Paul, is in fact carefully constructed and 'loaded with rhetorical figures'.[33]

Hardly anybody believes that the questions in 3.1-5 are to be taken at their face value. Paul does not crave information; the questions are rhetorical, to provoke interaction by the audience.[34] The 'biting and aggressive' style likewise serves a rhetorical purpose. Betz rightly explains: 'This insult, however, should not be taken too seriously. Such addresses were commonplace among the diatribe preachers of Paul's day.'[35] He even claims that Paul here presents a 'carefully prepared mixture of some logic, some emotional appeal, some wisdom, some beauty, and some entertainment' in order to affect his readers better than with too perfect and thereby suspicious logic.[36]

Galatians 4.12-20 is often called an 'erratic and irrational outburst', 'reflecting [sic] strong pathos'.[37] Paul is said to be overwhelmed by his own feelings. The main argument is that he does not continue with 'sachlich-theologische' argumentation, but refers to personal matters.[38] We meet 'deep affection, concern, and perplexity'.[39] The metaphors

30. See Betz, *Galatians*, pp. 54-55; Fung, *Galatians*, pp. 49-50.

31. Fung, *Galatians*, p. 129.

32. D. Guthrie, *Galatians* (NCB; Grand Rapids: Eerdmans, 1973), p. 91.

33. Longenecker, *Galatians*, p. 99.

34. For the functions of the rhetorical question, see W. Wuellner, 'Paul as Pastor: The Function of Rhetorical Questions in First Corinthians', in A. Vanhoye (ed.), *L'Apôtre Paul: Personnalité, style et conception du ministère* (BETL, 73; Leuven: Leuven University Press, 1986), pp. 49-77.

35. Betz, *Galatians*, p. 130; cf. also Longenecker, *Galatians*, p. 100. This consolation means, however, only scholars; for the original readers (as well as for modern hermeneutical purposes) the insult should be understood with full emotional force.

36. Betz, *Galatians*, p. 129.

37. H. Schlier, *Der Brief an die Galater* (MeyerK, 7; Göttingen: Vandenhoeck & Ruprecht, 4th edn, 1965), p. 208; cf. also Mussner, *Der Galaterbrief*, pp. 304-305; Longenecker, *Galatians*, p. 188; even Betz, *Galatians*, p. 221.

38. Mussner, *Der Galaterbrief*, pp. 304-305.

39. Longenecker, *Galatians*, p. 194.

'mother' and 'children' reveal particular depth of feeling on Paul's part.[40] We are given 'a glimpse into the heart of a true evangelist and pastor'.[41]

But at least here a red light ought to flash. The speech of a trained orator hardly happens to reveal something about his heart, nor does a carefully prepared letter. Our only picture of the author is that implicit in the text, and it serves a purpose: the *ethos* of the author is boosted and the reader is to be emotionally affected by the author's implied emotions.[42] Most commentators seem to have neatly fallen victim to this strategy.

Betz, although also himself calling this section a 'lighter' one, rightly remarks: 'What has not been recognized is the rhetorical character of this passage'.[43] In particular the stereotypical devices of mother,[44] *immutatio vocis*[45] and *dubitatio*[46] have duly affected—that is, misled— the scholars. Interestingly enough, Luther, who still possessed a certain medieval perception of rhetoric, rightly states: 'He does not miss any- thing'.[47] To pretend to be devoid of arguments is typical for an orator, and a well-designed device in Paul's strategy.[48]

Summarizing, we can say that Galatians as a whole is an impas- sioned, emotionally loaded letter. This can hardly be denied. The examples mentioned above are the most striking, but many minor features in the text support the impression.

There is, however, reason to doubt whether the *author himself* is overwhelmed by emotions. He presents himself in the text as per- plexed, uncalculating, straightforward and impassioned; the letter seems to be an instant response, a natural primitive reaction, to alarm-

40. Guthrie, *Galatians*, p. 121; Ridderbos, *The Epistle of Paul*, p. 170.

41. Longenecker, *Galatians*, p. 197.

42. Kraftchick, 'Ethos and Pathos Appeals', pp. 227-28, finds this device often in Galatians.

43. Betz, *Galatians*, p. 221.

44. Betz, *Galatians*, p. 233.

45. Betz, *Galatians*, p. 236; Martin, *Antike Rhetorik*, pp. 353-55.

46. Betz, *Galatians*, pp. 236-37; Lausberg, *Handbuch der literarischen Rhetorik*, I, pp. 383-84, §§776-78; Quintilian, 9.2.19.

47. Paul 'as a genuine orator presents his case with great care and faith—all in order to call them back to the truth of the Gospel and to win them away from the false apostles' (M. Luther, *Werke* [Kritische Gesamtausgabe (WA) XL; Weimar: Böhlau, 1911], p. 652).

48. Betz, *Galatians*, p. 237.

ing news from the congregations. Yet a closer look reveals that this purposeful impression is consciously produced by utilizing effective contemporary rhetorical means. One would expect more unorthodox ways of expressing perplexity if the apostle actually were in frenzy.

Of course it is possible that Paul was carried away by his emotions; perhaps he had learned his rhetoric so well that he could neatly follow the rules even in a furious state. But is this plausible? Another explanation is that the apostle knew exactly what he was doing. Irrespective of the feelings in his own mind (which we cannot reach), the apostle was able carefully to compose a letter, aimed for maximum effect among the addressees.

But in both cases it seems odd if he had lost control over the theological contents of his letter, which we have reason to believe were far more important for him than the art of persuasion as such. Whether or not his theology in Galatians is contradictory and confused, it seems clear that Paul's exceptional theological utterances cannot be explained away by referring to his state of mind. The apostle must be held fully responsible for what he dictated.

3. *Coerced by the Villains?*

Even if Paul was not confused when composing the letter, there is another explanation for his eccentric theological statements. The letter is confusing since it is a hasty response to an acute situation. The Judaizing antagonists[49] have launched an attack from Jerusalem[50] on Pauline congregations, importing a radically different theology. Paul has to react rapidly and forcefully in order to regain his position[51] among the addressees, and to save the genuine Christian doctrine.[52] This haste explains why his theology in the letter is somewhat exag-

---

49. The majority of scholars are inclined to see the antagonists as Judaizing Christians. Other hypotheses (that they are local Jews, Gentile converts, gnostics, zealots, pneumatics, etc.) have not gained wider support. For an overview, see Longenecker, *Galatians*, pp. lxxvii-c; Fung, *Galatians*, pp. 3-9.

50. Longenecker, *Galatians*, p. xcv. Or at least they may have been in contact with Jerusalem (Fung, *Galatians*, pp. 8-9).

51. According to Ridderbos, *The Epistle of Paul*, p. 18, it is a traditional view that the antagonists were attempting to 'cut off the effect of Paul's work', directly challenging Paul's status (p. 15); Longenecker, *Galatians*, p. xcv, although they claimed not to be opposing him .

52. Cf. Ridderbos, *The Epistle of Paul*, pp. 15-18.

gerated. The theology is less important than winning the battle. This, in turn, indicates either a careless or an opportunistic attitude on the part of the apostle.

But was the situation too urgent to produce proper theology? According to Longenecker, one of our main sources for the situation in Galatians is the opening statement: 1.6-9.[53] However, the rhetorical function of these verses, although within the *exordium*,[54] is already that of a *narratio*: the speaker describes the situation in seemingly neutral terms, in order to prepare for his forthcoming arguments. This is one of the most effective means of persuasion.[55] Therefore these verses must be read with great suspicion.

For many scholars one of the clearest proofs of the apostle's haste is 1.6 (οὕτως ταχέως). It shows for them that the exigency of Galatians was acute.[56] However, this expression is of rhetorical origin[57] and 'should not be used too quickly to date the letter'.[58] It rather refers to the ease with which the addressees were allegedly won over by the antagonists.[59]

Another sign of the haste is the vicious nature of the antagonists, whose rapid invasion seems to have posed an imminent danger to the congregation. Unfortunately, our only source for the antagonists' conduct is Paul's polemic attack on them, and there are risks in such 'mirror reading'.[60] It is likely that the one-sided dispute yields an unbalanced picture of the antagonists and even of the whole situation.[61]

53. Longenecker, *Galatians*, p. xcv; another source is the postscript in 6.11-18.

54. Cf. Betz, *Galatians*, pp. 44-45. Against him I claim that the epistolary opening phrases, 1.1-5, also serve as *exordium*—Betz's inability to recognize this is due to his misunderstanding of the relationship between rhetoric and epistolography (see L. Thurén, *The Rhetorical Strategy of 1 Peter with Special Regard to Ambiguous Expressions* [Åbo: Åbo Academy Press, 1990], pp. 60-61).

55. See J.D. O'Banion, 'Narration and Argumentation: Quintilian on *Narratio* as the Heart of Rhetorical Thinking', *Rhetorica* 5 (1987), pp. 325-51; L. Thurén, 'Risky Rhetoric in James?', *NovT* 37 (1995), pp. 262-84 (271).

56. See Guthrie, *Galatians*, p. 61; Ridderbos, *The Epistle of Paul*, pp. 15, 46-47; Fung, *Galatians*, p. 44; Longenecker, *Galatians*, p. lxv.

57. Mussner, *Der Galaterbrief*, p. 53 n. 54.

58. Betz, *Galatians*, pp. 47-48.

59. Thus Rohde, *Der Brief des Paulus*, pp. 38-39.

60. J.M.G. Barclay, 'Mirror-Reading a Polemical Letter: Galatians as a Test Case', *JSNT* 31 (1987), pp. 73-93; Longenecker, *Galatians*, p. lxxxix.

61. W. Schmithals, *Paul and the Gnostics* (trans. J. Steely; Nashville: Abingdon Press, 1972), p. 18, even argues that Paul did not know the situation very well, and

Longenecker warns us of the difficulty of such an approach, but laments that this is the only way to proceed.[62] Barclay, too, is aware of the problem. He even acknowledges the rhetorical nature of the text, and provides seven criteria for assessing the reliable facts.[63] However, he fails to see the most obvious factor affecting the description of the antagonists: the technique called *vituperatio*.

Knowledge of *vituperatio* brings us a means for a critical reading of such a polemic. In antiquity, as in modern cultures, there were certain conventional ways of vilifying the antagonists and of adjusting the situation at hand to suit the wishes of the speaker. A comparison with such conventions explains many things.

Classical forms of vilification are found throughout the letter. Du Toit's study has highlighted some common customs of this persuasive device in both religious and philosophical treatises.[64] The author was supposed to use standard labels when describing his opponents.[65] In fact, the technique was so well known to both partners in communication, that no one took them at their face value.[66] They were either hyperbolical or purely fictive. Thus it is an elementary mistake to regard such stereotypical labels as historical information.

Almost every device presented in du Toit's article on vilification can be found in Galatians.[67] The antagonists are censured for their *hypocrisy* (2.13) and labeled with a ψευδ-prefix (2.4);[68] they are accused of *sorcery* (3.1)[69] and of *moral depravity* (6.12-13, even 2.4)[70] or a *perversive influence* (1.7; 5.10; 5.12);[71] they are presented as *ludicrous*

W. Marxsen, *Introduction to the New Testament* (trans. G. Buswell; Oxford: Basil Blackwell, 1968), p. 53, claims that he misunderstood the whole thing.

62. Longenecker, *Galatians*, p. lxxxix.

63. Barclay, 'Mirror-Reading', pp. 73-93.

64. For other literature, see also Thurén, 'Hey Jude!', p. 458 n. 45.

65. L.T. Johnson, 'The New Testament's Anti-Jewish Slander and the Conventions of Ancient Polemic', *JBL* 108 (1987), pp. 419-41 (432-33).

66. See Johnson, 'The New Testament's Anti-Jewish Slander', pp. 423-33; A. du Toit, 'Vilification as a Pragmatic Device in Early Christian Epistolography', *Bib* 75 (1994), pp. 403-12 (411).

67. Another good example is the letter of Jude; see Thurén, 'Hey Jude!'.

68. Du Toit, 'Vilification', p. 405.

69. Du Toit, 'Vilification', p. 407.

70. Du Toit, 'Vilification', p. 408.

71. Du Toit, 'Vilification', p. 409.

characters (5.12)[72] and threatened with *eschatological judgment* (1.8-9; 5.10).[73] To 'reveal' the opponents' *secret intentions* is also an effective means of impugning their trustworthiness (2.4; 6.13).

The purpose of such statements was not to describe the antagonists, but to signal that they are the bad guys. Their *ethos* was decreased in order to dissociate the addressees from them.[74] By such defamation the author wants to alienate the addressees from the antagonists, to protect them from their influence.

Were the antagonists foreigners? Longenecker presents as a *communis opinio* that the antagonists were not local, since the apostle so frequently distinguishes them from the addressees. As the strongest evidence he adduces the use of the word τινες.[75] However, this is a common device for such a task, having clearly a pejorative function in Gal. 1.7 and 2.12.[76]

Hong argues that since the antagonists are mentioned in the third person and the addressees in the second, the former must be intruders.[77] If, however, the separation of the two groups was Paul's main goal, the distinction of the persons tells us nothing about their origin. If the antagonists were a group within the congregation, such a distinction is precisely what Paul should have made in order to protect the addressees from their influence.

Further proof that the antagonists were not natives could be 2.4, in which they are claimed to have *infiltrated* and *intruded* among the addressees to *spy*.[78] But even these images belong to standard labels.

72. Du Toit, 'Vilification', p. 410. He refers to W. Lütgert (*Gesetz und Geist. Zur Vorgeschichte des Galaterbriefes* [BFCT, 22.6; Gütersloh: Bertelsmann, 1919], pp. 31ff.) as the worst example of deriving historical data from vilifying labels. Lütgert finds the Cybele-cult behind this verse.

73. Du Toit, 'Vilification', p. 410.

74. Cf. du Toit, 'Vilification', p. 412.

75. Longenecker, *Galatians*, p. xciv.

76. Cf. du Toit, 'Vilification', p. 406. For more on alienation as a persuasive device in Galatians, see A. du Toit, 'Alienation and Re-identification as Tools of Persuasion in Galatians', *Neot* 26 (1992), pp. 279-95.

77. I.-G. Hong, *The Law in Galatians* (JSNTSup, 81; Sheffield: JSOT Press, 1993), p. 117.

78. Longenecker, *Galatians*, p. 51, claims that these are 'of course' Paul's own terms, meaning that the opponents did not so regard themselves, and in a sense this may be true. However, the terms themselves are hardly of Pauline origin.

Derived from military and political language[79] they are used also in 2 Pet. 2.11 and Jude 4. The villains are presented as obscure strangers or 'undercover agents', whereas the addressees are good citizens. Even these labels tell us more about the goals of the author than the actual circumstances in the congregation. The fact that Paul condemns his opponents as intruders does not mean that they actually were such. Thus Munck's thesis—that the antagonists were Paul's own converts, who under the influence of the Old Testament and the news from Jerusalem were attracted by Jewish customs—cannot easily be refuted.[80]

We can conclude that these stereotypical devices do not provide us with much reliable historical information about the antagonists. It is possible that they were dishonest, hypocritical newcomers to the congregation with evil intentions. But this is not undoubtedly indicated in the text. Instead, the technique used tells us something important about Paul's purpose: to dramatize the situation and to alienate the antagonists from the addressees in order to exclude their influence. But the very same labels could have been used by the opponents about Paul himself.

To sum up: the letter may give the impression of haste, but nothing in the situation actually indicates that Paul was in too much of a hurry to think before writing.

4. *The Antagonists' Theology Described?*

We have reason to believe that just as Paul's stereotypical 'description' of the antagonists' ethics, motives or social status presumably did not match exactly with reality—and was never even meant to be taken as so doing—so his implications of their theological standpoint are also exaggerated. Although the antagonists' teaching could not be derided as easily as their way of life—there was always the risk of losing one's credibility—even theological description can be distorted so that it does not depict the antagonists' actual teaching. As with any caricature, this could be easily seen by the audience without ruining the goal. There is no reason to think either that the speaker believes in the caricature or that he is lying to the audience.

Paul's description of the antagonists has often been interpreted as a

79. Betz, *Galatians*, pp. 89-91.
80. J. Munck, *Paul and the Salvation of Mankind* (London: SCM Press, 1959), p. 131. This is, of course, not to say that Munck is necessarily right.

characterization of Judaism. But is this reasonable? By rhetorical polarization and *synkrisis*[81] Paul highlights the antithesis between salvation through the law and the central elements of Christianity. In many instances Paul claims that righteousness through the law excludes Christ, grace, faith and promise: Gal. 2.16, 21; 3.2-5, 6, 11, 12, 14, 17, 18, 21-25; 5.4. There is indeed a 'sharp distinction between two sets of concepts'.[82]

Räisänen shows how this antithetical technique has led Christian exegetes to produce 'a desolate picture of "late Judaism"', which is still widely accepted, although it is only a 'vicious caricature' (*sic*).[83] Only after the studies of Moore, Limbeck and Sanders are we slowly learning that this picture is false.[84]

Räisänen first acknowledges that Paul only speaks of Christian Judaizers, not of Jews,[85] and asks whether Paul is at all to be blamed for the later Christians' distorted picture of Judaism.[86] But failing to answer this seemingly rhetorical question,[87] he nevertheless ends up by stating that Paul attacked the law 'as *the Jewish* gateway to righteousness'.[88] He claims that 'Paul either (implicitly, at least) gives an inaccurate picture [of Palestinian Judaism], or else bases his view on insufficient and uncharacteristic evidence'.[89]

But Galatians does not visualize Jewish soteriology.[90] We find no indication that Paul would have tried to convince his addressees, or that he is neutrally describing the faith of his Judaizing opponents, let alone Palestinian Judaism. It is not Paul, but the modern exegetes' unnatural, static way of reading his writings that gives a picture of a postulated

---

81. For the device and its use in Hebrews, see C.F. Evans, *The Theology of Rhetoric: The Epistle to the Hebrews* (London: Dr Williams's Trust, 1988); T.W. Seid, 'The Rhetorical Form of the Melchizedek/Christ Comparison in Hebrews 7' (PhD Dissertation, Brown University, 1996).

82. Räisänen, *Paul and the Law*, p. 163.

83. Räisänen, *Paul and the Law*, pp. 164-65, 168.

84. Räisänen, *Paul and the Law*, pp. 165-68.

85. Räisänen, *Paul and the Law*, p. 162.

86. Räisänen, *Paul and the Law*, p. 168.

87. Instead, Räisänen, *Paul and the Law*, p. 168, rephrases his question with a wholly different problem: 'is Paul's critical attitude toward Torah rooted in *anthropology* or *Christology*?' (his emphasis).

88. Räisänen, *Paul and the Law*, p. 177; my emphasis.

89. Räisänen, *Paul and the Law*, p. 181.

90. Against Räisänen, *Paul and the Law*, p. 184.

religion attempting to gain righteousness through the Law.[91]

Speaking of the views of his opponents, Paul does not actually attribute to them the overstated legalistic soteriology which he is discussing. On the contrary, they are said *not* to fulfill the law, and are alleged to be interested in circumcision *not* in order to gain salvation, but to avoid persecution because of Christ (6.12-13). If Paul sought to imply that his opponents agreed with the position, which is presented in the letter as an antithesis to his own theology, he would hardly describe them in this way.

Instead, the 'legalistic' soteriology is composed and presented by Paul himself. It reflects a pedagogically overstated, theoretical view of possible consequences of the antagonists' theology. In order to counteract somebody's ideas, it is often effective to exaggerate and redefine them in order to reveal their 'true nature'. This may not be fair, but is at least good rhetoric.

This is exactly what Paul is doing with his opponents. He sees the antagonists' theology as 'yeast', and his mission is to show how it can 'leaven the whole batch of dough', namely, the Christian theology (or the addressees' faith) (Gal. 5.9).

Thus, we do not need Sanders's research to perceive the burlesque nature of the idea of salvation through the law: a glance at the persuasive techniques of Galatians suffices. The caricature is not due to later interpreters, but was produced already by Paul himself. By driving the views of his opponents *ad absurdum*, Paul portrays the possible result of their theology. Only thereby can he show why the opponents' seemingly Christian teaching is incompatible with his own.

Summing up this far, we cannot conclude from the information in Galatians that the outward situation in the congregation was particularly dramatic. The individuals whom Paul opposes were probably not religious and ethical monsters; their version of Christianity hardly differed much from that of Paul. We do not know whether they came from elsewhere or whether they just represent ideas inherent in the congregation. Probably neither they nor Paul's (other) addressees saw the situation as urgent.

Consequently some commentators argue that there is no indication that the opponents presented themselves as especially hostile to Paul.[92]

91. Cf. Räisänen, *Paul and the Law*, p. 188.

92. See especially G. Howard, *Paul's Crisis in Galatia* (SNTSMS, 35; Cambridge: Cambridge University Press, 1979), pp. 1-19.

Whereas Jewett believes that they were just pretending to be on Paul's side,[93] Howard wonders whether they even had any intention of opposing the apostle.[94] At least it is probable that the antagonists saw themselves as representives of orthodox Christianity.[95]

5. *Galatians as Dramatization*

Why, then, is Galatians such a frantic letter? As a literary phenomenon, the emotional, aggressive and dramatizing character of Galatians is primarily a matter of *style*, not direct evidence of the apostle's actual feelings. The scholars' inability to see this is attributable to negligence of style in modern exegetical research. As stylistic studies formerly tended to be technical classifications of devices, paying little attention to the pragmatic function of the style, even the emergent rhetorical research has put this subject at a disadvantage.[96]

In fact, stylistic matters should often be given priority when studying New Testament texts, as they can reveal the author's goal. The style of a particularly rhetorically conscious text was never fortuitous; instead it was an important means of persuasion. Thus stylistic features should not be seen naively as errors.

In Galatians, the agonizing style fits well into the rhetorical exigency, as does the pompous style of 2 Peter. It was the apostle who sought trouble and controversy. It is obvious that Paul himself assessed the situation as serious. The seemingly slight shift in the teaching—the question of certain religious rites—was for him theoretically decisive.

The argumentative situation is difficult, however, since the addressees fail to think similarly. Paul has to mobilize all his rhetorical skills to polarize and dramatize the situation, in order to paint a stark picture and force the addressees to choose between the alternatives.

This requires him to alienate the addressees from the antagonists as effectively as possible (exactly what he accuses his antagonists of

93. Longenecker, *Galatians*, p. xciii.
94. Howard, *Paul's Crisis*, pp. 1-19.
95. Betz, *Galatians*, pp. 89-91.
96. I have discussed this issue more thoroughly at our Pretoria conference, using 2 Peter as a test case: L. Thurén, 'Style Never Goes out of Fashion: 2 Peter Re-evaluated', in S.E. Porter and T.H. Olbricht (eds.), *Rhetoric, Scripture and Theology: Essays from the 1994 Pretoria Conference* (JSNTSup, 131; Sheffield: Sheffield Academic Press, 1996), pp. 329-47.

trying to do in 4.17), and to widen the theological gap as much as he can. Some specific tools for this purpose can be detected.

a. *Labeling the Opponents*

From the aforesaid heavy use of vilification as a device I have already concluded that Paul assumes that the addressees did not look askance on his antagonists or their theology. They did not find the situation as especially critical or dramatic. The device is thereby also a tool for *dramatizing* the situation, for seeking confrontation with the opponents.

b. *Mighty Expressions*

When in 1.16-22 Paul highlights the different origin of his gospel, it is evident that he emphasizes his independence from the apostles in Jerusalem and the distance between him and them.

But the point is often not so much what Paul says, but how he says it: Paul recommends an uncompromising attitude. The dissuasive, emotional emphasis is evident in the gently modifying expressions of the *narratio*. Thus, when Paul proclaims that he 'opposed Kephas [κατὰ πρόσωπον] *to his face*' (2.11), the point is not that he and Peter had different opinions, but the thespian, aggressive way he told this to Peter.[97] Similarly, in 2.5 Paul adds a stark, almost melodramatic, adverb: 'We did not give into them, *even for a moment* [πρὸς ὥραν]'.[98]

The confrontation is depicted by the use of hyperbole, at its best or worst. If somebody does not agree with Paul, he is immediately ἀνάθεμα, *cursed* (1.8-9). Paul received no Christian education whatsoever from any man (1.12-20). He was very advanced in Judaism and persecuted the Christians, καθ' ὑπερβολήν (1.13-14), etc.

c. *Absolute Theology*

5.2-3 and 5.9 express the same absolute, climactic attitude concerning

97. The commentators tend to be so excited about the episode itself that they miss this stylistic feature: Rohde, *Der Brief des Paulus*, pp. 100-105; Fung, *Galatians*, pp. 106-109. Longenecker (*Galatians*, pp. 62-72) even undermines the expression. The exceptions include Mussner (*Der Galaterbrief*, p. 137 n. 15), who referring *inter alia* to Polybius translates 'rückhaltslos, in aller Öffentlichkeit' and Betz, *Galatians*, p. 106 n. 443. But even they do not dwell on the message of the exceptional expression.

98. Fung observes the absolutist role of the expression (*Galatians*, p. 94), whereas usually the scholars preoccupied with theology neglect the powerful signal given thereby.

theology: 'If you let yourselves be circumcised, Christ will be of no use to you at all'. The slightest deviation from Paul's doctrine will ruin everything, since 'a little yeast leavens the whole batch of dough'. What the addressees (and possibly the antagonists) see as completing Paul's message, or possibly regard as a slightly different nuance, is presented by the apostle as an enormous error and deviation.

In the *peroratio*, the author usually writes openly, without unduly complicated strategies.[99] In Galatians, we find too obvious a contradiction. Previously Paul claimed unconditionally and emphatically: 'If you receive circumcision, Christ will do you no good at all...every man who receives circumcision is obligated to keep the entire law' (5.2-3). As a symbol of deviation from Paul's version of Christianity circumcision can ruin everything. But in the *peroratio* he rephrases a slogan.[100] 'Neither circumcision nor uncircumcision means anything [οὔτε τί ἐστίν]' (6.15): A minor surgical operation as such means nothing.

Taken at their face value, the verses reveal an enormous inconsistency and logical break. However, their rhetorical nature is too obvious to be misunderstood. It sounds as if Paul admitted that he has overreacted to the question about circumcision. What is really important is not this question but Christ. Yet he has tried to show that this little 'yeast' can be fatal for the Galatians.

To conclude it can be stated that the text does not indicate that Paul saw any dramatic difference in the practical life between the two versions of Christianity in Galatia. He attempts to make his addressees aware of the theoretical, theological difference, and does so by dramatizing rhetoric.

The emotional, exaggerating and dramatizing style befits the dissuasive goal of the epistle. The disturbing, impassioned ambience is intended to enable the addressees to perceive the imminent danger beneath a calm surface. By creating an urgent, black-and-white situation the apostle invites the addressees to take a stand. Thus the style simply meets the rhetorical exigency of the text.

We cannot know whether Paul's ultimate motives were purely theological or whether they had pertained chiefly to his personal authority.[101] But the immediate aim of Galatians is clear: to dramatize the

---

99. See Thurén, 'Risky Rhetoric in James?', p. 273.

100. Longenecker, *Galatians*, pp. 295-96.

101. Against du Toit ('Alienation', pp. 279-80), who only makes emphatic claims, but provides no arguments. We can never reach the possible, unspoken, intentions of the author.

situation. The apostle sought thereby to regain his absolute theological authority over the congregations, which in turn was needed for renewing the addressees' 'allegiance to the one and only true gospel'. In this difficult task Paul hardly acted without thought. The letter is a stylistic and rhetorical masterpiece, and there is no reason to doubt that the same applies to its theology.

But simultaneously: here the very rhetorical techniques enable us to see Paul's theology. This kind of rhetorical absolutizing of the actual, in practice similar alternatives—Paul or the local 'Judaizing' Christians as authority—*is theology*. Paul attempts to display as vividly as possible the different religious, principal structures of thought behind the practical life.

6. *Conclusion*

Instead of making another rhetorical analysis of Galatians, I have made use of existing studies. Thereby, I have attempted to filter the effect of various persuasive techniques from expressions in the letter, which are commonly utilized for the acquisition of historical and theological information. I hope that this kind of a study enables the theology of Galatians to be compared more easily with, for example, Romans. Whether or not Professor Dunn agrees with my rhetorical interpretation of Galatians, he at least can no longer claim that such a perspective is irrelevant for studying Pauline theology.

Part IV

RHETORICAL INTERPRETATION OF HEBREWS AND IGNATIUS

SYNKRISIS IN HEBREWS 7:
THE RHETORICAL STRUCTURE AND STRATEGY

Timothy W. Seid

At the eleventh hour of my doctoral research on synkrisis (comparison) in Hebrews, I happened to come across the article 'Hebrews as Amplification' by Thomas H. Olbricht.[1] You can imagine my anxiety as I read, expecting to find my 'original contribution to scholarship' already in print. Fortunately, although Dr Olbricht came close to my conclusions, I still think I have something significant to add.[2]

In fact, several scholars have mentioned synkrisis in relation to Hebrews. Harold Attridge begins his section on Heb. 3.1-6 by saying, 'Thus this new segment of the text begins, as did the first, with a synkrisis or comparison'.[3] He gives no description of what he means by the transliterated Greek term σύγκρισις. David Aune also uses this term regarding Hebrews. In his opinion, 'The rhetorical strategy of the author is based on a comparison (*synkrisis*) between the old and the new'.[4] Again, there is no elaboration on what this term means beyond the simple translated meaning of comparison. In an unpublished paper, Lee Zachary Maxey briefly identifies several portions of Hebrews as containing synkrisis.[5] The only person who describes what synkrisis is and how it functions in Hebrews does so in an unlikely book and in an

1. Thomas H. Olbricht, 'Hebrews as Amplification', in S.E. Porter and T.H. Olbricht (eds.), *Rhetoric and the New Testament: Essays from the 1992 Heidelberg Conference* (JSNTSup, 90; Sheffield: JSOT Press, 1993), pp. 375-87.

2. See 'The Rhetorical Form of the Melchizedek/Christ Comparison in Hebrews 7' (PhD Dissertation, Brown University, 1996).

3. Harold W. Attridge, *The Epistle to the Hebrews: A Commentary on the Epistle to the Hebrews* (Hermeneia; Philadelphia: Fortress Press, 1989), p. 104.

4. David E. Aune, *The New Testament in its Literary Environment* (LEC; Philadelphia: Westminster Press, 1987), p. 213.

5. Lee Zachary Maxey, 'The Preacher as Rhetorician: The Rhetorical Structure and Design of Hebrews 12:4-13' (Unpublished paper for The Institute for Antiquity and Christianity at the Claremont Graduate School), pp. 77-78.

unlikely place.[6] Günther Zuntz, in his *The Text of the Epistles*, discusses synkrisis as follows:

> I ought perhaps to have said that one of the reasons, with me, for regarding Hebrews as, originally, a homily is the excessive use which it makes of the rhetorical method of *synkrisis*. This is a traditional device of encomiastic Greek and Latin rhetoric: the person, or object, to be praised is placed beside outstanding specimens of a comparable kind and his, or its, superiority ('ὑπεροχή') urged (type: 'Hercules overcame the lion, but you...'). The student of Hebrews who peruses, for example, Lucian's 'Praise of the fly' can hardly fail to be amused by the close analogies of method in this humorous piece of writing; beginning with τοσοῦτον ἀπαλώτερα ἔχουσα τὰ πτερὰ ὅσον κτλ. (Luc. I), cf. Heb. i. 4 τοσούτῳ κρείττων γενόμενος ἀγγέλων ὅσῳ κτλ. F. Focke ('Synkrisis', in *Hermes*, viii, 1923, 327 ff., esp. 335 ff.) has put this traditional device of the rhetorical schools (see, for example, Quintilian ii. 4. 21) into a larger context. The classical paradigm, already with Aristotle, was Isocrates, *Euagoras* (esp. 34 ff. and 66: τίνα γὰρ..., cf. Heb. i. 5). Aristotle himself (*Rhet.* i. 9, 1368a 20) gives the recipes for this and other devices for 'magnification' (αὔξησις). The rhetorical handbooks of the Roman period, such as Theon and Hermogenes, develop them; the schools practised them; writings such as Plutarch's *De virtute Alexandri* and laudatory speeches like the Latin panegyrics, and Eusebius' of Constantine, live by them. And so does Hebrews, in contrasting Jesus, and his Church, with angels, Moses, Melchizedek, high-priests, the synagogue, the 'heroes of faith', &c. At the same time, Hebrews is materially a midrash on, mainly, Pss. 94 and 109 and Jer. 31.30 ff. It is a midrash in rhetorical Greek prose—it is a homily.[7]

Zuntz's conclusions speak to the precise problem of identifying the literary genre of Hebrews. Does Hebrews contain midrash with its concomitant rabbinic hermeneutical methodology, or does Hebrews conform to some type of Greek rhetoric—or is it both?

I have followed the logic which suggests that one should first look to the tradition of the language within which a document was written. This is especially germane to the study of Hebrews since its Greek is recognized to be highly polished in its vocabulary, grammar and figures

---

6. Cited by F.F. Bruce, *The Epistle to the Hebrews* (NICNT; Grand Rapids: Eerdmans, 1964), p. xlviii n. 111. C.F. Evans also builds on Zuntz in his brief monograph *The Theology of Rhetoric: The Epistle to the Hebrews* (London: Dr Williams's Trust, 1988).

7. Günther Zuntz, *The Text of the Epistles* (London: British Academy, 1953), p. 286.

of speech, and the Greek documentary evidence precedes the appearance of Jewish midrash. Indeed, it is generally recognized that rabbinic hermeneutics was built upon the principles of Greek logic and argumentation.[8] It makes sense to look first to the primary (and prior) linguistic tradition, and only when it provides no satisfying points of similarity should one investigate other literary influences.

I have argued elsewhere that midrash is not an appropriate designation for Hebrews.[9] In short, I demonstrate that it is an ambiguous term:

8.   Saul Lieberman, *Greek in Jewish Palestine* (New York: Jewish Theological Seminary of America, 1942; repr. New York: Feldheim, 1965); *idem, Hellenism in Jewish Palestine* (New York: Jewish Theological Seminary, 1962); *idem*, 'How Much Greek in Jewish Palestine?', in H. Fischel (ed.), *Essays in Greco-Roman and Related Talmudic Literature* (New York: Ktav, 1977), pp. 325-43; David Daube, 'Rabbinic Methods of Interpretation and Hellenistic Rhetoric', *HUCA* 22 (1949), pp. 239-64; Martin Hengel, *Judaism and Hellenism* (trans. John Bowden; Philadelphia: Fortress Press, 1981), p. 81; E.E. Hallewy, 'The Writers of the Aggada and the Greek Grammarians', *Tarbiz* 29 (1959–60), pp. 47-55; *idem*, 'Biblical Midrash and Homeric Exegesis', *Tarbiz* 31 (1961–62), pp. 157-69, 264-80.

9.   The secondary literature consulted includes Lewis M. Barth, 'Reading Rabbinic Bible Exegesis', in W.S. Green (ed.), *Approaches to Ancient Judaism: Studies in Liturgy, Exegesis, and Talmudic Narrative*, IV (BJS; Chico, CA: Scholars Press, 1983), pp. 81-93; Renée Bloch, 'Midrash', in W.S. Green (ed.), *Approaches to Ancient Judaism: Theory and Practice*, I (trans. Mary Howard Callaway; BJS; Missoula, MT: Scholars Press, 1978), pp. 29-50; Shaye J.D. Cohen, *From the Maccabees to the Mishnah* (LEC; Philadelphia: Westminster Press, 1987); Michael Fishbane (ed.), *The Midrashic Imagination: Exegesis, Thought and History* (Albany: State University of New York, 1993); M. Gertner, 'Midrashim in the New Testament', *JSS* 7 (1962), pp. 267-92 (268-69); Joseph Heinemann, 'The Art of Composition in Leviticus Rabbah', *HaSifrut* (1969–70), pp. 808-34; *idem*, 'Profile of a Midrash: The Art of Composition in Leviticus Rabbah', *JAAR* 39 (1971), pp. 141-50; Martin S. Jaffee, 'The "Midrashic" Proem: Towards the Description of Rabbinic Exegesis', in Green (ed.), *Approaches to Ancient Judaism*, IV, pp. 95-112; R. LeDéaut, 'A propos d'une définition du midrash', *Bib* 50 (1969), pp. 395-413; Jacob Neusner, 'History and Midrash', *Judaism* 9 (1960), pp. 47-54; *idem, What Is Midrash?* (Guides to Biblical Scholarship; Philadelphia: Fortress Press, 1987); Gary G. Porton, 'Defining Midrash', in J. Neusner (ed.), *The Study of Ancient Judaism. I. Mishnah, Midrash, Siddur* (New York: Ktav, 1981), pp. 59-92; Gary G. Porton, 'Midrash: Palestinian Jews and the Hebrew Bible in the Greco-Roman Period', *ANRW* 19.2, pp. 103-38; *idem, Understanding Rabbinic Midrash: Texts and Commentary* (Hoboken, NJ: Ktav, 1985); Anthony J. Saldarini, 'Judaism and the New Testament', in E.J. Epp and G.W. MacRae (eds.), *The New Testament and its Modern Interpreters* (The Bible and its Modern Interpreters; Philadelphia: Fortress Press, 1989), pp. 27-54; Richard S. Sarason, 'Toward a New Agendum for

in its vague sense of 'commentary' it is not very helpful; in its proper usage it refers to a body of literature for which there is virtually no evidence prior to the third century. All attempts to discover an early form of midrash contained in synagogue sermons is based only on conjectural literary evidence and on an inadequate understanding of first-century synagogues.[10]

There is, however, much literary evidence for synkrisis. Descriptions of synkrisis are to be found in Aristotle's *Ars Rhetorica* (e.g. 1368a19-29), *Rhet. ad Alex.* 1441a28–30, and Quintilian's *Institutio Oratoria* 2.4.21, as well as the *Progymnasmata* of Theon, Hermogenes and Aphthonius. It can be illustrated by its usage in encomium—as Olbricht correctly identified it—with Isocrates's *Helen* 24–25 and *Evagoras* 37–39 and in its independent function, for example, as appendixes to the *Lives* of Plutarch.

Synkrisis is the comparison of two subjects of similar quality and is characterized by comparative exchanges (often with the μέν...δέ construction) which praise (or censure) one subject by drawing parallels to a model subject often using the common topics of encomium in order to persuade the audience to modify their character and behavior accordingly.

Through the course of trying to prove the existence of synkrisis in Hebrews 7, I began to see it occurring throughout Hebrews. Others have identified the hortatory sections of Hebrews but have considered the rest of Hebrews to be exposition of a midrashic nature. Instead of viewing this alternation in Hebrews as exposition/exhortation, I have labeled this synkrisis/paraenesis. As a result, I offer the following outline of Hebrews and then give a survey of the document given this rubric:[11]

the Study of Rabbinic Midrashic Literature', in E. Fleischer and J. Petuchowski (eds.), *Studies in Aggadah, Targum and Jewish Liturgy in Memory of Joseph Heinemann* (Jerusalem: Magnes Press, 1981), pp. 55-73; E. Stein, 'Ein jüdisch-hellenistischer Midrasch über den Auszug aus Ägypten', *MGWJ* 78 (1934), pp. 241-52; Geza Vermes, 'Bible and Midrash: Early Old Testament Exegesis', in P.R. Ackroyd and C.F. Evans (ed.), *The Cambridge History of the Bible* (3 vols,; Cambridge: Cambridge University Press, 1970), I, pp. 199-231; Addison G. Wright, 'The Literary Genre Midrash', *CBQ* 28 (1966), pp. 105-38, 415-57; Solomon Zeitlin, 'Midrash: A Historical Study', *JQR* 44 (1953), pp. 21-36.

10. Cohen, *From the Maccabees*, p. 111.

11. Some of the main treatments on the structure of Hebrews include David Alan Black, 'The Problem of the Literary Structure of Hebrews: An Evaluation and

Outline of Hebrews

Angels (1.1–2.18):	Synkrisis of Son and Angels (1.1-14)
	Paraenesis (2.1-18)
Moses (3.1–4.16):	Synkrisis of Moses and Christ the Son (3.1-6)
	Paraenesis (3.7–4.16)
Aaron (5.1–6.20):	Synkrisis of Aaron and Christ (5.1-10)
	Paraenesis (5.11–6.20)
Melchizedek (7.1–8.3):	Synkrisis of Melchizedek/Christ and Levitical
	Priesthood (7.1-25):
	Paraenesis (7.26–8.3)
Covenant (8.4–10.18):	Synkrisis of First Covenant and New Covenant
	(8.4–10.18)
	Paraenesis (10.19–12.29)
Epistolary Appendix (13.1-25)	

Nevertheless, I wish to focus here on Hebrews 7, since the interpretation of it is paradigmatic for an understanding of the rest of the book.

Commentators interpret this section as a midrash because of the quotation of Scripture. Yet they describe the chapter as a comparison.

a Proposal', *GTJ* 7 (1986), pp. 163-77; Louis Dussaut, *Synopse structurelle de l'épître aux Hébreux: Approache d'analyse structurelle* (Paris: Cerf, 1981); George H. Guthrie, *The Structure of Hebrews: A Text-Linguistic Analysis* (NovTSup, 73; Leiden: E.J. Brill, 1994); R. Gyllenberg, 'Die Komposition des Hebräerbriefs', *SEÅ* 22–23 (1957–58), pp. 137-47; Barnabas Lindars, 'The Rhetorical Structure of Hebrews', *NTS* 35 (1989), pp. 382-406; Linda Lloyd Neeley, 'A Discourse Analysis of Hebrews', *Occasional Papers in Translation and Textlinguistics* 3–4 (1987), pp. 1-146; Olbricht, 'Hebrews as Amplification', pp. 375-87; James Swetnam, 'Form and Content in Hebrews 1–6', *Bib* 53 (1972), pp. 368-85; *idem*, 'Form and Content in Hebrews 7–13', *Bib* 55 (1974), pp. 333-48; *idem*, 'On the Literary Genre of the "Epistle" to the Hebrews', *NovT* 11 (1969), pp. 261-69; T.C.G. Thornton, 'Review of *La structure littéraire de l'épître aux Hébreux* by Albert Vanhoye', *JTS* 15 (1964), pp. 137-41; Walter Überlacker, *Der Hebräerbrief als Appell: Untersuchungen zu exordium, narratio und postscriptum* (ConBNT, 21; Stockholm: Almqvist & Wiksell, 1989); Leon Vaganay, 'Le plan de l'épître aux Hébreux', in L.H. Vincent (ed.), *Memorial Lagrange* (Paris: J. Gabalda, 1940), pp. 269-77; Albert Vanhoye, 'Discussions sur la structure de l'épître aux Hébreux', *Bib* 55 (1974), pp. 349-80; *idem*, *La structure littéraire de l'épître aux Hébreux* (Studia Neotestamentica; Paris: Desclée De Brouwer, 1963); *idem*, 'Literarische Struktur und theologische Botschaft des Hebräerbriefs (1.Teil)', *SNT* 4 (1979), pp. 119-47; *idem*, 'Literarische Struktur und theologische Botschaft des Hebräerbriefs (2.Teil)', *SNT* 5 (1980), pp. 18-49; *idem*, *Structure and Message of the Epistle to the Hebrews* (trans. James Swetnam; Subsidea Biblica, 12; Rome: Pontifical Biblical Institute, 1989).

Attridge, for example, refers to it six times as comparison. Buchanan twice calls it a comparison. This statement from Fitzmyer is indeed ironical: 'Before turning to the new data, I must stress with several modern writers that the detailed comparison of Christ and Melchizedek in Heb. 7 is an excellent example of a midrash on Gen. 14.18-20'.[12] Actually, it is an excellent example of a comparison and only appears to have some things in common with midrash.[13] Upon closer examination, the features of this chapter do not function as a midrash would but do cohere as elements of a σύγκρισις.

My procedure will be to demonstrate the features of ch. 7 that indicate synkrisis. The most important indications are the common topics and the structure of comparative exchange. The overall tenor of the passage is indicative of Greek rhetoric and philosophical argumentation. There is no need to appeal to later rabbinic texts in order to understand the argument and concepts in ch. 7.

If one studies the rhetorical handbooks and model speeches, and then reads the actual speeches, one will generally find less rigidity, more spontaneity and a general adaptation of the guidelines to the particular situation and subject. Plutarch, for example, does not follow the same rigid set of topics for each of his comparisons. He finds whatever marks the individuals as similar and draws comparisons on that basis. There is, however, a tendency to formulate the comparative exchanges based on common topics. What we find in ch. 7 is this same type of practice. The author has built his comparisons based on those things which are points of similarity in order to show the superiority of the priesthood of Melchizedek to that of the Levitical priesthood and, consequently, since Jesus' priesthood is equal to that of Melchizedek, that Jesus is a superior high-priest. The main purpose of this argument is not so much a polemical or dogmatic one, but it consists of moral exhortation: since Jesus is a superior high-priest, he is able to provide a constancy of mediation by which the people of God will be able to endure temptation

12. Joseph A. Fitzmyer, *Essays on the Semitic Background of the New Testament* (London: Chapman, 1971), pp. 221, 222 (appeared earlier as 'Now This Melchizedek [Hebr 7:1]', *CBQ* 25 [1963], pp. 305-21).

13. Bloch distinguishes the function of this 'midrash' from others in that the author wished to draw from the biblical texts apologetic arguments rather than answers to actual questions (Renée Bloch, 'Midrash', in *Supplément au Dictionnaire de la Bible*, V, col. 1279; repr. in Renée Bloch, 'Midrash', in Green [ed.], *Approaches to Ancient Judaism*, I, pp. 29-50).

to sin and the hardship of suffering in order to remain faithful to God to the very end.

The basic outline of 7.1-25 is given below:

1. Introduction (7.1-4)
   a. Narration (7.1-2a)
   b. Meaning of Name (7.2b)
   c. Poetic Description of Topics (7.3)
      1. Parentage and Genealogy (7.3a)
      2. Birth and End of Life (7.3b)
      3. Office Remains in Perpetuity (7.3c)
   d. Introductory Statement: Greatness of Melchizedek (7.4)
2. Comparative Exchanges (7.5-25)
   a. Action: First Done (7.5-7)
   b. Status (7.8-10)
   c. Tribal Ancestry (7.11-17)
   d. Achievements (7.18-25)
      1. Introduction of Better Hope (7.18-19)
      2. Guarantee of Better Covenant (7.20-22)
      3. Long Lasting and for Others (7.23-25)

The following discussion is not intended to be a full exegetical treatment of every aspect of this rather long section. I shall develop a reading of the text which places it within its rhetorical context.

1. *Introduction (7.1-4)*

In the first four verses, the author establishes the basis for the comparison. He has already quoted the text concerning Melchizedek several times. He left off with this at 5.10 and has come back to this subject in 6.20. The quotation from Ps. 110.4 has three main points: (1) the one addressed is called a high-priest; (2) he holds the office 'forever' (εἰς τὸν αἰῶνα); (3) it is a Melchizedekan order of priesthood.

a. *Narration (7.1-2a)*

[1] οὗτος γὰρ ὁ Μελχισέδεκ, βασιλεὺς Σαλήμ, ἱερεὺς τοῦ θεοῦ τοῦ ὑψίστου, ὁ συναντήσας Ἀβραὰμ ὑποστρέφοντι ἀπὸ τῆς κοπῆς τῶν βασιλέων καὶ εὐλογήσας αὐτόν, [2] ᾧ καὶ δεκάτην ἀπὸ πάντων ἐμέρισεν Ἀβραάμ.

[1] For this one is the *Melchizedek, King of Salem...a priest of the Most High God,* the one who *met Abraham returning from the slaughter...of the kings ...* and who *blessed* him, [2] to whom also Abraham divided *a tenth from all.*

The author first explains who this character is with a narration constructed from the Gen. 14.17-19 account. In the translation above, words taken from the Genesis text are italicized, and ellipses designate where something has been left out from the original account. Whether the author was being selective or simply remembered the account the best he could is impossible to know. In any case, it is a concise statement of the events having to do with Melchizedek.

Aristotle described narration in ceremonial oratory—to which comparison is related—as not being continuous but intermittent:

> There must, of course, be some survey of the actions that form the subject-matter of the speech. You will have to recall well-known deeds among others; and because they are well known, the hearer usually needs no narration of them; none, for instance, if your object is the praise of Achilles; we all know the facts of his life—what you have to do is to apply those facts. But if your object is the praise of Critias, you must narrate his deeds, which not many people know of. The narration should depict character; to which end you must know what makes it do so. One such thing is the indication of moral purpose; the quality of purpose indicated determines the quality of character depicted and is itself determined by the end pursued (*Rhet.* 1416b–1417a).

Usually there is no need for a comparison to begin with a narrative or description. Comparisons are normally made of stock figures from history and mythology. In the case of Plutarch's comparisons in the *Lives*, the biographical sections preclude any need for narration within the comparisons. Plutarch does, however, begin the comparisons with a statement referring to what has been learned about the subjects for comparison:

> This is what I have learnt of Romulus and Theseus, worthy of memory [ἄξια μνήμης]. It seems, first of all… (*Thes.-Rom. synk.* 1.1).

> Having thus finished the lives [διεληλύθαμεν βίον] of Lycurgus and Numa, we shall now, though the work be difficult, put together their points of difference as they lie here before our view. Their points of likeness are obvious… (*Lyc.-Numa synk.* 1.1).

> We have here had two lives [οἱ μὲν οὖν βίοι τῶν ἀνδρῶν τοιαύτην ἔχουσιν ἱστορίαν] rich in examples (πολλὰ καὶ καλὰ παραδείγματα), both of civil and military excellence. Let us first compare the two men in their warlike capacity (*Per.-Fab. synk.* 1.1).

> Having described all their actions [δεκκειμένων δὲ τῶν πράξεων] that seem to deserve commemoration, their military ones, we may say, incline

the balance very decidedly upon neither side. They both, in pretty equal measure... (*Cor.-Alcib. synk.* 1.1).

Such being the story of these two great men's lives [τοιούτων δὲ τῶν κατὰ τὴν ἱστορίαν ὄντων], without doubt in the comparison very little difference will be found between them [δῆλον ὡς οὐκ ἔχει πολλὰς διαφορὰς οὐδ' ἀνομοιότητας ἡ σύγκρισις] (*Aem.-Tim. synk.* 1.1).

These are the memorable things I have found in historians [ἀναγραφῆς ἄξια τῶν ἱστορημένων] concerning Marcellus and Pelopidas. Betwixt which two great men, though in natural character and manners they nearly resemble each other... (*Pel.-Marc. synk.* 1.1).

Having mentioned the most memorable actions [ἀξίων μνήμης] of these great men, if we now compare [παρατεθείς] the whole life of the one with that of the other, it will not be easy to discern the difference between them... (*Arist.-Cato Maj. synk.* 1.1).

First then, as for the greatness of the benefits [μεγέθει τῶν εὐεργεσιῶν] which Titus conferred on Greece, neither Philopoemen, nor many braver men than he, can make good the parallel [παραβάλλειν] (*Phil.-Flam. synk.* 1.1).

Having completed [διεληλύθαμεν] this Life also, come we now to the comparison [σύγκρισιν]. That which was common to them both was that they were founders of their own greatness... (*Lys.-Sulla synk.* 1.1).

In the comparison [ἐν δὲ τῇ συγκρίσει πρῶτον] of these two, first, if we compare [παραβαλλόμενος]... (*Nic.-Crass. synk.* 1.1).

These are the most remarkable passages that are come to our knowledge [μνήμης ἄξια παρειλήφαμεν] concerning Eumenes and Sertorius. In comparing [συγκρίσει] their lives, we may observe that this was common to them both... (*Sert.-Eum. synk.* 1.1).

Thus having drawn out the history of the lives [ἐκκειμένων οὖν τῶν βίων] of Agesilaus and Pompey, the next thing is to compare them (*Ages.-Pomp. synk.* 1.1).

Having given an account [διηγήσεως] severally of these persons, it remains only that we should take a view of them in comparison with one another [ἐκ παραλλήλου τῶν βίων] (*Ag./Cleom.-Gracchi synk.* 1.1).

These are the most memorable circumstances recorded in history [ἃ...ἄξια μνήμης...τῶν ἱστορουμένων] of Demosthenes and Cicero which have come to our knowledge (*Demosth.-Cic. synk.* 1.1).

There are noble points in abundance in the characters of these two men, and one to be first mentioned is their attaining such a height of greatness upon such inconsiderable means [τοῦ μεγίστους ἐλαχίσταις ἀφορμαῖς γενέσθαι] (*Dion-Brut. synk.* 1.1).

From these examples it is evident that Plutarch introduced his synkriseis with a statement regarding the history and narrative of the subjects for comparison. In his situation the lives of the subjects had already been told. The author of Hebrews first gives a brief history of what is significant regarding Melchizedek.

Hebrews 7.1-2 is not a quotation, but only an allusion. The author does not use any introductory formula. The words are not an exact quotation of any extant text. It appears to be only a selective rendering highlighting the salient features of the events surrounding this figure Melchizedek, about whom the only other information is the reference in the psalms. It functions as a narrative upon which the comparison will be made.

b. *Meaning of Name (7.2b)*

> πρῶτον μὲν ἑρμηνευόμενος βασιλεὺς δικαιοσύνης ἔπειτα δὲ καὶ βασιλεὺς Σαλήμ, ὅ ἐστιν βασιλεὺς εἰρήνης.

> First of all, [Melchizedek] is in one way interpreted 'king of righteousness', but then also in another way 'king of Salem', which means 'king of peace'.

What is most peculiar about this verse is that the author makes no use of this word study. Virtually no relevance comes from it. There is no development of the concept of righteousness; there is no clear application of Salem with Jerusalem; there is virtually no argument built on kingship and messianism. All that is given is a pedantic etymological and philological treatment of the name Melchizedek. It is much less than we would expect if this were a true midrash in the rabbinic style.[14]

Certainly the rabbis were not the only ones to play with the meaning of names. Philo, for example, frequently gives the meaning of names in his *De congressu* (2, 20, 25, 30, 36, 40, 41-47, etc.). It is also part of Greek rhetoric. Aristotle described this form of argument based on names:

> Another line is to draw meanings from names. Sophocles, for instance, says, 'O steel in heart as thou art steel in name'. This line of argument is common in praise of the gods. Thus, too, Conon called Thrasybulus rash in counsel. And Herodicus said of Thrasymachus, 'You are always bold

---

14. Attridge refers to it as 'standard Jewish interpretations' and also notes the way in which the author does not develop these themes (*The Epistle to the Hebrews*, p. 189).

in battle'; of Polus, 'you are always a colt'; and of the legislator Draco that his laws were those not of a human being but of a dragon, so savage were they. And, in Euripides, Hecuba says of Aphrodite, 'Her name and Folly's lightly begin alike', and Chaeremon writes, 'Pentheus—a name foreshadowing grief to come' (*Rhet.* 1400b.6).

Theon also makes it part of encomium:

> It is clever sometimes to compose an encomium on the basis of the meaning of names, the same name, or namesakes, if it is not altogether coarse and ridiculous. And so, on the basis of the meaning of names: for example, Demosthenes, that he was, so to speak, the strength of the people. On the basis of the same name: when someone happens to have the same name as a man who has already been honored. On the basis of namesakes: for example, Pericles surnamed Olympian because of the greatness in his accomplishments (*Progymn.* 9.49-55).[15]

What we find in Heb. 7.2 is more in keeping with this tradition in Greek rhetoric than it is with the foundation for midrash.

c. *Poetic Description of Topics (7.3)*

Comparisons normally proceed along a standard set of topics. They typically follow a chronological order, but this is not always the case. In the *Rhetoric to Alexander* we find a clear delineation of the order of topics which should be covered (1440b.14–1441b.3; cf. *Rhet. ad Her.* 3.7.13–8.15).[16] Similar topics are covered by Theon and the other progymnasmatic writers. Birth is one of the first topics. The *Rhetoric to Alexander* next has genealogy (1440b.24). A broad topic under which many items may be discussed is achievement (πρᾶξις).

The topics which Plutarch covers in his comparisons are wide-ranging, but still typical of encomium. One will find such topics as achievements, actions, ancestors, battles, wars, military exploits, victories, trophies, birth, character, childhood, death, education, faults, friends, gifts, benefactions, habits, honor, innovations, laws enacted, marriage, wife, children, family, office, parents, policies (domestic, civil), rearing, rule, supernatural favor, titles, virtues, voyages, wealth and youth.

---

15. James R. Butts, 'The Progymnasmata of Theon: A New Text with Translation and Commentary' (PhD Dissertation, Claremont Graduate School, 1986), p. 473.

16. This is discussed in the section on the *Rhetoric to Alexander* in chapter 4 of my dissertation.

Throughout the rest of Hebrews 7, there is an attention given to these common topics. An examination of the function of these topics will provide a better explanation for the flow of the text than has been given by appeals to midrash and rabbinic hermeneutics.

1. *Parentage and Genealogy (7.3a).*

ἀπάτωρ, ἀμήτωρ, ἀγενεαλόγητος,

Without mention of father, mother, or genealogy.

Verse 3 is recognized for its 'quasi-poetic flavor'.[17] The asyndeton construction (without intervening conjunctions) is forceful by its terseness. The first two words are linked together by their isocolon (equal number of syllables), and are connected with the third by alliteration.

Attridge attributes the interpretive device which infers these characteristics of Melchizedek to an argument from silence found in both 'Philo and rabbinic exegetes'.[18] The assumption is that the author of Hebrews is making a theological statement that Melchizedek did not have a mother or father because there is no mention of them. This is indeed a strange exegetical twist by the author, if that is in fact what he means. The references Attridge gives to Philo (*Leg. All.* 2.55; 3.79; *Abr.* 31) do not have the same implications. The reference to the Talmud is even less satisfying.

Commentators since the publication of H.L Strack's and Paul Billerbeck's *Kommentar zum Neuen Testament aus Talmud und Midrasch* have cited the rabbinic dictum *Quod non in Thora, non in mundo.*[19]

17. Attridge, *The Epistle to the Hebrews*, pp. 189-90. There is no need to construct a form-critical hypothesis about an early hymn being used by the author here. This is as if to say that a prose author is incapable of writing in a poetic fashion. It is interesting that these three epithets appear in *Apoc. Abr.* 17.10 (Attridge, *The Epistle to the Hebrews*, p. 190 n. 54, and Hans-Friedrich Weiss, *Der Brief an die Hebräer* [MeyerK; Göttingen: Vandenhoeck & Ruprecht, 1991], p. 377 n. 16, both have the reference as 17.9; according to R. Rubinkiewicz in 'Apocalypse of Abraham: A New Translation and Introduction', in *OTP*, I, p. 697, it appears as 17.10) in a hymn to the God of Israel. The relationship between this text and Hebrews is difficult to assess.

18. Attridge, *The Epistle to the Hebrews*, p. 190.

19. Str–B, III, pp. 694-95. See, e.g., F. Schröger, *Der Verfasser des Hebräerbriefs als Schriftausleger* (BU, 4; Regensburg: Regenburger, 1968), p. 136; Attridge, *The Epistle to the Hebrews*, p. 190; George Wesley Buchanan, *To the Hebrews: Translation, Comment and Conclusions* (AB, 36; Garden City, NY:

Although Spicq does give a reference to *Sanh.* 107b and *Gen. R.* 65,[20] others give the supporting evidence for this rabbinic principle in Philo.[21] This confusion is the result of a wrong approach to Hebrews.

Hans-Friedrich Weiss draws attention to this weakness:

> Against such an interpretation is, above all, the fact that the two titles ἀπάτωρ and ἀμήτωρ quite generally in the ancient world—including both the Greco-Hellenistic and the Jewish—have the meaning of 'divine predictions', thus denoting respectively the divine origin and nature.[22]

It is argued that since these terms are found in Greek literature, there is little need to find parallels elsewhere. This still assumes that the author of Hebrews is involved in a doctrinal discussion about the divinity of Melchizedek.

F.F. Bruce makes an interesting comment in this regard. If you were to put the point to the author of Hebrews that Melchizedek came from a 'dynasty of priest-kings in which he had both predecessors and successors', he would have agreed, but would have considered it irrelevant to his purposes.[23] Bruce adds,

> The important consideration was the account given of Melchizedek in holy writ... Melchizedek remains a priest continually for the duration of his appearance in the biblical narrative; but in the antitype Christ remains a priest continually without qualification.[24]

Although Bruce comes about it a different way, this is precisely the textual argument the author is making. The loose translation given above attempts to highlight the significance of this. The author of Hebrews is following the normal pattern of drawing comparisons according to the common topics. If his point is that Melchizedek is immortal because he existed apart from the disadvantages of mortal

Doubleday, 1972), p. 119; Ceslaus Spicq, *L'épître aux Hébreux* (2 vols.; EBib; Paris: J. Gabalda, 1952–53), II, p. 209; Paul Ellingworth, *The Epistle to the Hebrews: A Commentary on the Greek Text* (NIGTC; Grand Rapids: Eerdmans, 1993), p. 358; Bruce, *Hebrews*, p. 136.

20. Spicq, *L'épître aux Hébreux*, II, p. 209 n. 3.

21. 'L'argument de silence, qui applique à l'écriture le principe juridique: Ce qui ne peut être produit est regardé comme inexistant, est utilisé par les Rabbins. Il est couramment mis en œuvre par Philon dans son exégèse biblique' (Spicq, *L'épître aux Hébreux*, II, pp. 208-209 n. 4).

22. Weiss, *Der Brief*, p. 377.

23. Bruce, *Hebrews*, p. 137.

24. Bruce, *Hebrews*, pp. 137-38.

parentage, then why also mention that Melchizedek was 'without genealogy'? What is the point if this is a theological argument about divinity and immortality? In fact, the reference to genealogy in v. 6 makes it clear that the point is that his genealogy is not from any tribe, especially not from Levi. It makes more sense that the author has this combination of parentage and genealogy which is so typical in Greek rhetoric.[25] These topics continue in the next phrase.

2. *Birth and End of Life (7.3b).*

μήτε ἀρχὴν ἡμερῶν μήτε ζωῆς τέλος ἔχων

neither mention of birth nor having mention of death

The rhythmic language continues in this polysyndeton 'neither...nor' construction. In addition, the author appears to use homoioteleuton by forming the same sound at the end of the phrases. This highly stylized and poetic clause presents two more of the common topics found as introductory in encomia and in comparisons.

The birth and death of individuals are almost always mentioned in comparisons. In Aphthonius's model comparison of Achilles and Hector, this plays an important role. Their births are mentioned first in the comparison—it follows a chronological order. At the end of the comparison, birth and death are discussed together:

καὶ γεγονότες ἄμφω παρὰ θεῶν, ἐκ θεῶν ἀνηρέθησαν· ὅθεν γὰρ τὸ γένος, καὶ τὸ τοῦ βίου τέλος εἰλήφασιν· ὅσον δὴ παραπλήσιον βίος καὶ θάνατος, τοσοῦτον Ἕκτωρ Ἀχιλλεῖ παραπλήσιος.

And both, having sprung from gods, were taken off by gods; whence they drew their beginning, they also derived the end of their lives. To the degree that there was similarity in life and in death, by that degree is Hector on a par with Achilles.[26]

In this case, Aphthonius is trying to show the greatness of Hector by

25. Aphthonius, in his model comparison of Achilles and Hector, traces the genealogy of Achilles (son of Peleus, Peleus of Aeacus, and Aeacus of Zeus) and of Hector (Priam and Laomedon, Laomedon from Dardanus, Dardanus of Zeus). The *Rhetoric to Alexander* discusses the proper way to employ genealogy (1440b.29–1441a.12).

26. Aphthonius, *Progymn.* 10., in C. Waltz (ed.), *Rhetores Graeci*, I (Stuttgart and Tübingen: J.G. Cotta, 1832), p. 100, lines 15-18. Trans. R. Nadeau, 'The Progymnasmata of Aphthonius in Translation', *Speech Monographs* 19 (1952), pp. 277-78.

comparing him to Achilles. The final comparative exchange emphasizes the similarity of birth and death.

Much of the difficulty in interpreting 7.3b arises from what appears
to be the author's claim that Melchizedek is a semi-divine being. This
sends scholars scrambling to find parallels in the Qumran literature
(11QMelch), 2 *Enoch*, and in the Nag Hammadi tractate *Melchizedek*
(*Melch.* 9.1).[27] Although it is not central to the overall argument, it is
contended that the author of Hebrews is only making note of what is—
or is not—in the narrative of the Genesis account. The frame of reference is the passage in the psalms ('a priest forever'), and the impetus is
the pattern of the common topics for comparison.

3. *Office Remains in Perpetuity (7.3c).*

ἀφωμοιωμένος δὲ τῷ υἱῷ τοῦ θεοῦ, μένει ἱερεὺς εἰς τὸ διηνεκές.

but in comparison to the Son of God, he remains a priest in perpetuity.

This poetic description of Melchizedek culminates in 7.3c. A major
topic in the comparison of Melchizedek is the office of priest. The per-
petual condition of this office will become the focus in the succeeding
comparative exchanges. What is more important here than the topic is
the verb with which the author begins this final clause.

The KJV reads 'but made like unto the Son of God...' This translation has tended to influence the reading of the text. It implies the idea of
creation: God created Melchizedek to be like the Son of God. A better
grammatical translation of the verb is 'being likened' or 'resembling'.
The term could be translated idiomatically as 'in comparison'. Support
for this interpretation is Plato's use of the word in *Rep.* 517a-b:

ταύτην τοίνυν, ἦν δ' ἐγώ, τὴν εἰκόνα, ὦ φίλε Γλαύκων, προσαπτέον
ἅπασαν τοῖς ἔμπροσθεν λεγομένοις, τὴν μὲν δι ὄψεως φαινομένην
ἕδραν τῇ τοῦ δεσμωτηρίου οἰκήσει ἀφομοιοῦντα, τὸ δὲ τοῦ πυρὸς ἐν
αὐτῇ φῶς τῇ τοῦ ἡλίου δυνάμει·

This image then, dear Glaucon, we must apply as a whole to all that has
been said, likening the region revealed through sight to the habitation of
the prison, and the light of the fire in it to the power of the sun.

We could translate this, starting at 517b, 'comparing, on the one hand,
the region revealed through sight to habitation of the prison, and, on
the other hand, the light of the fire in it to the power of the sun'. The

---

27. See Attridge's excursus in *The Epistle to the Hebrews*, pp. 192-93.

context is clearly that of drawing comparisons. Plato uses this word in this way again in *Rep*. 564b:

δὴ ἀφομοιοῦμεν κηφῆσι, τοὺς μὲν κέντρα ἔχουσι, τοὺς δὲ ἀκέντροις.

We were likening them to drones, some equipped with stings and others stingless.

Again, the context is comparison, 'we are comparing them to drones—some, on the one hand, have stingers, and, on the other hand, some are stingless'. Finding parallels in Plato is more credible than appeals to the Talmud, Dead Sea Scrolls and Nag Hammadi.

There is only a need for such far-reaching studies if the meaning is that Melchizedek was created a semi-divine being. It must be pointed out, however, that the tense here is present, not past. With both the meaning of the word, the tense of the verb, and the context of the passage, the best understanding is the one we have presented. Paraphrased, 'Since, in the text of Genesis, Melchizedek is being compared to the Son of God, he remains a priest even today'.

The difficulty of this passage is reflected in the commentaries. Moffat puts the wording this way, ' "made to resemble" (*i.e.* in scripture)'.[28] Attridge is hesitant and tries to show both sides of this issue. What he says is highly instructive and will be quoted fully:

> While the function of the comparison between Melchizedek and Christ is clear, the precise nature of the comparison and the status of Melchizedek himself is not. Exegetes have long been divided on the issue of whether Melchizedek is simply a scriptural symbol or a heavenly being of some sort. In support of the first alternative is the fact that the comparison proceeds primarily on a literary level. Melchizedek is 'likened' to Christ, and it is 'testified' that he lives. The author appears to be deliberately noncommittal about the figure of Melchizedek himself. Furthermore, he does not advance any explicit speculation about Melchizedek. He neither explains how his 'eternal priesthood' relates to that of Christ, nor does he polemicize against him as a rival to Christ. He would appear, like Philo, to be uninterested in the person of Melchizedek himself and only concerned with what he represents.[29]

Leaving aside Attridge's constant reference to this passage as comparison in spite of his explicit designation of midrash, he expresses well

28. James Moffatt, *A Critical and Exegetical Commentary on the Epistle to the Hebrews* (New York: Charles Scribner's Sons, 1924), p. 93.

29. Attridge, *The Epistle to the Hebrews*, p. 191.

the problem with the text. These problems are dissipated when understood in the context of synkrisis.

d. *Introductory Statement: Greatness of Melchizedek (7.4)*

θεωρεῖτε δὲ πηλίκος οὗτος ᾧ [καὶ] δεκάτην Ἀβραὰμ ἔδωκεν ἐκ τῶν ἀκροθινίων ὁ πατριάρχης.

Now observe how great is this one to whom Abraham the 'first-father' gave a tenth from his spoils.

As illustrated above in the catena of introductory passages from Plutarch, a constant theme is the greatness of the individuals being compared. This is the precise goal of comparison. In Heb. 7.4, the author calls the audience to 'listen' to him extol the greatness of Melchizedek.[30] He will do this by a series of comparative exchanges which center on the topics applicable in this case.

2. *Comparative Exchanges (7.5-25)*

Almost the rest of Hebrews 7 (vv. 5-25) is constructed around comparative exchanges. The topics follow the order of action, status, ancestry and achievements. The first comparative exchange shows that the Melchizedek of Genesis is superior to the Levites of Numbers. After this the comparative exchanges will prove the superiority of Jesus as a high priest like Melchizedek.

a. *Action: First Done (7.5-7)*

⁵ καὶ οἱ μὲν ἐκ τῶν υἱῶν Λευὶ τὴν ἱερατείαν λαμβάνοντες ἐντολὴν ἔχουσιν ἀποδεκατοῦν τὸν λαὸν κατὰ τὸν νόμον, τοῦτ' ἔστιν τοὺς ἀδελφοὺς αὐτῶν, καίπερ ἐξεληλυθότας ἐκ τῆς ὀσφύος Ἀβραάμ·
⁶ ὁ δὲ μὴ γενεαλογούμενος ἐξ αὐτῶν δεδεκάτωκεν Ἀβραάμ, καὶ τὸν ἔχοντα τὰς ἐπαγγελίας εὐλόγηκεν. ⁷ χωρὶς δὲ πάσης ἀντιλογίας τὸ ἔλαττον ὑπὸ τοῦ κρείττονος εὐλογεῖται.

⁵ On the one hand, those of the sons of Levi who receive the priesthood have a commandment, according to the law, to take a tithe from the people, that is, their brothers, though having derived from the loins of Abraham.

---

30. A similar phraseology is *4 Macc.* 14.13: θεωρεῖτε δὲ πῶς πολύπλοκός 'And consider how comprehensive...'

⁶ On the other hand, the one whose genealogy is not traced from them received tithes from Abraham and blessed him who had the promise.
⁷ Without dispute, the lesser is blessed by the greater.

The Levitical law provides for the priests to tax the people. They are, the author points out, descendants of Abraham. The *touché* is that Melchizedek did one better. He received a tithe from Abraham himself —and gave *him* a blessing.

These verses are clearly constructed as a comparative exchange. The μέν...δέ construction and the pronominal articles are apparent features. The subject shifts from one to the next. The literary style is typical of synkrisis.

One of the first topics after discussing the external and bodily qualities was actions—a quality of the soul. Theon defines one of the reasons for an action being praiseworthy as having been done first.[31] Aristotle also places importance on this:

> There are, also, many useful ways of heightening the effect of praise. We must, for instance, point out that a man is the only one, or the first, or almost the only one who has done something, or that he has done it better than any one else; all these distinctions are honourable (*Rhet.* 1368a.4).

This attribute characterizes the comparative exchange here. Melchizedek was the first priest and, as such, received tithes before the Levitical priests.[32]

Commentators are confused by the 'lesser/greater' statement of our author. As Attridge says, 'It is hardly self-evident that the "lesser" is always blessed by the "greater" since there are numerous biblical examples of inferiors blessing their superiors'.[33] The author's comment in 7.7 is not a maxim, specific or general. It is a judgment based on the comparison.

Plutarch illustrates this aspect of comparison already discussed above. Frequently he states his judgment about whether one or the other of the subjects is greater:

31. Theon, 'On the Encomium and the Denunciation' (*Progymn.* 9.36).
32. This characteristic actually pervades Hebrews in the word ἀρχή and its compound forms. The term 'high priest' denotes the priest 'first in line', but could also have the connotation of 'first in time'.
33. Attridge, *The Epistle to the Hebrews*, p. 196.

⁵πλήθει δ' οὐδ' ἄξιον παραβαλεῖν τοῖς ἐπὶ Λεύκολλον συνελθοῦσι τοὺς ὑπὸ Κίμωνος κρατηθέντας. ⁶ὥστε πάντῃ μεταλαμβάνοντι δυσδιαίτητον εἶναι τὴν κρίσιν· ἐπεὶ καὶ τὸ δαιμόνιον ἀμφοτέροις ἔοικεν εὐμενὲς γενέσθαι, τῷ μὲν ἃ χρὴ κατορθοῦν, τῷ δ' ἃ φυλάττεσθαι [χρὴ] προμηνῦον, ὥστε καὶ τὴν παρὰ τῶν θεῶν ψῆφον αὐτοῖς ὑπάρχειν ὡς ἀγαθοῖς καὶ θείοις τὴν φύσιν ἀμφοτέροις.

There is no comparison between the numbers which came against Lucullus and those subdued by Cimon. All which things being rightly considered, it is a hard matter to give judgment. For supernatural favour also appears to have attended both of them, directing the one what to do, the other what to avoid, and thus they have, both of them, so to say, the vote of the gods, to declare them noble and divine characters.³⁴

The language of 7.7 is typical of comparison. It is obvious that the words 'lesser' and 'greater' are comparatives. The statement is indicative of the judgment of superiority that takes place in comparisons.

Commentators who continually try to find parallels in rabbinic literature suddenly use rabbinic citations to argue against the author of Hebrews at this point based on the assumption of doctrinal exposition that the author is stating a universal truth.³⁵ Is Hebrews rabbinic or isn't it? This inconsistency underlines the weakness of the traditional approach.

b. *Status (7.8-10)*

⁸καὶ ὧδε μὲν δεκάτας ἀποθνήσκοντες ἄνθρωποι λαμβάνουσιν, ἐκεῖ δὲ μαρτυρούμενος ὅτι ζῇ. ⁹καὶ ὡς ἔπος εἰπεῖν, δι' Ἀβραὰμ καὶ Λευὶ ὁ δεκάτας λαμβάνων δεδεκάτωται, ¹⁰ἔτι γὰρ ἐν τῇ ὀσφύϊ τοῦ πατρὸς ἦν ὅτε συνήντησεν αὐτῷ Μελχισέδεκ.

⁸And here, on the one hand, men who have since died receive tithes. On the other hand, there, it is testified, Melchizedek is living. ⁹One might almost say that, Levi, who received tithes, through Abraham also paid tithes. ¹⁰For he was yet in the loins of his great grandfather when Melchizedek met him.

The rhetorical structure of the comparative exchange is again evident. On the inferior side are the Levitical priests. They are depicted as those who, at the time of the author, have died. Yet, in the biblical text, one

34. Plutarch, *Cim.-Luc. synk.* 3.5-6.
35. Attridge, *The Epistle to the Hebrews*, p. 196 (cf. n. 134); Buchanan (*To the Hebrews*, p. 121) does not actually cite any texts, he simply says 'Rabbis did not concur...'

can read of them receiving tithes. In contrast, with regard to Melchizedek, there in that text in Genesis there is no mention of him having died. With tongue in cheek, so to speak, the author quips that it is as though the Levitical priests paid tithes in Abraham.

This comparative exchange proves Melchizedek's status or reputation, his δόξα. Theon lists this among the external qualities in his section on encomium (9.18) and also in his section on comparison (10.15). The priesthood of Melchizedek, on this basis, is presented as superior to the Levitical priesthood. The author now turns to show that Jesus has a priesthood superior to the Levitical in view of the fact that he has been appointed as a priest in the order of Melchizedek.

c. *Tribal Ancestry (7.11-17)*

[11]εἰ μὲν οὖν τελείωσις διὰ τῆς Λευιτικῆς ἱερωσύνης ἦν, ὁ λαὸς γὰρ ἐπ᾽ αὐτῆς νενομοθέτηται, τίς ἔτι χρεία κατὰ τὴν τάξιν Μελχισέδεκ ἕτερον ἀνίστασθαι ἱερέα καὶ οὐ κατὰ τὴν τάξιν Ἀαρὼν λέγεσθαι; [12]μετατιθεμένης γὰρ τῆς ἱερωσύνης ἐξ ἀνάγκης καὶ νόμου μετάθεσις γίνεται.

[13]ἐφ᾽ ὃν γὰρ λέγεται ταῦτα φυλῆς ἑτέρας μετέσχηκεν, ἀφ᾽ ἧς οὐδεὶς προσέσχηκεν τῷ θυσιαστηρίῳ. [14]πρόδηλον γὰρ ὅτι ἐξ Ἰούδα ἀνατέταλκεν ὁ κύριος ἡμῶν, εἰς ἣν φυλὴν περὶ ἱερέων οὐδὲν Μωϋσῆς ἐλάλησεν. [15]καὶ περισσότερον ἔτι κατάδηλόν ἐστιν, εἰ κατὰ τὴν ὁμοιότητα Μελχισέδεκ ἀνίσταται ἱερεὺς ἕτερος, [16]ὃς οὐ κατὰ νόμον ἐντολῆς σαρκίνης γέγονεν ἀλλὰ κατὰ δύναμιν ζωῆς ἀκαταλύτου, [17]μαρτυρεῖται γὰρ ὅτι σὺ ἱερεὺς εἰς τὸν αἰῶνα κατὰ τὴν τάξιν Μελχισέδεκ.

[11]Therefore, if indeed the Levitical priesthood under which the people had received the law was able to bring people to full maturity, what further need would there be for another priest to be raised up according to the order of Melchizedek and not to be named according to the order of Aaron? [12]For when there is a transformation of the priesthood, there occurs out of necessity also a transformation of law.

[13]For he of whom we speak is part of a different tribe from which no one has attended the altar. [14]For it is evident that our Lord sprang from Judah about which tribe Moses said nothing regarding a priest. [15]And it is consequently even more apparent, if a different priest arises according to the likeness of Melchizedek, [16]who has become a priest not according to a law of a fleshly command, but according to the force of an interminable life. [17]For it is testified, 'You are a priest forever according to the order of Melchizedek'.

The comparative exchange in 7.11-17 is delimited based on the switch in subject. Verses 11 and 12 have to do with the Levitical priesthood. The subject changes at 7.13. Since a new comparative exchange begins with 7.18, this one is confined to 7.11-17. The particle μέν is used for emphasis in 7.11 rather than as a marker emphasizing a sentence or clause in distinction to another as in a μέν...δέ construction. This construction is not necessary for a comparative exchange, but usually does occur.

The topic is ancestry. This, again, is fundamental to encomia and to comparison (Theon, 9.15-19; 10.13-17; Hermogenes, 8.10). In Aphthonius's comparison of Achilles and Hector, he compares their ancestry:

> καὶ προγόνου γεγονότες Διός, πατράσι παραπλησίοις ἐχρήσαντο. Ἀχιλλεῖ μὲν γὰρ πατέρες Αἰακὸς καὶ Πηλεύς· ὧν ὁ μὲν αὐχμῶν ἐξαιρεῖται τοὺς Ἕλληνας, ὁ δὲ Λαπίθας ἀελὼν, ἆθλον τῆς ἀρετῆς θεᾷ συνοικεῖν ἐκληρώσατο. Ἕκτορι δὲ πρόγονος ὑπῆρχε Δάρδανος, θεοῖς τὸ πρώην συνδιαιτώμενος. πατὴρ δὲ Πρίαμος, κρατῶν πόλεως τετειχισμένης ὑπὸ θεῶν· ὅσον δὴ παραπλήσιον τὸ θεοῖς συνοικεῖν καὶ συνδιαιτᾶσθαι τοῖς κρείττοσι, τοσοῦτον Ἕκτωρ Ἀχιλλεῖ παραπλήσιος.

> And having been born with Zeus as a progenitor, they had forefathers nearly alike. For the ancestors of Achilles were Aeacus and Peleus, of whom the former freed the Greeks from want and the latter was allotted marriage with a goddess as a prize for his prowess in overcoming the Lapithes. On Hector's side, Dardanus was a forefather who formerly lived with the gods, and his father, Priam, was in command of a city whose walls were built by gods. To the degree that there was similarity in living with the gods and association with superior beings, by that degree is Hector about equal to Achilles.[36]

Having traced the genealogy of Achilles and Hector, Aphthonius compares the ancestry of each of them and what is significant about the group of people from whom they descended.

Plutarch also covers this topic of ancestry:

> ἔτι δ' οἱ *μέν*, ὅτε λαμπρότατον εἶχεν ἡ Ῥώμη καὶ μέγιστον ἀξίωμα, [καὶ] καλῶν ἔργων ζῆλον ὥσπερ διαδοχὴν ἀρετῆς πατρῴας καὶ προγονικῆς ᾐσχύνθησαν ἐγκαταλιπεῖν· οἱ *δὲ* καὶ πατέρων τἀναντία προῃρημένων γεγονότες, καὶ τὴν πατρίδα μοχθηρὰ πράττουσαν καὶ νοσοῦσαν παραλαβόντες, οὐδέν τι διὰ ταῦτα τὴν πρὸς τὸ καλὸν ἀπήμβλυναν ὁρμήν.

36. Aphthonius, *Progymn.* 10, in Waltz (ed.), *Rhetores Greci*, I, p. 99, lines 8-17. Trans Nadeau, 'The Progymnasmata', p. 277.

Besides, the Gracchi, happening to live when Rome had her greatest repute for honour and virtuous actions, might justly have been ashamed, if they had not also left to the next generation the noble inheritance of the virtues of their ancestors. Whereas the other two had parents of different morals, and though they found their country in a sinking condition, and debauched, yet that did not quench their forward zeal to what was just and honourable.[37]

This comparative exchange follows the typical pattern. The ancestry is noted only with relationship to moral character, rather than specifically to any actions or achievements.

While it would press the matter too much to think that the author of Hebrews is simply discussing the tribal relationships of the priesthood because it is the next topic, it is not unimaginable that his consideration of the common topics brought these relationships to his attention. If the nature of Jesus as priest is significant; and the concept of first to do something is important along with one's ancestry; combine that with the text which has Melchizedek as representative of an eternal priesthood which would characterize the messianic figure; and this Melchizedek was the first priest described in Scripture; and Jesus does not come from the priestly tribe, then it follows that one would draw a comparison of the tribal ancestry of Jesus to that of the Levites. This connection works itself out here in this comparative exchange dealing with ancestry.

The author claims the superiority for the priesthood of Jesus because it is based on the priestly order of Melchizedek. It is not a priesthood which has its inception grounded in a 'fleshly' commandment of the law. The argument being developed is that the people of God were cut short of reaching their goal of entering the promised land. The author of Hebrews is drawing this parallel to exhort his audience not to fall short of reaching their goal of full maturity, both morally and spiritually. Since the people of God did not achieve this, it is concluded that the fault is with the system which did not help them progress. In contrast to this, Jesus brings about a system which will enable the faithful to come to maturity, τελείωσις. This concept is brought out more fully in the next section.

d. *Achievements (7.18-25)*
The central topic of encomia is achievements. The *Rhetoric to Alexan-*

---

37. Plutarch, *Ag./Cleom.-Gracchi synk.* 1.3-6.

der (1441b.4-13) places the discussion of achievements as the main topic for praise regarding a person's adulthood. Usually this type of comparison in Plutarch has to do with the achievements in government, in the enactment of laws, in building programs, in benefactions to the people, innovations in society, victory in foreign affairs, advancement in politics, and those actions which are memorable and long-lasting.

The author of Hebrews, after having introduced Jesus into this comparative section—though not by name until v. 22—goes on to formulate three comparative exchanges which set forth his achievements. These are three ways in which Jesus is found to be superior in His role as priest to the Levitical priests. The first two achievements are based on the praiseworthiness of having been the only one to do something (Theon, *On Encomium* 9.35-38).

1. *Introduction of Better Hope (7.18-19).*

[18]ἀθέτησις μὲν γὰρ γίνεται προαγούσης ἐντολῆς διὰ τὸ αὐτῆς ἀσθενὲς καὶ ἀνωφελές, [19]οὐδὲν γὰρ ἐτελείωσεν ὁ νόμος,
  ἐπεισαγωγὴ δὲ κρείττονος ἐλπίδος, δι' ἧς ἐγγίζομεν τῷ θεῷ.

[18]For, on the one hand, there is a repeal of a preceding commandment because of the weakness and ineffectiveness of it. [19]For the law did not bring anyone to the intended goal.

On the other hand, there is a subsequent better hope, through which we do approach close to God.

In this comparative exchange, the author once again begins to use the μέν...δέ construction. We also find the significant comparative term κρείττων. The achievement which sets Jesus apart is that he has introduced a 'better hope'.

Our reading of the text here continues to keep in mind the textual argument the author has been developing. It is the rhetorical structure that helps to define the argument. Traditionally, 7.18 is understood to be, as Attridge puts it, 'not simply an amendment of the Law, but its definitive "abrogation"'.[38] The 'abrogation' is of a particular commandment, not the Law as a totality. How could this be when the author of Hebrews himself says, using the same word as in 7.18, 'Anyone who abrogates [ἀθετήσας] the Law of Moses without mercy will be put to death on the basis of two or three witnesses' (10.28)? The difficulty with the Law, the ceremonial system involving the Levitical

---

38. Attridge, *The Epistle to the Hebrews*, p. 203.

priesthood, is that it fails to bring people[39] to the intended goal of full maturity. The failure in chs. 3 and 4 was the failure of the people of God to enter God's rest. The author says nothing about the failure of the message, it was the disobedience of the people that prevented them from making progress. Likewise here, the people are not brought to the level of fulfillment. Its 'weakness' and 'ineffectiveness' are connected to its fleshly and temporal nature.

The other side of the comparative exchange maintains the balance. What is inferior in the one is shown to be superior in the other. The converse of οὐδὲν γὰρ ἐτελείωσεν ὁ νόμος is that there is a 'better hope'. This refers to the effectiveness of Jesus as high priest to bring a person near to God. The comparison is meant to encourage the audience to endure their present suffering and remain faithful. Jesus will be able to help them to 'make it home', so to speak.

2. *Guarantee of Better Covenant (7.20-22).*

[20]καὶ καθ᾽ ὅσον οὐ χωρὶς ὁρκωμοσίας, οἱ *μὲν* γὰρ χωρὶς ὁρκωμοσίας εἰσὶν ἱερεῖς γεγονότες,
[21]ὁ *δὲ* μετὰ ὁρκωμοσίας διὰ τοῦ λέγοντος πρὸς αὐτόν, ὤμοσεν κύριος, καὶ οὐ μεταμεληθήσεται, σὺ ἱερεὺς εἰς τὸν αἰῶνα, [22]κατὰ τοσοῦτο [καὶ] κρείττονος διαθήκης γέγονεν ἔγγυος Ἰησοῦς.

[20]And what about the oath! For the former, on the one hand, are become priests without an oath.
   [21]The latter, on the other hand, became a priest with an oath because of what was said to Him, 'The Lord has sworn and will not equivocate, "You are a priest forever" '. [22]In this way Jesus has become the pledge of a better covenant.

The litotes (double negative) construction forcefully introduces the subject of the oath. As in Plutarch's comparisons, the pronominal article appears in conjunction with the μέν...δέ construction (here translated, 'the former...the latter'). On the basis of the oath stated in Ps. 110.4, the author concludes that Jesus' priesthood is superior. The Levitical priests did not have this quality. It is this 'oath' that ensures that Jesus' priesthood is eternal. As such he is a pledge of a better

---

39. The neuter οὐδέν may also apply to people. 'The neuter forms are often used of persons' (H. Smyth, *Greek Grammar* [Cambridge, MA: Harvard University Press, 1956], §2736). Ellingworth takes it as 'nothing' but concedes 'no one' is grammatically allowable, 'Chrysostom understood "nothing" as "no one", and the author's main concern is clearly with people' (*Hebrews*, p. 381).

agreement. It is the achievement of having been the only one to accomplish a thing.

3. *Long Lasting and for Others (7.23-25).*

²³καὶ οἱ μὲν πλείονές εἰσιν γεγονότες ἱερεῖς διὰ τὸ θανάτῳ κωλύ-εσθαι παραμένειν·

²⁴ὁ δὲ διὰ τὸ μένειν αὐτὸν εἰς τὸν αἰῶνα ἀπαράβατον ἔχει τὴν ἱερωσύνην. ²⁵ὅθεν καὶ σῴζειν εἰς τὸ παντελὲς δύναται τοὺς προσερ-χομένους δι᾽ αὐτοῦ τῷ θεῷ, πάντοτε ζῶν εἰς τὸ ἐντυγχάνειν ὑπὲρ αὐτῶν.

²³And the priests, on the one hand, are become many on account of being prevented from continuing due to death.

²⁴On the other hand, He has an indissoluble priesthood because it remains 'forever'. ²⁵Wherefore, he is also able to preserve to the fullest degree those who approach God through Him, always living in order to intercede for them.

In the final comparative exchange of this section, the author concludes with the topic of Jesus' achievement of holding the office of priest for all time. In contrast to the Levitical priests who continue to die off, Jesus has done what others could not do. As a priest in perpetuity he is able to bring those who approach God through him to the state of full maturity. Those who approach God through Jesus will not fall, but be safely brought to the consummation of their spiritual existence. As a priest who lives forever, Jesus is able to perform the priestly function of intercession on their behalf. An achievement which is done for the sake of others is highly regarded. In this comparison, Jesus is shown to be superior by virtue of an achievement which is long-lasting, which others are unable to do, and which was performed for the benefit of others.

The paraenesis that climaxes this synkrisis makes the judgment that the superior priest is the one who has offered a one-time sacrifice, who is not weak in susceptibility to death, and who, on the basis of God's oath, will remain as priest forever. The Son who has experienced the trials of life and remained faithful to God is the one who has been exalted to heaven where God serves as high-priest. The crucial words for the audience are 'we have such a High Priest' (8.1). It is true that synkrisis is often, as Aphthonius described it, an encomium with a denunciation (*Progymn.* 10), but the goal of a positive synkrisis is to persuade the audience to accept the judgment of who or what is superior and to emulate those characteristics. The methodology that stresses the expository sections of Hebrews also tends to emphasize the negative aspect of the comparison. Comparisons are to be made with items which are considered to be equal. Aphthonius remarks that it is ridiculous to compare an obviously inferior subject to one which is clearly superior. Comparisons are drawn between subjects concerning which there is difficulty assessing which is superior. The author tells his audience what the main point is in the recapitulation 'we have such a high priest'. It is a logical fallacy to assume the converse.

Not only has the structure of this section in Hebrews been proven to be that of the genre synkrisis, it has additionally been shown that the author of Hebrews here follows to a great degree the common topics of epideictic oratory. This approach has provided a basis for a better understanding of the text. It is an approach that, as much as possible, reconstructs the patterns of argumentation as they existed in the first century. I have only been able to touch upon the many and great implications this reading of the text can have for our overall interpretation of the theology of Hebrews.

AUTOBIOGRAPHY AND RHETORIC:
ANGER IN IGNATIUS OF ANTIOCH

Mary W. Patrick

If one can see through the hyperbole of which Ignatius is a master practitioner, one can ask: 'What makes Ignatius mad?' and 'Who is he mad at?' After some ground-clearing rhetorical analysis, this essay will answer 'deficient hospitality resulting in disrespectful assertion of an insufficiently christocentric hermeneutic' and 'Philadelphians'. The first section offers a rhetorical analysis of Ignatius's *Philadelphians*, and prepares the way for the second section which addresses two historical questions concerning Ignatius and his opponents.

1. *Rhetorical Analysis of Ignatius,* Philadelphians

The distinctiveness of the letter Ignatius wrote to the Philadelphians from Troas appears clearly in a comparison of the rhetorical situation of *Philadelphians* to that of his letter to the Romans.[1] What warrant does Ignatius have for writing a letter? What can he reasonably hope to accomplish by a letter, in this particular situation? In his letter to the

---

1. The discussion of rhetorical situation is substantial. The article that initiated recent discussion is L. Bitzer, 'The Rhetorical Situation', *Philosophy and Rhetoric* 1 (1968), pp. 1-14. Other contributions include W. Beale, 'Rhetorical Performative Discourse: A New Theory of Epideictic', *Philosophy and Rhetoric* 11 (1978), pp. 221-46; A. Brinton, 'Situation in the Theory of Rhetoric', *Philosophy and Rhetoric* 14 (1981), pp. 234-48. Bitzer defines rhetorical situation as 'a complex of persons, events, objects and relations presenting an actual or potential exigence which can be completely or partially removed if discourse, introduced into the situation, can so constrain human decision or action as to bring about the significant modification of the exigence' ('The Rhetorical Situation', p. 3). For extension of the theory and incorporation into exegetical procedure, see D.L. Stamps, 'Rethinking the Rhetorical Situation: The Entextualization of the Situation in New Testament Epistles', in S.E. Porter and T.H. Olbricht (eds.), *Rhetoric and the New Testament: Essays from the 1992 Heidelberg Conference* (JSNTSup, 90; Sheffield: JSOT Press, 1993), pp. 193-210.

Romans, written from Smyrna, Ignatius addresses a church with which he has no prior acquaintance. The communication is entirely one-way: Ignatius does not respond to the Romans; he draws arguments primarily from his own experience. The result is a ferocious concentration on a single argument. By contrast, in his letter to the Philadelphians, written from Troas, Ignatius addresses a church he had visited in person. The communication in his letter is part of a larger conversation.

The conversation with the Philadelphians had two stages prior to Ignatius's letter, with different participants. The initial encounter had involved Ignatius and two groups of Philadelphians, one a group of people who argued with him. Since that time there has been a second stage of the conversation: messengers from Antioch[2]—Rheus Agathopous and Philo—have heard the story of Ignatius's visit from the various Philadelphian points of view. They have reported to Ignatius both what the Philadelphians said and their own evaluation of the situation in the church at Philadelphia.

Far from the one-way communication involved in sending an initial message, the formal elements in this complex rhetorical situation include:

1. Ignatius;
2. Philadelphians who did not argue with Ignatius;[3]
3. Philadelphians who argued with Ignatius;
4. Rheus Agathopous and Philo;
5. Philadelphians who 'received' them;[4]
6. Philadelphians who 'dishonored' them;
7. factional infighting in Philadelphia independent of Ignatius;[5]
8. attempts to manipulate Ignatius in relation to local politics;
9. possible disinformation by Philadelphians;
10. possible misperception by messengers.

It is likely, though not entirely certain, that the people who dishonored the messengers were the same people who had argued with Ignatius.

2. The messengers are cited explicitly in Ignatius, *Phld.* 11.1.
3. Only some (τις) argued, 8.2. Plurals are used to refer to them in Ignatius, *Phld.* 8.2 but their number cannot be discerned.
4. Ignatius, *Phld.* 11.1 mentions both this category and the next.
5. Both this item and the next interpret the attempt to 'deceive' Ignatius (μέ τινες ἠθέλησαν πλανῆσαι), Ignatius, *Phld.* 7.1.

The subject matter of the rhetorical situation is no less complex than the formal elements. We may identify five subjects involved in the rhetorical situation, any one of which may permit the writing of a letter:

1. news about Philadelphia;
2. news about Antioch;
3. the treatment of travelers;
4. misunderstanding by Philadelphians;
5. misunderstanding by Ignatius.

The elements so identified will be inspected in turn.

First of all, hearing news about someone calls them to mind and thereby may occasion a letter, according to epistolary theory and practice. The fact that news came from Philadelphia[6] is, for this reason, occasion for a letter.

The second subject, the news from Antioch, is good news. The church at Antioch is 'at peace'.[7] It is a reasonable inference that factionalism has been replaced by what Ignatius elsewhere calls 'unity'.[8] The news from Antioch, then, confirms Ignatius's central message about unity, vindicating what he has said and validating his own authority 'as a man set on union' (Ignatius, *Phld.* 8.1).[9] On the basis of

6.   The news from Philadelphia was reported orally by Rheus Agathopous and Philo (οἳ καὶ μαρτυροῦσιν ὑμῖν, *Phld.* 11.1).

7.   Ignatius, *Phld.* 10.1. The same news is reported with variations in each of the other letters written from Troas (*Smyrn.* 11.2; *Pol.* 7.1). Especially instructive is the statement that it has 'received its own greatness and its own constitution has been restored' (*Smyrn.* 11.2).

8.   The appeal for unity 'may well represent the central concern of the letters of Ignatius', W. Schoedel, *Ignatius of Antioch* (Hermeneia; Philadelphia: Fortress Press, 1985), p. 21. There are only three critical commentaries on Ignatius's letters in English (Lightfoot in 1885 [1889], Grant in 1966, Schoedel in 1985) and two in German (Zahn in 1873, Bauer in 1920 with a second edition by Paulsen in 1985). Bauer has made Lightfoot available in German; Grant has built on Lightfoot and made Bauer available in English; Schoedel, the first full-scale commentary in a century, has accumulated the results of his predecessors and added to them substantially. On this basis, I have regarded Schoedel as a reliable representative of the critical tradition. On the rhetoric of factionalism and reconciliation, see M.M. Mitchell, *Paul and the Rhetoric of Reconciliation: An Exegetical Investigation of the Language and Composition of 1 Corinthians* (Louisville, KY: Westminster/John Knox Press, 1993).

9.   There is no difference in meaning for Ignatius between 'union' (ἕνωσις) and 'unity' (ἑνότης).

the news from Antioch, Ignatius is prepared to speak confidently, forthrightly and earnestly to the Philadelphians about the hazards of factionalism and the benefits of unity.

The third subject, the treatment of travelers, stands as a barrier to friendly communication with the Philadelphians. Ignatius's favorite phrase for referring to a cordial reception is 'You have refreshed me in every respect',[10] an expression conspicuously absent in *Philadelphians*. In its place we find: 'I thank God for you that you received them, as the Lord also received you. But may those who dishonored them be redeemed by the grace of Jesus Christ' (Ignatius, *Phld.* 11.1). Both lack of cordiality and Ignatius's strategy for overcoming the barrier to communication erected by it are apparent here: Ignatius distinguishes 'those who dishonored' from the 'you' who 'received them'. The cordiality of the latter group, however minimal, permits further communication. A hint that Ignatius himself was not cordially received appears in *Phld.* 6.3, 'I thank my God that I am in clear conscience as concerns you and that no one can boast either in private or in public that I burdened anyone in anything great or small'.

The fourth subject is that the Philadelphians had misunderstood Ignatius's sermon. Ignatius may well have learned of their misunderstanding for the first time from Rheus Agathopous and Philo. The Philadelphians mistook his oft-repeated admonition to unity[11] with the bishop for an indictment of their factionalism. They thought that because someone from their congregation had informed him that certain people were schismatics, he had singled out those people for censure. This simple mistake is easily remedied by an explanation in ch. 7; explanation is a good reason to write a letter.

The fifth subject also derives from the report of the messengers. Some members of the congregation at Philadelphia had claimed Ignatius's message was unscriptural. At the time he thought the argument was over what, in fact, was written in the 'archives', a matter of quoting Old Testament passages.[12] Now he realizes that the dis-

---

10. κατὰ πάντα με ἀνέπαυσεν occurs in Ignatius, *Eph.* 2.1, *Magn.* 15.1, *Trall.* 12.1, *Smyrn.* 9.2 and 12.1; the same formula appears with respect to other people in *Rom.* 10.2 and *Smyrn.* 12.1.

11. The Philadelphians had no knowledge, of course, of the admonitions Ignatius would address from Smyrna to the churches of the Meander valley: *Magn.* 6–7, *Trall.* 1.2–3.2, *Eph.* 3–10.

12. W. Schoedel, 'Ignatius and the Archives', *HTR* 71 (1978), pp. 97-106.

agreement was over the definition of 'archives', and seizes the opportunity to prove his case anew (Ignatius, *Phld.* 8.2–9.1); correcting his
argument is another good reason to write a letter.

From within this enormously complex rhetorical situation, Ignatius
planned his letter, initiating a third round in their conversation. As far
as anyone knows, Ignatius had the last word. We can infer the decisions
he made and the order in which he made them from the rhetorical situation, from epistolary and rhetorical theory and from the letter he
finally wrote to the Philadelphians. The first decision Ignatius made
was that the coolness of the relations between himself and the
Philadelphians did not preclude writing a letter. The next decision was
to write one which envisages most of the addressees as friendly.
Epistolary theory and practice encourage Ignatius to write his letter on
a single subject.[13] Indications that he decided on 'unity' as his subject
matter may be found throughout the letter.

Ignatius nowhere states that he had, in fact, preached 'unity' and
engaged in an argument about unity when he had visited Philadelphia.
He gives the content of his sermon as 'Attend to the bishop and the
presbytery and the deacons' (*Phld.* 7.1), a theme elsewhere associated
with appeals to unity.[14] In Ignatius, *Magn.* 6.2, to cite an outstanding
example, he wraps unity, division and bishops into a single admonition,
'Let there be nothing among you which is able to divide you, but be
united to the bishop'.

Ignatius does not specifically state the subject his opponents challenged. It makes sense, however, to argue that they challenged the subject matter of his sermon rather than some other topic. The evidence
that the sermon was about unity may be supplemented by Ignatius's
new argument, *Philadelphians* 9, addressed to the people he had argued
with previously. In Ignatius, *Philadelphians* 9, Christians and Old Testament figures alike enter 'into the unity of God' (εἰς ἑνότητα θεοῦ)
through the one 'who alone [μόνος] is entrusted with the secrets of
God'.

The next decision Ignatius made was the species of rhetoric to use.

---

13. Demetrius, *Eloc.* 231 (περὶ ἁπλοῦ πράγματος) may be supplemented by
admonitions in the context to avoid exaggerated complexity of subject matter and
ornamentation.

14. Schoedel, *Ignatius of Antioch*, p. 22: 'Closely related to the theme of unity
are Ignatius' reflections on the ministry'.

He had need of all three.[15] He needed epideictic for praise of unity and denunciation of schism; he needed deliberative to explain himself and to argue again the point previously argued;[16] he needed judicial to defend himself against the charge in *Phld.* 7.1 that he is a tool of someone who gave advance information. He uses all three in appropriate places. Epideictic appears in *Phld.* 1.1–6.2, judicial in *Phld.* 6.3–8.1, deliberative in *Phld.* 8.1–9.1. In spite of the shifts in species of rhetoric Ignatius outlines a single argument, 'The Relevance of Preaching "Unity"'.

The outline Ignatius decided upon consists of the amplifications of two themes (*Phld.* 1.1–4.1; 5.1–6.2) followed by an oration (*Phld.* 6.3–9.1). The oration he writes is a correction of the one actually delivered in Philadelphia. In it he treats the same subject matter but does so in a manner designed to meet directly both the objections he encountered and those reported to him. The amplification of the themes follows the order prescribed in *Rhet. ad Her.* 4.43.56; the corrected oration follows the standard outline of a speech.

We are now in a position to follow Ignatius's decisions as the outline is amplified into the extant letter. Ignatius prefers juxtaposition to the use of conjunctions to signal his moves and is notoriously promiscuous in his proliferation of metaphors. As a consequence, discerning outlines is a high-risk venture. Historical critics have given content subtitles related to changes in metaphor and ignored the possible reasons for the order of statements; my working hypothesis is that each shift of metaphor potentially marks a new segment of composition. I have sought to classify transitional materials as introductions, to label clauses in accordance with appropriate patterns and to identify hermeneutical remarks and summaries. Fortunately, Ignatius writes on one topic per letter or gives titles to major sections of letters; fortunately, too, he supplies each letter with a summary; unfortunately, the unmarked summaries are often as cryptic as what they summarize.

The first theme and its amplification is *Phld.* 1.1–4.1:

---

15. G. Kennedy, *New Testament Interpretation through Rhetorical Criticism* (Chapel Hill, NC: University of North Carolina Press, 1984), p. 19; S. Stowers, *Letter Writing in Greco-Roman Antiquity* (LEC, 5; Philadelphia: Westminster Press, 1986), pp. 51-52.

16. This is true even if his sermon was epideictic, 'In Praise of Unity'.

res: Of which bishop I know[17] that he obtained a ministry for the community, not of himself, nor yet through any human beings, nor yet for vainglory, but in the love of God the Father and the Lord Jesus Christ, by whose gentleness I was struck, who though silent can effect more than they who talk vanity;

ratio: for he is attuned to the commandments as a cithara to its strings. Therefore my soul blesses his godly mind, knowing that it is virtuous and perfect, (also) his freedom from disturbance and his freedom from wrath, as one living in all godly gentleness.

res pronuntiata: Children of the light of truth, flee division and false teachings. Where the shepherd is, there follow as sheep.

contrarium. For many specious wolves take God's runners captive by evil pleasure, but they will have no place in your unity.

simile: 3.1. Refrain from evil plants which Jesus Christ does not cultivate, because they are not a planting of the Father.

hermeneutical explanation: not that I have found division among you, but a filtering out).

exemplum: 3.2. For all who are of God and Jesus Christ, these are with the bishop; and all who repent and come to the unity of the church, these too will be of God, that they may live according to Jesus Christ.

res iudicata: 3.3. Be not deceived, my brothers: if anyone follows a schismatic, he does not inherit the Kingdom of God; if anyone walks in a foreign doctrine, this person does not conform to the passion.

conclusio: ch. 4. Be eager, then, to celebrate one eucharist; for one is the flesh of our Lord Jesus Christ, and one the cup for union through his blood; one the altar, just as one the bishop along with the presbytery and deacons, my fellow slaves; that whatever you do, you may do it in a godly way.

Ignatius begins his letter to the Philadelphians by amplifying a theme drawn from the character of the bishop. Ignatius does not think highly of the bishop but is determined to put the best possible face on a bad situation. Omission of the bishop's name is evidence of Ignatius's evaluation of the bishop's ineffectiveness. The most Ignatius can say for the man is that his ineffectiveness is better than speaking vanity. The bishop's gentleness (ἐπιείκεια) is a lack of administrative courage, and his silence (σιγή) constitutes a failure to intervene rhetorically in a

17. See Schoedel, *Ignatius of Antioch*, p. 195, on opening the body of the letter with a relative clause. Except where indicated, the translation is Schoedel's.

social situation produced by the articulation of alternative opinions held by congregational leaders. The plurals in Ignatius's description of the alternative to the bishop refer to a group of unnamed leaders in the church whose vain chatter (τῶν μάταια λαλούντων) has produced sub-groups within the church. The result of the bishop's ineffective leadership is that only some people can be described as 'at one with the bishop and with the presbyters and deacons with him' (Ignatius, *Phld.* Inscr.) but it is to these people that the letter is addressed.[18]

Ignatius draws his theme from the real character of the bishop ('tuned to the commandments', 1.2) because the real character of the bishop is 'virtuous and perfect'. By formulating the matter in this way Ignatius subsumes the character of the bishop under final headings[19] and thus gives it authority. Rephrasing his theme in the format in which he wishes to amplify it, Ignatius addresses directly those who are with the bishop, naming them 'children of the light of truth', and transforms his theme into an admonition to 'flee division' (φεύγετε τὸν μερισμόν). The definition of 'division' is 'bad teaching'. Working from the formulation in 2.1, Ignatius amplifies his theme (*Phld.* 2.2–4.1).

Ignatius's amplification differs only slightly from that recommended in *Rhet. ad Her.* 4.43.56: he argues from topic of the contrary, citing the danger of wolves, from an analogy with dangerous plants and from an example of people who belong to the bishop.[20] He adds two elements, an argument from the topic of authority which contains a quotation from Paul (1 Cor. 6.9-10), and a hermeneutical evaluation, 'Not that I found division among you, but a filtering out' (3.1). He calls attention to this second element by three compositional techniques: (1) although it uses the key word μερισμός, he does not locate it near the *res pronuntiata*, φεύγετε τὸν μερισμόν, which it explains; (2) he addresses his audience directly (παρ' ὑμῖν) and speaks of himself in first person (εὗρον); (3) he uses an unusual word, ἀποδιϋλισμός, to characterize the state of the congregation. Schoedel has argued cogently that the

---

18. Schoedel, *Ignatius of Antioch*, p. 195.

19. See B. Mack, *Rhetoric and the New Testament* (Minneapolis: Fortress Press, 1990), pp. 37-38 for a discussion of the adaptation of 'final topics' to Christian use.

20. On the difficulties of finding Christian historical examples and the consequent use of 'whoever' in place of historical figures of the distant past, see Mack, *Rhetoric and the New Testament*, pp, 40-41.

unusual term comes from terminology for the preparation of wine,[21] but he has not considered the rhetoric of using an unusual word to evoke audience response. By all three compositional techniques Ignatius draws attention to his statement. Although he has urged his addressees to flee division, he does not want anyone to leave the congregation. He assures them that the congregation as such is not characterized by division but by a process of separation. He wants his addressees to read everything he says in light of his evaluation and to make decisions accordingly. What is important is to be located where the bishop is when the filtering is complete.

Ignatius's conclusion (ch. 4) draws out the consequences for his audience, repeating the numeral 'one' five times and specifying unity as association with the bishop.

The second theme and its amplification is in *Phld.* 5.1–6.2:

> *introduction:* 5.1. My brothers, I overflow in my love for you, and greatly rejoicing I watch out for your safety—not I, but Jesus Christ in whom, though I am bound, I fear all the more, since I am still imperfect; but your prayer will make me perfect unto God that I may attain the lot in which I was shown mercy, having fled to the gospel as to the flesh of Jesus and to the apostles as to the presbytery of the church.

> *res:* And let us also love the prophets

> *ratio:* because they also made their proclamation with the gospel in view and set their hope on him and waited for him in whom by believing they were also saved,

> *res pronuntiata:* being in the unity of Jesus Christ, saints worthy of love and worthy of admiration, attested by Jesus Christ and numbered together in the gospel of the common hope.

> *contrarium:* 6.1. But if anyone expounds Judaism to you, do not listen to him; for it is better to hear Christianity from a man who is circumcised than Judaism from a man uncircumcised;

> *simile:* both of them, if they do not speak of Jesus Christ, are to me tombstones and graves of the dead on which nothing but the names of men is written.

> *exemplum:* 6.2. Flee, then, the evil arts and plots of the ruler of this age, lest, battered by his opinion, you grow weak in love;

> *conclusio:* but all of you, come together with undivided hearts.

21. Schoedel, *Ignatius of Antioch*, pp. 166-67.

The composition of the introduction is strongly marked by self-refer-ence[22] and by elaborate regard for his addressees. Ignatius tells his addressees how to interpret this theme and its amplification: he is watching out for their safety. Then he carefully makes his addressees as much responsible for him as he is for them: their prayer for him will link them to him. The lengthy and elaborate introduction is a clue that what follows is a singularly delicate matter, one close to Ignatius's heart.

What is at stake in Philadelphia is nothing less than the status of the Old Testament prophets (*Phld.* 5.2). Ignatius regards them as Christians and thinks his addressees may hold a different opinion. The status of the Old Testament prophets is the subject matter of the vain chatter which the bishop has tolerated (1.1) and from which the addressees are to flee (2.1). Theological discussion of the status of Old Testament prophets is the evil pleasure (2.2) which threatens the unity of the church in Philadelphia.

Amplification of the theme appears in ch. 6: arguments from the topics of the contrary and of the similar in *Phld.* 6.1 and by example in 6.2. The real danger of a non-christocentric interpretation of the Old Testament is that it may weaken the bonds of Christian love which con-stitute the unity of the church. From its effect, the weakening of love, especially with respect to his own case, Ignatius pronounces non-christocentric interpretation an evil art of the ruler of this age (6.2).

Ignatius stamps his conclusion with urgency, using a strong adversa-tive (ἀλλά), an inclusive direct address (πάντες...γίνεσθε) and reitera-tion of his key term μερισμός now applied to the wellsprings of human attitude and behavior. The conclusion confirms Ignatius's principle: solidarity concerning all that is Christian, including the Old Testament prophets and his own case, is the highest value.

What follows, beginning in *Phld.* 6.3, is a speech, designed to per-suade the Philadelphians of Ignatius's views concerning Christian unity, the proper interpretation of the Old Testament and the relation of the two in his case. In the process, Ignatius defends himself against

---

22. J. Perkins, in 'The "Self" as Sufferer', *HTR* 85.3 (1992), pp. 245-72, apply-ing the categories of M. Foucault, suggests that Ignatius is part of a cultural move-ment, which uses 'representations of bodily pain and suffering to construct a new subjectivity of the human person' (p. 246); 'The focus on the body in Ignatius... should not be interpreted as aberrant, but as part of a far-reaching cultural discourse that constructed new locations for social control and power' (p. 247).

charges which arose, after he had left, from their misunderstanding of what he had said, and adjusts his previous argument to meet objections which he had not understood fully when they were first raised. For the first of these tasks he uses judicial rhetoric in *Phld.* 6.3–8.1; for the second he uses deliberative rhetoric in *Phld.* 8.1–9.1. To outline the speech we adopt Aristotle's prescription: 'The necessary parts of a speech are the statement of the case and proof. These divisions are appropriate to every speech, and at the most the parts are four in number—introduction, statement, proof, epilogue' (*Rhet.* 3.13.4).

> *introduction:* 6.3. I thank my God that I am clear in conscience as concerns you and no one can boast either in private or in public that I burdened anyone in anything great or small.
>
> And I pray for all among whom I spoke that they may not have it as a witness against them.

Ignatius's introduction, partly in the form of a prayer, is filled with self-reference. The prayer associates Ignatius with God, adding to his stature, and dissociates him from all partisans in Philadelphia. He is in good conscience that nothing he did or said in Philadelphia contributed to the problems to which the early part of his letter refers. The constraints of his own difficult situation did not force him into dependency (ἐβάρησα) on any partisan group (called 'boasters'). The final sentence names what follows as reluctant judicial rhetoric,[23] a court case against his addressees which he prays he will eventually lose when they change their policy.

> *statement of the case:* ch. 7; 8.1A. For although some desired to deceive me at the fleshly level, yet the Spirit, which is from God, is not deceived; for it knows whence it comes and whither it goes and it exposes hidden things.
>
> I cried out while among you, I spoke with a loud voice—the voice of God: 'Attend to the bishop and the presbytery and the deacons'.
>
> Those who suspected me of saying this because I had advance information about the division of some—he is my witness in whom I am bound that I did not learn it from any human being.
>
> It was the Spirit who made proclamation, saying these words:
>
> (1) Do nothing without the bishop
> (2) Keep your flesh as the temple of God
> (3) Love union

---

23. Schoedel calls this a 'strong warning', Schoedel, *Ignatius of Antioch*, p. 205.

(4) Flee divisions

(5) Be imitators of Jesus Christ as he himself is of his father.

I, then, did my part as a man set on union. Where there is division and anger, God does not dwell.

To state his case Ignatius sets out a narrative of the events, told for the purpose of proving his case. One easily infers that he is accused of preaching his sermon because someone had given him advance information. He neither affirms nor denies he had talked with members of the congregation before his sermon. He claims, however, that the sermon was the prophetic work of the Spirit, quite independent of any prompting from the congregation. Evidence of the Spirit is the loud voice,[24] specifically identified as God's. The summary of his sermon is a variant on the theme of 'unity' which he often uses.[25] Further testimony that his sermon was inspired is supplied by calling upon Christ as witness. A final piece of evidence is recital of oracles, introduced by the early Christian messenger formula, λέγον τάδε.[26] The oracles, composed in a literary form suitable for oracles of the period,[27] are the themes Ignatius amplifies into sermons.

At this point Ignatius looks back over the narrative, summarizing what is agreed upon as a result of the narrative. He takes it to be proven beyond disagreement that he spoke in Philadelphia in a way appropriate to 'a man set on union'. The point to be adjudicated is the broader one, whether the Spirit spoke the truth. Ignatius phrases the issue in a manner calculated to secure the sympathy of his hearers for his side of the case: 'God does not dwell where there is division and anger' (οὗ δὲ μερισμός ἐστιν καὶ ὀργή, θεὸς οὐ κατοικεῖ, 8.1). The composition of the summary of the narrative is linked to the formulation of the issue by the tandem conjunction, μέν... δέ, making the ἕνωσις on which Ignatius is set the opposite of μερισμός. If Ignatius proves his case, he will have proved that God does not dwell in Philadelphia and the Christians there are beyond hope. Because such a result is both theologically anomalous and pastorally unacceptable, Ignatius changes course. The argument he offers in support of his statement of the case is delib-

24. D. Aune, *Prophecy in Early Christianity and the Mediterranean World* (Grand Rapids: Eerdmans, 1983), pp. 291-92 n. 5.

25. Ignatius, *Magn.* 3–5; *Trall.* 2.1–3.2; *Eph.* 3–10 are major expositions of the theme of 'Unity'.

26. Aune, *Prophecy in Early Christianity*, p. 292.

27. Aune, *Prophecy in Early Christianity*, p. 293.

erative, designed to persuade his addressees to change their policy in order to avoid the verdict to which his case is leading.

> *proof:* 8.1B–9.1. (Introduction) All, then, who repent the Lord forgives, if they turn in repentance to the unity of God and the council of the bishop. I believe the grace of Jesus Christ who will remove every bond from you.

> (general principle: 8.2A): I exhort you to do nothing from partisanship but in accordance with Χριστομαθίαν.

Ignatius adopts, in a hermeneutical introduction, the premise that repentance is always available. To prove the truth of what he had previously declared in Philadelphia, 'Attend to the bishop and to the presbytery and deacons', and to target his original point anew, he formulates a deliberative proof, παρακαλῶ δὲ ὑμᾶς μηδὲν κατ᾽ ἐρίθειαν πράσσειν, ἀλλὰ κατὰ χριστομαθίαν (*Phld.* 8.2). A deliberative proof should compare norms or courses of future action, prefer the better of the alternatives and urge a policy directed to the better (*Rhet. ad. Her.* 3.2). The indications that Ignatius's proof is deliberative are: (1) the verbs μετανοῦσιν and παρακαλῶ indicate change; (2) two norms are set forth, κατ᾽ ἐρίθειαν and κατὰ χριστομαθίαν; (3) the preferred norm receives striking formulation, χριστομαθίαν. The verb πιστεύω confirms Ignatius's intent to formulate a persuasive argument.[28] χριστομαθίαν is a word Ignatius has made up to summarize the argument which follows in 8.2b–9.1. Devising a new word attracts the attention of the hearer who cannot avoid seeking a definition of χριστομαθίαν in what follows.

> (a complete argument 8.2B–9.1) *introduction:* I heard some say 'If I do not find (it) in the archives, I do not prove (it) in the Christian message'.[29]

28. J. Kinneavy, *Greek Rhetorical Origins of Christian Faith: An Inquiry* (New York: Oxford University Press, 1987), argues the convergence of the related terms πείθω and πιστεύω in the Hellenistic era. 'It is the hypothesis of this book that a substantial part of the concept of faith found in the New Testament can be found in the rhetorical concept of persuasion, which was a major meaning of the noun *pistis* (faith or *persuasion*) and the verb *pisteuein* (to believe) in the Greek language at the period the New Testament was written' (p. 43). BAGD, *s.v.* 'πιστεύω', separates the meanings of πιστεύω into (1) be convinced of something and (2) trust, in the sense of religious belief. Acts 28.24, καὶ οἱ μὲν ἐπείθοντο τοῖς λεγομένοις οἱ δὲ ἠπίστουν, is a fine example of the convertibility of πιστεύω and πείθω.

29. Translation here is more literal than Schoedel's: '"If I do not find [it] in the

And when I said 'It is written', they answered me 'That is just the question'.

1. *proposition:* But for me the archives are Jesus Christ, the inviolable archives are his cross and death and his resurrection and faith through him—in which, through your prayers, I want to be justified.

2. *reason:* The priests are good; yet better the high priest entrusted with the holy of holies.

3. *proofs of the reason:*
(a) who alone is entrusted with the secrets of God

(b) since he is the door of the Father through which enter Abraham and Isaac and Jacob and the prophets and the apostles and the church.

4. *résumé:* All these—into the unity of God.

Ignatius composes a formal argument like those he had written to persuade the Romans and for which analysis follows *Rhet. ad Her.* 2.18.28. The introduction to the argument reports a conversation he had in Philadelphia. The report is extremely condensed and notoriously difficult to interpret. The bits of information which follow will help clarify the report, the conversation reported and the persuasion Ignatius intends to effect by his letter.

Ignatius has made use of stasis theory[30] in deciding how to argue. Stasis theory sets out a pattern of questions, each requiring a 'yes' or 'no' answer, for the speaker to ask in sequence in the process of planning an argument. If it is to be used at all, it is used after all possible arguments are invented and provides the criteria for eliminating some possible arguments in preference to others. The first question is: is the issue a matter of fact? If it is, the stasis for the speech is the stasis of fact. If it is not, the speaker proceeds to the next major question: is the issue a matter of definition? If it is, the stasis for the speech is the stasis of definition. If it is not, the speaker proceeds to the next major question. As his reply indicates, Ignatius had thought at the time the question raised was a matter of fact. He had responded to an objection by quoting Scripture and abbreviates that response in his letter, citing only the quotation formula, 'It is written',[31] and omitting the references.

archives, I do not believe [it to be] in the gospel"' (ἐὰν μὴ ἐν τοῖς ἀρχείοις εὕρω, ἐν τῷ εὐαγγελίῳ οὐ πιστεύω) (*Ignatius of Antioch*, p. 207).

30. For a general treatment of stasis theory, see G. Kennedy, *The Art of Persuasion in Greece* (Princeton, NJ: Princeton University Press, 1963), pp. 306-14.

31. Ignatius uses the formula with a quotation in *Eph.* 5.3 and *Magn.* 12. The

That he now thinks the issue is a matter of definition can be seen from the fact that he invents a term, χριστομαθίαν, which requires definition. In the same way, he formulates the proposition with the unusual term 'archives', another term which requires definition.

Schoedel has established firmly what many have held, that the term 'archives' refers to the Old Testament.[32] 'It is written', the quotation formula used by early Christians—including Ignatius—for quoting Scripture, confirms his identification. 'Gospel' does not, however, in Ignatius's lifetime, refer to all or a part of what is now called the New Testament, but must refer to the oral message of Christianity.[33] The clue to the meaning of the verbs εὕρω and πιστεύω lies in their connection to oral speech. Both verbs are related to the technical vocabulary of Greek rhetoric: εὕρησις is the 'finding' or 'inventing' of arguments, πίστις is 'proof'.[34]

By applying these antecedents we may explain the reported conversation with relative adequacy. Some group had refused to accept Ignatius's proof of the importance of paying attention to the bishop because no discussion of 'paying attention to the bishop', or even of 'unity' in general, can be found in any Old Testament text. Ignatius had thought his interlocutors were not aware of the way early Christians had applied key Old Testament texts and proceeded to quote some.[35] He treated the question as a matter of fact. Upon further reflection and perhaps from what Rheus Agathopous and Philo have reported Ignatius now perceives his interlocutors as having a view of the Old Testament

use is the same in Mt. 2.5, 4.4, 4.6, 4.7, 4.10 and many other places in the New Testament.

32. Schoedel, 'Ignatius and the Archives'.

33. Schoedel, *Ignatius of Antioch*, p. 208 n. 6; H. Rathke, *Ignatius von Antiochien und die Paulusbriefe* (TU, 99; Berlin: Akademie Verlag, 1967), pp. 26-28; H. Paulsen, *Studien zur Theologie des Ignatius von Antiochien* (Forschungen zur Kirchen- und Dogmengeschichte, 29; Göttingen: Vandenhoeck & Ruprecht, 1978), pp. 56-58; H. Koester, *Synoptische Überlieferung bei dem apostolischen Vätern* (TU, 65; Berlin: Akademie Verlag, 1957), pp. 24-61; and *idem*, *Ancient Christian Gospels: Their History and Development* (Philadelphia: Trinity Press International, 1990), pp. 7-8; R. Gundry, 'EUAGGELION: How Soon a Book?', *JBL* 115 (1996), pp. 321-25.

34. C. Andersen (ed.), *Lexicon der Alten Welt* (Zürich: Artemis, 1965), *s.v.* 'Rhetorik', by H. Hommel, cols. 13-44.

35. Schoedel, *Ignatius of Antioch*, p. 210 n. 19 mentions Nestle's enumeration of 15 quotations or allusions to Ps. 117(118) in the New Testament.

which differs from his own. He now perceives the question as a matter of definition. Consequently, he now proves his own definition of the Old Testament to show that unity in general, and paying attention to the bishop in particular, are entailed as a logical consequence.

The first words of the proposition indicate clearly that Ignatius's argument is in the stasis of definition. It is a personal definition but not, he thinks, a private one. That it is personal is shown by 'for me' and the final clause. That he thinks it is not a private definition can be seen by the fact that he gives a reason.[36] What he sets out is a radically christo-centric view of Scripture. The single high-priest who is entrusted with the Holy of Holies is more advantageous for salvation than the plurality of priests in the Jerusalem temple. Ignatius offers two closely related proofs of the priority of the high-priest. First, the high-priest is custo-dian of divine secrets; secondly, the high-priest controls access to God. That it is in Scripture that the high-priest is found is shown by the char-acters who enter. The sequence begins with the patriarchs in their narrative order followed by the prophets,[37] and then by the apostles and the church. The history of salvation which Ignatius constructs here bears for him the significance he gives it: proof of the christocentricity of Scripture or, alternatively, as he puts it in the résumé, proof that unity is the content of Scripture. And, in the final analysis, χριστομαθίαν means unity exhibited in both gracious hospitality and a christocentric hermeneutic.

> *summary:* 9.2
> Now the Gospel has something distinctive: the coming of the Savior, our Lord Jesus Christ, his suffering and resurrection; for the beloved prophets made their proclamation with him in view; but the gospel is the completion of incorruptibility. All things together are good, if you believe with love.

Ignatius concludes the body of the letter with a summary[38] of the argument. The first clause summarizes chs. 1–4; the second, 5.1–6.2; the third, the oration 6.3–9.1. Thus, the first three clauses summarize individual segments of his letter, the final one is a general summary.

In 5.1–6.2, Ignatius treats the status of the biblical prophets directly, characterizing them as having 'made their proclamation with the gospel

---

36. The reason of the proposition reveals that Ignatius has a christology some-what related to that of Hebrews.

37. Concerning whom Ignatius had admonished the Philadelphians in 5.2.

38. Schoedel, *Ignatius of Antioch*, p. 210.

in view' (εἰς τὸ εὐαγγέλιον κατηγγελκέναι). In 9.2, he repeats the characterization almost verbatim: they 'made their proclamation with him in view' (κατήγγειλαν εἰς αὐτόν). Clearly, the second clause of 9.2 sums up the second of the three sections of the body of the letter.

In 6.3–9.1, Ignatius argues the case that the single high-priest is more advantageous than the plurality of priests because the high-priest gives saving access to the unity of God. The high-priest 'completes' or 'perfects' what the priests did. In this way, the 'completion of incor-ruptibility' in the third clause of 9.2 repeats the argument in 6.3–9.1, the third section of the body of the letter.

The pattern of the summary requires the first phrase of 9.2 to sum up chs. 1–4, the amplification of a theme formulated in 2.1, 'flee division and bad teaching'. Amplification emphasized the unity which consti-tutes the flight from division; the summary in 9.2 anchors the flight from bad teaching christologically.

By drawing together the summary, the final clause sums up the entire body of the letter. The theme of unity, Old Testament prophets and issues of interpretation constitutes a single argument (πάντα ὁμοῦ) which is persuasive to Christians united by the bonds of love. The final phrase, ἐν ἀγάπῃ πιστεύητε (9.2), echoes in composition the introduc-tion to the proof πιστεύω τῇ χάριτι (8.1); in each the verb carries rhetorical overtones.

> *introduction:* 10.1. Since it has been reported to me that in accordance with your prayer and the compassion which you have in Christ Jesus the church at Antioch in Syria is at peace,
>
> 1. *proposition:* it is right for you as a church of God to appoint a deacon to undertake there an embassy of God to rejoice with them when they have assembled and to glorify the name.
>
> 2. *reason of the proposition*: 10.2. Blessed in Jesus Christ is he who will be counted worthy of such a service, and you too will be glorified.
>
> 3. *proof:* It is not impossible for you to do this for the name of God if you want to, just as the neighboring churches have sent bishops and others presbyters and deacons.

To the body of the letter Ignatius appends an independent argument concerning the propriety (πρέπον, 10.1) of an embassy to Antioch. If the Philadelphians undertake to send someone to Antioch they will need to work together in such a way as to cure the factionalism of the congregation.

news: 11.1. As to Philo the deacon from Cilicia, a man witnessed to, who is even now serving me in the word of God with Rheus Agathopous, an elect man, who has followed me from Syria, having said farewell to life, both of whom also bear witness for you, I too thank God for you that you received them as the Lord also receives you. But may those who dishonored them be redeemed by the grace of Jesus Christ.

greetings: 11.2. The love of the brothers at Troas greets you whence I also write you through Burrhus who was sent with me by the Ephesians and Smyrneans as a token of honor. The Lord Jesus Christ will honor them, in whom they have hope in flesh, soul, spirit, faith, love, concord. Farewell in Jesus Christ, our common hope.

News from the messengers provides occasion for the letter. That some, at least, of the Philadelphians made them welcome, gives occasion for Ignatius to make a positive remark; that only some failed the elementary obligations of hospitality limits his criticism.[39]

2. *Quest for the Historical Opponents*

Much scholarship on the Ignatian letters has been directed to the opponents Ignatius combats in his letters.[40] Did he deal with Judaizers, Docetists, Gnostics, antinomian anarchists, rationalists or some combination? How many kinds of opponent were there, and where did they live? Doctrinal controversy is an abiding interest of theologians and has fueled interest in Ignatius for centuries. Where intellectual historians reign, ideological controversy remains the proper object of inquiry. What interests historical theologians may not drive history, however, and in this essay I venture a reconsideration based on rhetorical analysis. Two questions commonly asked of Ignatius's epistles will be addressed here: how many categories of opponent did Ignatius encounter? How ought the opponents to be characterized?

The place to start a search for the historical opponents of the historical Ignatius is the letter to the Philadelphians, in which the rhetorical situation is rich and complex and the references, while cryptic, appear to refer to things that happened. The way to start, in my opinion, is the

39. Schoedel, *Ignatius of Antioch*, p. 214; and R.M. Grant, *Ignatius of Antioch* (Apostolic Fathers, 4; New York: Nelson, 1966), p. 109, discuss the messengers. For the role of Burrhus, see Schoedel, *Ignatius of Antioch*, pp. 45, 214 and Grant, *Ignatius of Antioch*, p. 32.

40. For an up-to-date bibliography, see S. Wilson, *Related Strangers: Jews and Christians 60–170 C.E.* (Minneapolis: Fortress Press, 1995), pp. 360 nn. 90-96.

rhetorical analysis with which I began this essay. By this rhetorical analysis, or some other, we clear the ground for historical analysis, setting before ourselves the perspectives of speaker and audience(s) and the rhetorical exigence resolvable by the discourse.[41]

Summation of the results of rhetorical analysis relevant to a quest for historical opponents follows Aristotle's categories: ἦθος, πάθος, λόγος (*Rhet.* 1.2.3), indicating, respectively, author, audience and subject matter. The strength of Ignatius's character appears in his willingness to revisit the occasion on which he lost an argument, to explain himself and attempt reconciliation with opponents.[42] It is a measure of his control of his ἦθος that anger is so little in evidence.

What drives the letter is issues of hospitality and the honoring or dishonoring of a guest. In letters to churches from the Meander Valley which sent delegations to greet him at Smyrna and to the host church in Smyrna, Ignatius overflows with gratitude for the way in which he has been treated. He evaluates the churches in close relation to their attention to his needs. How large a delegation have they sent? How substantial is the contribution they have made to his well-being? Substantial contributions are evaluated as evidence of Christian maturity and readiness for advanced metaphysical theology.[43] Ignatius's *Philadelphians* is the obverse of the same coin. Analysis of the rhetorical situation shows Ignatius to have received a grudging welcome in Philadelphia and little respect when he preached. He regarded the argument following his sermon as a sign of disrespect and was deeply offended. Further news (11.1) from Philadelphia has given him reason to write a letter, but no reason to alter his evaluation.

At two key points in his letter Ignatius speaks plainly and precisely about his own theological agenda and method. The first is his self-definition for the benefit of those whom his manner and style had confused: 'I then did my part as a man set on union' (ἐγὼ μὲν οὖν τὸ ἴδιον ὡς ἄνθρωπος εἰς ἕνωσιν κατηρτισμένος, 8.1). The second corrects his

---

41. For another, less exegetical, rhetorical analysis, see D. Sullivan, 'Establishing Orthodoxy: The Letters of Ignatius of Antioch as Epideictic Rhetoric', *The Journal of Communication and Religion* 15 (1992), pp. 71-86.

42. It is worth noting that the self-deprecating statements which characterize the self-references written from Smyrna (Ignatius, *Magn.* 14; *Trall.* 12.3; 13.1; *Eph.* 21.2.) are little in evidence in this letter. See Schoedel, *Ignatius of Antioch*, pp. 13-14 on the matter of self-effacement in general.

43. The kind of theology in *Eph.* 11–19 but refused in *Trall.* 5.

previous argument, clarifying his own hermeneutic, 'But for me the archives are Jesus Christ' (ἐμοὶ δὲ ἀρχεῖά ἐστιν Ἰησοῦς Χριστός, 8.2). The import for either theological agenda or theological method of his intense concern with Old Testament prophets is less clearly articulated.

πάθος (audience). Ignatius's considerable pastoral skills are in evidence in *Philadelphians*, transmuting anger at lack of hospitality into persuasive technique. He overlooks, for example, the Philadelphians' lack of welcome in order to have sufficient structures of friendship in place to warrant a letter. He also overlooks the leadership vacuum in Philadelphia.

One of the most important of Ignatius's pastoral strategies is involving his audience in his own project, of which evidences appear in 5.1, 5.2 and ch. 10. The hermeneutical introduction, 5.1, contains a string of qualifying and amplifying phrases filled with self-reference. Again, at the beginning of 5.2, he attempts to include his addressees, 'Let us also love the prophets' (ἀγαπῶμεν...), and makes his bonds a leadership tool. He intends to secure unity in prayer and then, as a secondary effect of the unity in prayer, to induce his opponents to agree with his theology and to accord him in his absence the honor they had denied him in his presence.

A further instance of the technique of involving the Philadelphians in his project is the solicitation of an embassy to Antioch in ch. 10. He challenges them to take on a big project which will unite them, thus achieving in practice what they do not value in theory.

Ignatius's pastoral skills also appear in *Phld.* 6.3–9.1, where he rejects the judicial species of rhetoric. The decision to change species of rhetoric is made in public so that the addressees can see where his judicial case is leading and hope that his conclusion can be avoided. His deliberative case gives them an option, a way out, a chance to repent. The change of species in midstream is not only a clever move involving a high level of rhetorical skill but also one involving a high level of pastoral skill, creating options where none existed.

λόγος (subject matter). The intellectual component, Ignatius's hermeneutic, is spelled out in *Phld.* 5.2–6.1 and chs. 7–9. From the fact that Ignatius regards only the Old Testament as something needing interpretation we may infer that he regarded only the Old Testament as Scripture.[44] Whatever hermeneutical key Ignatius uses here it is a key

---

44. Whatever early Christian writings he knew were not included in the concept

to unlock the Old Testament. The key he insists upon is 'Jesus Christ'. That is, Ignatius insists upon a christocentric interpretation of the Old Testament, in which Christ is the criterion by which the heroes of the Old Testament are admitted to the presence of God on equal footing with 'the apostles and the church' (9.1).

We get very limited glimpses of how such a hermeneutic would work in the interpretation of any specific text. The discussion of the Old Testament prophets in 5.2 gives a general overview in language more nearly operational than any used elsewhere, however, 'The prophets made their proclamation with the gospel in view'.[45] For historical reconstruction it is important to observe that Ignatius's hermeneutic does not stand alone. Always it is correlated with a highly incarnational christology and an ethics embodied in whole-hearted cooperation in the hospitable practices subsumed under the term love, as the summary (9.2) shows.

I am now in a position to answer the first question: how many kinds of opponents did Ignatius encounter? To begin the reconstruction of the historical identity of the opponents of Ignatius, four observations arise directly from rhetorical analysis of Ignatius's *Philadelphians*:

1. Someone in Philadelphia argued with Ignatius.
2. The subject of the argument was Old Testament prophets.
3. Someone in Philadelphia 'dishonored' (11.1) Ignatius's friends at a later date.
4. Ignatius was offended, using 'deceive' (7.1), 'boast' (6.3) and 'speak vanity' (1.1) to refer to them to their faces.

To these four observations two more, derived inferentially from correlation of the rhetorical situation of Ignatius, *Philadelphians*, with that of the other epistles, may be added:

'archives', nor did 'gospel' mean to him written accounts of any sort. Certainly 1 Corinthians was securely stored in his memory.

45. Presumably, the prophets are honored not only for predicting Christ but also for wisdom which accords with Christian paraenesis, for oracles of judgment appropriate to the Last Judgment and for enduring persecution like Christ and Ignatius. No mention is made of a third division of the Hebrew canon, which might be taken to indicate the size of Ignatius's Old Testament were it not for his quotations from Proverbs. It is possible he included among the prophets a rather wide range of authors, including Moses, David and Solomon. The only two direct quotations from the Old Testament are Prov. 3.34 in *Eph.* 5.3 and Prov. 18.17 in *Magn.* 12. Each has the quotation formula γέγραπται (so Rathke, *Ignatius*, p. 24).

5. Ignatius talked about the same Philadelphians in Smyrna, contrasting the cordiality of his reception in Smyrna with his earlier and substantially less friendly reception in Philadelphia.
6. Ignatius also talked about the Philadelphians in Troas, where he received oral reports from Philo and Rheus about their behavior and about the Smyrneans' perception of them, and from which he dictated his letters to Philadelphia and to Smyrna.

To these six observations, let me propose three more, identifying opponents referred to obliquely in letters other than that to Philadelphia with the historical opponents with whom he had argued in Philadelphia:

7. The debaters in Philadelphia are satirized in the counter-example in Ignatius, *Magn.* 8–10 of a church which does everything wrong.[46]
8. From the Philadelphians' lack of christocentricity and lack of hospitality Ignatius creates for the Trallians, as an *exemplum,* a dangerously insubstantial christology (Ignatius, *Trall.* 10).[47]
9. Based on what he heard from Philo and Rheus, Ignatius warns the Smyrneans to avoid gossip concerning the erring Christians in Philadelphia (Ignatius, *Smyrn.* 5–7).[48]

The answer, then, to the historical question asked most frequently is 'Ignatius had one set of opponents: Philadelphians deficient in hospitality and christocentricity'.

It will be noted that I am extremely reluctant to base historical conclusions on rhetorical *exempla* or *contraria*. It is for this reason that I have declined to discern historical Docetists in an *exemplum* in

46. I argued this point in a paper delivered to the Pauline epistles section at the 1994 SBL Annual Meeting, 'How Ignatius Read Paul: The Rhetorical Use of Gal. in Ign. *Magn.* 8–10' and repeat part of that argument below.

47. Ignatius infers from the small size of the Trallian delegation that a renewal of concentration on the incarnation is needed, lest they become as the Philadelphians are. The rhetorical analysis leading to the conclusion that the Docetists are an *exemplum* appeared in a paper I delivered at the 1993 SBL Annual Meeting, 'Ignatius as Example: Ignatius *Trallians* 10 in Rhetorical Context'.

48. Because the hospitality of the Smyrneans, who served as hosts for Ignatius's many visitors and who joined with the Ephesians in supporting his epistolary endeavors (*Phld.* 11.2), is beyond reproach, as is their theology (*Smyrn.* 1), the people to be avoided must be opponents about whom Ignatius spoke during his stay in Smyrna.

Trallians 10 and historical Judaizers in an elaborated counter-example in *Magnesians* 8–10. I will even claim the authority of Aristotle in support of my principled reluctance, adducing the definition 'Persuasion is produced by the speech [λόγος] itself, when we establish the true or apparently true [ἀληθὲς ἢ φαινόμενον] from the means of persuasion applicable to each individual subject' (*Rhet.* 1.2.6). The ἢ φαινόμενον gives pause, does it not? It seems to me that speakers and authors are as likely to construct composite or typical exemplars as they are to describe meticulously the historically particular and that readers and audiences often prefer the apt to the accurate.[49]

If rhetorical criticism appears to be making a historical sceptic of me with respect to one of the questions usually asked and answered, the probabilities are that it will similarly affect my view of the second of the questions to be addressed here: appropriate characterization of the opponents. What should the historical opponents of the historical Ignatius be called? Most scholars have termed them 'Judaizers'.[50]

A recent treatment of the relations of Jews and Christians in the relevant period, offering a careful assessment of the current state of the quest for the historical opponents of Ignatius, will serve as an example of modern historical scholarship.[51] In a section concerning 'Gentile Judaizers', Wilson offers five conclusions about Ignatius and his opponents with varying degrees of certainty: (1) 'Some (if not all) of the Judaizers were Gentile in origin' with the added suggestion that they had been Gentile God-fearers attached to a synagogue; (2) 'The Judaizers had a particular view of the scriptures, and were especially inclined to dispute any Christian beliefs that they could not find in

---

49. For review of the evidence from the handbooks advising speakers and authors to shape the narrative to match the argument, see R. Hall, 'Historical Inference and Rhetorical Effect: Another Look at Galatians 1 and 2', in D.F. Watson (ed.), *Persuasive Artistry: Studies in New Testament Rhetoric in Honor of George A. Kennedy* (JSNTSup 50; Sheffield: JSOT Press, 1991), pp. 310-14.

50. D. Sullivan, 'Establishing Orthodoxy', p. 75, referring to E. Harrison (ed.), *Baker's Dictionary of Theology* (Grand Rapids: Baker Book House, 1960), offers what I take to be a typical statement: 'The most pressing problem for the young Church at this time was the presence of two heretical groups—the Judaizers and the docetists. The Judaizers were a party in the early Church, made up mostly of Pharisees who insisted that Gentiles had to become Jews before they could become Christians.' Wilson, *Related Strangers*, pp. 159-60 and p. 358 nn. 70-75, deals with primary sources and defines terms more adequately.

51. Wilson, *Related Strangers*, pp. 163-65, from which the quotations derive.

them', to which he adds probable Sabbath observance, docetic christology and 'a distinctive view (and separate celebration) of the Eucharist';
(3) 'The dispute seems to have been over both belief and practice'; (4)
'The Christian community may have been split into factions…but they
were recognizably part of the same group'; (5) The opponents 'blurred
the boundaries between Judaism and Christianity and thus compro-
mised the distinctive identity of the latter'. Rhetorical analysis of
Ignatius, *Philadelphians*, will require modification of this characterization of Ignatius's historical opponents in several respects.

It is clear, to begin with, that Ignatius does not use the term
'Judaizer' in his letter to the Philadelphians. The only use in the corpus
is the infinitive in *Magn.* 10.3. It is equally clear, in the second place,
that the term 'Judaizer' is not the self-designation of Ignatius's opponents in Philadelphia or of any other Christians. Who, after all, would
call themselves 'Ecclesia of Christian Fake Jews' or 'Assembly of
Wannabee Jews'? Rather, Ignatius has borrowed the term 'Judaizer'
from Paul's description of his argument with the Christians in Antioch
(Gal. 2.11-14) and has used it in his letter to the Magnesians to characterize non-local opponents in a negative way.[52] It is clear, in the third
place, that neither Paul nor Ignatius uses the term in letters directed to
the opponents themselves. This third observation suggests the rhetorical
force of the term: both Paul and Ignatius use it for blame. The context
is epideictic, in each case. Modern historical scholars have, in their
turn, borrowed the term for purposes of scientific description and
therein lies the problem. Historians need a descriptive term and the
ancient use of 'Judaizers' may lead us to mistake hype for fact and
blame for description.

We may summarize the results of rhetorical analysis relevant to the
characterization of the historical Philadelphian opponents in four
observations:

1. The opponents started an argument following Ignatius's
    sermon.
2. The argument was about Scripture.
3. The subject of the sermon to which they objected involved the
    christocentric interpretation of the Old Testament prophets.

---

52. For Paul, see J. Hester, 'Placing the Blame: The Presence of Epideictic in
Galatians 1 and 2', in Watson (ed.), *Persuasive Artistry*, pp. 281-307.

4.   They treated Ignatius, and later his friends, as unwelcome intruders.

Ignatius has created from these data a model. The first three observations yield a model which looks something like proto-Mishnaic Jews. The final observation makes them look just plain rude. Is there any other characteristic we can discern?

When Ignatius composed a satirical portrait of a church gone wrong for the Magnesians, he used the model of the impolite and hermeneutically impaired Christians in Philadelphia and modified it significantly. There is no mention of arguing or of textual interpretation and hermeneutics, but he has added the verb 'to judaize'. The resulting portrait is both hypothetical and comic and I need to say a little more about each category.

Comedy is signaled at the end of *Magnesians* 8–10 by 'It is ridiculous…'[53] and by the piling up of terms in the introduction: 'erroneous opinions…old fables which are useless' (ἑτεροδοξίαις…μυθεύμασιν τοῖς παλαιοῖς ἀνωφελέσιν οὖσιν, 8.1). Further evidences of comedy include: the verbal overload and excessive length of the interrogative sentence in 9.1-2; the *reductio ad absurdum* in 10.1 addressed to putative Judaizers; the invention of a trial by odor from the traditional image of salting food in 10.2. And, while Schoedel translated σαββατίζοντες as 'keeping Sabbath', and 'living κατὰ κυριακήν' as 'living according to the Lord's Day', would not 'sabbatizing' and 'Sundayizing' serve as well in 9.1?[54]

There are two pieces of evidence that the case is hypothetical. The

---

53.   ἄτοπόν ἐστιν… (10.3). The classic definitions of comedy specify incongruous juxtaposition based on social class not moral virtue: Aristotle, *Poetics* 2.1: ἐπεὶ δὲ μιμοῦνται πράττοντας, ἀνάγκη δὲ τούτους ἢ σπουδαίους ἢ φαύλους εἶναι τὰ γὰρ ἤθη σχεδὸν ἀεὶ τούτοις ἀκολουθεῖ μόνοις, κακίᾳ γὰρ καὶ ἀρετῇ τὰ ἤθη διαφέρουσι πάντες ἤτοι βελτίονας ἢ καθ᾽ ἡμᾶς ἢ χείρονας (Since living persons are represented these must necessarily be either good men or inferior—thus only are characters normally distinguished, since ethical differences depend on vice and virtue—that is to say either better than ourselves or worse or much what we are); and 5.1: ἡ δὲ κωμῳδία ἐστὶν ὥσπερ εἴπομεν μίμησις φαυλοτέρων μέν, οὐ μέντοι κατὰ πᾶσαν κακίαν, ἀλλὰ τοῦ αἰσχροῦ ἐστι τὸ γελοῖον μόριον (Comedy, as we have said, is a representation of inferior [people], not indeed in the full sense of the word bad, but the laughable is a species of the base [or ugly]). Text and translation are from LCL.

54.   Schoedel, *Ignatius of Antioch*, pp. 118-127 (118).

first is the conditional forms.[55] The second is the use of first-person plurals.[56] Ignatius includes himself among the putative Judaizers to encourage his addressees to join in the charade.

One modest detail of the otherwise comic portrait in Ignatius, *Magnesians*, sheds additional light on appropriate characterization of the Philadelphians who argued with Ignatius. Ignatius mentions Old Testament prophets in only two places in his letters, *Magn.* 8.2 and 9.2 and *Phld.* 5.2, in each case in a *ratio*. To the observation that Ignatius says the Old Testament prophets were 'saved' (*Phld.* 5.2), we may now add the observation that Ignatius says they were saved by being 'raised from the dead' (*Magn.* 9.2) following 'persecution' (ἐδιώχθησαν, *Magn.* 8.2).[57]

From inspecting his treatment of Old Testament prophets in the two letters we learn something important about both Ignatius and his opponents. Viewed in rhetorical perspective, the fact that Ignatius accepts the Jewish legend that prophets were martyred and supplements it with the Christian gloss that martyred prophets were raised from the dead by Christ means that Old Testament prophets are models for Ignatius's own life. Here is a fundamental principle of Ignatius's intensely self-referential theology: what Christ did for prophets who were persecuted for being Christians ahead of time he will surely do for the persecuted bishop of Antioch—if only he can remain faithful until death.

Viewed in rhetorical perspective, the Philadelphians, as a congregation, failed to deal with the self-referentiality involved in Ignatius's enthusiasm for martyred prophets. If the self-interested character of the principle had been apparent, it is possible that the congregation was divided because opponents blamed Ignatius as a self-absorbed ideologue and non-opponents failed to counter the debaters in order to offer honor, hospitality and pastoral care to Ignatius. In the absence of evidence of epideictic in Ignatius's account of the opponents' case, the case that the Philadelphians understood the self-referentiality of Ignatius's attachment to Old Testament prophets is weak. For this reason, it seems better to leave the cause of factionalism in abeyance and to say, in general terms, that the Philadelphians had failed to

55. εἰ μέχρι νῦν in 8.1, εἰ in 9.1 and ἐάν in 10.1.

56. 8.1, 9.1 and 10.1. The only other first-person plural in the letter is in *Magn.* 1.1.

57. For persecution as the fate of prophets, see Mt. 5.11-12, Acts 7.51-52 and commentaries. Schoedel, *Ignatius of Antioch*, p. 119.

respond to their guest in a pastorally effective way.

As a consequence of this excursion through *Magnesians* 8–10, I am now in a position to formulate a fifth characteristic of the historical Philadelphians who argued with Ignatius—inadequate pastoral sensitivity—to revise the list of characteristics and to assess the term 'Judaizers' as a characterization of Ignatius's historical opponents. Thus:

1. The opponents started an argument following Ignatius's sermon.
2. The argument was about Scripture.
3. The subject of the sermon to which they objected involved the christocentric interpretation of the Old Testament prophets.
4. They treated Ignatius, and later his friends, as unwelcome intruders.
5. The congregation was not pastorally sensitive to the self-referentiality of Ignatius's sermon.

Clearly, neither lack of pastoral sensitivity nor lack of hospitality has anything to do with Judaism or an enthusiasm for Jewish practices of any kind. Engaging a preacher in dialogue and intellectual debate over Scripture and its interpretation might well have something to do with Judaism. When Ignatius uses the verb 'to judaize' to blame the Philadelphians (albeit not to their faces) for misunderstanding him, he reveals his intellectual grasp of the first three characteristics and his compositional or stylistic cleverness in blaming. He also reveals his existential fragility: when his attempt to place his own status as a martyr-elect in a theological context was treated as subject for intellectual debate, he regarded the challenge as blame-worthy personal rejection and lack of hospitality.

When modern scholars use the term 'Judaizers' to characterize Ignatius's opponents in the debate at Philadelphia, they take Ignatius's satire at face value, turn pastorally insensitive debaters into ideologically coherent heretics and treat the terminology of blaming as description. It is not clear to me as a historian that either Ignatius or his friends were actually treated in Philadelphia in a way that anyone on the scene would identify as overtly impolite and inhospitable. Rather, rhetorical analysis has yielded a historical picture of misunderstanding on both sides and a letter attempting reconciliation.

At least in this instance and for at least one rhetorical critic, the effect of rhetorical analysis has been to render historical reconstruction difficult and historical conclusions tenuous. We have been able to see that Ignatius had one category of opponent, people in Philadelphia who argued against his christocentric interpretation of Old Testament prophets. We have not, however, been able to discern an ideology of the opponents. Rather, they have seemed not to understand the importance Ignatius attaches to what he says.

3. *Conclusion*

The first section of this essay undertook an elaborate analysis of the rhetoric of Ignatius, *Philadelphians*, printing a translation of the text and commenting on it section by section. The second section used the rhetorical analysis developed in the first section in pursuit of two historical questions commonly asked and answered by scholars of Ignatius's letters: how many kinds of opponents did Ignatius have? How should his opponents be characterized?

It will be noted that the results of the rhetorical analysis with which this essay began is characterized by amplitude, by the locating of multiple premises and conclusions, by the discerning of the reference of juxtaposed terms and metaphors, by the formulation of large themes and theological principles, by the positing of constructed audiences and their persuasion. By contrast, the results of historical reconstruction using the rhetorical analysis tends to the minimal. Gone are heretical sects of intruders with their antibishops, counter-eucharists and coherent theological agendas. In their place, there appear miscommunication, misunderstanding and failure to respond with adequate sensitivity. The discontinuity of the results is odd. Different analytical procedures have yielded results of varying scope and the decision to deploy rhetorical analysis in the service of historical reconstruction has given a decidedly unheroic look to Ignatius and those Christians who debated with him in Philadelphia.

INDEXES

INDEX OF REFERENCES

OLD TESTAMENT

CHRISTIAN AUTHORS

INDEX OF AUTHORS

JOURNAL FOR THE STUDY OF THE NEW TESTAMENT
SUPPLEMENT SERIES